Congress and the People

Congress and the People
Deliberative Democracy on Trial

Donald R. Wolfensberger

The Woodrow Wilson Center Press
Washington, D.C.
The Johns Hopkins University Press
Baltimore and London

Editorial offices:
The Woodrow Wilson Center Press
One Woodrow Wilson Plaza
1300 Pennsylvania Avenue, NW
Washington, D.C. 20004-3027
Telephone 202-691-4010
www.wilsoncenter.org

Order from:
The Johns Hopkins University Press
P.O. Box 50370
Baltimore, Maryland 21211
Telephone 1-800-537-5487
www.press.jhu.edu

Printed in the United States of America on acid-free paper ♾
First paperback printing 2001

2 4 6 8 9 7 5 3 1

Library of Congress Cataloging-in-Publication Data

Wolfensberger, Donald R.
Congress and the people : deliberative democracy on trial / Donald R. Wolfensberger.
p. cm.
Includes bibliographical references and index.
ISBN 0-8018-6307-4 (hardcover)
1. United States. Congress—History. 2. United States. Congress—Reform—History.
3. Democracy—United States. I. Title.
JK1021 .W64 1999
328.73'09—dc21

99-050675

ISBN 0-8018-6726-6 (pbk.)

The Woodrow Wilson International Center for Scholars

Lee H. Hamilton, Director

ABOUT THE CENTER

The Center is the living memorial of the United States of America to the nation's twenty-eighth president, Woodrow Wilson. Congress established the Woodrow Wilson Center in 1968 as an international institute for advanced study, "symbolizing and strengthening the fruitful relationship between the world of learning and the world of public affairs." The Center opened in 1970 under its own board of trustees.

In all its activities the Woodrow Wilson Center is a nonprofit, nonpartisan organization, supported financially by annual appropriations from the Congress, and by the contributions of foundations, corporations, and individuals. Conclusions or opinions expressed in Center publications and programs are those of the authors and speakers and do not necessarily reflect the views of the Center staff, fellows, trustees, advisory groups, or any individuals or organizations that provide financial support to the Center.

To my parents, Homer and Lucille Wolfensberger, and my wife, Monty

Contents

Acknowledgments

First and foremost, I want to thank the Woodrow Wilson International Center for Scholars for making my stay there and this book possible. The Center's director, the late Dr. Charles Blitzer, was kind enough to expedite my application for a position as a guest scholar soon after the Christmas holidays in 1997. This enabled me to move into my new quarters right after my retirement as a staff member of the House of Representatives. By making the transition from the House on the Hill to the Castle on the Mall virtually overnight, I was able to tackle my new assignment with the same rigor and discipline that had become second nature in the Congress.

The people at the Wilson Center were wonderful in orienting me to a new life as a budding author and rusty scholar: Dr. Michael J. Lacey, director of the U.S. Studies Division, and his assistant, Susan Nugent; Joe Brinley, director of publications; Zed David and his staff in the library; my research assistants, Amy Goad and Manisha Desai; the other support staff of the Center who were always friendly, helpful, and encouraging; and all the fellows and scholars whose wealth of knowledge and intellectual curiosity inspired me.

I am also very grateful to my students in the "Congress and Legislative Behavior" honors course at the American University in the fall of 1997 for helping to stimulate my thinking further about the Congress. Although the book project was temporarily shelved in favor of course preparation, the hiatus proved to be a critical period for sifting and testing all the ideas and theories garnered from books against the truths and lessons derived from my years on the Hill.

Last, but not least, I want to thank Walter Oleszek of the Congressional Research Service and former representative Tony Beilenson for taking the time to read the book and provide helpful comments. That goes double for my wife, Monty—my best editor, proofreader, critic, and friend.

Introduction

If a book is like a journey, then a good introduction is your travel brochure, itinerary, and invitation, all rolled into one. Your tour guide, the author, should tell you why he chose (and why you should want) to take this particular trip, what you can expect to see and learn along the way, and what the ultimate destination is.

As I soon discovered when I arrived at the Woodrow Wilson Center as a guest scholar in February of 1997, writing a book can be a winding, pathfinding adventure with no certain landmarks or destination. My initial book proposal, tentatively titled *To Restore the People's House: A Memoir and a Mandate*, was to chronicle my personal involvement in congressional reform efforts as a staff member of the House of Representatives over nearly three decades. I planned to relate how the institution had changed during that period, and what still needs to be done to ensure that our system of government retains its vital connection to the people.

But before plunging into writing that book, I had to turn my attention to a more immediate project. I had promised to prepare a paper on "Congress and the Threat of Direct Democracy" for a panel on the "Twenty-First-Century Congress" at the annual meeting of the American Political Science Association. I soon found that to write such a paper with any authority, I needed to learn a lot more about how the people have viewed their Congress for more than two hundred years and how Congress, in turn, has regarded the people. Have we been on an inevitable and irreversible march toward direct democracy as our Republic has grown and matured, as some strongly argue? Or does our history show a quite different path: an acceptance by the people of representative democracy that frees them to pursue their individual interests and happiness while vigilantly watching their government to hold it accountable?

Before I could confidently assess where we are today, let alone where our form of government might be going, I had to journey back to our very origins as a Republic. The paper thus expanded into a book, this book, and much of the material originally planned for the tome on recent congressional changes (absent the personal memoir) was incorporated.

The past may not always foretell the future, but I do believe the motto carved in the marble exterior of the National Archives building: "What's Past Is Prologue." The founding and subsequent development of this nation are a good introduction to its present and future. The American political system has evolved over the past two centuries in an ongoing tug and pull between the democratic impulse for greater individual liberty, rights, and sovereignty, and the constitutional imperative for national unity, purpose, stability, and security.

These are not mutually exclusive or opposing forces. Indeed, the Declaration of Independence makes clear that governments are established to secure the unalienable rights of citizens to life, liberty, and the pursuit of happiness, "deriving their just powers from the consent of the governed." The preamble to the Constitution reaffirms that government is the creation and instrument of "We the People" to "secure the Blessings of Liberty to ourselves and our Posterity." But it also recognizes the other purposes of constitutional government: "to form a more perfect Union, establish Justice, insure domestic Tranquility, provide for the common defence, [and] promote the general welfare."

This duality might best be explained by using the analogy of a colonial-era whale-oil lantern. (One model, the "agitable burner," was invented in the same year the Constitution was written.) The people have carefully designed the lantern both to regulate and to protect the flame of individual liberty and to light the way for the nation's progress into the future's uncertain darkness. They have entrusted certain of their members with responsibility to maintain and operate the lantern. If it is not properly tended to the flame will die, or it will burn so fiercely that the lantern is destroyed. This is the balance of which Woodrow Wilson wrote in an essay for the *Atlantic Monthly* at the beginning of this century:

> There are many things . . . which we have found to be conditions precedent to liberty—to the liberty which can be combined with government. . . . We know, for one thing, that it rests at bottom upon a clear experimental knowledge of what are in fact the rights of individuals, of what is the equal and profitable balance to be maintained between the right of the individual to serve himself and the duty of government to serve society.[1]

The continuous interplay between the democratic impulse for liberty and the constitutional imperative for order has been a creative tension: it has produced a vast expansion of individual rights and freedoms and the growth of a strong and modern nation-state.

Will this seemingly inexorable march of democracy and national progress continue, and, if so, where it will take us in the twenty-first century? Many political commentators and futurists see some form of direct democracy as the wave of the future—an inevitable offshoot of the information-age revolution that is surging toward the millennium, transforming everything in its path.

Electronic information gathering and interactive decision making, combined with declining public trust in the institutions of government, will lead, they predict, to an irresistible demand for more direct public involvement in policy making at all levels of government. Given the relative success of the century-old experience with state initiatives and referendums, and the information age's potential for an electronically enlightened and interactive electorate, the day cannot be far off, they tell us, when voters will simply pick up their remotes and legislate.

A variety of terms has been used to describe this brave new world of legislator-citizens: cyberdemocracy, teledemocracy, the electronic republic, electronic democracy, and electronic town hall meetings. The proponents of a national, direct democracy come in all political and ideological stripes. They include presidential hopefuls at one time (Patrick Buchanan, Ross Perot, and Jack Kemp), futurists (Heidi and Alvin Toffler), consumer activists (Ralph Nader), and political analysts (Kevin Phillips)—to name a few.

In his book *The Electronic Republic*, Lawrence Grossman, former president of the Public Broadcasting Service and NBC News, asserts that electronic democracy is inevitable. It is not a question of whether "the transformation to instant public feedback through electronics is good or bad, or politically desirable or undesirable," because, "[l]ike a force of nature, it is simply the way our political system is heading."[2]

Graeme Browning in her book *Electronic Democracy* tells of the 1994 accreditation by Canadian authorities of the Democratech Party of British Columbia. This party advocates turning all government decisions over to the people because, according to its Web site, "with modern, instantaneous communications, the people can directly make their own decisions, relegating politicians to the scrap heap of history."[3] Whether the party was intentionally paraphrasing Trotsky—opponents of communism relegated to the "dustbin of history"—I do not know, but the concept fits neatly with the communist ideal of the state. The state supposedly will wither away, leaving behind a pure democracy of the people—perhaps, in this case, a dictatorship of the cybertariat. Lenin's observation that "Communism is Soviet Power plus the electrification of the whole country" might even be paraphrased by the Democratech Party: "direct democracy is people power plus the wiring of the nation."[4]

While no party devoted exclusively to electronic, direct democracy has yet emerged in the United States, Ross Perot, more than anyone else in recent times, popularized the notion of national, electronic town hall meetings. At the University of Richmond on October 15, 1992, citizens were allowed to question Perot and the other presidential candidates in an electronic town hall format. Perot gave the audience his vision of how to build a consensus and make decisions in the electronic age:

> This is going to take, first, building a consensus at grassroots America. Right from the bottom up, the American people have got to say they want it. And at that point, we can pick from a variety of plans and develop new plans. And the way you get things done is bury yourselves in the room with one another, put together the best program, take it to the American people, use the electronic town hall—the kind of thing you're doing right here tonight—build a consensus and then do it and then go on to the next one. But don't just sit here slow dancing for four years doing nothing.[5]

Perot's novel idea to convert the presidency into a television anchor post for citizen decision making on national problems sparked some public interest at first but did not catch on with the other candidates, let alone the Congress. That is not to say that Congress has always ignored calls for more direct involvement in government by citizens. As this book will recount, various proposals for national initiatives and referendums have been considered by the Congress from time to time, though none has succeeded, mainly because of the lack of any widespread public support.

For a variety of reasons, national direct democracy, even on a limited basis, is not the inevitable wave of the future. First, to permit the people to initiate and/or vote on national laws would require a constitutional amendment. A constitutional amendment requires not only the approval of two-thirds of both houses of Congress that jealously guard their constitutional lawmaking prerogatives, but also ratification by three-fourths of the states, the smaller of which could be seriously harmed by a nationwide popular vote that gives the more populous states a substantial upper hand.

Second, it is unlikely that the people really want such additional responsibilities. Notwithstanding some public opinion polls that show slight majority support for a national initiative process, the idea runs contrary to the democratic impulse that strongly supports our current constitutional arrangement of representative democracy. The impulse is more about being left alone by government than it is about being an integral part of the governing process.

And third, the state initiative and referendum process has been radically transformed from its original concept as a democratic safety valve of last resort. Today the valve is open all the way all the time. The result is a torrent of special-interest-driven and industry-run fire hose fights. This disturbing development should make anyone—even the staunchest supporters of the state process—reluctant to apply it nationally.

Congress has been sporadically responsive to the democratic impulse of a people distrustful of, but dependent upon, our constitutional system of elected officials to safeguard their individual freedoms. Congress has never felt particularly threatened by a democratist impulse for rule by the masses except to the extent that strong and popular presidents have positioned themselves over the Congress as being the only true embodiment of the popular will—a threat that became at least a partial reality during the era of the "imperial presidency," roughly between 1933 and 1973.

The most potent spur to action by the Congress has always been the threat of rejection at the polls through frequent elections. Congress has taken seriously the democratic impulse to keep elected representatives as close to the people as possible. It has been responsive to this impulse by expanding and protecting their individual rights and freedoms, and by internally reforming the institution to make it more efficient, effective, accessible, and accountable to the people, as well as to make it a coequal with the executive branch.

In Chapter 5, "The Initiative and Referendum Movement," the book suspends its congressional focus to examine the emergence of these direct democracy devices in certain states at the turn of the twentieth century and Woodrow Wilson's conversion from an opponent to a supporter of their use. At one point on his road to the White House, Wilson even expressed support for a national referendum process. But he soon drew back when his supporters became alarmed that he was being radicalized. Had he pressed such a view, the line against direct democracy may not have been drawn at the states, and a national initiative, or at least referendum, process might be a reality today.

Wilson's ultimate rejection of national initiatives and referendums did not spare him during his own presidency from a national movement for a referendum on the conflict that became World War I, a story told in Chapter 6. Nor did the concept's failure to catch on prevent its re-emergence prior to World War II. Among the leaders of both movements was Bob LaFollette of Wisconsin—Sen. Bob LaFollette, Sr., in the first instance and his son, "Young Bob," in the second.

While turning a cold shoulder to letting the people legislate directly, Congress has been open, from time to time, to reforming its own internal operations to improve its policy performance and enable the institution to be more responsive and accountable to the people. Very seldom, though, have such self-improvements been self-initiated. They have usually been in response to public frustration over legislative lethargy or institutional scandals. Sometimes congressional majorities have ignored public demands for them to change their ways and paid dearly by losing control of one or both houses. The Democrats' loss of control of the House and Senate after the 1994 elections is a recent example.

The latter half of this book examines reform efforts leading up to the Republican takeover of Congress in 1995. In particular, it examines the "sunshine paradox": the more Congress opened its doors and windows to the people (with committee hearings, floor debates, and votes in both arenas carried directly to the people via C-SPAN television and a congressional Internet site), the lower it dropped in public confidence and approval.

Republicans promised to reverse this trend in declining public trust when they assumed control of the 104th Congress. Numerous institutional changes were incorporated in their campaign manifesto, "The Contract with America," unveiled in September of 1994. It pledged that a Republican Congress would help to "restore the bonds of trust between the people and their elected representatives," "transform the way the House works," "restore accountability to Congress," and "end its cycle of scandal and disgrace."[6] This book takes a close look at the origins of these proposals, the people involved in their development and adoption, and their relative degrees of success and failure in practice.

Most of the time the American people do not pay close attention to what Congress does or does not do, let alone *how* it does its business. This lack of attention contributes to the suspicion that Congress is up to no good, cutting secret deals with the special interests at the expense of the public interest and the "little guy."

Because there is an element of truth in this perception—politics, after all, is about mediating between competing factions and trying to accommodate as many constituency interests as possible—the image of a misbehaving Congress is not easily dispelled. Indeed, it is often reinforced by skimpy and selective media accounts that highlight only negative aspects of the system while ignoring the positive. Consequently, public confidence in Congress, like other institutions of authority in modern times, suffers.

Especially for the last quarter of a century, since the twin nightmares of Watergate and Vietnam, observers have worried that this erosion of trust in government could prove fatal to our system. A final breakdown in trust certainly could lead to a radical, even violent change in the way we govern ourselves, though there is no evidence that the people have lost faith in the basic constitutional principles and structures. Indeed, because of a better economy in recent times, more people see the country headed in the right direction. Even the Congress is seen as doing a better job (at least compared with its performance in 1994). And the federal government is enjoying slightly higher levels of public trust and confidence, though a majority still view it unfavorably.

As members of Congress will be the first to admit from their own experience and that of their former colleagues, complacency is a dangerous thing. The people's ability to change things dramatically, at the drop of a ballot, continues to drive congressional behavior. The principal challenge for Congress continues to be how to remain responsive to the people and their problems while maintaining the proper balance between individual liberty and national stability and progress. The former calls on the representative character of the system, while the latter calls on the need for deliberation to determine what the national interest is and to act on it. Although individual members are perfecting the art of representation, the institution is falling farther and farther behind in its ability to deliberate on major issues. Instantaneous communications and polling threaten the ability of Congress to operate in a truly deliberative setting. "Virtual" direct democracy—representatives simply serving as funnels for public whims and passions—poses a greater threat today than does "actual" direct democracy. Virtual direct democracy undermines the founders' idea of a deliberative body of citizens chosen by the people to "refine and enlarge the public views" into "the true interest of their country."[7]

It is my hope that the reader will enjoy this journey through our history, especially through the last three decades of dramatic change in the Congress, as much as I did. The book traces this history through a series of selected stories involving a rich cast of characters both inside and outside Congress. Where possible, it lets them speak directly about the causes, convictions, and challenges that motivated them. The small parts they played in this vast and still unfolding mosaic we call representative democracy will help us understand how we got where we are today as a nation, and how we as individuals might affect where we are headed.

Restoring deliberative democracy will be one of the greatest tests our country will confront in the new century. It has been on trial since our founding as a nation. If history is any guide, the ongoing tensions between the people and their elected representatives, as told in these pages, will continue to reflect the resilience and adaptability of our system of government.

Notes

1. Woodrow Wilson, "The Ideals of America," in the *Atlantic Monthly* 90 (December 1902): 721–34. See also *The Public Papers of Woodrow Wilson: College and State*, vol. 1, ed. Ray Stannard Baker and William E. Dodd (New York: Harper & Brothers, 1925; Kraus Reprint Co., 1970), 436–37.

2. Lawrence K. Grossman, *The Electronic Republic: Reshaping Democracy in the Information Age* (New York: Penguin Books, 1995), 154.

3. Graeme Browning, *Electronic Democracy: Using the Internet to Influence American Politics* (Wilton, Conn.: Pemberton Press, 1996), 84. Browning does not go on to tell how the Democratech Party fared in the 1994 elections.

4. Vladimir Ilyich Lenin, "New External and Internal Position and the Problems of the Party," *Report, 1920, to the Eighth Congress of the Communist Party*, in *Collected Works*, vol. 31 (Moscow: Progress Publishers, 1927), 487–518.

5. Remarks of Ross Perot, "Second Presidential Debate: Voters Grill Candidates in Unprecedented Format," *Congressional Quarterly Almanac, 1992*, vol. 48 (Washington, D.C.: Congressional Quarterly, 1993), 115-A.

6. *Contract with America: The Bold Plan by Rep. Newt Gingrich, Rep. Dick Armey, and the House Republicans to Change the Nation*, ed. Ed Gillespie and Bob Schellhas (New York: Times Books/Random House, 1994), 7–8.

7. James Madison, "Federalist No. 10," in *The Federalist Papers* (New York: Mentor Books, 1961), 62.

1

Making a Constitution

PERHAPS no other figure from the Revolutionary War era more embodies the democratic impulse for limited government and individual rights than Thomas Jefferson. As the author of the Declaration of Independence, with its emphasis on individuals' "unalienable rights" and governments constituted by the people to safeguard those rights, Jefferson provides a useful sounding board on whether the constitutional designs considered in 1787 were in harmony with the Spirit of '76.

As the U.S. ambassador to France at the time, Jefferson could not participate directly in the Constitutional Convention's deliberations in Philadelphia. Nevertheless, he kept track of proposals through frequent correspondence and was not hesitant to comment on them, before, during, and after the Convention—a one-man Greek chorus.

Jefferson was not particularly enthusiastic about the need for a new Constitution to replace the Articles of Confederation that governed the newly independent country from March of 1781 until March of 1789. Writing to fellow Virginian Edward Carrington from Paris on August 4, 1787, Jefferson said:

> I confess, I do not go as far in the reforms thought necessary, as some of my correspondents in America; but if the convention should adopt such propositions, I shall suppose them necessary. My general plan would be, to make the States one as to everything connected with foreign nations, and several as to everything purely domestic.[1]

While admitting to "all the imperfections of our present government" under the Articles of Confederation, Jefferson praised it as "the best existing, or that ever did exist."[2]

In a letter to John Adams of Massachusetts on November 13, 1787, two months after the new Constitution had been submitted to the states, Jefferson expressed some misgivings about the document: "[T]here are things in it which stagger all my disposition to subscribe to what the assembly has proposed." Chief among these were the inadequate size of the House of Representatives to manage foreign and federal affairs and the unlimited terms of the president: "Like a bad edition of a Polish King," the president "may be elected from four years to four years, for life."[3]

By the time Jefferson wrote to James Madison of Virginia on December 29, 1787, he seemed more disposed to support the new Constitution in most respects and elaborated on those provisions he particularly liked, including the division of the government into three separate branches; the "greater House being chosen by the people directly"; the proportional representation of the people in the House and the equal representation of the states in the Senate; the voting by person rather than by states in the Congress; and the presidential veto authority. Jefferson then went on to discuss two things that he did not like about the Constitution: "the omission of a bill of rights" and "the abandonment in every instance, of the principle of rotation in office, and most particularly in the case of the President."[4] Jefferson was not alone. The issues of term durations and limits for both the executive and legislative branches were fiercely debated at the Constitutional Convention of 1787.

Under the Articles of Confederation, the delegates to the Congress of the Confederation were appointed by their state legislatures for annual terms. (In a six-year period no delegate could serve for more than three years.) Moreover, the Articles contained "a power reserved to each state, to recall its delegates, or any of them, at any time within the year, and to send others in their stead for the remainder of the year."[5] Although delegates were apportioned by population of their states, each state had only one vote in the Congress.

On May 31, 1787, after the Constitutional Convention decided without discussion or dissent that there should be two branches of the new legislature, a resolution proposing popular election of the first branch of the legislature was debated.

According to Madison's notes on the debate, Roger Sherman of Connecticut opposed the election by the people and favored appointment by the state legislatures on grounds that "the people immediately should have as little to do as may be about the Government. They want information and are constantly liable to be misled." Elbridge Gerry of Massachusetts also opposed the resolution: "[T]he evils we experience flow from the excess of democracy. The people do not want virtue, but are the dupes of pretended patriots."[6]

George Mason of Virginia, however, strongly supported the popular election of the lower house. Since "it was to be the grand depository of the democratic principle of the government," it "ought to know and sympathize with every part of the community." James Wilson of Pennsylvania agreed: "No government could long subsist without the confidence of the people." Madison echoed these sentiments, terming "the popular election of one branch of the National Legislature essential to every plan of free Government."[7]

The resolution carried, five states to two, with Connecticut divided. The question was reopened on June 6 when Charles Pinckney of South Carolina proposed "that the first branch of the national Legislature be elected by the State Legislatures, and not by the people." James Wilson weighed in on the side of the people:

> The government ought to possess not only the force, but secondly the mind or sense of the people at large. The Legislature ought to be the most exact transcript of the whole Society. Representation is made necessary only because it is impossible for the people to act collectively.[8]

Pinckney's resolution was rejected, three states to eight.

On June 12 the Convention took up the issue of terms of office for the first branch of the legislature. Sherman and Oliver Ellsworth, also from Connecticut, proposed annual terms; Edward Rutledge of South Carolina, "every two years"; and Daniel of St. Thomas Jenifer of Maryland "every three years." Madison seconded the motion for terms of three years. "Instability is one of the great vices of our Republics to be remedied," he said. A three-year term "will be necessary, in a government so extensive, for members to form any knowledge of the various interests of the states to which they do not belong." But Gerry argued strongly for "annual elections as the only defence of the people against tyranny."[9] Three years were agreed to by an 8-4 vote.

On June 13, 1787, the Committee of the Whole issued a report on the plan for the new government.[10] After further debate on June 18, the plan provided for a popularly elected House with two-year terms, a Senate elected by the state legislatures for seven-year terms, with no limitation on terms for members of either house; and a president to be chosen by the national legislature for a single, seven-year term.[11]

On June 18 Edmund Randolph had offered an amendment to reduce the term of members of the popularly elected House from three to two years. Madison reiterated his earlier argument that frequent elections, whether annual or biennial, would be inconvenient for the representatives, especially the new members, who would need time "to acquire that knowledge of the affairs of the States in general without which their trust could not be usefully discharged." Sherman said he preferred annual elections but would be content with biennial. According to Madison's notes, Sherman "thought the representatives ought to return home and mix with the people" because if they remained at the seat of government "they would acquire the habits of the place which might differ from those of their constituents." The amendment for two-year terms was adopted, 7-2.[12]

Another important issue for the Convention was eligibility to vote for representatives to the Congress. On August 7 Gouverneur Morris of Pennsylvania moved to strike the language that made eligibility the same as that for electors of the lower house of their state legislature, thereby restricting the vote to freeholders (landowners). John Dickinson of Delaware spoke in favor of the Morris motion because he considered property holders "the best guardians of liberty." Confining the vote to them was "a necessary defense against the dangerous influence of those multitudes without property and without principle with which our country like all others, will in time abound."[13]

Ben Franklin disagreed: "[W]e should not depress the virtue and public spirit of our common people." They "displayed a great deal during the war . . . [and] contributed principally to the favorable issue of it." Moreover, "the sons of a substantial farmer, not being themselves freeholders, would not be pleased at being disenfranchised, and there are a great many persons of that description."[14] After considerable debate the Morris motion was rejected, 1-7.

The question of the president's term also stirred controversy. For weeks the delegates wrestled over just what role, if any, the national legislature or the people should play in the choice of the executive. At issue was the relationship between the first two branches.

On July 17 a motion to provide for the election of the president by the people was rejected by a vote of one state to nine. The Convention then passed unanimously the wording of the Randolph plan that the executive be chosen by the national legislature. After the Convention postponed consideration of a seven-year term for the executive, William Houston of New Jersey offered a motion to strike from the Randolph plan the ineligibility of the executive for a second term. According to Madison's notes on the debate, Gouverneur Morris was the only delegate to speak on the motion: "The ineligibility proposed by the clause as it stood tended to destroy the great motive to good behavior, the hope of being rewarded by a reappointment. It was saying to him [the executive], make hay while the sun shines."[15]

The motion carried, 6-4. On July 19 a motion was offered by Alexander Martin of North Carolina to reinsert the one-term limit on the executive. This time the debate was tied to whether the executive should be elected by the legislature. After a motion was adopted to make the executive subject to election by electors chosen by the states, a vote was taken on whether to make the executive ineligible for a second term. This time the motion was rejected by a 2-8 vote. On July 24 Martin and Gerry moved to reinstate the one-term limit on the executive. To enhance the chances for passage of his motion, Martin suspended its consideration and moved to make the executive term eleven instead of seven years. Gerry suggested fifteen years, only to be trumped by Rufus King of Massachusetts who said twenty years was "the medium life of princes." Another delegate chimed in with eight years.[16]

Wilson suggested that the executive be chosen by electors chosen by lot from the national legislature. "This is committing too much to chance," warned Gerry. "If the lot should fall on a set of unworthy men, an unworthy Executive must be saddled on the Country."[17] Mason was later to comment on this option: "Among other expedients, a lottery has been introduced. But as the tickets do not appear to be in much demand, it will probably not be carried on."[18]

On July 25 Ellsworth moved that the executive be appointed by the legislature, except if standing for a second term, in which case he would be chosen by electors appointed by the state legislatures. In discussing the motion, Madison reviewed all the alternatives that had been laid before the Convention. After dismissing selection by both the national and state legislatures, he said that "the remaining mode was an election by the people or rather by the qualified part of them, at large." Madison told the delegates that he liked this mode the best despite "all its imperfections"—namely, the people would prefer a candidate from their own state and this would disadvantage the smaller states, and the people would favor the more populous northern states over the southern states.[19]

To this Ellsworth replied, "The objection drawn from the different sizes of the States is unanswerable. The citizens of the largest states would invariably prefer the candidate within the state; and the largest states would invariably have their man."[20] However, John Dickinson of Delaware agreed with Madison, admitting he "had long leaned towards an election by the people which he regarded as the best and purest source."[21] Ellsworth's motion was defeated, 4-7.

Pinckney then offered a motion that the executive be chosen by the legislature but not be eligible for election for more than six years in any twelve years. Mason approved the idea, saying that such limits on consecutive terms had the sanction of experience in the instance of the Congress and some of the executives of the states. The Pinckney motion was narrowly rejected, 5-6.

On July 26 Mason moved to reinstate the one-term limit on a seven-year executive chosen by the national legislature. The motion passed, 7-3. A month later the Convention revisited the question of how the president should be chosen. It rejected election by the people (a 2-9 vote) and election by electors chosen by the people (a 5-6 vote). It was not until September 7 that the Convention reached agreement. The president would be chosen by electors appointed in a manner determined by each of the states, with the number of electors equal to the total number of national representatives and senators. The president would serve a four-year term without limit on the number of terms that could be served. Clearly, the issue of the president's election and time in office was among the most difficult for the Convention, consuming as it did several days of debate over a three-month period and, by one count, some sixty ballots.[22]

Another issue involving the degree of authority to give to the people arose. Who should ratify the new Constitution—the people at large or the state legislatures? Randolph favored ratification by conventions of delegates chosen by the people, but Gerry expressed reservations, noting that in the eastern states, the Confederation had been sanctioned by the people themselves, and "the people in that quarter have at this time the wildest ideas of government in the world."[23] On June 12 Randolph's ratification plan passed, 6-3.

The idea of popular ratification was a novel one. Only Massachusetts and New Hampshire had submitted their state constitutions to town meetings for approval.[24] The issue of who should ratify the new Constitution was revisited on August 31. Madison spoke for ratification by conventions of the people, "the fountain of all power." By resorting to them, he said, all difficulties would be resolved.[25] The Convention agreed to ratification by only nine states (as opposed to all thirteen as required by the Articles of Confederation for revising that document). The Convention then agreed, 10-1, that the new Constitution should be subject to ratification by conventions in each state.

The issue of including a bill of rights in the Constitution was hardly broached until near the end of the Convention. On August 20 Charles Pinckney had submitted to the Convention what amounted to a thirteen-paragraph bill of rights. But, according to Madison's notes, "these propositions were referred to the Committee on detail without debate or consideration of them by the House."[26]

The issue was not resurrected until September 12 when one delegate observed that no provision was made in the Constitution for trial by juries. This led Mason to say that he "wished the plan had been prefaced by a Bill of Rights," since "it would give great quiet to the people."[27] Gerry immediately moved for a committee to be appointed to prepare a bill of rights, and Mason seconded the motion.

Sherman rose in opposition. He was "for securing the rights of the people where requisite," but the "State Declarations of Rights are not repealed by the Constitution" and therefore are sufficient. Mason countered that "the Laws of the U.S. are to be paramount to the State Bills of Rights." With that brief debate, Gerry's motion was voted and rejected, 0-10, with Massachusetts abstaining.[28]

Five days later, on September 17, 1787, the Constitution was signed by all members present except Randolph, Mason, and Gerry. It was sent on to the

Congress of the Confederation, which forwarded it to the states for ratification ten days later.

During the ensuing debate over ratification, the proponents and opponents of the proposed Constitution came to be known as the Federalists and Anti-Federalists, respectively. The most famous of the former group included Alexander Hamilton and John Jay of New York, and James Madison of Virginia. They published eighty-five letters in New York City newspapers under the heading of "The Federalist" and the pseudonym of Publius. The most famous tracts of the Anti-Federalists, also published in New York, appeared under the pseudonyms of Cato (thought by some to be New York's governor, George Clinton) and Federal Farmer.

The two sides differed among other things over whether the proposed House of Representatives would be truly representative of the people. One of the letters from a Federal Farmer put it in the following terms:

> The people of this country, in one sense, may all be democratic; but if we make the proper distinction between the few men of wealth and abilities, and consider them, as we ought, as the natural aristocracy of the country, and the great body of the people, the middle and lower classes, as the democracy, this federal representative branch will have but very little democracy in it.[29]

This was one of Jefferson's stated concerns, as we have seen, though he did not side with the Anti-Federalists during the ratification campaign. Jefferson's other stated concerns were also the main themes of the Anti-Federalists in their opposition to the Constitution—the prospect of an overly powerful executive and the lack of a bill of rights.

The perfunctory consideration and rejection of a bill of rights by the Constitutional Convention turned out to be a nearly fatal miscalculation. Shortly after the Constitution was signed, Mason sent his list of objections to George Washington. Perhaps because they had been scribbled on a committee report, Mason's views were given the status of a minority dissent and were rushed into print in the *Pennsylvania Packet* on October 4 under the heading "George Mason's Objections." The short work began with the words "There is no Declaration of Rights."[30] As historian Robert Rutland notes, Mason's "first sentence struck home. Through the next ten months, try as they might, supporters of the Constitution (soon glorying in the name 'Federalist') never were able to dispel the fears created by Mason's opening war cry."[31]

For whatever reason, the famed authors of the Federalist—Madison, Hamilton, and Jay—did not bother in their early letters to engage the Anti-Federalists on the bill of rights controversy. Although their series of letters to the public began to appear in New York City newspapers on October 27, 1787, it was not until Federalist No. 84, the next-to-last letter, that Hamilton undertook to explain why a bill of rights had not been included in the Constitution (this letter probably did not appear until after the last state, New York, had ratified the Constitution on July 26, 1788). In Federalist No. 84 Hamilton acknowledged the fuss that had been created over the issue: "the loud clamours against the plan of the convention, on this score." If the protests were well founded, he said, "no epithets of reprobation will be too strong for the constitution of this State," which also lacked a bill of rights. But both constitutions, according to Hamilton, "contain all which, in relations to their objects, is reasonably to be desired."[32]

Referring to the proposed Constitution, he wrote:

> Here, in strictness, the people surrender nothing; and as they retain everything they have no need of particular reservations. . . . Here is a better recognition of popular rights than volumes of those aphorisms which make the principal figure in several of our State bills of rights and which would sound much better in a treatise of ethics than in a constitution of government.[33]

According to Madison historian Rutland, "At first, Madison was not mindful of the hue and cry over an omitted bill of rights." Washington had sent Madison a copy of Mason's pamphlet, "and in reply Madison ignored the one which had the most public impact to dwell on matters of less substance."[34]

The first five states to ratify the Constitution had done so expeditiously in December of 1787 and January of 1788: Delaware, Pennsylvania, New Jersey, Georgia, and Connecticut. In none was the lack of a Bill of Rights an apparent stumbling block. However, the next state to ratify, Massachusetts, on February 6, 1788, did recommend that "certain amendments and alterations in the said Constitution" be introduced to "remove the fears and quiet the apprehensions of many of the good people of this Commonwealth and more effectually guard against an undue administration of the Federal Government."[35] There followed nine specific recommendations, including one calling for smaller House districts, and several others relating to taxes and the rights of citizens.

Since the proposed amendments were merely recommendations for consideration after the new government was in operation, Madison, in a letter to Washington, referred to them as "a mere blemish . . . in the least offensive form."[36]

Although Maryland ratified the Constitution on April 28 without recommending further amendments to the document, South Carolina, in its ratification resolution on May 23, followed the lead of Massachusetts in proposing amendments after the new government was formed. But more disturbing to Madison was news from his home state of Virginia that Patrick Henry, in league with George Mason, was attempting to wreck the ratification process by making a package of amendments, including a bill of rights, a prior condition for ratification. Madison hurried home to Virginia from New York to become a candidate for the Richmond ratification convention that was to begin on June 2. Moreover, Madison would learn from Hamilton that the New York and Virginia Anti-Federalists were attempting to collaborate in passing an identical set of conditional amendments.[37]

After considerable debate Madison and his allies secured Virginia's ratification of the Constitution with unconditional amendments attached on June 25 by a vote of 89 to 79. The final product of the Virginia ratifying convention is a masterful study in compromise. It consisted of two resolutions. The resolution of ratification contained the Federalists' philosophy that every power not granted to the people by the Constitution "remains with them and at their will," and therefore, that "no right of any denomination can be canceled abridged restrained or modified" by the Congress or president acting in any capacity except where such powers are granted by the Constitution for such purposes. The resolution goes on to list just two examples of these essential rights implicitly reserved to the people—"the liberty of Conscience and of the press."[38]

The second resolution adopted by the Virginia Convention listed proposed constitutional amendments for consideration by the Congress as soon as it assembled. Attached was a twenty-part "Declaration or Bill of Rights asserting and securing from encroachment the essential and unalienable Rights of the People." Included in this listing of rights were provisions affecting persons elected to the first two branches of government. In order that such elected officials may be "restrained from oppression by feeling and participating the public burthens, they should at fixt periods be reduced to a private station, return into the mass of the people." The listing further proposed that "the people have a right peaceably to assemble together to consult for the common good, or to instruct their Representatives; and that every freeman has a right to petition or apply to the legislature for redress of grievances."[39]

Following the "Declaration or Bill of Rights" to be included in the Constitution were a listing of twenty "Amendments to the Body of the Constitution." While there was no specific amendment on rotational term limits for representatives or senators, as was suggested for both branches, there was a specific proposal that the president should not hold office "for more than eight years in any term of sixteen years."[40]

New York followed suit a month later on July 26, 1788, adopting two resolutions similar to those adopted by Virginia: a ratifying resolution that included a declaration of rights reserved to the states and the people, and a resolution instructing their representatives to Congress to seek ratification of certain specified additional amendments to the Constitution. The former declaration included the right of the people "to instruct their Representatives" and "to petition or apply to the legislature for redress of grievances." The latter amendments included provisions limiting senators to no more than six years in office in any twelve-year period; the right of the legislatures of the states to recall their senators; and the ineligibility of the president for a third term.[41]

The state of New Hampshire had actually beaten Virginia to the punch by ratifying the Constitution five days earlier on June 21. New Hampshire's resolution, like Massachusetts's ratifying resolution, recommended that certain alterations and provisions be introduced into the Constitution—namely, a twelve-part bill of rights.[42]

North Carolina and Rhode Island would not ratify the Constitution until November of 1789 and May of 1790, respectively—well after the new government was under way. Rhode Island had earlier flouted the mode of ratification prescribed by the Constitutional Convention (and directed by the Congress) that the proposed Constitution "be submitted to a Convention of Delegates, chosen in each State by the People thereof, under the Recommendation of its Legislature, for their Assent and Ratification."[43] Instead, the Rhode Island legislature called for a public vote of the people. This was the first instance in the fledgling Republic of a popular referendum on a major national question. According to one historical account:

> Fearing the inevitable, Providence merchants boycotted the voting and the Antifederalist triumph was complete, as the Constitution was defeated in the only state where citizens voted directly in their town meetings, 2,708 to 237.[44]

Notes

1. *The Life and Selected Writings of Thomas Jefferson*, ed. Adrienne Koch and William Peden (New York: The Modern Library, 1944), letter to Edward Carrington, Paris, Aug. 4, 1787, 427.
2. Ibid.
3. Ibid., letter to John Adams, Nov. 13, 1787, 435.
4. Ibid., letter to James Madison, Dec. 29, 1787, 437–38.
5. *Documents Illustrative of the Formation of the Union of the American States*, ed. Charles C. Tansill, H. Doc. 398, 68th Cong., 1st sess. (Washington, D.C: U.S. Government Printing Office, 1927), 28.
6. Ibid., 125.
7. Ibid., 126.
8. Ibid., 160.

9. Ibid., 192–93.

10. The committee of the whole, consisting of all members of the parent body, is a device that originated in the British parliament to keep proceedings secret from the crown by replacing the Speaker (thought to be the crown's agent) with a chairman as presiding officer. As adapted by the colonial legislatures and subsequent American conventions and congresses, it retained its usefulness as a forum for free discussion and voting that would not be made part of the official journal. Its recommendations were still subject to review and final action by the parent body. See also Don Wolfensberger, "Committees of the Whole: Their Evolution and Functions," *Congressional Record*, 103d Cong., 1st sess., Jan. 5, 1993, H27–31. The British origins of the committee of the whole are also discussed in Chapter 7.

11. Ibid., 201–3. On June 12, the Committee of the Whole had adopted an amendment by Pinckney without objection or apparent debate striking from the Randolph (or Virginia) Plan a provision that would have limited members of the first branch of the legislature to not more than one term without an unspecified interval of time, and would have subjected them to recall (pp. 195 and 953).

12. Ibid., 254–56.

13. *Documents Illustrative of the Formation of the Union*, 488.

14. Ibid., 490.

15. Ibid., 396.

16. Ibid., 444.

17. Ibid., 447.

18. Ibid., 456–57.

19. Ibid., 451.

20. Ibid., 452.

21. Ibid., 454–55.

22. Catherine Drinker Bowen, *Miracle at Philadelphia: The Story of the Constitutional Convention, May to September, 1787* (1966; reprint, Boston: Little, Brown and Co., 1986), 189.

23. *Documents Illustrative of the Formation of the Union*, 166.

24. Bowen, *Miracle*, 228.

25. *Documents Illustrative of the Formation of the Union*, 650.

26. Ibid., 571–73.

27. Ibid., 716.

28. Ibid.

29. *Origins of the House of Representatives: A Documentary Record*, ed. Bruce A. Ragsdale (Washington, D.C.: U.S. Government Printing Office, 1990), 52–53. See also "Letters from the Federal Farmer, No. 3," *The Complete Anti-Federalist*, ed. Herbert J. Storing (Chicago: University of Chicago Press, 1981), 235–36.

30. Robert A. Rutland, "Madison's Career Peak: The Federal Convention of 1787," in *Papers on the Constitution*, ed. John W. Elsberg (Washington, D.C.: Center of Military History, United States Army, 1990), 40.

31. Ibid.

32. Alexander Hamilton, "Federalist No. 84," *The Federalist Papers* (New York: Mentor Books, 1961), 513.

33. Ibid.
34. Rutland, "Madison's Career Peak," 41.
35. *Documents Illustrative of the Formation of the Union*, State of Massachusetts resolution of ratification, 1018.
36. Rutland, "Madison's Career Peak," 44.
37. Ibid., 44–45.
38. *Documents Illustrative of the Formation of the Union*, State of Virginia resolution of ratification, 1027.
39. Ibid., 1029–30.
40. Ibid., 1032.
41. Ibid., State of New York resolutions of ratification, 1037, 1041, 1042.
42. Ibid., State of New Hampshire resolution of ratification, 1024–27.
43. Ibid., "Resolution of the Federal Convention Submitting the Constitution to Congress, September 17, 1787," 1005.
44. Rutland, "Madison's Career Peak," 44.

2

The Bill of Rights: Madison Gets Religion

THERE is no apparent record that James Madison made any binding commitment to future action by the new Congress on a bill of rights and other proposed amendments to the Constitution as the price for ratification by the Virginia Convention. However, his hand was forced on the issue when he ran for a seat in the new House of Representatives against his good friend James Monroe. Rumors had circulated among Baptists in his district that he did not favor a bill of rights or specific guarantees of religious freedom. To dispel these rumors, Madison wrote a letter to a Baptist minister in Culpeper County, admitting that he had not seen the need for a bill of rights. However, "circumstances are now changed," he explained:

> The Constitution is established on the ratification of eleven States and a very great majority of the people of America; and amendments, if pursued with a proper moderation and in a proper mode, will be not only safe, but may serve the double purpose of satisfying the minds of well meaning opponents and of providing additional guards in favor of liberty. Under this change of circumstances, it is my sincere opinion that the Constitution ought to be revised.[1]

He added that such rights should include "all the essential rights, particularly the rights of Conscience in the fullest latitude, the freedom of the press, trials by jury, security against general warrants, etc."[2] That commitment apparently appeased the doubters since Madison went on to beat Monroe by a comfortable margin.

The First Congress was supposed to convene on March 4, 1789, but it was not until April 1 that the House achieved a quorum and could proceed with business. Madison became the de facto legislative floor leader. After electing a Speaker and adopting its rules, the House passed essential legislation on tax revenues, the regulation of commerce, and the establishment of various executive departments. The press of this business did not distract Madison, however, from his commitment to a bill of rights. He had been compiling a list of all the suggested constitutional amendments that had been submitted by the state ratifying conventions. A pamphlet was produced revealing 209 specific recommendations from six state ratifying conventions for amendments to the Constitution. New York's ratifying convention had even gone so far as to call for a second convention to draft the amendments. President Washington, in his inaugural address to the Congress on April 30, 1789, which Madison is thought to have drafted, took cognizance of this strong sentiment on the part of the states for alterations in the Constitution:

> Besides the ordinary objects submitted to your care, it will remain with your [Congress's] judgment to decide how far an exercise of the occasional power delegated by the fifth article of the Constitution is rendered expedient at the present juncture by the nature of objections which have been urged against the system, or by the degree of inquietude which has given birth to them.[3]

Washington did not offer any specific recommendations for amendments, placing his "entire confidence in your [the Congress's] discernment and pursuit of the public good." But he did caution the Congress "to avoid every alteration which might endanger the benefits of a united and effective government, or which ought to await the future lessons of experience, a reverence for the characteristic rights of freemen and a regard for the public harmony."[4]

Not surprisingly, Madison scrupulously followed Washington's advice, winnowing the 209 proposals down to just 19. He avoided any major alterations in the structure of the government and focused instead on guaranteeing certain civil liberties—the long-awaited bill of rights. He presented the package to the House on June 8, 1789, and immediately moved that the House begin to consider it in the Committee of the Whole. Despite President Washington's support and Madison's steady commitment to presenting and passing the package, the Federalists were still not convinced of the necessity of the amendments and were therefore reluctant to consider them. The Anti-Federalists in Congress were also resistant, but for another reason: they did not think the amendments went far enough.

In arguing for immediate consideration, Madison noted that while the Constitution had been ratified by eleven of the thirteen states, "there is still a great number of our constituents who are dissatisfied with it; among whom are many respectable for their talents and patriotism, and respectable for the jealousy they have for their liberty." He continued: "We ought not to disregard their inclination, but on principles of amity and moderation, conform to their wishes and expressly declare the great rights of mankind secured under this Constitution."[5] After explaining the proposed amendments in some detail, Madison addressed the arguments that had been raised against a bill of rights.

The House did not resume consideration of the amendments until July 21. At that time a motion was made to refer the proposed amendments to a select committee of eleven, consisting of one representative from each state. Elbridge Gerry of Massachusetts, who had not signed the original Constitution, objected to a select committee on grounds that it would be under no obligation to consider other amendments that had been recommended by the states but excluded from Madison's package. The motion was consequently amended to clarify that the select committee consider both the amendments proposed by Madison and those other amendments proposed by the several states. The motion carried.[6]

The select committee reported its recommendations back to the House in virtually the same form recommended by Madison, making only minor alterations and consolidating the package from nineteen to seventeen amendments. The House began considering them on August 13, 1789, and did not complete its work until August 24 after an arduous debate and amendment process.

Perhaps the most interesting debate (certainly from the standpoint of this book on Congress and the people) occurred on an amendment offered by Rep. Thomas Tudor Tucker of South Carolina. The House was considering the following amendment recommended by the select committee: "The freedom of speech and of the press, and the right of the people peaceably to assemble and consult for their common good, and to apply for redress of grievances shall not be infringed." Tucker offered an amendment to insert, after "common good," the words "to instruct their representatives."[7]

As was noted earlier, both the New York and Virginia ratifying resolutions had included a recommendation recognizing the right of the people to instruct their representatives in Congress. Moreover, it was pointed out by Rep. Aedanus Burke of South Carolina during debate on [Tucker's] amendment that the "Constitutions of Massachusetts, Pennsylvania, and North Carolina, all of them recognize, in express terms, the right of the people to give instructions to their representatives."[8]

The debate on the Tucker amendment captures the various views of the members of the First Congress on the role of the representative, his relationship to his constituents, and the wariness of some in the House about the threat of direct democracy.

Rep. Thomas Hartley of Pennsylvania expressed regret that the amendment had even been offered since there was little danger of error given the shortness of House terms and the division of powers in the government. Moreover, it must be presumed that members have the confidence of the people during the period for which they are elected, "and if by misconduct they forfeit it, their constituents have the power of leaving them out at the expiration of that time—thus they are answerable for the part they have taken in measures that may be contrary to the general wish."[9]

Hartley went on to observe that "representation is the principle of our government; the people ought to have confidence in the honor and integrity of those they send forward to transact their business; their right to instruct them is a problematical subject." And he proceeded to explain why:

> We have seen it attended with bad consequences both in England and America when the passions of the people are excited, instructions have been resorted to and obtained to answer party purposes; and although the public opinion is generally respectable, yet at such moments it has been known to be often wrong; and happy is that Government composed of men of firmness and wisdom to discover and resist popular error.[10]

Hartley then pointed out the problems posed by instructions to a deliberative process in which "the great end of meeting is to consult for the common good." In his words:

> A local or partial view does not necessarily enable any man to comprehend it [the common good] clearly; this can only result from an inspection into the aggregate. Instructions viewed in this light will be found to embarrass the best and wisest men. . . . And were all the members to take their seats in order to obey instructions and those instructions were so various as it is probable they would be, what possibility would there exist of so accommodating each to the other as to produce any act whatever?[11]

Because "so many inconveniences and evils arise from adopting the popular opinions of the moment," Hartley hoped the government would not bind itself to such opinions by constitutional act or submit to their influence by oath. "If they do," he warned, "the great object which this Government has been established to attain will inevitably elude our grasp on the uncertain and veering winds of popular commotion."[12]

Rep. John Page of Virginia took the opposite view, noting that under a democracy, "whose great end is to form a code of laws congenial with public sentiment, the people's opinion ought to be collected and attended to." He went on:

> Our Government is derived from the people, of consequence the people have a right to consult for the common good; but to what end will this be done if they have not the power of instructing their representatives? Instruction and representation in a Republic appear to me to be inseparably connected; but were I the subject of a monarch, I would doubt whether the public good did not depend more upon the prince's will than the will of the people.[13]

Rep. George Clymer of Pennsylvania said the Tucker amendment was "utterly destructive of all ideas of an independent and deliberative body" and that its passage would render the Congress "a mere passive machine."[14]

Rep. Roger Sherman of Connecticut echoed these thoughts, saying that if members are guided by instructions, "there would be no use in deliberation; all a man would have to do would be to produce his instructions and lay them on the table, and let them speak for him."[15]

Elbridge Gerry, in an apparent reversal of his antidemocracy stance at the Constitutional Convention, supported a constitutional declaration that the people have the right to instruct their representatives. Such instructions "will form a useful fund of information for the legislature." And he went on:

> We cannot, I apprehend, be too well informed of the true state, condition, and sentiment of our constituents, and perhaps this is the best mode in our power of obtaining information. I hope we shall never shut our ears against the information which is to be derived from the petitions and instructions of our constituents. I hope we have never presumed to think that all the wisdom of this country is contained within the walls of this House.[16]

Rep. Michael Jenifer Stone of Maryland argued that if the instruction provision became part of the Constitution, any law passed by Congress would be of no force if a majority of the members had been instructed to the contrary. Instead of looking at the law itself, the judiciary would be forced to examine the instructions from the various parts of the Union. "It follows very clearly from hence," concluded Stone, "that the Government would be altered from a representative one to a democracy, wherein all laws are made immediately by the voice of the people."[17]

To this Gerry sarcastically responded that he "had always heard it was a democracy; but perhaps he was misled, and the honorable gentleman was right in distinguishing it by some other appellation; perhaps an aristocracy was a term better adapted to it."[18]

When the question on the Tucker amendment to allow people to instruct their representatives was finally called, it was rejected by a vote of 10 to 41.[19]

Before the House concluded its consideration of the constitutional amendments on August 25, Representatives Gerry and Tucker tried two other tacks to broaden the scope of amendments. On August 18 Gerry offered a motion to commit the package to the Committee of the Whole with instructions to consider all the other amendments proposed by the states. His motion failed, 16-34.[20] Tucker then tried a similar approach that specified which amendments should be considered in the Committee of the Whole. These included consecutive term limits on the president, representatives, and senators; annual elections of senators; and a limit on the government's authority for direct taxation. His motion failed on a voice vote.[21] The Senate consolidated the seventeen House proposals into twelve, which were submitted to the states on September 25, 1789. A little over two years later, in December of 1991, three-fourths of the states had ratified ten of the twelve amendments; the ten passed would be our Bill of Rights.[22]

By keeping his promise to see through the ratification of the Bill of Rights, Madison had a tremendous impact on the recalcitrant states of Rhode Island and North Carolina: they rethought their status outside the Union, and a full Union of thirteen states became a reality. Summarizing Madison's roles in the Constitutional Convention, the fight for ratification, and the adoption of the Bill of Rights by the First Congress, historian Robert Rutland exudes:

> He had done more than any other American to build the new ship of state, he had guided her into a safe harbor, and he had believed that her rigging and timbers were sound enough for the storms ahead. Madison was both the master builder and the pilot. The Union was saved, and the twin goals of the Revolution—liberty and self-government—were preserved for posterity.[23]

Notes

1. Robert A. Rutland, "Madison's Career Peak: The Federal Convention of 1787," in *Papers on the Constitution*, ed. John W. Elsberg (Washington, D.C.: Center of Military History, U.S. Army, 1990), 46.

2. Ibid.

3. *Inaugural Addresses of the Presidents of the United States: From George Washington, 1789, to George Bush, 1989*, S. Doc. 101-10, 101st Cong., 1st Sess. (Washington, D.C.: U.S. Government Printing Office, 1989), 4.

4. Ibid.

5. *Annals of the Congress of the United States, First Congress: The Debates and*

Proceedings of the Congress of the United States, comp. Joseph Gales Senior, Washington, D.C., June 8, 1789, 432.

6. Ibid., 662, 664–65.
7. Ibid., 733.
8. Ibid., 745.
9. *Annals of the Congress*, 733.
10. Ibid.
11. Ibid., 734.
12. Ibid.
13. Ibid.
14. Ibid., 735
15. Ibid., 735–36.
16. Ibid., 737.
17. Ibid., 739.
18. Ibid., 742–43.
19. Ibid., 747.
20. Ibid., 757.
21. Ibid., 761–62.
22. The two amendments not ratified would have increased the number of representatives and delayed any increase in the compensation of members of Congress until after the next election. The latter amendment, known as the Madison amendment because of his authorship of it, was ratified over two hundred years later by the requisite number of states on May 18, 1992. Three years earlier the Congress had given the Madison amendment on member's pay statutory force and effect by including it in the Ethics Reform Act of 1989.
23. Rutland, "Madison's Career Peak," 46.

3

The Right to Petition: The Long Drive

THE protections against laws abridging the freedom of religion, speech, and the press are perhaps the best known of the rights delineated in the First Amendment. But just as important in a democracy are "the right of the people peaceably to assemble, and to petition the Government for a redress of grievances." Like the freedom of religion, speech, and press, the rights of assembly and petition had rocky starts in our history and were subject to official abuse and neglect.

When James Madison initially presented his draft constitutional amendments to the First Congress on June 8, 1789, the applicable provision read:

> The people shall not be restrained from peaceably assembling and consulting for the common good; nor from applying to the Legislature by petitions, or remonstrances, for redress of their grievances.[1]

When the provision was reported back to the House from the select committee in August of 1789, the clause had been changed:

> and the right of the people peaceably to assemble and consult for their common good, and to apply to the Government for redress of grievances shall not be infringed.[2]

Although the House did not further amend the clause, the Senate replaced the word "applying" with the words "to petition," while retaining "Government" over Madison's original "Legislature."

The right of citizens to petition government for a redress of grievances traces back to chapter 61 of the Magna Carta in 1215. The right was subsequently used by the Parliament, which petitioned the king for a redress of grievances as a trade-off for meeting the financial needs of the monarch. This right eventually grew into the Parliament's right to dictate the king's response to such petitions. In 1414 the House of Commons declared itself to be "as well assenters as petitioners." And by 1669 the Commons had further resolved that every commoner in England had "the inherent right to prepare and present petitions" to it "in case of grievance." The Commons was "to receive the same" and judge whether the petitions "were fit to be received." Finally, the English Bill of Rights of 1689 asserted the right of subjects to petition the king and made "all commitments and prosecutions for such petitioning to be illegal."[3]

The right to petition the government for a redress of grievances was well ingrained in the English settlers who came to America's shores, and it took early root in the colonial and state legislatures, many of which adopted their own bills or declarations of rights. This, in turn, led to the demand for and eventual adoption of the Bill of Rights added to the Constitution in 1791.

Even before the First Congress began consideration of a bill of rights, the House adopted a rule on April 7, 1789, providing for the disposition of citizen and state petitions, the latter being known as memorials. The new House rule read as follows:

> Petitions, memorials, and other papers addressed to the House, shall be presented through the Speaker, or by a member in his place, and shall not be debated or decided on the day of their first being read, unless where the House shall direct otherwise; but shall lie on the table, to be taken up in the order they were read.[4]

According to one commentary, "during the first several decades of the federal government, before the development of a modern party system, petitions served as one of the most important means of communication between constituents and their representatives."[5] They were also an important source of legislative initiatives in the Congress. A petition from John Fitch of Philadelphia, sent on April 2, 1789, and laid before the Congress on May 13, requested a patent on a method of steam locomotion. The petition was submitted through James Madison in the House and William Samuel Johnson of Connecticut in the Senate. It was one of several petitions from citizens seeking patents that led to passage of the Patents Act in April of 1790.[6]

A petition from "Tradesmen, Manufacturers, and Others of the Town of Baltimore," laid before the Congress on April 11, 1789, discussed the problems of trade regulation and the need for some form of protection for new industries.

This and similar petitions were referred to the Committee of the Whole in the House during consideration of the Impost Act, which passed in July of 1789.[7]

According to the index for the combined *House Journal* for the First and Second Congresses, a total of 217 citizen petitions were filed in the first two Congresses during the years 1789 to 1792.[8] From the outset of the new Republic, the right of petition was considered an important means of citizen communication, involvement, and influence on the legislation of Congress. Members paid close attention to such entreaties.

Although the right to file petitions was well established with the first set of rules adopted by the House in 1789, Congress was not always willing to heed them. A case in point is the issue of slavery. The Constitution (Article I, section 9, clause 1) had specifically prohibited the Congress from taking any action restricting the slave trade in the original thirteen states prior to 1808. Moreover, Article V prohibited Congress from considering any amendment to the Constitution regarding slavery prior to 1808.

Notwithstanding that clear prohibition, petitions were received by the Congress before 1808 calling for the abolition of slavery. At that time the petitions were simply referred to committee and not acted on. As time went on, however, opposition to them by southern members increased. Antislavery sentiment and sectional strife grew in the wake of several slave uprisings.

The issue gained considerable momentum in the 1830s when the American Anti-Slavery Society organized a petition drive aimed at the Congress. According to one account:

> The society, thanks largely to the efforts of anti-slavery women, bombarded Congress with hundreds of thousands of petitions that called for ending slavery and the slave trade in the nation's capital, abolishing the interstate slave trade, adopting legislation barring slavery from western territories, and rejecting the admission of any new slave state.[9]

The problem of how to handle such petitions came to a head in December of 1835 when Rep. William Jackson of Massachusetts presented a petition calling for the abolition of slavery in the District of Columbia. Rep. James H. Hammond of South Carolina moved that the petition not be received. This set off a prolonged debate.[10]

While the debate was still raging on January 4, 1836, Rep. John Quincy Adams of Massachusetts, the only House member to have previously served as president of the United States (1825–28), entered the fray by presenting another petition from citizens of his state calling for the abolition of slavery and the slave trade in the District of Columbia. Rep. Thomas Glascock of Georgia offered a motion that the petition not be received. He cited as his authority *Jefferson's Manual:* "regularly a motion for receiving a petition must be made and seconded, and a question put whether it shall be received." Unconvinced, Adams responded that it was a "foundation principle that the House had no right to take away or abridge the constitutional right of petition."[11]

Finally, on February 4, 1836, Rep. Henry L. Pinckney of South Carolina proposed that the whole subject of petitions and slavery be referred to a select committee. The proposal was adopted and sent to a nine-member select committee that reported its recommendations back to the House on May 18. The following week after lengthy debate three resolutions were passed by the House. The first, adopted by a vote of 182 to 9, stated that the Congress had no constitutional authority to interfere with the institution of slavery in any of the states of the Confederacy. The second resolution, adopted 132-45, declared that the Congress ought not interfere in any way with slavery in the District of Columbia. And the third resolution, adopted by vote of 117 to 68, stated that all resolutions related to slavery should be laid on the table without being printed or referred, and that no further action should be taken on them.[12]

On January 19, 1837, Rep. Albert G. Hawes of Kentucky, in order to put an end to the discussions of the abolition of slavery that were taking a great deal of the time of the House, offered a resolution nearly identical to the third resolution adopted the previous year. It stated that "all petitions, memorials, resolutions, propositions, or papers relating in any way to slavery, shall, without being printed or referred, be laid upon the table, and that no further action be had thereon."

Undeterred by this, Adams, who had earned the nickname "Old Man Eloquent" for his unremitting attacks on slavery, arose in the House a few weeks later on February 6, 1837, and said that he had in his hand a petition signed by twenty-two persons, declaring themselves to be slaves. As it later developed, the petition was a forgery perpetrated by one of the southern members and intended as a joke on Adams. Adams did not disclose the contents of the petition, which called for his expulsion, and instead let members proceed on the assumption that it called for the abolition of slavery in the District of Columbia, as the earlier ones had.[13]

Adams posed a parliamentary inquiry to the Speaker as to what the disposition of the petition was under House rules. Immediately another member leapt to his feet and offered a resolution censuring Adams for "gross disrespect of the House." The censure resolution was debated and amended over the course of several days. Two resolutions were then put to a vote by the House. Both were rejected. The first resolution stated that any member who in the future presented a petition from slaves "ought to be considered as regardless of the feelings of the House, the rights of the Southern States, and unfriendly to the Union." The second resolution stated that since John Quincy Adams had disclaimed any intent to do anything disrespectful of the House and promised not to present such a petition in the future, all further proceedings in regard to his conduct were terminated.[14]

The matter was not over, however. Nine days later, on February 18, 1837, Rep. Amos Lane of Indiana moved to reconsider the votes by which the two resolutions had been rejected. The House eventually adopted two substitutes. The first substitute resolution, adopted 160-35, stated that the House could not receive the petition presented by Adams. The second substitute resolution, adopted by a vote of 162 to 18, stated that "slaves do not possess the right of petition secured to the people of the United States by the Constitution."[15]

On December 21, 1837, the new 25th Congress adopted a resolution similar to those adopted in previous Congresses. Petitions on slavery would be automatically laid on the table without being read or referred. On December 12, 1838, in that same Congress, several petitions on slavery were laid on the table, and the action was accompanied by a "declaration of the character of the Government under the Constitution, the rights of Congress in relation to slavery, etc."[16]

None of this stopped Adams from keeping the issue of slavery before the House. He simply found creative new ways to do so. On January 7, 1839, for instance, he presented to the House a petition asking for the appointment of a "committee on color" to whom "all officeholders and Members of Congress would be referred for an examination of their respective pedigrees in order that all persons having the least degree of colored blood in their veins might be expelled from office." Not surprisingly, a question was raised as to whether this was an attempt to ridicule the House, and therefore, whether the petition should be received. The House decided that it was not a proper or respectful petition, and voted 25 to 115 against receiving it.[17]

The following year, on January 28, 1840, after a lengthy debate the House adopted this standing rule (unlike the temporary orders that expired at the end of each Congress):

> No petition, memorial, resolution, or other paper praying the abolition of slavery in the District of Columbia or any State or Territory, or the slave trade between the States or Territories of the United States in which it now exists, shall be received by this House or entertained in any way whatever.[18]

Because the House rule on petitions required that they be read before any action was taken on them, such as whether to receive them or refer them to committee, a considerable backup of petitions was created. In 1838 and 1840 the House adopted temporary orders to relieve this congestion. The orders permitted petitions to be handed to the clerk of the House and, without being read, to be automatically disposed of by the Speaker, who would determine whether they should be received or referred. In both of those years, once the congestion had been relieved, the House rescinded its orders and thereby reverted to the standing rule of the House.

To pave the way for repealing the "gag rule" on slavery petitions, Adams offered the previous temporary orders as a standing rule of the House on March 29, 1842. At that time he had 150 petitions in his desk that he had been prevented from offering. The House adopted the rule under suspension of the rules, which required a two-thirds vote. As adopted, the rule read:

> That Members having petitions and memorials to present be permitted to hand them to the Clerk, endorsing the same with their names, and the reference or disposition to be made thereof, and that such petitions and memorials be entered on the Journal, subject to the control and direction of the Speaker, and if any petition or memorial be so handed, in which in the judgment of the Speaker is excluded by the rules, that the same be returned to the Member from whom it was received.[19]

The backlog of petitions was created by the reluctance of the House to consider or have read any petitions, notwithstanding the rule prohibiting the reading of any antislavery petitions and their automatic tabling. However,

> as soon as Mr. Adams' rule was adopted a flood of petitions was presented, the titles of which occupy twenty three pages of the Journal. Petitions relating to slavery were questioned by the Speaker and laid on the table. Thus was solved the problem of presenting petitions without consuming the time of the House.[20]

The previous year, on June 7, 1841, Adams had scored a temporary victory in rescinding the "gag rule" when he offered a motion that it not be adopted as part of the rules of the House until the Rules Committee had made its report on further changes in the rules. Although his motion was adopted, on the following day a motion was made to reconsider the vote setting aside the "gag rule." After six days of debate, the House reversed itself, and the rule was reinstated.

It would not be until the convening of the second session of the 28th Congress, on December 3, 1844, that Adams finally succeeded once and for all in rescinding the "gag rule" on antislavery petitions. His motion was adopted by vote of 108 to 80. That evening, reflecting on his triumph, Adams wrote in his diary: "Blessed, forever, blessed, be the name of God!" A week later a petition was received from the citizens of New York City calling for the abolition of slavery in the District of Columbia. The petition was received and referred by the Speaker to the Committee on the District of Columbia.[21]

Slavery was not abolished in the District of Columbia until the adoption of Henry Clay's Compromise of 1850—two years after Adams died at the age of eighty from a stroke suffered during debate on the House floor. And it would take a bloody Civil War before slavery was finally abolished nationwide with the ratification of the Thirteenth Amendment to the Constitution in 1865. But Adams died knowing that his successful effort to repeal the "gag rule" dealt slavery its first defeat and would help pave the way for the great debates on slavery in the next decade.

Exercising the Right: Resistance and Progress

The right of the people to petition their government for a redress of grievances has met with other obstacles over the course of American history. For instance, in 1894 General Coxey of Ohio organized a march on Washington by armies of unemployed persons to present petitions to Congress for jobs. Instead of receiving the petitions, the government arrested the leaders of the march.

During World War I, petitions for repeal of the espionage and sedition laws and against military recruiting measures resulted in imprisonment. A march of veterans on Washington in 1932 to petition for bonus legislation was considered by the government to be a threat to the Constitution. The U.S. Army was called out to expel the veterans and burn their camps.[22]

In more recent times the government has learned how to better accommodate large demonstrations of citizens who come to the nation's capital to petition their government for a redress of grievances. On August 28, 1963, 250,000 demonstrators participated in a "March on Washington" in support of civil rights. This activism bore fruit in the 1964 Civil Rights Act. On November 15, 1969, 250,000 people converged on Washington, D.C., for a "Vietnam Moratorium" rally—the peak of the antiwar protests. On May 9, 1970, 60,000 to 100,000 persons held an antiwar rally on the Ellipse behind the White House. Equal effort was given to influencing the Congress as "thousands of students and university officials streamed through Members' offices presenting petitions urging an end to U.S. military involvement in Southeast Asia."[23]

Smaller antiwar rallies organized by more radical protest groups in April and May of 1971 produced the only significant outbreaks of violence and arrests. On May 5 some 800 demonstrators were arrested at the U.S. Capitol and detained in R.F.K. Stadium. The charges against most of them were dropped after the first eight to be tried were acquitted.

On May 24, 1972, Rep. Bella Abzug (D-N.Y.) rose on the House floor to highlight an antiwar petition:

> We have petitioning us today outstanding citizens of this country, social leaders, leaders of the arts, sciences, and professions. They have come here to petition us to act immediately to cut off funds for the war and end our military activity in Indochina.[24]

She then asked unanimous consent of the House that "a representative of those citizens come in and have the opportunity to present a petition, and that we hear what those people, who are the conscience of this country and who represent a majority of the American people, have to say." To that the Speaker replied, "The gentlewoman's request is not in order." A "Parliamentarian's Note" indicates that "under Rule XXXII, clause 1, the Speaker does not have the authority to entertain a request to waive the rule pertaining to the privilege of admission to the floor."[25]

A survey of *House Journal* volumes in the second half of this century reveals a steady decline in the popularity and use of petitions as a method of influencing the Congress. Whereas in the 82d Congress (1951–53), 800 petitions were filed with the House, in the 87th Congress (1961–63), this number was nearly halved to 414, and in the 92d Congress (1971–73), the number had dropped to 287. There was a temporary bump in petitions filed in the House in the 92d Congress (1981–83) when 681 were presented—many of which advocated a popular "nuclear freeze." But the trend since then has been generally downward (see Table 3.1).

Ironically, the 226 petitions filed in the 103d and 104th Congresses combined is not much more than the 217 petitions filed in the House in the 1st and 2d Congresses combined, even though the nation's population has grown from 4 million to 260 million in the interim. The decline in the use of petitions can be ascribed to a number of factors. The most obvious is the increased use of "grass-roots" or "Astroturf" mass mailings to members of Congress promoted by special interests. These mailings, even though computer generated, are more likely to get attention and a response by a member if they are sent by individual constituents, than would be a single petition containing the same number of constituents' names. The petition would be filed with the clerk of the House, referred to a committee, and most likely forgotten.

Another factor is the ease of communication between a constituent and a representative not only by mail post, but by phone, fax, e-mail, telegram, and district office appointments. Those means of communication have all proven more effective in attracting attention and responses than the more formal petition. Since the mid-1970s, members of Congress have actually become proactive in soliciting constituents' grievances by scheduling regular district office hours and town hall meetings. Some members even have traveling office vans that make it easy for constituents to get in touch.

Modern Petition Techniques

Nevertheless, petitions can still serve as a photogenically dramatic way for a group to present its particular wishes or demands to Congress. Three examples of this were demonstrated early in the 105th Congress—one relating to Social Security, another to campaign finance reform, and the third to a constitutional amendment on flag desecration.

On February 25, 1997, a group of ten House and Senate Democrats, led by Senate minority leader Tom Daschle (D-S.D.), attended a press conference called by the National Committee to Protect Social Security and Medicare. The group accepted what the organization's press release described as "over 890,000 petitions urging the Congress to vote against a balanced budget amendment (BBA) which doesn't protect the Social Security Trust Fund." As the press release noted, "A dozen large boxes overflowing with petitions, were displayed at the event." The petitions were "signed by National Committee members from all fifty states and from every congressional district in the country."[26]

On the afternoon of the press conference, Sen. Harry Reid (D-Nev.) offered an amendment to the pending constitutional amendment (S.J. Res. 1) "to require that the outlay and receipt totals of the Federal Old-Age and Survivors Insurance and the Federal Disability Trust Funds not be included as a part of the budget totals."[27]

Table 3.1
Petitions Filed in the House of Representatives, 98th–105th Congresses (1983–99)

Congress	Years	Petitions filed
98th	1983–85	416
99th	1985–87	493
100th	1987–89	241
101st	1989–91	254
102nd	1991–93	176
103rd	1993–95	145
104th	1995–97	81
105th	1997–99	93

Sources: *House Journal*, various volumes; Congressional Record Indexes; Office of the Clerk of the House.

During the discussion of his amendment, Reid made the following reference to the petitions:

> Mr. President, we received today almost a million signatures from a group of senior citizens who signed these petitions in the last few days. They have a right to do that. Of course they do, because, Mr. President, American seniors are exercising a powerful right to stop a devastating wrong. The right to petition our Government for wrongs is guaranteed in the first amendment of the Constitution. This right is a cornerstone of our democracy and deserves to be enshrined in the Constitution, and it was. Giving Congress and the courts the power to permanently raid Social Security should not be guaranteed by the highest, most powerful legal document in our country.[28]

Earlier in the debate, Sen. Dianne Feinstein (D-Calif.), who had been present at the morning's press conference, also made reference to the petitions by noting:

> This morning we had signatures from 890,000 Social Security recipients, urging our opposition to any balanced budget amendment which does not protect Social Security. Those signatures represent just the current recipients today. People like my daughter, who is in her mid-thirties, is working and providing that money, said to me, "Mother, you know that isn't going to be there when I retire. Why don't you just let me have the money now. There are better things I can do with it. I could use it right now."[29]

At the end of the day the Reid amendment was tabled, 55-44. But several days later the constitutional amendment itself would fall one vote short of the required two-thirds majority for passage. Ironically, the petition was never formally filed with the secretary of the Senate (or the clerk of the House). But it had served its purpose as a valuable prop for a photo-op. Indeed, the day after the press conference the leading Capitol Hill newspaper, *The Hill*, ran a front-page picture showing the overflowing boxes of petitions and the caption "Senior Power: Sen. Dianne Feinstein displays petitions from senior citizens who oppose GOP version of balanced budget amendment."[30]

On February 12, 1997, another press conference was held—this one announcing a petition drive by two citizen groups, Common Cause and Campaign for America. Their goal was to collect 1,776,000 signatures on petitions urging congressional passage of campaign finance reform by the Fourth of July. The petition campaign, called "Project Independence," was termed by its organizers "the largest grassroots initiative ever." Citizens in all fifty states were asked to sign a "Declaration For Independence" from "the influence of special interest money." The joint press release announcing the petition drive noted that citizens could sign by calling a new toll-free number or by calling up the Common Cause World Wide Web site on their computers.[31]

The third petition drive in the 105th Congress attracted attention on June 12, 1997, during debate on a special rule for the consideration of a constitutional amendment to prohibit the physical desecration of the American flag. Rules Committee chairman Gerald B. Solomon (R-N.Y.), after explaining the debate and amendment procedures provided in the rule, went on to discuss the popular support for the constitutional amendment. He pointed out that forty-nine state legislatures had passed resolutions calling on Congress to pass the amendment. The proposed constitutional amendment "is not an idea that just a few people dreamed up," he said. "We are responding to the will of the overwhelming majority of the American people by restoring to the Federal Government power to protect the flag of this Nation."[32] He then called the attention of the House to the committee table at which he was standing:

> Stacked on this table right next to me now are more than 3 million signatures of people from all walks of life, and I would invite Members to come over and take a look at them—3 million signatures from my colleagues' congressional districts. These signatures were gathered by the American Legion and the Citizens Alliance.[33]

The flag constitutional amendment passed the House later that day by a vote of 310 to 114, twenty-seven votes over the two-thirds majority necessary.[34]

Computers or toll-free numbers can be used to gather signatures on petitions to Congress. This may spark a renewed interest in the use of this right to influence Congress. There is no requirement in House rules that all signatures on a petition must be original signatures. According to precedents and current practices, as long as the first name on the petition is an original signature, it does not matter whether the rest are or not.

A dispute did arise in the Senate on February 25, 1879, over whether the Senate could receive a petition that had been sent by telegraphic dispatch from someone purporting to be E. F. Smith, the secretary of the Constitutional Convention of the State of California. The Senate rule specified that "before any petition or memorial shall be received or read at the table it shall be signed by the petitioner or memorialist." Sen. James Blaine of Maine argued that as long as the senator or presiding officer presenting it "stood sponsor for it as an authentic memorial or telegraphic dispatch, it should be received as it might be the only means by which a distant community could exercise its right of petition." The vice president, the presiding officer who had originally laid the matter before the Senate, could not vouch for the authenticity of the dispatch. Thus he upheld the point of order that it not be received, even though one of the senators from California offered to vouch for it.[35]

The appearance of thousands of typed names of citizens on a petition may not cause a problem for the House or Senate in receiving the petition, so long as the first name is an original and verifiable signature. But the organizers who have gathered the names by phone or computer could be embarrassed if some names turn out to have been falsely submitted. Since there is no legal penalty for such filings, it is unlikely that the organizing group would take the trouble to verify each submission. But, for the future credibility of both the group and the process, some random verification will probably be advisable in this new electronic age.

Notes

1. *Annals of the Congress of the United States, First Congress: The Debates and Proceedings of the Congress of the United States*, comp. Joseph Gales Senior, Washington, D.C., June 8, 1789, 434.

2. Ibid., Aug. 15, 1789, 731.

3. *The Constitution of the United States of America: Analysis and Interpretation*, ed. Johnny H. Killian, S. Doc. 9916 (Washington, D.C.: U.S. Government Printing Office, 1987), 1142.

4. *Annals of the Congress*, April 7, 1789, 100.

5. *Origins of the House of Representatives: A Documentary Record*, ed. Bruce A. Ragsdale (Washington, D.C.: U.S. Government Printing Office, 1990), 145.

6. Ibid., 145–49.

7. Ibid., 149–51.

8. Under Article I, section 5, clause 3 of the Constitution, "each House shall keep a Journal of its Proceedings and from time to time, publish the same." The *Journal* records the actions of the body, including the introduction and referral of bills and resolutions, the filing of committee reports, and the receipt and referral of messages from the executive and memorials and petitions from states and citizens. Although the *Journal* records the texts and votes on motions and amendments, it does not include a transcript or summary of legislative debates. These are published in the *Congressional Record*.

9. Leonard L. Richards, "Adams, John Quincy," in *The Encyclopedia of the United States Congress*, ed. Donald C. Bacon, Roger H. Davidson, and Morton Keller (New York: Simon and Schuster, 1995), vol. 1, 7.

10. Paul S. Rundquist, "Petitions and Memorials," in ibid., vol. 3, 1541–42.

11. Asher C. Hinds, *Hinds' Precedents of the House of Representatives of the United States* (Washington, D.C.: U.S. Government Printing Office, 1907), vol. 4, sec. 3344, 276.

12. Ibid., 275–76.

13. For a more detailed description of this incident and the slavery petition controversy, see the excellent book by William Lee Miller, *Arguing about Slavery: The Great Battle in the United States Congress* (New York: Alfred A. Knopf, 1996).

14. Hinds, *Hinds' Precedents*, sec. 3342, 275.

15. Ibid.

16. Ibid., sec. 3346, 278; sec. 3343, 275.

17. Ibid., sec. 3352.

18. Ibid., sec. 3347, 278.

19. Ibid., sec. 3312, 264.

20. Ibid.

21. House Committee on Rules, *A History of the Committee on Rules*, committee print, 97th Cong, 2d sess. (Washington, D.C.: U.S. Government Printing Office, 1983), 44.

22. Killian, ed., *The Constitution of the United States*, 1143–44.

23. *Congressional Quarterly Almanac, 1970*, vol. 26 (Washington, D.C.: Congressional Quarterly, 1970), 931.

24. Lewis Deschler, *Deschler's Precedents of the United States House of Representatives*, H. Doc. 94-661, 94th Cong., 2d sess. (Washington, D.C.: U.S. Government Printing Office, 1977), vol. 7, chap. 24, sec. 10.2., 426.

25. Ibid.

26. National Committee to Preserve Social Security and Medicare, "Nation's Second-Largest Seniors Group Delivers Nearly One Million Petitions to Congress," media advisory, Feb. 25, 1997.

27. Reid Amendment No. 8 to S.J. Res. 1, Balanced Budget Amendment to the Constitution, *Congressional Record*, Feb. 25, 1997, vol. 143, no. 21, S1495.

28. Ibid., S1541.

29. Ibid., S1511.

30. *The Hill*, vol. 4, no. 8, Feb. 26, 1997, 1. No story accompanied the picture.

31. "Common Cause & Campaign for America Launch 'Project Independence'," joint press release, Feb. 12, 1997, from Common Cause's Web site.

32. Remarks of Rep. Gerald B. Solomon, *Congressional Record*, June 12, 1997, H3726–27.

33. Ibid., 3727.

34. The resolution was never voted on by the Senate in the 106th Congress, even though a similar resolution (S.J. Res. 40) was reported from the Senate Judiciary Committee on June 24, 1998, on a 11-7 vote. In the 105th Congress the House passed the constitutional amendment by a vote of 312 to 120 on June 28, 1995, but a Senate version fell four votes short of a two-thirds majority on Dec. 12, 1995, 63–36.

35. Hinds, *Hinds' Precedents*, sec. 3328, 270–71.

4

Congress and the Progressive Era

THE Progressive Era in the late nineteenth and early twentieth centuries was marked by growing social and economic upheaval in the nation. Yet for much of this period Congress intensely resisted organizational change or legislation of any kind. Power was dispersed among a highly decentralized committee system. During the 48th through 50th Congresses (1883–89), observes congressional historian George B. Galloway, "the House of Representatives had been reduced to a condition of legislative impotence by abuses of its then existing rules of procedure. Not only was its legislative output small and insignificant, but the use of dilatory motions combined with the disappearing quorum and a series of filibusters to make the House an object of public ridicule and condemnation."[1]

Another historian, Mark Wahlgren Summers, cites examples of this legislative impotence. In the 45th Congress (1877–79), the House Claims Committee was flooded with 913 small claims cases, yet it considered only a few due to a lack of clerical staff and money. Of those it considered, only 163 claims bills were reported to the House, and only a dozen were finally acted on by the Congress. In the 48th Congress (1883–85), 11,000 bills, filling hundreds of pages of the House calendar, died at the end of the Congress for lack of time, while others that moved to the Senate were never heard from again.

Summers attributes the legislative ineffectiveness of the period to a number of factors. First, too many legislators spent too much time trying to satisfy individual constituents' claims and needs. Second, the government suffered from a long period of divided control. From 1875 to 1895, Democrats held the House in every Congress but two, while Republicans held every Senate but one. Not until 1881 did one party control the White House and both houses of Congress, and not until 1889 did a Congress come under strong enough partisan control to put through a legislative program. Third, the rules of procedure, especially the "disappearing quorum" tactic, favored minority-party obstruction and hindered majority action. Finally, members of Congress, especially Democrats, were disposed against making laws without a pressing need.[2]

Public pressure began to build against the gridlocked Congress. A January 19, 1888, *Washington Post* editorial entitled "Slowly Doing Nothing" blasted the House for passing only four minor bills in six weeks and blamed the system of rules as "the prime cause for the wonderful inertia of this unwieldy and self-shackled body." The *New York Tribune* ran a series of editorials in January of 1889 that also attacked the system of rules as "Legislative Lunacy." The paper demanded they be amended "to permit the majority to control the business for which it is responsible." And the *Washington Post,* in April of 1889, editorialized against the "un-Democratic, un-Republican, and un-American rules of the House of Representatives which have submitted that body to a petty committee of debaters." The *Post* followed up with a nationwide survey of public opinion that supported its contentions about the futility, wastefulness, and complexity of House procedures.[3]

The Reed Rules

It would take a big man to turn the system around, and Republican representative Thomas Brackett Reed of Maine would prove to be that man in more ways than one. First elected to the House in 1876, the six-foot-three-inch, 275-pound Reed was as large in intellect, vision, and political acumen as he was in physical stature.

In late June of 1879, the House appointed a Committee on Rules "for the purpose of revising, codifying, and simplifying the rules of the House." The five-member select committee was chaired by Democratic Speaker Samuel J. Randall of Pennsylvania. On December 19 it issued a unanimous report that cited the "urgent" need for a "thorough revision of rules of the House" as a parliamentary and "practical business necessity" because of the tremendous changes that had taken place in the House over the years. The committee's principal objective, according to its report, was "to secure accuracy in business, economy of time, order, uniformity and impartiality, and to prepare if possible a simple, concise, and non-partisan code of rules." The committee went on to describe its report as a document "which should neither surrender the right of the majority to control and dispose of the business for which it is held responsible, or, on the other hand, to invade and restrict the powers of a minority to check temporarily, if not permanently, the action of a majority believed to be improper or unconstitutional."[4]

All told, the proposal slashed the number of House rules from 169 to 44 by eliminating 32 obsolete or unnecessary rules, condensing another 122 rules into 32, and retaining 12 in their entirety. The House began debating the package of rules changes on January 6, 1880, and continued to consider and amend it over the next two months to the exclusion of all other business. Finally, on March 2, 1880, it was adopted.[5]

During consideration of the rules package, an amendment was offered to allow the Speaker to judge whether a quorum was present under certain circumstances. It was hoped this would eliminate the problem of the disappearing quorum, used so often by the minority as an obstructionist tactic. Some opposed the amendment, fearing that a future Speaker might abuse the rule by claiming the presence of a quorum when one did not actually exist. The argument was sufficiently persuasive with members of both parties that on the following day, the amendment was withdrawn.[6] One of the members who spoke in adamant opposition was Representative Reed, then serving his second term. He argued that minorities had not abused the disappearing quorum. The device, he said, was necessary to prevent harmful or partisan legislation by the majority. A decade later Reed's words would come back to haunt him.[7]

One of the reforms passed in 1880 was to make the Rules Committee a permanent standing committee of the House. Until then it had been a temporary, select committee with the sole purpose of recommending to the House changes in the standing rules at the beginning of each Congress. In 1858 the Speaker was made a member of the Select Committee on Rules, and the following year its chairman—the first time the presiding officer of the House was a member of a committee, let alone its chairman. With the elevation of the Rules Committee to a standing committee in 1880, the Speaker retained his chairmanship as well as his authority to appoint all other members to that and other House committees. The new Rules Committee was given jurisdiction over "all proposed action touching on the rules and joint rules."[8]

While the 1880 rules revision did not mention disappearing quorums and dilatory motions, it provided a platform—the newly strengthened Rules Committee—for future Speakers to deal with those problems. Already a master of parliamentary skills, Reed was one of the first members to recognize the full potential of the Rules Committee. Republicans recaptured control of the House in the election of 1880. When the 47th Congress convened in December of 1881, Reed received eleven votes for Speaker in the Republican Caucus, losing to J. Warren Keifer of Ohio. Keifer appointed Reed to the chairmanship of the Judiciary Committee, and, when an opening occurred on the Rules Committee, Keifer appointed Reed to fill that slot.

Reed immediately set about to put his ideas for stricter majority rule into practice. In March of 1882, he presented reports from the Rules Committee to amend House rules by permitting a majority vote to gain the immediate consideration of business, regardless of its place on the calendar. The amendments met with minority obstruction and were never brought to a vote. Two months later, on May 27, 1882, Reed presented another rules change to the House to abolish dilatory motions during the consideration of contested election cases. On this occasion the Speaker upheld Reed's point of order against a minority attempt to block consideration of the rules change with a motion to adjourn, and the House proceeded to adopt the new rule.[9]

Reed struck a third blow for the cause toward the end of the 47th Congress in February of 1883. An important House tariff bill, with Senate-passed amendments, had been stuck at the Speaker's table for several weeks because Republicans lacked the necessary two-thirds votes to suspend the rules and send it to a House-Senate conference committee. Reed persuaded the Rules Committee to report a special rule that would permit the House to suspend the rules by majority vote during the remainder of the session and to take the bill from the Speaker's table, declare a disagreement between the houses, and ask the Senate for a conference. The proposal was so radical that even some Republicans objected, and on the first vote on the special rule, a disappearing quorum was utilized to block its adoption. But the next day sufficient votes for the measure were mustered to adopt the rule, and the tariff bill was rushed through conference and sent to President Chester Arthur who signed it on March 3, 1883. Reed's biographer, William A. Robinson, wrote that "whatever may be thought of the contents of the measure, regarded strictly as a matter of party strategy and parliamentary tactics, its passage was one of the most daring maneuvers of Reed's entire career, or for that matter, in the history of Congress."[10]

When the Democrats recaptured control of the House in the 48th Congress (1883–85), their newly elected Speaker, John G. Carlisle of Kentucky, used special order resolutions from the Rules Committee infrequently because there was still some question about their validity. Moreover, Carlisle's reluctance to dispose of dilatory motions and disappearing quorums led to further filibusters and legislative stalemate.[11] This in turn gave rise to the outcry in the press and the public about the system of rules that prevented Congress from taking necessary legislative action.

Joining that hue and cry was Reed, even though he was a member of the minority that was often guilty of employing the rules for obstructionist and dilatory purposes. But his views remained consistent. As minority leader in the 49th and 50th Congresses (1885–89), he held the same views expressed while he was in the majority: "the rules of the House are not for the purpose of protecting the rights of the minority, but to promote the orderly conduct of the business of the House."[12]

In the election of 1888, Republican Benjamin Harrison was elected president, and Republicans recaptured control of both houses of Congress, aided by their support for a more protectionist tariff policy. The 51st Congress would not convene until December of 1889. In the interim Reed wrote articles for two national magazines, outlining his plans to end dilatory motions and reestablish majority rule in the House. In the October 1889 issue of *North American Review*, in an article titled "Obstruction in the National House," Reed predicted the 51st Congress would try "to establish rules which will facilitate the public business—rules unlike those of the present House, which only delay and frustrate action."[13]

Reed was in a position to make such a prediction with some certitude since he was likely to be elected Speaker and thereby serve as Rules Committee chairman as well. On December 2, 1889, Reed was elected Speaker by twelve votes over Carlisle, with Republicans outnumbering Democrats in the House, 170 to 160. The following day the House referred the House rules of the previous Congress to the Rules Committee for recommended changes.

The fiercest test of wills in the new year arose when the House took up a contested election case in West Virginia, Smith versus Jackson. Consideration of the matter was promptly challenged by Democratic Minority Leader Carlisle. The question carried on a nonrecorded division vote with a clear quorum present. On the roll call vote that followed, the Democrats refused to vote. Action halted because of the lack of a voting quorum. It was at this point that Speaker Reed ordered the clerks to call the names of those members who were present but who had refused to vote. Reed then proceeded to call the names of those whom he had observed. This produced a great uproar from the Democrats. As one observer, Rep. Joseph Gurney Cannon of Illinois, recalled years later, Democratic representative William Breckenridge of Kentucky rushed down to the well of the House and shouted, "I deny the power of Speaker, and denounce it as revolutionary."[14]

Reed then ruled that members present but not voting should be counted toward a quorum under the constitutional meaning of the term. Points of order against Reed's ruling were raised by the Democrats and, according to Galloway, "debate continued for three days amid scenes of unprecedented turbulence and disorder." During the course of the battle, Reed issued another famous ruling: he would refuse to recognize members rising to make dilatory motions.

When the turmoil eventually subsided, Reed's rulings were upheld on a party-line vote. Exercising his authority as chairman of the Rules Committee, Reed asked the committee to incorporate his rulings and other ideas for majority action into the standing rules of the House. The new code of rules, known as the "Reed Rules," codified his rulings outlawing disappearing quorums and dilatory motions. In addition, they reduced the quorum requirement in the Committee of the Whole from a House majority to 100 members, authorized the Committee of the Whole to close debate on any section or paragraph of a bill under consideration, streamlined the order of business of the House, and gave the Speaker new authority to dispose of business on the Speaker's table by referring measures to committees without debate. The new rules were debated for four days by the House and adopted by a party-line vote of 161 to 144 on February 14, 1890.[15]

By his actions Reed had firmly established the concept of majority rule as well as party responsibility and accountability. Moreover, he had laid the groundwork for a strong speakership and a Rules Committee that together would set the legislative agenda for the House and expedite its business through the use of special order resolutions. Reed summarized these developments for his constituents as follows:

> Party responsibility has begun, and with it also the responsibility of the people, for they can no longer elect a Democratic House and hope the minority will neutralize their action or a Republican House without being sure that it will keep its pledges. If we have broken the precedents of a hundred years, we have set the precedents for another hundred years nobler than the last, wherein the people, with full knowledge that their servants can act, will choose those who will worthily carry out their will.[16]

Unlike Carlisle, Reed was not hesitant to use the Rules Committee's authority to report order-of-business resolutions as a means of taking up bills out of order and limiting debate and even amendments to them. On a major civil rights bill, the Federal Election Act, the Rules Committee reported a special rule that limited the time for general debate and set a date and time for a final vote. The rule passed over the strenuous objections of the Democrats. Similarly, on a bill providing for the purchase of silver the Rules Committee reported a special rule that prohibited the offering of a substitute amendment on free coinage of silver. The rule met with some resistance even within Republican ranks, but was narrowly adopted, 120-117.[17]

On special rules such as these, Reed caucused with the two other Republicans on the Rules Committee, Cannon and William McKinley of Ohio. Then before the committee meeting he would call in the two Democratic members on Rules. One of those members, Benton McMillin of Tennessee, recounted what happened. Reed would tell them: "Here is an outrage McKinley and Cannon and myself are about to perpetrate. You will have time to prepare your screams and usual denunciations."[18]

True to Reed's report to his constituents, the new system of rules permitted the majority party to carry out its legislative agenda and permitted the people to hold them accountable for it. The 51st Congress was very productive legislatively, with the House passing some 611 bills, many of considerable importance. But much of the legislation was seen as a means of simply passing government benefits to friends of the Republican Party through higher tariffs, the purchase of silver, generous pensions for veterans, rivers and harbors projects, reimbursement to northern states of monies paid during the Civil War, and high premiums on government bonds. The Congress came to be known as the "Billion Dollar Congress." Because most voters did not feel they had benefited from this largesse, the Republicans lost control of the House in the landslide 1890 elections. Democrats won 231 seats compared with only 88 for the Republicans and 14 for the populists.[19]

The Democrats elected Charles F. Crisp of Georgia as Speaker. In the new House's rules package from the Rules Committee, Crisp dropped some of Reed's innovations such as the anti-dilatory motion and quorum-counting rules. Other changes, however, strengthened the Rules Committee by allowing it to report at any time without notice and permitting its reports to be considered without intervening motions except one motion to adjourn.

Late in the 53d Congress (1893–95), the Democrats were forced to bring in an amendment restoring the quorum-counting rule. They also restored in practice the bar against dilatory motions. Prior to the adjournment of the 53d Congress in February of 1895, Crisp further strengthened the hand of the Rules Committee by ruling that it could make in order consideration of a bill not reported by the committee of jurisdiction.

Republicans recaptured the House in the 1894 landslide elections, and Reed returned to the Speaker's chair for the 54th and 55th Congresses (1895–99). In the 1896 presidential contest Governor William McKinley, who had served in the House as a member of the Rules Committee and chairman of the Ways and Means Committee, easily defeated the Nebraska prairie populist, Democrat William Jennings Bryan.

The Revolt against Cannon

By 1897 neither party was inclined toward legislative activism on domestic social or commercial matters, preferring to leave them to the market and states, except in dire circumstances. Reed resigned from his House seat in September of 1899 because of differences with President McKinley on the war with Spain over Cuba, the annexation of Hawaii, and the acquisition of Puerto Rico and the Philippines. Republican representative David B. Henderson of Iowa, described by one observer as a man of "moderate ability and rather weak of will power," served as Speaker for the next two Congresses, the 56th and 57th

(1899–1903).[20] Despite Henderson's lackluster leadership, the Rules Committee's influence continued to grow.

With Henderson's retirement in 1902, Republicans elevated to the speakership Joe Cannon of Danville, Illinois, an old hand in Congress. First elected to the House in 1872 at the age of thirty-six, Cannon was defeated in 1890 but reelected in 1892. When Republicans retook control of the House in the 1894 elections, Cannon was named chairman of the Appropriations Committee, and he returned to the Rules Committee where he had served between 1887 and 1891. Twice Cannon had run unsuccessfully for Speaker, losing to Reed in 1889 and to Henderson in 1899. Once elected Speaker, he made the most of it.

Cannon built on the powers Reed had developed as Speaker and Rules Committee chairman to gain near absolute control over his party, the House, and the legislative agenda. But in many ways he was Reed's opposite. Cannon was as wiry as Reed was rotund, preferring cigars and chewing tobacco to food. Whereas Reed used his powers to break obstructionism and move legislation, Cannon often used his powers to block the consideration of legislation he did not like. He was fond of observing that "everything is all right out West and around Danville. The country don't need any legislation."[21]

Cannon strictly maintained party discipline by deftly using the numerous powers of the Speaker—namely, to recognize members on the floor, schedule bills, and appoint committees and their chairmen. As time went on, the affectionate nickname of "Uncle Joe" became "Czar Speaker." After the assassination of President McKinley on September 14, 1901, Vice President Theodore Roosevelt became president. Roosevelt championed a more activist role for the presidency and the government. In keeping with the reform-minded mood of the country, Congress passed numerous important bills during Roosevelt's presidency (1901–9). Among them were the Newlands Reclamation Act, the Elkins Act ending discriminatory pricing by railroads, the Pure Food and Drug Act, and the Hepburn Act strengthening the authority of the Interstate Commerce Commission. The latter bill was the result of hard bargaining between Speaker Cannon, Senate Republican leader Nelson Aldrich, and President Roosevelt, who had to give up on tariff reform.[22]

As Cannon became less cooperative with Roosevelt and more resistant to mounting pressures for more activist government policies, discontent grew within in his own party's ranks among Progressives from the Midwest and West. Late in the 60th Congress the insurgents pushed for two amendments to House rules—one to provide for the election of committees by the House rather than their appointment by the Speaker, the other to establish a Calendar Tuesday to consider bills from committees without clearance by the Rules Committee.

Cannon and his stalwart allies countered with an amendment establishing a Calendar Wednesday for the same purpose, and it was adopted. But this did not satisfy the insurgents, and they prepared to offer more comprehensive rules changes at the beginning of the next Congress.[23]

When the 61st Congress convened on March 15, 1909, the traditional resolution adopting the rules of the previous Congress was offered by Cannon's top lieutenant on the Rules Committee, Rep. John Dalzell of Pennsylvania, who immediately moved the previous question to bring the matter to a final vote. Although the previous question was narrowly adopted, 193-189, the rules resolution was narrowly rejected, 189-193. This was an unprecedented setback for a Speaker at the beginning of a new Congress. Minority Leader Champ Clark of Missouri then gained recognition to offer an alternative set of House rules that removed the Speaker from the Rules Committee and provided for its enlargement from five to fifteen members to be elected by the House. Clark's resolution asked the committee to report back to the House by the following December with any further recommendations for changes in House rules. The resolution also removed the Speaker's authority to appoint members to committees, except for the Committee on Ways and Means and four minor housekeeping committees. Following Dalzell's earlier action, Clark immediately moved the previous question, thereby bringing the momentous resolution to a vote without debate.[24]

Cannon's forces were ready, however. They had carefully developed a counterstrategy with conservative Democrats. The previous question was rejected, 180-203. This meant someone else could be recognized to offer yet another version. Cannon recognized Democratic representative John J. Fitzgerald of New York, chief of the Tammany Hall delegation and a Rules Committee member, who offered a substitute amendment. Fitzgerald's substitute did not alter the composition of the Rules Committee or the Speaker's chairmanship of it. Instead, it prohibited the Rules Committee from reporting a special rule that would prevent the motion to recommit a bill. More importantly, it established the right of the minority to offer the motion. The Fitzgerald package also established a Consent Calendar that allowed any member to place a reported bill on the calendar and call it up. The package required a two-thirds vote of the House to set aside Calendar Wednesday.

Unlike Dalzell and Clark, Fitzgerald allowed debate to proceed on his amendment, and Minority Leader Clark took advantage of the opportunity:

> Mr. Speaker and gentlemen, this is one of the greatest days the House of Representatives has ever seen in a quarter of a century. It does not make any difference if you beat us by a few votes, or if we beat you by a few

votes; the jig is up with the House machine. [Applause on the Democratic side.][25]

Clark went on to predict that the Speaker's temporary victory on that day was just that:

Outside of this House the demand for the revision of these rules is insistent, strong, increasing; you may turn it down today and turn it back today, but the time is not far distant when the public opinion outside of this House will be overwhelming inside of this House. [Applause.][26]

After over two hours of debate, the Fitzgerald amendment was adopted, 211-173, and the resolution as amended passed by voice vote. But Clark's words proved to be prescient. Exactly one year and two days later, on March 17, 1910, the insurgents struck again. Republican representative George Norris of Nebraska called up a resolution that he said was "made privileged by the Constitution." The resolution would amend House rules to enlarge the Rules Committee to fifteen members, apportioned by state groupings, with the chairman to be elected by the committee. Moreover, the proposed rules change explicitly prohibited the Speaker from serving on the committee. Dalzell immediately raised a point of order against the resolution on grounds that it was not privileged. Instead of ruling immediately, Speaker Cannon allowed debate to continue at length on the point of order and the merits of the resolution, in hopes of rounding up sufficient supporters in the interim to defeat the resolution.[27]

Debate continued through the night. The following day Cannon's supporters offered two alternatives for a ten- and fifteen-member Rules Committee with the Speaker remaining a member. The insurgents rejected both as well as subsequent attempts by the stalwarts to adjourn the House. Finally, on March 19, after twenty-nine hours of debate, Cannon ruled to sustain Dalzell's point of order. Cannon based his decision on a previous ruling by Democratic Speaker Randall "that the proposition to amend the rules was not a case of constitutional privilege." Norris appealed the Speaker's ruling, and the House refused to sustain the ruling by a vote of 162 to 182, with thirty-four Republicans breaking ranks to join the Democrats. The House then took up the Norris resolution.[28]

One of the leaders of the maverick Republicans, Rep. John Nelson of Wisconsin, summed up the fight as follows:

Have we not been punished by every means at the disposal of the powerful House organization? Members long chairmen of important committees, others holding high rank—all with records of faithful and efficient service to their credit—have been ruthlessly removed, deposed, and humiliated before their constituents and the country because, forsooth, they would not cringe or crawl before the arbitrary power of the Speaker and his House machine.[29]

"We are fighting for the right of free, fair, and full representation in this body for our respective constituencies," Nelson continued. "We are fighting with our Democratic brethren for the common right of equal representation in this House, and for the right-of-way of progressive legislation in Congress."[30]

One of Cannon's top lieutenants, Rep. James R. Mann of Illinois, stoutly defended the Speaker. Since Reed left the House the Speaker "is the leader and strongest influence in the House," but "it is not true that Speaker Cannon or any other Speaker is an autocrat." Mann went on to say that while "some of us revile him temporarily," just as all great men are abused at times, "when the book of history of this generation shall have been written . . . the years of the Speakership of Mr. Cannon will stand out among the most brilliant in the history of our country."[31]

Despite the ardent defense of Mann and other Cannon backers, the House adopted the Norris resolution by a vote of 191 to 156, after amending it to provide for a ten-member Rules Committee elected by the House. This time forty-three Republicans joined with the Democrats. However, when Cannon graciously invited a motion that the speakership be vacated, and a Democrat obliged, bipartisanship ended: the motion was tabled by party-line vote. Even the Republicans opposed to Cannon were not interested in having a Democrat as Speaker.

The first House rules changes reported by the newly enlarged and elected Rules Committee reflected continuing agitation over measures being bottled up in committees and in the Rules Committee. On June 17, 1910, the House adopted a new discharge rule whereby any member could file a discharge motion with the Clerk on any bill referred to a committee. After seven days the member could call up the motion, and, if seconded by a majority of members, the motion to discharge the bill from committee would be debated for twenty minutes. The rule was adopted by a division vote. Subsequent Congresses modified the rule as follows: the measure to be discharged had to be pending in a committee at least thirty days and a majority of members had to sign a discharge petition to bring the motion to the floor. The right to discharge was also extended to special rules providing for consideration of measures stalled in committees.[32]

"Cannonism," the arbitrary exercise of power to thwart progressive legislation, together with the Republicans' failure to fulfill their 1908 campaign pledge to lower tariffs, led to a Democratic takeover of the House in the 1910 elections and laid the groundwork for Woodrow Wilson's election as president in 1912. When the Democrats took over the House in 1911, they elected Champ Clark as Speaker, and Oscar Underwood of Alabama as the majority leader and chairman of the Ways and Means Committee. They also adopted a further rules change that provided for the election by the House of all House committees, with majority committee nominations to be made by the Democrats of Underwood's Ways and Means Committee. The overthrow of the Speaker did not spell an end to party government or to the influence of the Rules Committee. "Czar Speaker" was replaced by "King Caucus"—the assembly of all House Democrats. Majority Leader Underwood was careful to consult the caucus to achieve maximum party unity, discipline, and success.

The Expansion of Individual Rights

The terms of the Declaration of Independence are quite clear: when a government is negligent in securing the rights of the people, it is the people's right to alter or abolish that government. By urging that the Constitution be amended before it had even been ratified, the American people demonstrated how seriously they took their right to alter the government to further secure their "unalienable rights."

The amendment of the Constitution over the past two centuries to expand individual rights is testament to the document's resiliency and durability in accommodating legitimate demands for alteration. The three post–Civil War amendments were ratified in rapid succession: the Thirteenth Amendment outlawing slavery in 1865; the Fourteenth Amendment extending civil rights nationally in 1868; and the Fifteenth Amendment giving the right to vote to all male citizens of voting age regardless of race, color, or previous servitude in 1870.

While those three amendments originated with the Congress in direct response to the post–Civil War situation, the Seventeenth and Nineteenth Amendments, providing for the direct election of senators and giving women the right to vote, respectively, were in response to popular pressures to strengthen representative democracy stemming from the reformist agitation of the Progressive Era.

The movement for direct election of senators began in the 1870s with various agrarian associations and organized labor. By 1909 the cause had been joined by the Democratic Party as well as by the Populists and Socialists. Some thirty-three state legislatures had petitioned Congress for the amendment (in the case of states, such petitions are called memorials), and twenty-nine states had adopted various means for allowing voters to express a senatorial preference. The House of Representatives was understandably more willing to move on the amendment than was the Senate. Over a three-decade period the House passed nineteen direct-election constitutional amendments, including five such resolutions between 1893 and 1902. The Senate finally passed a version of the amendment in January of 1911 in response to increased public pressures resulting from allegations that fifty-seven members of the Illinois state legislature had been bribed in connection with their selection of William Lorimer to the U.S. Senate. The House and Senate finally agreed on the same version of the amendment in May of 1912, and by April of the following year it had been ratified by three-fourths of the state legislatures.[33]

The Nineteenth Amendment, known as the woman's suffrage amendment, also had a long gestation period, beginning right after the Civil War. In 1866 and 1867 differing versions of the amendment were considered and rejected by the Senate and the House, respectively. Angry that the Fourteenth Amendment enfranchised only black men, Susan B. Anthony and Elizabeth Cady Stanton founded the Woman Suffrage Association in 1869. The "Anthony" amendment was introduced in each Congress beginning in 1878. While it was reported favorably in one or both houses between 1882 and 1886, it was not brought to a vote in either house until January of 1887, when the Senate easily defeated it.

The suffrage movement resumed in 1890 and refocused its efforts on the states. But by 1910 only four states had granted women the right to vote. Fortunes began to improve in 1910, when Washington State approved the women's franchise by referendum. Four other states followed suit between 1911 and 1913. The movement's attention turned once again to the Congress, beginning with a parade in Washington on the day before Woodrow Wilson's inauguration in 1913. That summer suffragists presented senators with 200,000 signatures in support of a constitutional amendment. This increased public pressure forced Congress to revisit the issue for the first time since 1887. In 1914 and 1915 the House and Senate rejected the amendment, but it at least gained majority support for the first time in both houses. In 1918, with President Wilson's backing, the amendment received exactly two-thirds votes in the House, but fell two votes short of that in the Senate. That same year three of four state referendums on the issue were successful (eight other states had given women voting rights the previous year). President Wilson convened a special session of the 66th Congress in May of 1919. The House easily passed the amendment on the opening day of the session, and, after some stalling, the Senate passed it fifteen days later. The amendment was ratified by the requisite three-fourths of the states on August 26, 1920.[34]

Decades passed before additional constitutional amendments expanded the franchise: the Twenty-third Amendment, extending to the residents of the District of Columbia the right to vote for president and vice president, ratified in

1961; the Twenty-fourth Amendment, abolishing the poll tax in federal elections, ratified in 1964; and the Twenty-sixth Amendment, extending the right to vote to eighteen-year-olds, ratified in 1971.

Many of the promises embodied in the Civil War–era amendments for black citizens would not be secured until the Supreme Court's 1954 decision outlawing school segregation and subsequent civil rights laws enacted by Congress in the 1960s. On the other hand, an Equal Rights Amendment to the Constitution to guarantee equality of rights between the sexes under state and federal laws, first introduced in 1923 by Rep. Daniel R. Anthony (R-Kan.), the nephew of Susan B. Anthony, would not be submitted to the states by Congress until 1972. In 1982 an extended deadline for ratification expired without ratification by three-fourths of the states.

Notes

1. George B. Galloway, *History of the United States House of Representatives*, H. Doc. 250, 89th Cong., 1st sess. (Washington, D.C.: U.S. Government Printing Office, 1965), 118. The "disappearing quorum" was a device whereby members present in the chamber would refuse to answer to their names when a quorum call was ordered, thereby preventing business from proceeding if a majority had not registered its presence.
2. Charles Wahlgren Summers, "History of Congress: The Age of the Machine (1872–1900)," in *The Encyclopedia of the United States Congress*, ed. Donald C. Bacon, Roger H. Davidson, and Morton Keller (New York: Simon and Schuster, 1995), vol. 2, 1006–7.
3. Galloway, *History of the United States House*, 118–19.
4. House Committee on Rules, *A History of the Committee on Rules*, committee print, 97th Cong., 2d sess. (Washington, D.C.: U.S. Government Printing Office, 1983), 49–50.
5. Ibid., 50.
6. Ibid., 59–60.
7. Charles W. Calhoun, "Reed, Thomas B.," in *The Encyclopedia of the United States Congress*, vol. 3, 1688.
8. House Committee on Rules, *A History of the Committee*, 46, 60.
9. Ibid., 61–62.
10. Ibid., 63.
11. Ibid., 64–65.
12. Galloway, *History of the United States House*, 119.
13. Ibid.
14. House Committee on Rules, *A History of the Committee*, 70.
15. Ibid., 72–73; Galloway, *History of the United States House*, 120–21.
16. Galloway, *History of the United States House*, 121.
17. House Committee on Rules, *A History of the Committee*, 74.
18. Summers, "History of Congress," 1010.
19. House Committee on Rules, *A History of the Committee*, 74–75.

20. Ibid., 82, quoting from Hubert Bruce Fuller, *The Speaker of the House* (Boston: Little, Brown, 1909), 248.

21. Richard B. Cheney and Lynn V. Cheney, *Kings of the Hill: Power and Personality in the House of Representatives* (New York: The Continuum Publishing Co., 1983), 127.

22. Morton Keller, "History of Congress: The Rise of the Modern State (1933–1964)," in *The Encyclopedia of the United States Congress*, vol. 2, 1017.

23. House Committee on Rules, *A History of the Committee*, 86.

24. *Congressional Record*, March 15, 1909, 19–22.

25. Ibid., 26.

26. Ibid.

27. House Committee on Rules, *A History of the Committee*, 88.

28. Ibid., 88–89.

29. Galloway, *History of the United States House*, 51.

30. Ibid.

31. Ibid.

32. House Committee on Rules, *A History of the Committee*, 118–22.

33. John D. Buenker, "Seventeenth Amendment," in *The Encyclopedia of the United States Congress*, vol. 4, 1810–11.

34. Cynthia Harrison, "Nineteenth Amendment," in ibid., vol. 3, 1467–69.

5

The Initiative and Referendum Movement

THE Progressive Era in the late nineteenth and early twentieth centuries not only produced constitutional amendments instituting the direct election of senators and the right to vote for women. It also gave rise to a resurgence of interest in new forms of direct democracy, namely, the initiative and referendum process for the popular enactment of laws. Nathan Cree, a populist activist, in his 1892 book *Direct Legislation by the People*, proposed a complex, two-step system for permitting voters to enact national laws. The people could first petition to put a specified law on the national ballot. If adopted at the general election, the proposed law would be subject to consideration and amendment by the Congress, but would not be subject to presidential signature or veto. The final form of the proposed law would then be put to the voters for approval at the next general election.[1]

The People's Party endorsed the proposed national initiative and referendum in its 1892 platform, as did the Socialist Labor and Nationalist Parties in that election and again in 1896.[2] J.W. Sullivan gave further impetus to the movement with the publication in 1893 of *Direct Legislation by the Citizenship through the Initiative and Referendum*, a book based on his firsthand observations of how the Swiss system of direct legislation worked. He was convinced that it could work just as well in the United States, and that it was not impractical or utopian.[3]

South Dakota enacted the first statewide initiative process in 1898. In 1900 Utah adopted the initiative and referendum process, but it did not enact enabling legislation until 1917. In the state of Oregon, William S. U'Ren, a populist organizer, founded the Oregon Direct Legislation League. U'Ren enlisted the backing of the Grange, Oregon Knights of Labor, the Portland Federated Trades, and the Farmer's Alliance in his campaign for a state initiative and referendum. After a nearly seven-year campaign U'Ren and his movement won the approval of the legislature in 1899 and 1901, and ratification by the people in 1902 by an 11-1 margin. Today twenty-six states plus the District of Columbia provide for some form of statutory or constitutional initiative or referendum by citizen petition; of those, eighteen states adopted the process between 1898 and 1918, including ten between 1912 and 1916—the peak of the Progressive Era in American politics. The latter surge is attributed in part to the embrace of these direct democracy devices by both Theodore Roosevelt and Woodrow Wilson.[4]

Wilson's Conversion

Woodrow Wilson's conversion to direct democracy came late in his career but then rather swiftly—if not on the road to Damascus, most surely on the road to the White House. For all of his academic life, Wilson ardently opposed the concept of giving the people power to initiate legislation. In a textbook published in 1891 titled *The State and Federal Governments of the United States*, he wrote this about the referendum: "it assumes a discriminating judgment and a fulness of information on the part of the people touching questions of public policy which they do not often possess," and "it lowers the sense of responsibility on the part of legislators."[5]

In 1907 Wilson commended James Callaway, a reporter for the *Macon Telegraph* in Georgia, for his article contrasting former New York senator David Bennett Hill's opposition to the initiative and referendum with former Democratic presidential candidate William Jennings Bryan's support. Wilson called Senator Hill's position "not only sound, but the only position which a thoughtful and well-informed student of American affairs can legitimately take."[6]

Wilson went on to write:

> There seems to me to be, moreover, another and entirely conclusive objection to the initiative and referendum, quite apart from their incompatibility with the principles of our system of government. A casual petition by a relatively small number of citizens and a vote by however large a number do not constitute an organic process at all. The only process by which law can be safely and thoughtfully produced is the organic process which brings those who frame it into face to face conference so that the contents of the law will not be made up of the views of a chance combination of persons, but of views beaten out by exchange of thought in actual debate.[7]

In November of 1909, speaking before the City Club of Philadelphia on political reform, Wilson argued against two of the "good government" reform ideas that were the most popular at the time: "The referendum," he insisted, "can be just as easily managed by the professional politician, to all intents and purposes, as the direct primary and the main election." And he went on to say, "If there is no delegation of power the people are helpless in the hands of those who have time and training in political lines, and all the remedies suggested simply throw a more complicated burden on the voters." In Wilson's view, "the only pathway of reform that is practicable is the pathway of simplification," which makes "all our processes so simple that busy men will have the time and opportunity to perform them." To him that meant "the Short Ballot, and I am going to talk about nothing else."[8]

During his campaign for governor of New Jersey, Wilson invited "any politician in the state" to meet in "a debate upon public platform upon a public question." In a letter dated October 6, 1910, his Socialist Party opponent, Wilson B. Killingbeck, accepted Wilson's invitation. Killingbeck suggested that they debate their differing views of democracy, including his view that "Government and Legislative Bodies should always be controlled by the use of the Initiative and Referendum and right of recall [a device whereby voters can remove an official from office]." When Wilson declined a few days later on grounds that he had no date free in his schedule, Killingbeck criticized Wilson for ignoring the important issues that matter to people—"the economic dependence which threatens the right to a living, the right to work, the right to have a home, wife and children living in comfort." Killingbeck continued: "You are a democrat. But is there not a test for real democracy these days of business imperialism? The initiative, referendum and recall—when and where have you favored these measures?"[9]

And yet it was not Killingbeck's challenges and chiding that brought Wilson around to supporting the initiative and referendum. It was more likely the entreaties from other sources. Shortly after his election as governor on November 8, 1910, Wilson received a letter from Sen. George Earle Chamberlain, who had been the governor of Oregon before coming to the Senate. Chamberlain tried to sway the new governor:

> I do hope you may be able to take a decided stand in favor of progressivism in the Democratic Party. The time is not far distant when both parties must stand for the Initiative and Referendum, a real Direct Primary law, a Corrupt Practices Act, and possibly the Recall, and would it not be possible for you to recommend these measures to the New Jersey Legislature?[10]

In response to citizens' demands, six or seven states had already followed Oregon and adopted these measures, Chamberlain explained. Moreover, he said, the people of other states were endeavoring to adopt them as rapidly as possible since they were "the only instrumentality through which the corrupt convention system can be abolished and the political boss be put out of commission." Finally, Chamberlain put in a good word for a Washington correspondent for some western papers, John Lathrop, who would soon be visiting Wilson to explain the operation of the initiative and referendum system in Oregon.[11]

A few days later Wilson received a letter from Sen. Robert Latham Owen, a progressive Democrat from Oklahoma, advising him that his name "is now being considered by many of the Democrats of the Nation as a possible Presidential Candidate in 1912." Owen commended Wilson on a letter he had written to the National Democratic Club on December 10: "Your letter indicates that you stand for a genuine representation of the people, and of public opinion." Owen then expresses some reservations:

> . . . but I have understood that you were opposed to the Initiative and Referendum. I hope, sincerely, that this is not true, or that, upon examination you may give adherence to the doctrine of direct legislation by the people. At all events, I wish to ask you the plain question, as to whether or not you approve the Initiative and Referendum, in any form, or would be willing to give it your support?[12]

Lathrop, the reporter, had the same question. He interviewed governor-elect Wilson on December 19, 1910, and three days later gave him additional documents and information regarding the operation of the initiative and referendum in Oregon and Oklahoma. In both states, he assured Wilson, the legislatures had the opportunity to amend laws proposed by the people. The initiative and referendum, he argued, "supply the means of bringing the government back to the people, and I hope that in your Inaugural address [as governor] you will take [a] decided stand in favor of it." And Lathrop explicitly tied Wilson's stand on direct democracy devices to his presidential prospects:

> I give you good cheer and renew my expression of faith that your position on the pending popular government issues . . . will instantly constitute you the inevitable leader for 1912. Just as certainly as can be, an advanced stand such as I indicate will, first, be to forward a mighty movement for political salvation and, second, make Woodrow Wilson President to succeed William H. Taft.[13]

On the very next day Lathrop mailed Wilson a copy of a letter he had sent to William Jennings Bryan, touting Wilson's presidential candidacy. Lathrop also enclosed samples of blank initiatives and a model state constitutional amendment providing for the initiative and referendum.[14]

Prior to his inauguration as governor, Wilson received at least two other letters urging him to embrace the initiative and referendum. The first, dated December 24, 1910, was from Democrat Daniel Kiefer, a retired Cincinnati businessman. Kiefer commended Wilson for backing the New Jersey senatorial candidate who had won the popular preference primary and confessed that he had been wrong to think Wilson was "the favorite candidate of plutocracy for the democratic presidential nomination." Kiefer went on to write:

> Since then I have come to feel that in all probability I was mistaken. While your reported opposition to such true democratic measures as the Initiative and Referendum leave something lacking in your democracy it is clear that the predatory [business] interests will not consider you the candidate for them. The party and the country need more men like you in places of power.[15]

Wilson responded promptly on December 26 saying Kiefer's letter had given him pleasure and had made him smile "to think that I should ever have been regarded as the Wall Street candidate for the Presidency." He added that while he had many friends on Wall Street, they never supposed for a moment that he would "be serviceable to any interest that would be opposed to the interest of the people and the country at large."[16] And he concluded: "The duty of public men in our time is so clear that I do not see how any one can miss his way." Wilson did not respond in his letter to Kiefer's comments on the initiative and referendum.

Wilson received another letter dated December 29 from Joseph Fels of Philadelphia, a wealthy soap manufacturer and founder of the Joseph Fels Fund of America, an organization devoted to promoting the single tax. (Kiefer was the chairman of the fund.) After expressing delight "to find that you are more progressive [than] I thought you were," Fels stressed the "necessity for 'People's Rule' in this country, and that control of legislation by the people is even of greater importance than control of Senatorial elections." Fels asked Wilson whether he had noted the growing demand for the initiative and referendum. "The people want power," he said, "because they feel the rights of the people are safe with the people." The whole world is growing into democracy "and outgrowing the old constitution and statutory clothes" that no longer fit any more than "the clothes as a boy will fit you now." Fels said, "The auction block method of enacting laws and of refusing to enact needed legislation is even more vicious than the auction block method of electing United States Senators." Fels concluded, "The votes in favor of the Initiative and Referendum show that the people demand 'People's Rule.'"[17]

As late as January 8, 1911, just nine days before his inauguration, Wilson had given no hint of having changed in his opposition to the initiative and referendum. Indeed, on that date the *New York Times Annual Financial Review* praised Wilson's "scheme of community lawmaking" because "it substitutes for the more radical propositions that have been put forward for the furtherance of popular participation in government—the initiative and the referendum in particular—what may be called popular representative government."[18]

Nevertheless, the lobbying by Lathrop, Owen, and Kiefer appeared to be influencing Wilson. In his inaugural address on January 17, 1911, Wilson included references to various popular democracy reforms that western leaders said would extend his presidential appeal in their region of the country. Lest anyone doubt his larger audience, Wilson first posed several questions on obtaining a representative government to serve the real interests of the people and not just those of their representatives or of a few special interests. "These are the queries," Wilson stated, "which have drawn the attention of the whole country to the subject of the direct primary, the direct choice of representatives by the people, without the intervening of the nominating machine." He went on to make the following appeal to the New Jersey legislature:

> I earnestly commend to your careful consideration in this connection the laws in recent years adopted in the State of Oregon whose effect has been to bring government back to the people and to protect it from the control of representatives of selfish and special interests. They seem to me to point the direction which we must also take before we have completed our regeneration of a government which has suffered so seriously and so long as ours has here in New Jersey from private management and organized selfishness.[19]

Later in the speech Wilson advocated specific political reforms, although he did not specifically mention the "I and R" words, initiative and referendum. In an interview given to the *New York Globe and Commercial Advertiser* that same day, however, Wilson did not deny that he had the initiative and referendum in mind when he mentioned Oregon's laws, nor did he disguise his interest in them and those of other western states.

> I think they have many laws out there [in the West] which have proven their worth, though I wouldn't care to go so far as to say they would apply equally well in New Jersey. I am particularly interested in their laws of initiative and referendum, their law of recall, and their preference law, binding the legislators to choose a senator of the people's choice.[20]

Wilson warmed further to the initiative and referendum a month later in an address to the Democratic Club of Philadelphia on February 21, 1911. Putting it quite bluntly this time, he said:

> If we cannot get the kind of legislation we want, we will have the initiative and referendum, and where they have been tried, it is found that the people have just as discriminating a knowledge of what is necessary as any recent legislature, at any rate, has exhibited.[21]

Wilson did not envision that state initiatives and referendums would be used frequently, let alone as a replacement for the state legislatures:

> My conviction is that . . . once this direct access of the people to the execution of their own purposes is accomplished, the initiative and referendum will not be the ordinary means of legislation. They will be the very salutary gun kept in the closet. The knowledge that if they do not represent, representatives will be dispensed with, will make representatives represent. In these measures, therefore, we are not dispensing with representative government, but making sure that we are going to have it.[22]

In late January 1911 Samuel Huston Thompson, Jr., a self-described independent Republican residing in Denver, Colorado, wrote to Wilson expressing support for him as the next president, "regardless of party." A former student of Wilson's at Princeton University, Thompson raised the issue of the initiative and referendum, which he said he had trouble accepting "because you grounded us in a constitutional law which certainly did not contemplate any such radical change." Thompson concluded his letter by asking Wilson whether it was possible for him to express his views on the subject "without injuring yourself publicly."[23]

Responding to another letter of Thompson's in March that apparently posed the same question, Wilson said, "My attitude towards the initiative, referendum and recall is this. My judgment was at first very much against them, but I have been very much impressed by the success with which they have been used in Oregon, and in my Inaugural address to the Legislature I commended the Oregon system very warmly to their study and consideration." Wilson added that the adoption of these devices in any particular state must be adapted to its particular conditions. In New Jersey the people were tired of unfulfilled campaign promises, Wilson said, and "it may be necessary for them to assume upon occasion, at any rate, direct control of legislation themselves."[24]

Wilson may well have had Thompson in mind when he spoke to prominent state business leaders in Norfolk, Virginia, on April 23, 1911. According to one news account:

> Governor Wilson took a bold stand for the initiative and referendum. He said for twenty years he lectured classes against it and then he went to looking for the truth concerning it. Now he regretted that he could

not apologize to the classes for the lectures he had made before he looked into the facts. "Believe in it? Of course, I do, because I believe we want to get control of our institutions again."[25]

Writing to Wilson from Cincinnati on April 21, 1911, Daniel Kiefer praised his change of heart:

> Your recent endorsement of the Initiative and Referendum after having been a strong opponent, marks you as a kind of man in public life that is much too rare, a man with the moral courage to openly admit that a position once assumed was a mistaken one.[26]

In May of 1911, Wilson embarked on a national speaking tour to test the presidential waters. His trip included stops in Missouri, Colorado, California, Oregon, Minnesota, North Carolina, and South Carolina. Throughout the tour he sprinkled his speeches with references to the initiative and referendum systems adopted in some of the western states as one means to restore government to the people. But he was not always consistent in the degree or intensity of his support.

The Morning Oregonian on May 18, 1911, reported that the founder of the "Oregon System," William S. U'Ren, had "quietly slipped down over the California line today" and had boarded Wilson's train on its way to Oregon to advise Wilson on "the political situation in the state." According to the articles Wilson had been "roped and tied by the man from Oregon City."[27]

In an interview with the reporter from the Oregon paper datelined Medford, Oregon, Wilson praised the people of Oregon for "developing the movement of popular government throughout the country." Wilson went on, "We of New Jersey have adopted many of your laws and hope later to secure the initiative and referendum."[28]

And, if he was quoted correctly, he broke radically new ground by suggesting that the referendum be extended to the national level:

> The laws of recent years adopted in this state seem to me to point the direction which the Nation must also take before we have completed our regeneration of a Government which has suffered so seriously and so long from private management and selfish organization. . . . To nullify bad legislation the referendum must be adopted and it is only a question of time until it will be extended to the Nation. The better education of the people through the various states, of which Oregon was the first, will enable them to pass intelligently upon National measures. In such manner will popular government be lifted from the ranks of theory to actuality and a democracy which represents the will of the people be established.[29]

Speaking before a large gathering at the Portland Armory on May 19, Wilson reminded his audience that Oregon had not adopted the initiative and referendum to supplant the legislature but to secure its lost contact with the people. And yet, said Wilson, "You have made no progress, for to make this movement a success you must purify your legislative assembly, and make it responsive. . . . To get results you must continue in your work by making the Legislature a truly representative body." He challenged the people to "establish some form of responsible leadership"; although leaders who invoke the initiative and referendum "can easily get a sufficiently large fraction of your people to put their names on his petitions . . . they are not leaders you choose and therefore you cannot hold them responsible." Unless the president and governors assume the role of leadership, the people will be "discontented." Wilson's solution was to get the legislators to run on the same platform as the executive: "You will then begin, when matters are debated freely and openly, to get things into such shape as to make the initiative and referendum unnecessary."[30] In essence, he was arguing for his long-favored British parliamentary system of government as an alternative to the initiative and referendum for ensuring accountability.

In Seattle, Washington, just a few days later Wilson told an interviewer that he was not sure the initiative and referendum should be adopted throughout the country: "in fact, they might be dangerous in some localities," such as where "there was a large preponderance of prejudiced vote." Moreover, he noted that the framers of these devices did not intend for them to be used regularly since "it would be too cumbersome to do all our legislation by the initiative and referendum. But they are a most efficient club to hold over our lawmakers."[31]

Back home in New Jersey, Wilson soon found that his enthusiastic embrace of the initiative and referendum during his tour of the western states had branded him a radical or worse in the eyes of some. On July 31, 1911, a New York *World* editorial suggested by a series of rhetorical questions that his political ambition was getting the best of him, as it had Democrat William Jennings Bryan, an unsuccessful presidential candidate in 1896, 1900, and 1908 who ardently supported the initiative and referendum.

> Does Gov. Wilson think that playing to the gallery will promote his Presidential candidacy? Does he believe that efforts to win Mr. Bryan's approval and to capture his following will increase his political strength? Is he Bryantizing himself? Is he preparing with his initiative, referendum and recall programme and his money trust bugaboo to swallow Mr. Bryan's entire Confession of Faith?[32]

One of Wilson's political advisers, William Frank McCombs, immediately forwarded the editorial to Wilson and asked him to clarify his comments on banks and trusts. On September 23, 1911, McCombs related to Wilson a conversation he had with the business manager of the *New York Times*, Louis Wiley, in which he asked Wiley what he thought of Wilson. Wiley responded, "He is a radical and his views are subject to change for political reasons." When pressed for specifics, Wiley cited Wilson's positions on the initiative, referendum, and direct primaries. To clarify Wilson's positions, McCombs agreed to set up a question-and-answer session with Wilson for publication in the *Times*.[33]

Wilson subsequently agreed to interviews with the New York *World* and the *New York Times*, both of which were published on December 24, 1911. The *Times* interviewer observed that when Wilson first appeared as an advocate of the initiative, referendum, and recall (except for the judiciary), "his public utterances gave rise to considerable astonishment" because they "were tempered with few, if any, qualifying statements" and "contrasted sharply with the views he had expressed in his lectures and his writings." The interviewer noted that in Wilson's book *The State* he had "condemned the system as an utter failure." But the interviewer went on to assure his readers that "Gov. Wilson is a firm believer in representative government in the accepted sense of the term," and that the proper ends of government can best be attained in a republic "only through the party system, if only pure and effective leadership is provided for and placed so that there can be no question of divided responsibility." Moreover, wrote the interviewer, Wilson "does not believe that direct legislation is practicable and desirable as a general proposition." Rather, it should be resorted to only in an emergency "as a scourge and a deterrent to promote righteousness among public officials and political bosses."[34]

The interviewer said Wilson was not interested in promoting the adoption of the initiative and referendum nationwide. In Wilson's words, "It is a National question only in the sense that it is of universal interest and that public men everywhere are seeking or trying to avoid the means by which public opinion may be made supreme in public affairs."[35]

The *Times* interview did not dispel fears in the East that Wilson held radical views. Friends and supporters in his native state of Virginia expressed concern over his positions on the initiative and referendum. One of his responses was reprinted in the Richmond *Times-Dispatch* and was accompanied by a lengthy editorial that concluded as follows:

> The position of Governor Wilson on all public matters is a matter of profound concern to his native State, to the Democratic party and to the whole country, and his letter on the initiative, referendum and recall will clear up many doubts and quiet many misgivings on the part of his friends and fellow-citizens in Virginia.[36]

As the presidential campaign proceeded in 1912, Wilson made far fewer references to the initiative and referendum than he had in 1911, and when he did mention those devices, he was always careful to qualify his position. Speaking before the Maryland General Assembly in March of 1912, Wilson referred to the initiative, referendum and recall as "one insistent issue constantly arising in our public discussion," but one that has "nothing to do with national politics." In direct contradiction to what he had told a Portland reporter the previous May, he stated:

> There is no central body of opinion in this country demanding the initiative and referendum or the recall with regard to national representatives, and the call for these things is acute only in those States where the people feel that they must have what they have somehow lost and wish to recover—a control over their own representatives.[37]

No one is suggesting that "direct legislation should be substituted for elective representation" to "create a new system of government." The object was to "recover lost control" by relying on the devices as a "reserve power to be resorted to when it became necessary."[38]

Addressing a large audience in Atlanta on April 17, 1912, Wilson referred to the initiative and referendum as "two words that send cold shivers down the backs of some people, but which are not calculated to chill the prudent." He hastened to add that there was no need to discuss the initiative and referendum in Georgia because it already had a representative legislature that was responsive to the will of the people.[39]

On June 11, 1912, Josephus Daniels, a prominent Democratic politician from North Carolina, wrote to Wilson on the need for a Democratic platform "that rings." He asked him to draft some planks "that would catch the attention and win the approval of the average man."[40]

In response Wilson sent Daniels both an outline and specific language for proposed planks on trusts, tariffs, currency, political organization, the direct election of senators (the constitutional amendment then pending ratification by the states), the physical valuation of railroad properties, direct primaries, the unit rule, commission government for the cities, immigration, and labor. In his proposed plank on the initiative, referendum, and recall, Wilson reiterated his view that they "do not fall within the field of national questions," but he added that "they are not inconsistent with the spirit of our institutions." The object of the initiative and referendum, he wrote, "is to control legislative action where the legislature of the state fails to respond to the stronger movements of public opinion."[41]

As it turned out, the Democratic Platform of 1912 did not contain Wilson's draft language on the initiative and referendum. Instead, in a section titled

"Rule of the People," it referred to the 1908 platform's "demand for a return to the rule of the people," which "has now become the accepted doctrine of a large majority of the electors."[42] The platform went on:

> We again remind the country that only by a larger exercise of the reserved power of the people can they protect themselves from the misuse of delegated power and the usurpation of government instrumentalities by special interests. For this reason the National Convention insisted on the overthrow of Cannonism and the inauguration of a system by which the United States Senators could be elected by direct vote.[43]

The platform concluded by reminding the people that the Democratic Party offers itself "as an agency through which the complete overthrow and extirpation of corruption, fraud, and machine rule in American politics can be effected."[44]

The Progressive Party's platform of 1912 also included a section titled "The Rule of the People." It urged on the states "the policy of the short ballot, with responsibility to the people secured by the initiative, referendum, and recall."[45]

When the Democratic Convention opened in Baltimore on June 25, House Speaker Champ Clark of Missouri seemed the likely winner of the presidential nomination. But a two-thirds vote of the delegates was necessary to win, and a four-way race was on between Wilson, Clark, Gov. Judson Harmon of Ohio, who had the support of New York's Tammany machine, and House Majority Leader Oscar Underwood of Alabama, who was sapping some of Wilson's southern support. Reacting to New York's switch from Harmon to Clark on the tenth ballot, William Jennings Bryan and his Nebraska delegation switched from Clark to Wilson on the fourteenth ballot. It was the populist, Bryan, a strong proponent of the initiative and referendum, whose support helped put Wilson over the top on the forty-sixth ballot in the early morning hours of July 2.

Not in attendance at the convention, Wilson delivered his acceptance speech from his New Jersey home in Sea Girt over a month later on August 7. In his speech he reviewed the party's position as reflected in its platform planks. While making no reference to the initiative and referendum, he did return to his central theme of restoring "the rule of the people" without which there can be no rule of right. That right in politics, he said, is "made up of the interests of everybody. And everybody should take part in the action that is to determine it." He specifically called for presidential primaries, the direct election of senators, and the full disclosure of campaign contributions. He said the party was working toward a very definite object: "the universal partnership in public affairs upon which the purity of politics and its aim and spirit depend."[46]

During the general election campaign, Wilson mentioned the initiative, referendum, and recall less frequently than he had in the previous year, but he still cited them as limited examples of how the people in some states had exerted new influence over their legislatures and lawmaking. Wilson correctly perceived Theodore Roosevelt, nominee of the new Progressive or Bull Moose Party, as a greater threat than the Republican nominee, incumbent president William Howard Taft. Both Wilson and Roosevelt supported the state initiative and referendum process, and both supported the recall of state officials, though Roosevelt supported the recall of judges as well, and Wilson did not. Wilson went on to win in an electoral landslide with 435 electoral votes compared with 88 for Roosevelt and 8 for Taft.

As governor of New Jersey, Wilson had succeeded in pushing through the legislature both the direct primary law and a corrupt practices law for elections. There is no indication from his papers that he ever submitted a constitutional amendment or legislative message calling for a state initiative and referendum process. Nevertheless, his belated support for these direct democracy devices around the country is credited not only with their passage in other states, but with helping to establish him nationally as a progressive reformer.

Notes

1. Thomas E. Cronin, *Direct Democracy: The Politics of Initiative, Referendum and Recall* (Cambridge: Harvard University Press, 1989), 164.
2. Ibid.
3. Ibid., 48.
4. Ibid., 50–51.
5. Woodrow Wilson, *The State and Federal Governments of the United States* (Boston: D.C. Heath & Co., 1891), 42.
6. *The Papers of Woodrow Wilson*, ed. Arthur S. Link (Princeton: Princeton University Press, 1974), vol. 17 (1907–8), letter from Woodrow Wilson to James Callaway, Oct. 30, 1907, 461.
7. Ibid.
8. *The Papers of Woodrow Wilson* (1975), vol. 19 (1909–10), "An Address on Political Reform to the City Club of Philadelphia," Nov. 18, 1909, 512.
9. *The Papers of Woodrow Wilson* (1976), vol. 21 (1910), letters from Wilson B. Killingbeck to Woodrow Wilson, Oct. 6, 1910, 267–69; Oct. 18, 1910, 351–53.
10. *The Papers of Woodrow Wilson* (1976), vol. 22 (1910–11), letter from George Earle Chamberlain to Woodrow Wilson, Dec. 12, 1910, 175.
11. Ibid.
12. Ibid., letter from Robert Latham Owen to Woodrow Wilson, Dec. 16, 1910, 208.
13. Ibid., letter from John E. Lathrop to Woodrow Wilson, Dec. 22, 1910, 247–48.
14. Ibid., letter from John E. Lathrop to Woodrow Wilson, Dec. 23, 1910, 255.
15. Ibid., letter from Daniel Kiefer to Woodrow Wilson, Dec. 24, 1910, 357–58.
16. Ibid., letter from Woodrow Wilson to Daniel Kiefer, Dec. 26, 1910, 261.

17. Ibid., letter from Joseph Fels to Woodrow Wilson, Dec. 29, 1910, 278–80.

18. Ibid., "To Solve Corporation Problems through State Laws," an interview in *The New York Times Annual Financial Review*, Jan. 8, 1911, 315.

19. Ibid., Inaugural Address of Gov. Woodrow Wilson of New Jersey, Jan. 17, 1911, 351.

20. Ibid., "Wilson to Attempt to Kill Lobby," by Virginia Tyler Hudson, *New York Globe and Commercial Advertiser*, Jan. 17, 1911, 354–55.

21. Ibid., Woodrow Wilson's address to the Democratic Club of Philadelphia, Feb. 21, 1911, 448–49.

22. Ibid., 449.

23. Ibid., letter from Samuel Huston Thompson, Jr., to Woodrow Wilson, Jan. 25, 1911, 375–76.

24. Ibid., letter from Woodrow Wilson to Samuel Huston Thompson, Jr., March 27, 1911, 521.

25. Ibid., "Acclaimed Democracy's Giant of the Hour at Pewter Platter Dinner," *Norfolk Landmark*, April 30, 1911, 597.

26. Ibid., letter from Daniel Kiefer to Woodrow Wilson, April 21, 1911, 578.

27. *The Papers of Woodrow Wilson* (1977), "A News Report and Interview: U'Ren First Gains Gov. Wilson's Ear; Visitor Is Impressed," the Portland *Morning Oregonian*, May 18, 1911, vol. 23 (1911–12), 60.

28. Ibid., 61.

29. Ibid.

30. Ibid., Wilson speech at Portland, Oregon, Armory, March 19, 1911, 71–72.

31. Ibid., "Woodrow Wilson Welcomed on His Visit to Seattle," an interview in the *Seattle Daily Times*, May 20, 1911, 77.

32. Ibid., "Is Woodrow Wilson Bryantizing?" New York *World* editorial, July 31, 1911, 243.

33. Ibid., letter from William Frank McCombs to Woodrow Wilson, Sept. 23, 1911, 355–56.

34. Ibid., "Woodrow Wilson Talks on Big Public Questions," *New York Times*, Dec. 24, 1911, 619.

35. Ibid., 619–20.

36. Ibid., excerpts from "Woodrow Wilson and Virginia," editorial in the Richmond *Times-Dispatch*, Dec. 18, 1911, 602.

37. *The Papers of Woodrow Wilson* (1977), vol. 24 (1912), an address to the General Assembly of Maryland, March 7, 1912, 234.

38. Ibid., 234–35.

39. Ibid., a news report of a campaign address in Atlanta, "Wilson Is Choice of Georgia; Over 7,000 Heard Him in Spite of a Heavy Downpour," *Atlanta Journal*, April 17, 1912, 339.

40. *The Papers of Woodrow Wilson* (1977), vol. 24 (1912), letter from Josephus Daniels to Woodrow Wilson, June 12, 1912, 472.

41. Ibid., "Planks for a Democratic Platform," sent by Wilson to Josephus Daniels about June 16, 1912, 476–81.

42. *National Party Platforms, Volume 1, 1840–1956*, comp. Donald Bruce Johnson (Urbana: University of Illinois Press, 1978), "Democratic Platform of 1912," 175.

43. Ibid.

44. Ibid.

45. Ibid., "Progressive Platform of 1912," 176.

46. *The Papers of Woodrow Wilson* (1978), vol. 25 (1912), a speech accepting the Democratic nomination in Sea Girt, New Jersey, Aug. 7, 1912, 15.

6

National Referendum Proposals and the Isolationist Impulse

ALTHOUGH eighteen states adopted the initiative and referendum between 1898 and 1918, momentum for such a process at the national level never developed, mainly because neither major political party was willing to go that far in co-opting the ideas of the populists. Wilson's brief flirtation with extending the referendum to the national level, as reflected in just one newspaper interview in Oregon, was quickly forgotten after he made clear that what was good for some states was not workable or desirable nationally.

A survey of constitutional amendments introduced in Congress providing for a national initiative and/or referendum process is especially revealing in this regard. Between 1895 and 1943, only seven constitutional amendments that would establish an initiative and referendum process of broad application were introduced in the House and Senate combined. On the other hand, 101 constitutional amendments were introduced in the Congress that limited national initiatives and/or referendums to specified issues (see Table 6.1).

The very first constitutional amendment on the initiative and referendum was introduced in 1895 by Sen. William Peffer, a Populist Party member from Kansas who had first been elected to the Senate in 1890. Peffer reminded some observers of a Hebrew prophet because of his long, flowing white beard. A young Theodore Roosevelt, however, did not regard Peffer with religious respect, having once denounced him as "a well-meaning, pinheaded, anarchistic crank."[1]

Peffer's amendment would have required Congress to put any legislative ini-

Table 6.1
Constitutional Amendments Introduced in the U.S. Congress Calling for National Initiatives and/or Referendums (1895–1943)

		House		Senate		
Congress	Years	Issue specific	General	Issue specific	General	Total
54th	1895–97	0	0	0	1	1
55th–59th	1897–1907	0	0	0	0	0
60th	1907–9	0	1	0	0	1
61st	1909–11	0	0	0	0	0
62d	1911–13	1	0	2	1	4
63rd	1913–15	3	0	3	0	6
64th	1915–17	2	0	2	0	4
65th	1917–19	1	0	2	0	3
66th	1919–21	9	0	2	0	11
67th	1921–23	7	0	3	0	10
68th	1923–25	3	0	5	0	8
69th	1925–27	1	0	1	0	2
70th	1927–29	3	0	0	0	3
71st	1929–31	6	0	0	0	6
72d	1931–33	6	0	1	0	7
73rd	1933–35	8	1	2	0	11
74th	1935–37	3	1	2	0	6
75th	1937–39	9	1	6	0	16
76th	1939–41	4	1	2	0	7
77th	1941–43	1	0	1	0	2
TOTAL		**67**	**5**	**34**	**2**	**108**

Sources: "Proposed Amendments to the Constitution of the United States Introduced in Congress, 1889 to 1926," S. Doc. 93, 67th Cong., 1st sess., April 5, 1936; "Proposed Amendments to the Constitution of the United States of America Introduced in Congress from the 69th Congress, 2d Session, through the 87th Congress, 2d Session (Dec. 6, 1926 to Jan. 3, 1963)," S. Doc. 163, 87th Cong., 2d sess. (1963).

tiative before the people at the next election upon the petition of one-fifth of the qualified electors in the United States or one-fifth of the state legislatures. What is more, most major laws passed by Congress that changed national policy, especially regarding foreign relations, taxation, public lands, and the monetary system, would have had to be approved by referendum of the people.[2] Senator Peffer was beaten in his bid for reelection in 1896 along with the Democrats' populist presidential nominee, William Jennings Bryan.

Six other general initiative and referendum constitutional amendments were introduced during the first half of the twentieth century. In the 60th Congress (1907–9), Rep. Elmer Lincoln Fulton, a one-term Democrat from Oklahoma, proposed that 8 percent of the voters in each of fifteen states could petition to initiate bills and constitutional amendments, and 5 percent in each of fifteen states could trigger a referendum on any matter passed by Congress. In the 62d Congress, Republican senator Joseph Bristow of Kansas proposed allowing a national referendum on any law proposed by the president that was ignored by the Congress. The four other constitutional amendments of general application were introduced by Rep. William Lemke, a Republican from North Dakota, in each of four successive Congresses, the 73d to 76th (1933–41). They allowed for national initiatives on any legislative matter.[3] None of the general measures received any consideration by the Congress.

The issue-specific constitutional amendments for a national initiative and/or referendum did not begin to catch on until the 62d Congress (1911–13), and then only on a gradual basis. In that Congress Senator Bristow called for a national referendum on any law held unconstitutional by the Supreme Court. Also during the 62d Congress, Rep. Victor Berger, a Socialist Party member from Wisconsin, introduced the most radical constitutional amendment ever proposed. Not only did the amendment provide for a referendum on any law passed by Congress upon the petition of 5 percent of the voters in three-fourths of the states. It also provided for the abolition of the presidency, the Supreme Court, and the Senate—leaving only the House of Representatives standing.[4]

Most of the issue-specific or limited initiative and referendum proposals introduced between 1911 and 1943—49 of the 101 constitutional amendments—authorized the people either to ratify constitutional amendments and/or initiate constitutional amendments. Several others addressed the issue of Prohibition. But the second most popular of the constitutional amendments (forty-two were introduced between 1914 and 1943) was a proposal to require the people to ratify by popular referendum any declaration of war; declarations resulting from a direct attack on the United States were usually excluded. Three such amendments were introduced prior to World War I, two during the course of that war, and another thirty-eight between 1922 and the outbreak of World War II.

The World War I Referendum Proposals

The first war referendum constitutional amendment was introduced by Rep. Richard Bartholdt, a Republican from Missouri, on July 21, 1914. That same Congress, on January 15, 1915, Democratic senator Robert Owen of Oklahoma introduced his own war referendum constitutional amendment, drawing partly on Bartholdt's version and partly on the ideas expressed in an article by the Socialist Allan L. Benson. Benson had suggested that those who vote for a war referendum be sent to the front first, regardless of age or sex.[5]

Perhaps the greatest impetus to the war referendum idea came from William Jennings Bryan, the three-time Democratic presidential nominee from Nebraska who was appointed secretary of state by President Wilson in 1912. On June 9, 1915, Bryan resigned as secretary of state in protest over a second warning note Wilson had sent to the German government following the sinking of the British vessel *Lusitania* by a German submarine. In his letter of resignation, Bryan made clear his reason:

> Alike desirous of reaching a peaceful solution of the problems arising out of the use of submarines against merchantmen we find ourselves differing irreconcilably as to the methods which should be employed.[6]

Wilson accepted Bryan's resignation by letter "with much more than deep regret" and "only because you insist upon its acceptance." And Wilson concluded by echoing their mutual goals. "Our objects are the same and we ought to pursue them together," he said. "We shall continue to work for the same causes even when we do not work in the same way."[7]

Little did Wilson realize at the time how much their views would diverge on how best to pursue peace. According to Professor Thomas E. Cronin, "Within a few days after his resignation, Bryan was lamenting the absence of a referendum mechanism in the Constitution, and a few months later he was urging that the Constitution be amended to provide for public votes on matters of war and peace."[8]

Wilson must have sensed where Bryan was headed after visiting with him at his home on June 18. The next day he wrote Edith Bolling Galt that he felt "uneasy" about visiting Bryan because he "could not do it with genuine cordiality; but I did it on the best political advice!" He went on to observe:

> No stranger man ever lived, and his naïveté takes my breath away. . . . He was full of enthusiasm about what he was doing for peace and about what he was going to do, and perfectly at his ease.[9]

Bryan was quick to confirm Wilson's perceptions of both his dedication to peace and his naïveté. On June 19, 1915, the day following his meeting with Wilson, Bryan spoke in New York at a peace rally organized by a group that turned out to be a front for the German embassy. Five days later Bryan addressed a pro-German throng in Madison Square Garden that called itself "One Hundred Thousand Friends of Peace." He spoke again to the Friends of Peace on Labor Day at a mass convention they organized in Chicago.[10]

These rallies were the platforms Bryan used in calling for a constitutional amendment to permit a public referendum on war. The war referendum idea became a rallying point for assorted groups of populists, socialists, pacifists, pro-Germans, anti-British, and isolationists. Cronin asserts that "a majority of American voters might have vetoed entry into World War I if it had come to a vote at that time."[11]

This may have been true during 1915, when U.S. policy was still one of strict neutrality, but public opinion began to shift as the war in Europe worsened. Wilson unveiled a new policy of military preparedness before a joint session of Congress in early January of 1916. Although Wilson enjoyed support in the eastern states for strengthening American defense capabilities, sentiment in other parts of the country ran from apathy to suspicion. To remedy this, Wilson embarked on a speaking tour in late January of 1916 that included Pittsburgh, Cleveland, Milwaukee, Chicago, Des Moines, Topeka, Kansas City, and St. Louis. At all stops enthusiasm and support reportedly ran high. On March 6, 1916, Rep. James Hay of Virginia, chairman of the House Military Affairs Committee, introduced the National Defense Act. This bill to bolster American military forces and industrial preparedness passed the House on March 23 by a vote of 403 to 2, and by June 3 it had cleared the Senate in modified form. A version reflecting a compromise between the houses was signed into law by the president.[12]

On March 24, 1916, the day after the preparedness bill passed the House, the Germans torpedoed the French steamship *Sussex* in the English Channel, an act that appeared to violate their pledges after the sinking of the *Lusitania*. Wilson delivered an ultimatum to the German imperial government on April 18, and the following day addressed a joint session of Congress to report on his actions. The Hearst newspapers, with anti-British movements under their patronage, reacted immediately in editorials proclaiming that only the people should decide on war.[13] Taking up on this theme, Republican senator Robert M. LaFollette from Wisconsin wrote in the next issue of his monthly *LaFollette's Magazine*:

> The day is coming when the people, who always pay the full price, are going to have the *final say* over their own destinies. . . . They who do the fighting will do their own deciding.[14]

Ten days after Wilson's address to Congress, on Saturday, April 29, 1916, LaFollette introduced a bill to provide for advisory elections on declarations of war.[15]

The LaFollette measure was a clever twist on the constitutional amendments previously introduced: it would require only a majority vote of both houses and presidential approval, as opposed to a two-thirds vote of both houses and ratification by three-fourths of the states for constitutional amendments. However, the effect would likely be the same given the prospect of a presidential veto of even an advisory referendum bill and the need for two-thirds of both houses to override a veto.

Under the terms of the LaFollette bill, if the president severed diplomatic relations with any foreign government, and 1 percent of the qualified electors in each of twenty-five states (or more) file petitions with the director of the census calling for a popular vote on whether to declare war with that country, ballots would be sent to all qualified voters to mark either "yes" or "no" as to whether the United States should declare war against that country. The ballots would be returned to the director of the census who would tabulate the results and report them to the clerk of the House, who would make them available to members of either house of the Congress.

Because the LaFollette bill assigned responsibility for the war referendum to the director of the census, it was referred to the Senate Committee on the Census. A jurisdictional dispute followed. On May 3, 1916, the Wednesday after the introduction of the LaFollette bill, the chairman of the Senate Foreign Relations Committee, William J. Stone of Missouri, offered a motion that the Committee on the Census be discharged from further consideration of the bill and that it be referred to his committee. Under Senate rules, consideration of the motion was postponed until Friday, May 5, at which time Stone renewed his motion.

Senator Stone was in a very delicate position. On the one hand, he was a committee chairman and a member of the president's party. On the other hand, he represented many German-American constituents. For more than a year German-Americans had been complaining to members of Congress that the State Department's "neutral" trade policy tilted in favor of the Allies. Pressure was brought on the government to force the Allies to allow the passage of cargoes to Germany, and bills were introduced to prohibit the sale of munitions to either side. Among the most vocal members were Democratic senator Gilbert M. Hitchcock of Nebraska, who had a large constituency of German-Americans in Omaha, and Representative Bartholdt, a naturalized German, who, as mentioned previously, had introduced the first war referendum constitutional amendment in 1914.[16]

Whether Stone objected to the referral of the LaFollette bill primarily out of committee turf considerations or because he thought his fight for control over the bill would play well with the large German-American population of St. Louis is not clear from the debate that ensued. But he made a strong case for the re-referral of the bill to his committee. "It seems so clear that a measure . . . which concerns and is intended to influence the action of the Congress of the United States in declaring war against a foreign country should go to the Committee on Foreign Relations," he argued. He was not interested, he insisted, in using the occasion of his motion to debate the pending diplomatic negotiations with the German government or the merits of the LaFollette bill itself. He was simply there to make the case that "the bill presents a question of policy which so intimately and directly concerns the most vital interests of this Government in dealing with foreign affairs that there ought not to be a moment's hesitation in the mind of any Senator that it ought to go to the committee appointed by this body to take charge of our foreign relations."[17]

What Stone had apparently not counted on was a small group of Republican senators who favored keeping the bill in the Census Committee. Senators Moses Clapp of Minnesota, William Borah of Idaho, George Norris of Nebraska, and even the bill's sponsor, Senator LaFollette, spoke out at length against a change. LaFollette asked Senator Norris whether it was "easily conceivable that the Committee on the Census might broaden the terms of this bill so as to provide for an expression from the qualified voters of the country upon any question relating to the public welfare?" When Norris answered, "It is," LaFollette replied, "Then surely it would remove any question as to the prerogatives of this special Committee on Foreign Relations."[18]

After debate had gone on for some time, Chairman Stone referred somewhat apologetically to the time consumed on his motion to discharge LaFollette's bill from the Census Committee. "The matter before the Senate, of course, is merely one of correct procedure under the rules and practice of this body, and perhaps is far less important for the moment than matters of legislation pending," which happened to be a "good-roads" bill. Stone said he had promised the manager of the roads bill that he would take only "20 or 30 minutes to dispose" of his motion, "but it seems now that there is likely to be a somewhat prolonged discussion." He consequently asked unanimous consent to withdraw his motion temporarily. "I will call it up tomorrow during the morning hour," he promised.[19]

However, Stone did not renew his motion on the following day or for the remainder of the Congress. Although LaFollette had succeeded in keeping his bill in the Census Committee, it languished there without receiving so much as a hearing, let alone a favorable report. Despite Senate inaction on his war referendum bill, LaFollette did not go quietly into the night on the issue of war.

On Monday, February 26, 1917, the last week of the 64th Congress, President Wilson appeared before Congress to request the enactment of a bill authorizing the arming of American merchant ships. Although Stone introduced the bill by request on the following day, he could not support it and turned over management of the bill to another senator. Beginning on Wednesday, February 28, LaFollette led a handful of senators in a filibuster of the bill that ran up to adjournment of the Congress at noon on March 4. That effort successfully blocked passage of the bill, even though it had passed the House by a vote of 403 to 13 on Friday, and 76 senators signed a manifesto inserted in the *Congressional Record* expressing their desire to vote for the bill.[20]

The German-American propaganda organ *Viereck's* (formerly known as the *Fatherland*), exuded, "When the history of these days comes to be chronicled, the names of Stone, LaFollette, Hearst, and Bryan will shine forth like beacon-lights—if our annals are written by an American pen."[21]

President Wilson naturally viewed the dissidents quite differently. In a strongly worded statement issued on March 4, the day the 64th Congress adjourned, he called them "a little group of willful men, representing no opinion but their own" and accused them of rendering "the great government of the United States helpless and contemptible." Taking direct aim at the Senate filibuster, Wilson observed:

> The Senate has no rules by which debate can be limited or brought to an end, no rules by which dilatory tactics of any kind can be prevented. A single member can stand in the way of action, if he have but the physical endurance. The result in this case is a complete paralysis alike of the legislative and executive branches of government.

Wilson concluded, "There is but one remedy," and that is "that the rules of the Senate shall be so altered that it can act. The country can be relied upon to draw the moral. I believe that the Senate can be relied on to supply the means of action and save the country from disaster."[22]

The president summoned the Senate into special session on the very next day, March 5, 1917. Although the Senate regarded its right of extended debate as practically sacred, by the end of the week it had succumbed to public pressure and after six hours of debate voted 76-3 to adopt a new cloture (or debate cut-off) rule. The rule provided that, upon the petition of sixteen senators and a two-thirds vote of the Senate, debate could be terminated on any matter after each senator was given up to one additional hour of debate.[23]

When Wilson addressed the Congress on April 2, 1917, to request a declaration of war, there was no filibuster in the Senate. The declaration passed the Senate two days later by a vote of 82 to 6, with LaFollette, Norris, and the four other "willful men" in opposition. It passed the House on April 6, 373-50.[24]

Despite his unpopular stand on the war, "Fightin' Bob" LaFollette was reelected to the Senate in 1922 by an overwhelming margin. As public disillusionment with the war grew, many viewed LaFollette as a heroic prophet. He ran for president as a Progressive in 1924, carrying only Wisconsin, but capturing one-sixth of the popular vote. He died in 1925 and was succeeded in the Senate by his son, "Young Bob" LaFollette, who carried forward his father's progressive and isolationist positions, even to the point of keeping the advisory war referendum proposal alive.

World War II and War Referendum Debates

As an isolationist mood reemerged after the First World War, interest in a popular referendum on declaring war was renewed. Between 1921 and 1941, thirty-eight war referendum constitutional amendments were introduced, as were numerous bills calling for advisory referendums. In 1924 both the Democratic and Progressive Party platforms contained planks endorsing a war referendum. However, during the 1920s, only two or three war referendum constitutional amendments were introduced in any Congress. In the 72d Congress (1931–33), none was introduced.

By the mid-1930s, though, as war clouds grew in Europe and the Far East, the proposal was revived and support began to grow. In the 73d Congress (1933–35), seven constitutional amendments were introduced calling for a popular vote on declaring war, although four of them were introduced by the same member, Rep. James Frear of Wisconsin, an eleven-term Republican who did not stand for reelection in 1934. In the 74th Congress, only two such amendments were introduced, one by Democratic senator Marvel Logan of Kentucky and the other by Rep. Louis Ludlow of Indiana, also a Democrat.[25]

Before his House service (1929–49), Ludlow had been a Washington correspondent for Ohio and Indiana newspapers. It is therefore highly likely that he had written about the senior LaFollette's war referendum efforts in 1916. In the 75th Congress, Ludlow introduced two war referendum constitutional amendments, as did "Young Bob" LaFollette in the Senate. Moreover, nine other House and Senate members introduced such amendments, including Sen. Champ Clark of Missouri (formerly Speaker of the House), Rep. Warren Magnuson of Washington, and Rep. Hamilton Fish of New York (the third of four Hamilton Fishes to serve in the Congress).

Ludlow's second amendment, introduced on February 5, 1937, just one month after the convening of the new Congress, had the most success, although it ultimately was defeated. On March 24, Ludlow introduced a special rule providing for the consideration of the constitutional amendment with six hours of debate and an open amendment process. And on April 6 he filed a discharge petition on the special rule. (Once a majority of House members have signed a discharge petition, the matter is placed on the Calendar of Motions to Discharge Committees. After pending there for at least seven legislative days, the motion to discharge is eligible for consideration on the second or fourth Monday of the month.) By December 14, 1937, Ludlow had collected 218 signatures on his petition, and the 218 names were entered in the *Congressional Record* on that date.[26]

Because the second session of the 75th Congress adjourned on December 21, Ludlow was not able to offer his discharge motion until after the third session convened on January 3, 1938. On the second Monday of the month, January 10, Ludlow offered his motion to discharge the special rule on his constitutional amendment. Under House rules, the motion could be debated for twenty minutes, which were divided between Ludlow and Rules Committee chairman John O'Connor of New York. In his opening remarks Ludlow called his resolution for referendum on foreign wars "a valuable contribution to the cause of peace" that would "mark an epochal advancement in the cause of popular rule." He closed by indicating that the supporters had agreed to some changes that he found acceptable, and that they would be explained later by Representative Fish, the ranking minority member of the Foreign Affairs Committee.[27]

O'Connor immediately yielded his time to House Speaker William Bankhead of Alabama, who vehemently opposed a constitutional amendment requiring a war referendum. He termed Ludlow's proposal "the gravest question that has been submitted to the Congress of the United States since I became a Member of it more than 20 years ago." Speaker Bankhead characterized the idea as a "radical and . . . revolutionary . . . attack upon the fundamental basic principle of a representative democracy for a free people." The Speaker went on to say that as much as he abhorred war, he was "unwilling to abandon the wisdom and judgment of the framers of our Constitution . . . and say that no longer are the people of this country willing to trust their chosen Representatives in the Congress of the United States to reflect their views, or to protect the security of the Republic."[28]

And then, to put the icing on the cake, the Speaker read into the *Record* a letter he had requested from President Franklin Delano Roosevelt as to his attitude on the matter. Dated January 6, 1938, the letter called the Ludlow resolution "impracticable in its application and incompatible with our representative form of government."

> Our Government is conducted by the people through representatives of their choosing. It was with singular unanimity that the founders of the Republic agreed upon such [a] free and representative form of government as the only practicable means of government by the people.

Roosevelt concluded by saying that the Ludlow amendment would "cripple any President in his conduct of our foreign relations" and would "encourage other nations to believe they could violate American rights with impunity." Rather than keeping the United States out of war, "I am convinced it would have the opposite effect."[29]

Unpersuaded, Representative Fish spoke next, observing that "every public poll taken shows that approximately 80 percent of the people favor a referendum before being involved in a foreign war."[30] He called the Ludlow amendment "the greatest peace proposal before Congress during the 18 years I have been a Member of the House." He warned that a vote against the discharge motion would be not only a vote to stifle debate "but also a vote of want of confidence in popular government, in our free institutions, and in a government by the consent of the governed. . . . The American people should have the inalienable right to decide this great issue of war or peace themselves."[31]

Majority Leader Sam Rayburn of Texas did not think the amendment was a great peace proposal—far from it. He put things bluntly by saying that if Congress passed the constitutional amendment, "it would make the most tremendous blunder it has ever made since the formation of our government under the Constitution" because "it would ultimately do more to plunge this country into war than any action the Congress of the United States could take."[32]

In concluding statements for each side, Chairman O'Connor and Rep. Gerald Boileau of Wisconsin gave their respective views on the wisdom of referendums. In O'Connor's words, those who favored the Ludlow amendment subscribe to a "pure democracy," which he termed "the Elysian fields of the demagog" who "there besports himself in his political nudism—the only friend of the 'peepul'—indifferent to the fact of government or his own country." Once you have this "pure democracy," O'Connor concluded, "the next step is dictatorship."[33]

Boileau, elected as a Republican in 1930 and as a Progressive since 1934, and a World War I veteran, took issue with the president and House leaders who "have made the point that a provision for a referendum is a threat to representative democracy." He pointed out that the precedent for a referendum had already been established by the Roosevelt administration's farm legislation, which allowed farmers to determine "whether or not they should lead little pigs to slaughter." Boileau continued: "It is fair and it is right that all of the people should be permitted by a referendum vote to determine whether or not the sons and the daughters of these same farmers, among other citizens, should be led to slaughter upon the battlefields of foreign countries."[34]

The president's intervention coupled with an all-out effort by House Democratic leaders proved to be decisive. When the vote was taken, Ludlow's motion to discharge the special rule from the Rules Committee was defeated, 188-

209. Voting for the motion to discharge were 111 Democrats, 64 Republicans, 8 Progressives, and 5 Farmer-Laborites. Voting against were 188 Democrats and 21 Republicans. Not voting were 23 members.

While this 1938 vote was the high-water mark for the war referendum movement, it was not the last gasp by any means. When the 76th Congress convened in January of 1939, only three war referendum amendments were reintroduced, those of Senators Clark and LaFollette, plus that of Representative Ludlow. This time LaFollette would take the spotlight, just as his father had twenty-three years earlier. On July 11, 1939, the Senate Judiciary Committee rejected a motion to favorably report the LaFollette constitutional amendment by a vote of 5 to 9. In the words of the committee report, "Notwithstanding the adverse vote, the committee believed the resolution one upon which the Senate should be permitted to vote," so it forwarded the resolution and report to the Senate "with amendments and without recommendation."[35]

Despite the charitable attitude of the Judiciary Committee, the Senate majority leadership was in no apparent hurry to expedite Senate floor consideration of the LaFollette amendment. On October 27, 1939, LaFollette took matters into his own hands by offering an advisory war referendum amendment to a pending neutrality resolution. Under the terms of the amendment, a national advisory election on the question of war or peace would be held prior to any declaration of war by the Congress except in the case of an attack or threatened attack on the United States, its territories, or any nation in the Western Hemisphere. The national advisory election would be called by the secretary of state if he received a written request from four or more members of a seven-member U.S. Referendum Election Board consisting of the president of the Senate and three members each from the Senate Foreign Relations and House Foreign Affairs Committees.[36]

LaFollette presented his case in simple terms:

> Mr. President, I cannot see how any Senator who believes in democracy, who believes in the extension of popular participation in government, can fail to support this proposal for a national advisory referendum prior to any declaration of an overseas war.[37]

He went on to say that popular referendums were more feasible than when the Constitution was drawn because rapid transportation and communication, the radio, newspapers, and the rising tide of literacy "have provided this country with an economic and an intelligent and a democratic environment which makes this further advance toward reposing the power in the hands of the people possible."[38]

One of the senators taking a contrary view was Sen. Thomas Connally, a Democrat from Texas, who reminded his colleagues that "the people sent us here to act as Senators, and not as manikins." Calling the referendum "an assault on the representative principle," Connally asked the following: "If we as a House of Representatives and a Senate have not sense enough to legislate on whether we are to go to war or not, we have not sense enough to legislate on anything else. Why not submit everything to a vote of the people?"[39]

He went on:

> Talk about a referendum. We get a referendum in the Senate every morning. When we go to our offices, when we open our mail, when we wait for the telegraph boy, when we go to the long-distance telephone, when we mingle with our people at home, we are having a referendum, . . . and if Senators are honest and patriotic they want to represent the views of the people, unless the people are absolutely wrong.[40]

Senator Norris, one of the senators who had voted against the World War I declaration of war, also opposed the LaFollette amendment: "I believe it is a fantasy, an illusion, that we can surmount the obstacle by submitting to the people the question of embarking on war." Referring to the World War I declaration, he said, "after going through that experience, the hell, the damnation, of those terrible, agonizing, and bitter days, I have reached the conclusion that if Congress had followed the dictates of its own conscience no war would have been declared." But Congress then was following popular sentiment. Norris added that his own constituents had been nearly unanimous in favor of declaring war. Indeed, "if there had been a referendum then, in my opinion, 95 percent of the voters would have voted for war." And that brought Norris to the central difference between an ordinary citizen casting a vote in a ballot box and a member of Congress shouldering the responsibility for the vote:

> Shoulder a reckless man with responsibility and he becomes a different individual. He then has a responsibility that sobers him. He must reason things out. For that reason the vote of a Senator is vastly different from the vote of the ordinary citizen who goes to the ballot box and casts his vote. We have the blood of our people resting upon us. We are thinking in a broader sense than we would think if we were in an election booth. We are different men.[41]

Mindful of the popular sentiment for war when the *Maine* was sunk and again when the *Lusitania* was sunk, Norris added, "We ought not to be taken off our feet by some emotional excitement which may occur any day and which has occurred in the past many times almost without a moment's notice."[42]

In closing the debate LaFollette said, "it may amuse Senators to hear this fundamental idea ridiculed," but "they cannot successfully, by ridicule, bury the inherent desire of the men and women, citizens of this country, to have some effective opportunity to express their opinion upon the most important, the supreme issue and decision which can come in the life of any generation of people."[43]

The amendment was then overwhelmingly rejected, 17-73. LaFollette's more stringent constitutional amendment requiring a war referendum was never considered by the 76th Congress. But at least "Young Bob" had served his father's legacy well by pressing the issue of the proper role of the people in deciding vital questions of war and peace.

Notes

1. Allan Nevins and Henry Steele Commager, *A Pocket History of the United States* (New York: Washington Square Press, 1956), 346.
2. M.A. Musmanno, "Proposed Amendments to the Constitution, 1889–1928," H. Doc. 551, 70th Cong., 2d sess., 173–74.
3. Ibid., 174–75.
4. Ibid., 174.
5. Thomas E. Cronin, *Direct Democracy: The Politics of Initiative, Referendum and Recall* (Cambridge: Harvard University Press, 1989), 166–67.
6. *The Papers of Woodrow Wilson*, ed. Arthur S. Link (Princeton: Princeton University Press, 1974), vol. 33 (April 17–July 21, 1915), letter from William Jennings Bryan to Woodrow Wilson, 375–76.
7. Ibid., letter from Woodrow Wilson to William Jennings Bryan, 376.
8. Cronin, *Direct Democracy*, 167.
9. *The Papers of Woodrow Wilson*, vol. 33, letter from Woodrow Wilson to Edith Bolling Galt, June 19, 1915, 422.
10. Frederic L. Paxson, *American Democracy and the World War: The Pre-War Years, 1913–1917* (New York: Cooper Square Publishers, 1966), 279–81.
11. Cronin, *Direct Democracy*, 168.
12. Paxon, *American Democracy*, 294–96.
13. Ibid., 274.
14. Ibid.
15. The bill was S. 5796. It authorized "the Director of the Bureau of the Census under certain conditions to prepare and distribute blank ballots, and to receive and count marked ballots and report to the Congress the result of an advisory vote." See *Congressional Record*, April 29, 1916, 7018.
16. Paxon, *American Democracy*, 203–4.
17. *Congressional Record*, May 5, 1916, 7451–52.
18. Ibid., 7455.
19. Ibid., 7455–56.
20. Paxon, *American Democracy*, 399–401.
21. Ibid.
22. *The Papers of Woodrow Wilson* (1983), vol. 41 (Jan. 24–April 6, 1917), "A Statement," 319, 320.

23. Ibid., 402.
24. Ibid., 419.
25. Musmanno, "Proposed Amendments to the Constitution, 1889–1928," and "Proposed Amendments to the Constitution of the United States of America Introduced in Congress from the 69th Congress, 2d Session, through the 87th Congress, 1926 to Jan. 3, 1963," S. Doc. 163, 87th Cong., 2d sess. (Washington, D.C.: U.S. Government Printing Office, 1963).
26. *Congressional Record,* Dec. 14, 1937, "Motion to Discharge Committee," 1517–18.
27. *Congressional Record,* Jan. 10, 1938, 277.
28. Ibid.
29. Ibid.
30. Later in the debate Rep. Knute Hill of Washington cited a Gallup Poll that showed more than 70 percent favorable to the Ludlow amendment. Ibid., 282.
31. Ibid., 278.
32. Ibid., 281.
33. Ibid., 282.
34. Ibid.
35. S. Rept. 750, 76th Cong., 1st sess., "Proposing an Amendment to the Constitution of the United States for a Referendum on War," a report to accompany S.J. Res. 84, July 11, 1939.
36. For the text of LaFollette's amendment, see the *Congressional Record,* Oct. 27, 1939, 986–87.
37. Ibid., 987.
38. Ibid.
39. Ibid., 992.
40. Ibid.
41. Ibid., 995.
42. Ibid., 996.
43. Ibid., 999.

7

The Dawning of the Sunshine Seventies

Publicity is justly commended as a remedy for social and industrial diseases. Sunlight is said to be the best of disinfectants; electric light the most efficient policeman.

Louis D. Brandeis
Harper's Weekly

THROUGHOUT its history the Congress has reformed itself for a wide variety of reasons: to right an imbalance with the executive branch, to restore public confidence in the wake of scandals or legislative gridlock, to become more adaptable to changing domestic and international conditions, to renew its accountability to the people, to increase its ability to make informed and responsible decisions based on greater knowledge and deliberation, or to redistribute internal power to achieve more desirable legislative outcomes. Most significant reform efforts are pursued with a combination of these goals in mind, even though members and scholars alike have recognized their conflicting nature.[1] That which promotes greater responsibility and deliberation, for instance, may undermine the institution's ability to be more responsive, representative, or efficient. Increasing Congress's independence and coequal status with the executive branch may make it more difficult to break legislative gridlock through cooperation and compromise.

Speaker Thomas Reed's rules against an obstructionist minority in 1890 and the revolt against a more conservative Speaker, Joe Cannon, in 1910 were both aimed at unclogging legislative arteries to speed the flow of legislation favored by a congressional majority. Both were couched in terms of letting the people's representatives implement the will of the people.

The congressional reform revolution of the 1970s was the culmination of efforts begun in the previous decade to modernize the Congress and restore it as a coequal branch with the executive. Three main obstacles had blocked reform and a more responsive Congress in the early and mid-1960s: the seniority system that entrenched conservative southern Democrats in committee chairmanships, the Senate filibuster, and the House Rules Committee.

By the end of the 1970s, the reformers had succeeded beyond their wildest dreams. Committee chairmanships were elective positions, fewer votes were required to end filibusters, and the House Rules Committee was firmly under the control of the majority leadership. Moreover, power had been dispersed with the growth of a semiautonomous subcommittee system. Congress created a new congressional budget process, budget office, and war powers limits to counter executive branch dominance. And it opened committee meetings and hearings to the people, publicized committee and floor votes, and welcomed television cameras into committee and House floor sessions.

The Origins and Effects of Reform

This chapter focuses on the origins and effects of the reforms of the 1970s. They are usually categorized under the rubric of "sunshine" or "antisecrecy" reforms or "government in the sunshine." Their roots are traceable to the good government reforms propounded during the Progressive Era in American politics. But it was not until the 1970s that substantial steps were taken to open congressional proceedings to the public. While most of the changes Congress made during this period were not in response to any great outpouring of public sentiment—more than one observer has noted that "congressional reform has no constituency"—they did have the support of various interest groups as well as of editorial writers and columnists. But more important, they were seen by their supporters within the Congress as a necessary step to keep the Congress close to the people and thereby to enhance public understanding of the institution and its decisions.

Congress and Secrecy

Nothing in the Constitution requires public sessions of Congress, let alone public hearings of its committees or public votes. In fact, the Constitution makes no mention of committees at all. One of the first decisions of the First Continental Congress in September of 1774 was to keep its proceedings secret, the custom of the colonial assemblies. Likewise, the Constitutional Convention's proceedings in 1787 were secret. However, one of the rules proposed for the Convention would have permitted any member to call for the yeas and nays on any matter voted and the printing in the minutes of the names for and against. According to James Madison's notes, Rufus King of Massachusetts objected to the rule on grounds that it was unnecessary since acts of the Convention were not binding on constituents. Moreover, he argued that such a record of votes would be "improper as changes of opinion would be frequent in the course of the business and would fill the minutes with contradictions." George Mason seconded King's objection. A record of the opinion of members "would be an obstacle to a change of them on conviction," and, when promulgated in the future, "must furnish handles to the adversaries of the Result of the Meeting."[2] The rule was subsequently dropped by unanimous consent.

The House of Representatives in the First Congress did not open its doors to the public until April 8, 1789, a full week after the session began. The Senate, however, did not open its meetings to the public until December of 1795, and then only for legislative business.[3] It was not until June of 1929, at the suggestion of Sen. Robert LaFollette, Jr., of Wisconsin, that Senate sessions for so-called executive business (namely, the consideration of presidential nominations and treaties) were opened as well.[4]

The House did retain one curious relic from the British House of Commons—the "committee of the whole House" (see Chapter 1). This committee is a procedural convenience whereby the entire membership of the lower house first considered and amended legislation before finally reporting it back to the House for final action. The device had been created in the British House of Commons in the seventeenth century to permit discussion in secrecy of the king's budget requests, with a chairman presiding other than the Speaker, since the latter was considered an agent of the Crown. The device was attractive in the American colonial assemblies for much the same reason, and it was adopted by the Continental Congresses, the Congress of Confederation, and the Constitutional Convention.

The Constitution (Article I, section 5, clause 3) requires each house to keep a journal of its proceedings and publish it from time to time (except such parts as are determined to require secrecy). "The Yeas and Nays of the Members of either House on any question shall, at the desire of one fifth of those Present, be entered on the Journal." While the Constitution does not provide for a Committee of the Whole House, its establishment was among the first four rules adopted by the House of Representatives in April of 1789.

Although secrecy from the Crown was no longer a factor in the new American Republic, and the Committee of the Whole operated in public view, it did retain the practice from the Commons of taking nonrecorded votes by "tellers"—persons who counted members as they filed down the aisles in the chamber (one aisle for proponents and one for opponents of the pending proposition). The constitutional provision for obtaining a recorded vote by a demand for the "yeas" and "nays" is not construed as applying to the committees of the House, even to one consisting of all House members (the Committee of the Whole). The policy of nonrecorded votes in the Committee of the Whole remained part of House rules until 1971, even though the British House of Commons had changed its rules in the 1830s to permit recorded votes in its committees of the whole.[5]

House and Senate committees conducted most of their hearings and all of their meetings in private during the first century of the Republic based on the parliamentary concept that the work of committees was advisory in nature and was not to be discussed elsewhere, especially by the parent chamber, until the committee had filed a formal report. In the early twentieth century, with the construction of new House and Senate office buildings, more space became available for committees to hold public hearings, and many began the practice on a selective basis. But committee meetings to "mark up" or amend pending bills continued to be held in closed, executive sessions.

Progressivism and Publicity

Part of the Progressive Era's legacy was its emphasis on "publicity" as a prerequisite of good and effective government at all levels. This was based on the notion that most decisions were made behind closed doors by the party bosses and big money interests. If such decision making occurred in the open, officials presumably would have to pay attention to public opinion and act accordingly.

In a presidential campaign speech in 1912 titled "Let There Be Light," Woodrow Wilson said that in order to put government back on its "right basis, substituting popular will for the rule of guardians," a first necessity "is to open the doors and let in the light on all affairs which the people have a right to know about" and which have been "too secret, too complicated, and too round-about." Wilson believed "government ought to be all outside and not inside," and he called publicity "one of the purifying elements of politics."[6]

Unlike his conversion to the initiative and referendum, which came late in his public life, Wilson's opposition to secrecy in government began in his early years as a political science student. In his 1885 book *Congressional Government*, written as his doctoral thesis while at Johns Hopkins University in Baltimore, Wilson made these observations:

> The House sits, not for serious discussion, but to sanction the conclusions of its Committees as rapidly as possible. It legislates in its committee-rooms; not by the determinations of majorities but by the resolutions of specially-commissioned minorities; so that it is not far from the

> truth to say that Congress in session is Congress on public exhibition, whilst Congress in its committee-rooms is Congress at work.[7]

But Wilson warned that such committee deliberations "cannot take the place or fulfill the uses of amendment and debate by Congress in open session" because "the proceedings of the Committees are private and their discussions unpublished," thereby thwarting "the most essential object of all public discussion of public business [which] is the enlightenment of public opinion."[8]

Republican representative Victor Murdock of Kansas echoed the need for greater openness in House proceedings in 1908, two years before the successful revolt against Speaker Joseph Cannon of Illinois by insurgent Republicans and reform-minded Democrats (see Chapter 4). During debate on a postal appropriations bill on March 3, Murdock expressed frustration over how a committee chairman can often override the decisions of his own committee or of the House when a bill goes to conference with the Senate. Such unfair legislative procedures, however, would soon be corrected, he predicted:

> How it will come I do not know but I believe that its first manifestation will be a public demand for simplification of the rules, for the election of the Committee on Rules by the House, and for a larger membership of the committee, and eventually a demand that the doors of all committee rooms be opened, that all proceedings in committee and all votes in committee be recorded and be made accessible to the membership of the House and the public. [Applause.][9]

Murdock was prescient on all counts, though fulfillment of some of his predictions took longer than others. Two years later the Speaker no longer chaired the Rules Committee or had the authority to appoint its members. But more than sixty years would pass before committee meetings and hearings were opened to the public and committee votes publicized. For whatever reasons, the progressives' good government push for greater publicity in Congress did not become a central factor in the rules reforms adopted when Cannon was overthrown in 1910, or when the Democrats took over the House the following year.

In fact, real decision making on major legislation moved from closed committee rooms to the closed meetings of the Democratic Caucus deftly led by House Majority Leader Oscar Underwood (1911–15). Underwood would hammer out the legislative details in secret caucus sessions and then force the caucus product through committee (especially the Ways and Means Committee, which he chaired). The House, under strict rules of party instruction and discipline, usually jumped to Underwood's tune.

This is exactly the type of system Wilson considered ideal a quarter of a century earlier. In *Congressional Government* he praised behind-the-scenes deliberations in caucus and committees:

> Rather than imprudently expose to the world the differences of opinion threatened or developed among its members, each party hastens to remove disrupting debate from the floor of Congress, where the speakers might too hastily commit themselves to insubordination, to quiet conferences behind closed doors, where frightened scruples may be reassured and every disagreement healed with a salve of compromise or subdued with the whip of political expediency.

To Wilson, "the silvern speech spent in caucus secures the golden silence maintained on the floor of Congress, making each party rich in concord and happy in cooperation."[10]

Wilson's complaint, then, was not so much about secrecy as it was about where and by whom the secret decisions were made. On the one hand, he advocated greater public deliberation as essential to public enlightenment and education; on the other hand, he supported secret, legislative policy making in the caucus as essential to party cohesion and discipline. Therein lay the central contradiction of his thesis.[11]

Once they gained control of the House in the 62d Congress (1911–13), the Democrats may have realized that openness was not necessarily their best avenue for governing effectively as a new majority. When complaints were raised against the secret rule of "King Caucus" in 1913, Wilson's first year as president, Speaker Champ Clark had the following rebuttal:

> All this talk of secrecy is of no avail. . . . The people of the United States want to know what the Congress does. They are much more interested in results than in the methods by which those results are obtained.[12]

The Progressive Party platform of 1912 maintained its commitment to open government, including the Congress, notwithstanding the more progressive nature of Speaker Clark's House. In a section titled "Publicity and Public Service," the Progressive platform pledged the party "to legislation compelling the registration of lobbyists; publicity of committee hearings except on foreign affairs, and recording of all votes in committee."[13]

Renewed Pressures for Reform

Following the demise of "King Caucus" during President Wilson's second term, the Congress settled back into a system of committee government with power devolving from party leaders to committee chairmen who held their positions based on their seniority in Congress. Even the House Rules Committee, which had continued to cooperate with the majority leadership in scheduling legislation through President Franklin Roosevelt's first term, became an independent power unto itself beginning in 1937, dominated by a conservative coalition of southern Democrats and Republicans. President John F. Kennedy and Speaker Sam Rayburn attempted to change this conservative tilt in 1961 by enlarging the Rules Committee from twelve to fifteen members, adding two more liberal Democrats and one Republican. The rules change was narrowly adopted on January 31, 1961, 217-212. But even this move did not produce instant results in terms of expediting Kennedy's New Frontier legislation.

Pressures continued to build both inside and outside the Congress for more comprehensive reforms of the legislative branch. The titles of books published during this period reflect the growing frustration with Congress: *The Deadlock of Democracy* (1963); *Obstacle Course on Capitol Hill* (1964); *Congress: The Sapless Branch* (1964); *House Out of Order* (1965); and *Congress in Crisis* (1966).[14] Although there was a break in the legislative logjam between 1964 and 1966, as President Lyndon B. Johnson scored multiple successes in steering his Great Society program through Congress, the demand for systemic reforms of Congress persisted in the 1970s. These demands increased as Congress became wary of an "imperial presidency" and more vulnerable to charges of being a mere "rubber stamp" of the president.

Bipartisan support for congressional reform led to the formation of the Joint Committee on the Organization of Congress, headed by Democratic senator Mike Monroney of Oklahoma and Rep. Ray Madden of Indiana. It was patterned after a successful 1945–46 joint committee effort cochaired by Sen. Robert LaFollette, Jr., and then-representative Mike Monroney. In its final report to Congress on July 28, 1966, the joint committee cited the need for its proposed reforms:

> The Congress of the United States is the only branch of the Federal Government regularly and entirely accountable to the American people. Indeed, it is the people's branch. Our constitutional system is based on the principle that Congress must effectively bring to bear the will of the people on all phases of the formulation and execution of public policy. However, it is becoming more and more difficult for any collective decision-making entity like Congress to meet its responsibilities.[15]

The report went on to pinpoint the lack of "organizational effectiveness" as the reason for Congress's inability to carry out well its basic modern functions of legislation, oversight, and representation. Many of the joint committee's recommendations were embodied in the Legislative Reorganization Act of 1970. This landmark legislation launched the congressional reforms of the seventies, transforming the institution more than any event or series of events since the overthrow of Speaker Cannon. The joint committee recommended opening committee meetings and hearings to the public, making committee chairmen more responsive to committee members, publishing roll call votes in legislative reports, increasing committee staff resources, strengthening fiscal controls, and reorganizing the congressional research arm of the Library of Congress.

Five sets of supplemental views were filed by various members of the joint committee to its final report. One of the additions was made by Democratic representative Ken Hechler of West Virginia, a political science professor and former official in the Franklin Roosevelt and Truman administrations. He recommended providing more information to visitors to the nation's capital and to congressional galleries, electronic voting on certain major issues, closed-circuit-television broadcasting of floor sessions to members' offices, and publicly televising selected debates on the House and Senate floors. All three House Republican members of the joint committee concurred in the latter recommendation for public televising of floor proceedings.[16]

After the joint committee issued its report on July 28, 1966, a special Senate committee (composed of the Senate members of the former joint committee) reported a modified bill to the Senate. The bill was drafted following a hearing at which committee chairmen and ranking minority members were permitted to offer their views. However, no further action was taken by either house in the 89th Congress due to the lateness of the session. Early in the 90th Congress Senator Monroney reintroduced the modified Senate bill. It easily passed the Senate on March 7, 1967, by a vote of 75 to 9 after six weeks of debate and the consideration of seventy-nine amendments, only thirty-nine of which were adopted. Most of them dealt with committee procedures. Many of the amendments that addressed contentious issues, such as the filibuster, the selection of committee chairmen, and the Senate's rulemaking powers, were defeated.[17]

The Senate-passed bill was referred to the House Rules Committee, which held a hearing on it but took no further action in the 90th Congress. Speaker John McCormack of Massachusetts and senior committee chairmen opposed the "committee bill of rights," even the version watered down by Senate amendments. Efforts to reach an accommodation with the Speaker and his committee allies produced seven subsequent versions—all to no avail. The Democratic leadership's partisan efforts to block and gut the bipartisan reform bill incensed minority House Republicans, who rebelled with various attention-getting tactics on and off the House floor through the rest of 1967 and 1968. These Republican guerillas, known as "Rumsfeld's Raiders" after their leader, Illinois representative Donald Rumsfeld, even tried to block the final adjournment of the 90th Congress by stalling tactics late into the evening. Again their efforts were futile and hardly noticed outside the Capitol's environs. It was

Rumsfeld, in frustration, who coined the saying "congressional reform is an issue without a constituency."[18]

Ironically, the moribund reform bill was resuscitated in the 91st Congress by Democrats. Dissatisfied with their aging party and committee leadership and the lack of opportunities to make a mark, young Democrats urged their senior colleagues to take a fresh look at the joint committee's recommendations. One of the concessions they won from Speaker McCormack and Rules Committee chairman William Colmer of Mississippi was to bring the congressional reform bill to the House floor. As one of the Speaker's aides put it, "Congressional reform has become a symbolic thing to many members, and it's awfully difficult to resist under those circumstances. I think the Speaker has become reconciled to having a bill."[19]

On April 22, 1969, Colmer appointed a five-member special subcommittee of the Rules Committee to study and redraft the joint committee's legislation. Rep. B.F. Sisk of California, one of the two new Democrats added to the Rules Committee in 1961, chaired the subcommittee. In late October the subcommittee presented a draft to the House for further comments, which were received during eight days of hearings.

But it was not until June 17, 1970, that the Rules Committee finally reported a bill to the floor, H.R. 17654, the Legislative Reorganization Act of 1970. The committee also reported an open rule on the bill. This meant that any member of the House could offer germane amendments to the bill following six hours of general debate. All told, some sixty-five amendments would be offered during eleven days of consideration between mid-July and mid-September (with August off for the summer recess).

The House Rules Committee's bill was more faithful to many of the joint committee's procedural reforms than were earlier compromise versions floated in the previous Congress. According to the Rules Committee's report, the bill attempts to "write into the rules of the House democratic and equitable committee practices, many of them followed now by most committees." The report said the bill would "open more committee proceedings to the public" and "under stringent regulation, permit broadcasting of committee hearings."[20] The Rules Committee had avoided "a number of controversies that bogged down the Legislative Reorganization Act of 1967," such as changes in committee jurisdictions or proposals dealing with seniority. Those issues are more properly related to "party practices and customs than to formal rules, structure, and resources of Congress."[21]

Specifically, the Rules Committee's bill required committees to fix a regular meeting day at least once a month; provided a means by which a committee majority could call a special meeting on a specified matter if a chairman refused; required business meetings and hearings to be open to the public unless a committee majority voted otherwise; permitted the minority party on a committee to call its own witnesses during one day of hearings; authorized committees to adopt rules permitting the televised broadcasting and photographing of their hearings by majority vote; and required committees to announce and publish in their reports on public bills the results of recorded votes (meaning the total number of votes cast for and against) to order the measure reported to the House.

The Bipartisan Sunshine Coalition

The bill reported by the House Rules Committee was extensively amended. At the center of the amendment process was a bipartisan reform coalition headed by fourth-term Democrat Sam Gibbons of Florida, chairman of the Democratic Study Group (DSG) Task Force on Congressional Reform, and third-term Republican Barber Conable of New York. The group decided to confine its efforts to 10 floor amendments (out of some 200 submitted), at the heart of which were several antisecrecy reforms. When unveiling the package on July 8, 1970, Gibbons and Conable observed that "secrecy undermines the democratic process and saps public confidence in the House as a responsive and effective legislative body."[22]

The idea of making antisecrecy reforms the centerpiece of the bipartisan package was the brainchild of DSG staff director Richard P. Conlon, a former newspaper reporter who sensed that the antisecrecy theme would appeal to journalists. It did. The subsequent full-court lobbying campaign attracted the support of the AFL-CIO, National Education Association, Americans for Democratic Action, the National Committee for an Effective Congress, the National Farmers Union, and the Anti-Defamation League. And it generated dozens of editorials around the country, many of which were later inserted in the *Congressional Record*.[23] As two political scientists would later observe:

> Probably not since the revolt against Speaker Cannon in 1910 had the nation's press taken such an interest in congressional procedures. Whether or not the general public evinced any deep interest in the question is doubtful. Rumsfeld's remark about the lack of a reform constituency must be recalled. But this time, at least, a few influential outside voices were heard.[24]

The most important of the sunshine amendments was offered by Democratic representative Thomas P. "Tip" O'Neill, Jr., of Massachusetts and Republican representative Charles Gubser of California. It provided for recorded teller votes in the Committee of the Whole (where most House floor amendments are offered and disposed of). O'Neill and Gubser were both elected to the House in 1952, but that is when any similarity ended until their joint sunshine effort. Gubser, a hawkish member of the Armed Services Committee, was as conservative as O'Neill was liberal. O'Neill, a former speaker of the Massachusetts House, was well along on the leadership track, having served on the Rules Committee since his sophomore term in 1955–56.

O'Neill first presented the recorded teller vote amendment during the Rules Committee's markup of the reform bill. It was defeated on a 6-6 tie vote. On July 27, 1970, O'Neill offered the amendment on the House floor on behalf of himself, Gubser, and their 180 cosponsors. He explained that most of the important votes of the House are taken in the Committee of the Whole. He cited the recent examples of votes on the antiballistic missile system, the supersonic transport plane, and the invasion of Cambodia—all of which were nonrecorded votes in the Committee of the Whole. He went on:

> The secrecy of the Committee of the Whole has allowed too many Members to duck issues, to avoid the perils of controversial votes. But that is not in the spirit of this Nation, nor of this Congress. Our duties to the Nation and to the people we represent make this amendment necessary. We are primarily and most importantly legislators. And if the work of legislation can be done shrouded in secrecy and hidden from the public, then we are eroding the confidence of the public in ourselves and in our institutions.[25]

Representative Gubser called the nonrecorded teller vote "a relic of a passing era where the Federal Government was limited, and did not entwine itself so intricately with each individual citizen and his welfare." And he continued:

> Those days are gone and they will never return. Today we deal in a highly complex relationship between the people and their government. . . . We should and we can take the time to let the public know how we vote on each and every issue.[26]

One of the big boosts for the amendment during debate came from Majority Whip Hale Boggs of Louisiana. Noting that the British House of Commons had permitted recorded votes in the Committee of the Whole 138 years ago, Boggs said:

> Unfortunately, with never a King to fear and only the public to serve, the rule has been retained in the House of Representatives. We did so because we said it helped expedite the often slow legislative process. Unfortunately, it has also been used [as] a shelter from the public eye.

> I do not believe representative government can afford the luxury of a shelter from the public eye. The American people are entitled to know the recorded judgment of each Member on the great issues of our time. We cannot ask our people to respect our institutions unless the institutions themselves are self-critical and self-reforming.[27]

After a lengthy debate and the rejection of several amendments, the House adopted the O'Neill-Gubser amendment by voice vote. As amended, it also authorized the future use of electronic voting to replace calling the roll of members orally. The House began taking roll call votes on amendments in the Committee of the Whole beginning in January of 1971. By the beginning of the following Congress, the electronic voting system had been installed and tested. Use on a regular basis began on January 23, 1973.[28]

Sunshine Rules Governing Committees

Although the bill reported by the Rules Committee provided for open committee meetings and hearings in the House unless a committee by majority vote determined otherwise, the bipartisan coalition identified several loopholes that could easily be exploited by committees. There was nothing to prevent a committee from voting to close meetings or hearings for the rest of a Congress. And there was no requirement that a quorum be present when a committee voted, or that the vote be recorded. To remedy this, on July 14, 1970, Rep. William Hathaway, a third-term Democrat from Maine, received unanimous consent to offer two amendments. Both amendments would require that a committee majority quorum be present when it voted to close a meeting or hearing, that the vote could apply only to that day's meeting or hearing and not to future ones, and that the vote be conducted by roll call in public session.

The proposals ran into a buzz-saw of opposition from more senior members, especially committee chairmen who recounted how difficult it was to round up a majority of committee members to do anything, but especially for a hearing where only two members could constitute a quorum. Rep. Wayne Hays of Ohio, a Democrat in his eleventh term, concurred with an Education and Labor Committee member on the difficulty of writing legislation in public session: "What the gentleman is saying in effect is that you cannot write legislation with a lobbyist sitting at every Member's elbow, and that is exactly what would happen here." To this, Hathaway responded: "On the contrary, that is just the situation that prevails when you have a secret meeting, because only the lobbyists have access to the Members."[29]

Rep. George Mahon of Texas, chairman of the Appropriations Committee, agreed with Hays's assessment:

> The silent majority is not going to be present at the open markups of the bills; they are going to be too busy and too occupied otherwise. But if you have open markup on bills . . . do you not think that the special interests will be there? The silent majority will not be there, but the special interests will be well represented.[30]

After extensive debate the House adopted an amendment to delete the requirements for a majority quorum and roll call vote to close committee hearings and meetings. The amended Hathaway amendment was then rejected by a teller vote of 102 to 132. Three years later, on March 7, 1973, the House amended its rules along the lines of Hathaway's amendment. In order to close a meeting or hearing, a majority of the committee must be present and a roll call vote taken. The reasons for closing a hearing were limited to national security or personal privacy matters. (The Senate adopted a similar rule in 1975.) At the beginning of the 104th Congress on January 4, 1995, the House rule was further amended to apply the same conditions to the closing of committee meetings (that is, for national security and personal privacy reasons only). Broadcast coverage of any public hearing or meeting became an automatic right rather than a matter to be determined by committee vote.[31]

On the same day in 1970 that the Hathaway amendment was rejected by the House, another sunshine amendment affecting committees succeeded. It was offered by Rep. Dante Fascell, a Democrat from Florida. Whereas the bill reported from the Rules Committee required that a committee report contain only the numerical results of any record vote to report a measure, the Fascell amendment required that the results of each roll call vote taken by a committee be made available for public inspection in the offices of the committees. In concluding his explanation of the amendment, Fascell said, "This is an important and vital reform in the rules of this House and will instill knowledge and confidence in the American people whom we serve and further a great democratic tradition of an open society."[32]

Fascell's amendment was adopted by voice vote after one modification. Rep. H. Allen Smith of California, the ranking Republican on the Rules Committee, offered an amendment to reinsert the original committee language requiring inclusion in the committee report of the numerical results of a roll call vote to report a bill.

The Senate to its credit in 1970 retained the language from the original joint committee recommendation that all roll call votes taken in committee on a measure be published in the committee report. It was not until 1995 that the House adopted a similar rule requiring that committee roll call votes on any amendments offered during markup, as well as on motions to report a measure, be published in the committee report on that measure.[33]

Televised Proceedings: Pro and Con

The bill reported by the House Rules Committee in 1970 authorized televised committee hearings, something Rep. David Worth Dennis, a freshman Republican from Indiana, adamantly opposed. On July 20 he offered an amendment that would strike that authorization from the bill.

Up until 1970, neither house had a rule either permitting or prohibiting televised committee hearings. The Senate had been allowing TV broadcasting as a matter of practice since the late 1940s. In 1952 and again in 1955, Speaker Sam Rayburn ruled that committees could not televise their hearings since it was not specifically authorized by any House rule, though the ban was briefly lifted by Republican Speaker Joe Martin of Massachusetts in 1953–54.[34]

Dennis said he believed in "adequate publicity" but not in television in committee hearings because of the "physical disruption" it would cause:

> I certainly do not want to sit for a couple of hours in a committee room with those bright lights in my eyes. I do not like photographers stepping in between the committee and the witness during the testimony of the witness, and all the rest of the physical disruption that you are necessarily going to have in the committee.[35]

Dennis foresaw another problem with televised committee hearings. Television "overemphasizes because it cannot get all of the action, and it is bound to . . . emphasize a rather small part," he argued. Moreover, said Dennis, some members, "perhaps all of us," are in varying degrees "prima donnas" who "will be spending more time making hay on the television camera than in doing the business that we are sent there to transact."[36]

A Harvard law school graduate, Dennis likened congressional hearings and courtroom trials. Although the Constitution "has always provided that trials in courts shall be public . . . almost universally the courts have rejected the television broadcasting . . . because it interferes with the orderly transaction of the public business in the courts."[37] Rep. James Cleveland, a New Hampshire Republican, disagreed with the analogy. Although "proceedings in the courts are adversary proceedings . . . in many of our hearings they are for the purpose of getting information not only for the members of the committees but for the people of the country, who are after all our ultimate court, certainly our jury."[38]

The Dennis amendment was narrowly rejected by a teller vote, 93-96. Ironically, the most important hearings Dennis would participate in as a member of Congress, the House Judiciary Committee's impeachment hearings involving President Richard M. Nixon, were closed not only to broadcast coverage, but to the public as well out of deference to the rights and reputations of witnesses. However, on July 22, 1974, just two days before the committee began its public deliberations on three articles of impeachment, the House voted

346-40 to extend the authority for television, radio, and photographic coverage to meetings as well as hearings. Not surprisingly, Dennis voted against the resolution. That same afternoon the Judiciary Committee took advantage of the new rule and voted 31-7 to open its impeachment debates to broadcast coverage.[39]

Moreover, on August 7, 1974, the House adopted another resolution from the Rules Committee to permit the broadcast coverage of House floor debates on the articles of impeachment. This time the vote was 385-25, with Dennis and three other Judiciary Committee Republicans voting against.[40] The following evening Nixon announced his resignation as president.

Other Significant Reform Efforts

The 1970 bipartisan reform group had decided to stay away from changing rules affecting the internal distribution of power within the House, such as the practice of choosing the most senior member of a committee as its chairman. As the Rules Committee report had pointed out, such matters were best left to the party caucuses. However, some members of both parties disagreed. On July 28, 1970, Rep. Henry Reuss, a Wisconsin Democrat, offered an amendment to end seniority as the sole consideration in the selection of committee chairmen. Republican representative Fred Schwengel of Iowa then offered a substitute to permit the majority party members of each committee to select a chairman from among their three most senior members on the committee. The Schwengel amendment was rejected on a 28-196 teller vote, and the Reuss amendment was subsequently defeated, 73-160.[41]

The House Democratic Caucus adopted the Reuss amendment the following January as part of its rules, together with a provision allowing any ten members of the caucus to force a separate vote on any nominee for chairman. The caucus rule was further revised in 1973 to permit one-fifth of the caucus to force separate votes on each nominee for chairman; and in 1975 to provide for automatic separate votes on chair nominees. Three committee chairmen were subsequently rejected by the caucus.

The Democrats also adopted a caucus rule change in 1971 to allow Democrats on each committee to select subcommittee chairmen. And in 1973 the caucus established a bidding procedure within committee caucuses for choosing subcommittee chairmen, set subcommittee jurisdictions and budgets, and gave subcommittee chairmen semiautonomous authority from their full committee chairmen to select staff and set subcommittee agendas—the so-called subcommittee bill of rights.

This democratization and dispersal of power within the House, coupled with a large influx of Democratic freshmen in 1975 (the "Watergate Babies"), provided new opportunities for policy innovation and participation by junior

House members. The reforms also presented party leaders with new challenges—namely, how to maintain some semblance of party discipline and policy coherence.

The reform revolution of the mid-1970s set the stage for future changes that opened the Congress to the people even more. The most significant of those reforms, televising House and Senate floor proceedings, are examined in the next chapter.

Notes

1. See, for instance Leroy N. Rieselbach, *Congressional Reform: The Changing Modern Congress* (Washington, D.C.: CQ Press, 1994).

2. *Documents Illustrative of the Formation of the Union of the American States*, ed. Charles C. Tansill, H. Doc. 398, 68th Cong., 1st sess. (Washington, D.C.: U.S. Government Printing Office, 1927), 111.

3. Donald A. Ritchie, "Galleries," in *The Encyclopedia of the United States Congress*, ed. Donald C. Bacon, Roger H. Davidson, and Morton Keller (New York: Simon and Schuster, 1995), vol. 2, 897.

4. Paul S. Rundquist, "Secrecy of Congress," in ibid., vol. 4, 1775.

5. For a more detailed discussion of the origins, development, and operation of the Committee of the Whole, see Don Wolfensberger, "Committees of the Whole: Their Evolution and Functions," *Congressional Record*, 103d Cong., 1st sess., Jan. 5, 1993, H27–31.

6. Woodrow Wilson, "Let There Be Light," in *The New Freedom: A Call for the Emancipation of the Generous Energies of the People* (New York: Doubleday, Page & Co., 1913), 111–15.

7. Woodrow Wilson, *Congressional Government: A Study in American Politics* (1885; reprint, Baltimore: The Johns Hopkins University Press, 1981), 69.

8. Ibid., 71.

9. *Congressional Record*, March 3, 1908, 2837.

10. Wilson, *Congressional Government*, 211–12.

11. For a more detailed discussion of these contradictions, see Gerald B.H. Solomon and Don Wolfensberger, "The Decline of Deliberative Democracy in the House and Proposals for Reform," *Harvard Journal on Legislation* 31 (Summer 1994): 329–33.

12. Ibid., 338.

13. *National Party Platforms, Volume 1, 1840–1956*, comp. Donald Bruce Johnson (Urbana: University of Illinois Press, 1978), "Progressive Platform of 1912," 176.

14. James MacGregor Burns, *Deadlock of Democracy* (Englewood Cliffs, N.J.: Prentice-Hall, 1963); Robert Bendiner, *Obstacle Course on Capitol Hill* (New York: McGraw-Hill, 1964); Joseph S. Clark, *Congress: The Sapless Branch* (New York: Harper & Row, 1964); Richard Walker Bolling, *House Out of Order* (New York: Dutton, 1965); and Roger H. Davidson, David M. Kovcenock, Michael K. O'Leary, *Congress in Crisis: Politics and Congressional Reform* (Belmont, Calif.: Wadsworth Publishing Company, 1966).

15. "Organization of Congress," Final Report of the Joint Committee on the

Organization of the Congress, S. Rept. 1414, 89th Cong., 2d sess., July 28, 1966 (Washington, D.C.: U.S. Government Printing Office, 1966), 1.

16. Ibid., "Supplemental Views of Mr. Hechler," 80–81.

17. John F. Bibby and Roger H. Davidson, *On Capitol Hill: Studies in the Legislative Process*, 2d ed. (Hinsdale, Ill.: The Dryden Press, 1972), 256.

18. Ibid., 259.

19. Ibid., 260–61.

20. "Legislative Reorganization Act of 1970," H. Rept. 91-1215 of the Committee on Rules on H.R. 17654, "To improve the operations of the Legislative Branch of the Federal Government, and for other purposes," 3.

21. Ibid.

22. Bibby and Davidson, *On Capitol Hill*, 265.

23. Ibid., 264, 269–70.

24. Ibid., 270.

25. *Congressional Record*, July 27, 1970, 25796.

26. Ibid., 25799.

27. Ibid., 25800.

28. *House Rules and Manual, One Hundred Fourth Congress*, H. Doc. 103-342, 103d Cong., 2d sess. (Washington, D.C.: U.S. Government Printing Office, 1995), sec. 774(b) footnote, 552.

29. *Congressional Record*, July 14, 1970, 24049.

30. Ibid.

31. *House Rules and Manual, One Hundred Fourth Congress*, sec. 708, House Rule XI, clause 2(g), 461–65. The history of the rule is cited in a footnote at 464–65.

32. *Congressional Record*, July 14, 1970, 24054.

33. H. Res. 6, sec. 209, 104th Cong., adopted Jan. 4, 1995. See House Rule XI, clause 2(l)(2)(B), *House Rules and Manual, One Hundred Fourth Congress*, sec. 713(d), 472.

34. Ronald Garay, *Congressional Television: A Legislative History* (Westport, Conn.: Greenwood Press, 1984), 50–52.

35. *Congressional Record*, July 20, 1970, 24971.

36. Ibid.

37. Ibid., 24974.

38. Ibid.

39. On H. Res. 1107, "Broadcasting of Committee Meetings," see *Congressional Quarterly Almanac, 1974*, vol. 31 (Washington, D.C.: Congressional Quarterly, 1975), 878.

40. On H. Res. 802, "Broadcasting of Impeachment Proceedings," see ibid., 892.

41. *Congressional Quarterly Almanac, 1970*, vol. 26 (Washington, D.C.: Congressional Quarterly, 1971), 455.

8

A Window on Congress: Televising Floor Debates

By agreeing to the resolution [to televise its floor debates], the House reaffirmed its commitment to open government and to a fundamental tenet of democracy—that the success of popular, representative government depends upon an informed electorate. Since the American electorate gets a good deal of its information via radio and television, giving the broadcast media access to the complete proceedings of the House will give the people a major means for acquiring significant information about public affairs, about decisions of the House of Representatives, and about the institutional role and responsibilities of the House.

House Report

THESE words, contained in a 1978 report giving the Speaker final authority to move forward on televising House floor debates, seem a self-evident enough justification today for bringing Congress into the television age.[1] But getting the House to that point had been a major battle spanning three Congresses and involving multiple committees and subcommittees and numerous studies and reports. Key House leaders had to be dragged kicking and screaming into the twentieth century so that the people's house might be seen and heard in the people's houses. The Senate took even longer to cross that bridge—seven more years to be precise.

The temporary bump in congressional approval ratings resulting from television coverage of the 1973 Senate Watergate committee hearings and the 1974 House Judiciary Committee's impeachment proceedings gave new impetus to calls for televising House and Senate floor sessions. But the initial interest in televising Congress came earlier in the decade. Congressional Democrats, frustrated with President Richard Nixon's mastery of the airwaves in defending his policies, had objected to the relatively minor exposure their opposing views received. In short, the interest in television's influence on government and public opinion was a natural extension of concern over the perceived imbalance between the legislative and executive branches and what might be done about it. With Nixon's resignation in 1974 and the weakening of the presidency, that rationale lost much of its force.

The Joint Committee on Congressional Operations

The Joint Committee on Congressional Operations was authorized by the Legislative Reorganization Act of 1970 for the purpose of "strengthening Congress, simplifying its operations, improving its relationships with other branches of the United States Government, and enabling it better to meet its responsibilities under the Constitution of the United States."[2] Its chairman was Democratic representative Jack Brooks of Texas, a former member of the 1965–66 Joint Committee on the Organization of the Congress. In December of 1972 he requested the Congressional Research Service (CRS) to prepare a study of how Congress could use the communications media more effectively to communicate with the American people. The resulting study was released in early 1974 as a joint committee print titled "Congress and Mass Communications: An Institutional Perspective." It had been prepared under a CRS contract with John G. Stewart, a political scientist, a former aide to Senator and Vice President Hubert Humphrey, and, most recently, the director of communications for the Democratic National Committee (1970–72).[3]

The preface to the 1974 report was written by Joint Committee chairman Lee Metcalfe of Montana and Vice Chairman Brooks. (The chairmanship of the joint committee rotated between the houses with each new Congress.) As the reason for the study they cite Congress's "substantial stake in being able to communicate with the American people effectively" as a "co-equal and independent branch of the Federal Government."[4] The stakes had been raised considerably by the "massive and highly sophisticated use of mass communications by the President and the Executive branch." Each new administration contributed "to the growing imbalance between executive and legislative power." This gave the president "a unique potential for dominating the communications media and, ultimately, public discussion of critical policy issues." Indeed, the president can appear on prime-time television on all three networks by simple request. But Congress, "even if it is controlled by the party which does not control the White House, is given no such routine access."[5]

The preface goes on to note survey findings that the people have only the vaguest notions of the constitutional role played by Congress or how it carries out its legislative responsibilities. Yet the same findings show that Americans favor "a shift in influence in our democratic system toward their national legislature."[6]

The report documents this case made in the preface. Harris polls from 1965 through 1971 are cited. They show that the public's assessment of Congress's performance reverses from positive (excellent, very good) to negative (fair, poor): with 64 percent positive and 26 percent negative in 1965 (the height of President Lyndon Johnson's Great Society legislative juggernaut), to just 26 percent positive and 63 percent negative in 1971.[7]

The report also cites the differences in public support for a policy before and after a president appears on network television to defend it. The effects of appearances by Presidents Kennedy, Johnson, and Nixon are captured in Harris surveys from 1963 to 1970. For instance, public support for Nixon's announced incursion into Cambodia in 1970 rose from 7 percent to 50 percent after he explained his policy on network television. President Nixon's television appearances in 1973 relating to Watergate "would seem to provide an exception to this pattern," the report adds. "The mass communications media cannot automatically generate popular support for any position a President chooses to adopt." According to the report, the president's explanations of Watergate were offset in part by the televised hearings of the Senate Watergate committee. The hearings would "bring to popular attention a version of the facts that often conflicted with the President's version." Indeed, "the opportunity for Congress to go directly to the people in this instance was one factor in President Nixon's relative lack of success in his televised appearances."[8]

Coverage of the Watergate crisis was an exception to the usual imbalance between presidential and congressional exposure on television. Much of the report addresses how Congress can equalize its treatment by broadcasters. A chapter titled "Legislative Initiatives" gives considerable attention to 1970 hearings by the Commerce Committee's Subcommittee on Communications. Sen. J. William Fulbright favored amending the Communications Act to require broadcasters to carry the views of authorized representatives of the House and Senate on important public issues at least four times a year.[9]

The chapter "Congress and Broadcast Access" discusses fairness and equal time doctrines of the Federal Communications Commission and how Congress might gain access to the airwaves using them as a legal basis. The report predicts that the imbalance in access between the Congress and the president "eventually . . . will be corrected, at least in part, by legislation or by reaching some kind of voluntary agreement with the broadcast networks."[10]

In the final chapter, "Choices for Change," the report revisits Senator Fulbright's proposal for mandatory network carriage of congressional responses or programs, and variations thereon. The concern is expressed that if Congress allows for some broadcast coverage of its floor debates, this would be used by networks "as evidence under the fairness doctrine for refusing congressional spokesmen an opportunity to reply directly to broadcast appearances by the President."[11] The ability of Congress to respond to the president "is guaranteed only if Congress amends the Communications Act." Barring some kind of voluntary arrangement on a trial basis, "it would seem that legislative action is necessary."[12] The final chapter also discusses the various arguments for, and means of, broadcasting House and Senate floor proceedings.

From February to April of 1974, the Joint Committee on Congressional Operations conducted six follow-up hearings on the topic of "Congress and Mass Communications." Fifty-one witnesses appeared, including twelve House and Senate Members (eight Democrats and four Republicans), and twenty-four representatives of the broadcast and print media. Most of the testimony focused on the proposal to provide broadcast coverage of House and Senate floor debates. Support was almost unanimous, with differences only on how best it could be accomplished.

However, some cautionary words were offered, especially by members of the joint committee themselves in their opening statements. Vice Chairman Brooks, for instance, questioned whether broadcast coverage "would increase or decrease the public's understanding" since "such coverage for the most part would be confusing and of no interest at all." Moreover, he questioned whether there was an imbalance of television coverage between the president and Congress since Congress consists of 539 "independent individuals," and "although there is the leadership in both Houses, it is obvious that no one person can speak for all of the Members and rarely for the majority."[13]

Rep. James Cleveland of New Hampshire, the top House Republican on the joint committee, observed that "the best way for Congress to improve its public image is to improve its public performance." He called communications a "medium" that "cannot consistently manufacture facts" nor "for long distort or suppress them."[14]

Sen. Edmund S. Muskie of Maine, while supporting some means of unfiltered public exposure of Congress to the public through television, called attention to shortcomings in network coverage of committee hearings. "We all know that conflict makes news," he said. "We also know that a televised shouting match usually concentrates more on the exchange of insults than the exchange of ideas." In fact, "a congressional investigation receives more attention when important voices—but not necessarily significant questions—are raised." Moreover, "the bulk of our productive work in the Senate," what Muskie called "the actual exercise of legislating," receives little attention from the media. In committees with open markup sessions, "private interests have been well represented in the audience—as lobbyists—while the public interest—in the form of journalists—has been noticeably absent." He concluded on this point that "a clash of opinion is innately more newsworthy than the resolution of those differences."[15]

Sen. Walter F. Mondale of Minnesota, also a supporter of televising Congress, warned that "no reforms in structure or exposure of the Congress will totally cure the widespread feeling that Government is no longer responsive or accountable to the people." Televised proceedings cannot "eliminate the feeling of distrust from which the Congress is now suffering," which is due in part to "the inevitable fallout of a climate of Watergate, of energy shortages, and of soaring inflation." Nevertheless, Congress should move ahead with reforms "which will at least make the American public aware of honest attempts the Congress is making to deal with the problems that affect Americans most deeply."[16]

Rep. John B. Anderson of Illinois, chairman of the House Republican Conference and a proponent of televising Congress, cautioned against "expecting too much of any reforms" and attributing "too much power and potential to the media in the power struggle between the branches." In so doing, said Anderson, we may mistake the media for the message with the inevitable result being "a tendency to shape the message, in this case the legislative process, to fit the media." Anderson concluded that "the media is not the message nor the answer." In short, the "way for Congress to make the news is to make news. The way to redress the balance is to redress it—by action."[17]

One of the media witnesses was Neil MacNeill, congressional correspondent for *Time* magazine. In comparing broadcast coverage of the president and Congress, MacNeill observed that "the closed political branch of the Government receives greater press attention than the open branch, the Congress." This paradox "suggests that you will look in vain for public popularity and approval by opening still further your proceedings—by, for example, allowing the televising of floor debates in the Senate and House of Representatives."[18] He then made the essential argument for opening Congress:

> In an open society, openness is a virtue in itself. In a free society, the public business is the public's business—and the public should know all there is to know about it. Openness in itself will bring public understanding—but it will not necessarily bring Congress either public approval or popularity.[19]

The networks' representatives naturally opposed any statutorily mandated access by Congress to respond to the President or otherwise present a congressional perspective on national problems. Instead they argued strongly for Congress to open some or all of its debates to the broadcast media. By the time the joint committee's hearings ended on April 10, 1974, Chairman Metcalfe felt it necessary to clarify in his closing statement their purpose. "It has been inaccurately perceived by some observers that the primary motivation of the Joint Committee and other Members of Congress during these hearings is somehow to gain for Congress amounts of television and radio air time equal to that granted by the networks to the President and his spokesmen," Metcalfe said. Although the restoration of the balance of power between the Congress and the executive branch "is of prime concern to many Members of Congress and American citizens, the gaining of equal air time by Congress is certainly low on the list of priorities motivating these hearings."[20]

Metcalfe also refuted the charge that Congress was trying to "use the media to increase [its] public popularity and approval of voters." That line of thought, he said, was "off-target, for Congress is not seeking a journalistic facelift." Rather, the joint committee was trying to find ways to make "the more important functions of Congress better understood by the people through improved coverage by the press and broadcast media." Any evaluation of members' work "should continue to be based on the substantive performance of Congress."[21]

The following fall, on October 10, 1974, the joint committee filed an "interim report" titled "Broadcasting House and Senate Proceedings." Based on its hearings and studies, the joint committee found that the potential for bringing more information to the people through broadcast coverage was substantial, that the experience of other legislatures permitting such coverage had been favorable, and that the technology of communications was sufficiently advanced to provide for televising without disrupting floor proceedings. The interim report urged Congress to "move forward with a carefully designed but limited test to determine the ultimate feasibility and desirability of a permanent system for broadcasting activities in the House and Senate Chambers." The test was to be conducted in a nonpartisan manner during the first session of the 94th Congress (1975).[22]

The only person on the ten-member joint committee filing a dissenting view to the report was Republican senator Jesse Helms of North Carolina. He warned of "the radical concept of democracy that is inherent in this proposal" to televise congressional sessions, and said this concept "of direct or plebiscitary democracy" had been wisely rejected by the Framers of the Constitution. According to Helms, the proposal for congressional television "seeks to impose upon the legislative process an aspect of direct democracy that undermines representative government" because it would "seriously impair the ability of Members to perform their legislative duties in an atmosphere of free, open, and robust debate" and would "act as a deterrent to the exercise of individual judgment."[23]

How did Helms see the prospect of congressional television transforming representative democracy into direct democracy? In his words:

> It is not difficult to envision Members scrambling to the floor to get before cameras in order to impress the voters back home instead of persuading other Members, producing much oration and little debate.

In short, Helms thought television would force a member to reflect public opinion rather than "exercise his own judgment, even when it may not be popular to do so." If a member were simply to reflect public opinion, said Helms, "there would be no need of a legislative body" since "public policy could then be established through public opinion polls." Helms went on to undermine his argument, however, by making another criticism—namely that televising floor sessions would not accurately reflect the legislative process since, "to a great extent, floor activities are often a pro forma condensation and summation of countless days and weeks of committee hearings, executive sessions, conferences and reports."[24]

In the first session of the 94th Congress, on October 7, 1975, the Joint Committee on Congressional Operations, chaired by Representative Brooks, issued its final report on Congress and mass communications titled "A Clear Message to the People." In the report the joint committee reiterated its recommendation that "both Houses move as rapidly as possible to begin this experiment" of a "carefully conceived test" of broadcasting House and Senate floor proceedings. The report termed the broadcast proposal "the most practical, immediate, and direct way to enhance public understanding of congressional activities." The report also recommended that "all committees and conference committees open their hearings to broadcast coverage whenever such coverage will not detract from the legislative business at hand."[25]

Senator Helms again filed "separate views" in which he termed as naive the assumption that broadcasting would enhance public understanding of Congress. He questioned whether the public possessed "the sophisticated knowledge of parliamentary procedure" or "necessary background information on legislation to acquire a proper understanding of floor proceedings." Instead, he suggested that "broadcasting of floor proceedings might create more confusion than understanding."[26]

Earlier in the session, on March 3, 1975, Chairman Brooks and the seven other House members of the joint committee reintroduced a resolution to implement their proposal to televise House floor proceedings. Identical resolutions were cosponsored by 100 House members. Other resolutions were introduced by Representative Anderson, a member of the Rules Committee. On April 16 and June 17, 1975, the Rules Committee held hearings on the Brooks resolution.[27]

To explore the methods and procedures to be used in a test program, the Rules Committee established an Ad Hoc Subcommittee on Broadcasting, chaired by Democratic representative Bernie Sisk of California. Other members included Democrats Morgan F. Murphy of Illinois, Andrew Young of Georgia, and Claude Pepper of Florida; and Republicans John B. Anderson and Del Clawson of California. There followed a long and drawn-out struggle between the ad hoc subcommittee and Speaker Carl Albert's negotiating agent, Majority Leader Thomas P. "Tip" O'Neill, Jr., over who should control the cameras of the new House system—the House itself or some private broadcast entity such as a network pool. The matter would not be finally resolved until the second session of the succeeding Congress in 1978, and House floor proceedings would not be televised until early in the 96th Congress in 1979.

The Rules Committee Imbroglio

Representatives Sisk and Anderson took their new responsibilities on the Ad Hoc Subcommittee on Broadcasting quite seriously and immediately set to work to prepare for further hearings and an eventual set of recommendations for the full committee's consideration. Sisk assigned his administrative assistant, Tony Coelho (who would later succeed Sisk in Congress in 1979), to coordinate the staff effort, and Anderson assigned his Rules Committee associate staffer, this author, to head the minority staff work.

It was only much later that a Rules Committee majority staffer informed this author that Speaker Albert and Majority Leader O'Neill intended for the proposal to be "studied to death" in the ad hoc subcommittee and never reported to the full committee, let alone to the House. Neither had bothered to inform Sisk of that intent, at least not until it was too late, so he and Anderson plowed ahead tenaciously.

On November 19, 1975, Sisk, Anderson, and three other subcommittee members introduced House Resolution 875.[28] The main differences between this resolution and the Brooks proposal (House Resolution 269) were over who would provide the coverage and who would oversee its operation. The Sisk resolution authorized a network pool to provide full coverage under a contract with the House, with appropriate fees charged to the House and other broadcast entities for access to the coverage. The Rules Committee would retain oversight authority of the system through a Broadcast Advisory Board appointed by the chairman and consisting of members of the committee, plus the majority and minority leaders as ad hoc, nonvoting members. The Brooks resolution, on the other hand, gave control over the system to the House Commission on Information and Facilities, chaired by Brooks, under a United Nations–type arrangement whereby the cameras and equipment would be owned and operated by the institution itself.

Based on several comments and suggestions presented at hearings in early December, the subcommittee adopted additional amendments to the Sisk resolution and on February 4, 1976, voted to report the resolution to the full committee. The report was filed as a committee print on February 23.[29]

However, on February 24 the subcommittee members were called to a meeting with the Speaker and Majority Leader, both of whom expressed concerns about the resolution. Their main objections were that it infringed upon the Speaker's prerogatives to control the House chamber by mandating that the Clerk of the House enter into a contract with a specified party—the network pool. According to one staff source, O'Neill warned members at the meeting, "If you think the public's rating of Congress is low now, just wait till we get TV."[30]

O'Neill's resistance to televising the House was later confirmed in his memoir, *Man of the House*, in which he said many members' attitudes about TV were shaped by coverage of the national conventions:

> If a guy was reading a newspaper, they'd always show a close-up of him. If a delegate was picking his nose or scratching his ass, that's what you'd see. If somebody had a bald head, you could be sure of getting a close-up view of the shiny spot. No wonder so many of us were skittish. After all, why should the greatest legislative body in the world allow itself to be demeaned and humiliated before millions of people?[31]

After several staff-level discussions between representatives of the Speaker and the subcommittee, tentative agreement was reached on a package of amendments that was adopted by the subcommittee on March 4. Essentially the amendments would transfer from the Rules Committee to the Speaker the responsibility for implementing the new broadcast rule, create a bipartisan Broadcast Advisory Board to assist the Speaker in that responsibility, and delete all references in the resolution to the network pool arrangement.[32]

Even though the subcommittee adopted these changes to accommodate all of the leadership's expressed concerns, O'Neill reportedly approached Sisk on the House floor the following week and urged him not to bring up the resolution at the full committee's scheduled meeting on March 24. In remarks inserted in the *Congressional Record* on March 22, Anderson said he was "at a loss to explain why the Democratic leadership might still be working against opening our floor proceedings to broadcast coverage" since "a party which calls itself Democratic can hardly be opposed to openness and letting the people participate more directly in their representative form of Government—especially in our Bicentennial Year." Anderson called on the Speaker "to renounce these reports of your opposition and announce your full support for House broadcasting so that this resolution can be cleared for a House vote by the Rules Committee.[33] One subcommittee aide thus explained the leadership's continued resistance despite the accommodations that had been made:

> Our impression was that if we acceded to those changes, we'd be okay. . . . I think Albert and O'Neill were shocked when we gave in. They thought they'd be major items with us and that a compromise would break down over those issues.[34]

Despite O'Neill's reported pressures, the Rules Committee went ahead with its March 24 meeting. After taking statements from both Sisk and Anderson in support of the revised resolution, the committee debated its merits and questioned the chairman on aspects of the proposal. One of the members of the subcommittee, Clawson, who up until then had remained largely silent on the issue, strongly opposed any televised coverage of House debates:

> The temptations of television are seductive, but they may also be destructive. The risks are many and serious. Instead of informing our people, televised House proceedings may confuse them. Instead of educating it may bore them and make them impatient. Instead of polishing the image of the House, the consequences of broadcasting may further tarnish it. Instead of maintaining the dignity of the House, television may encourage circus antics. Instead of improving the legislative process, television may degrade it. And instead of enhancing the democratic process, television may corrode and cheapen it.[35]

Perhaps appropriately, the afternoon session of deliberations by the Rules Committee was covered by a network pool of cameras. The concern most often expressed by the members was that the proposal did not guarantee that broadcasters would provide a fair and balanced treatment of the floor debates in their news reports. One of those expressing that concern was Rep. John Young of Texas, a Democrat, who offered a motion to recommit the resolution to the subcommittee. Rep. Richard Bolling of Missouri offered a substitute that the resolution be recommitted to subcommittee with instructions to report back more information on two alternative means of coverage—"one by public television and the other [by] in-House procedures, and . . . a specific target date for the beginning of the coverage and distribution." The Bolling substitute was rejected, 4-11. At that point Anderson attempted to offer a substitute motion to report the Sisk resolution to the House, but he was ruled out of order. The Young motion was then adopted, 9-6, with seven Democrats and two Republicans in support, and four Democrats and two Republicans in opposition. Of the six Sisk subcommittee members, Representatives Young and Clawson voted to recommit the resolution; Representative Pepper, the only absentee, indicated for the record his support for the Sisk resolution.[36]

Prior to the two votes, Sisk informed his colleagues that it was his intention, if the resolution was recommitted, to reconvene the subcommittee and report back to the full committee in a "reasonable time" so that it could still be passed that year. "We are not keeping it under the rug," he promised. "I still believe in this cause and I am going to continue to fight for it."[37]

True to his word, Sisk wrote to all subcommittee members on April 5 to reiterate his intention to take further action and he solicited their thoughts and ideas "on possible approaches we might take on this matter." In the meantime subcommittee member Pepper had polled all House members on the proposition of broadcasting. Of the 346 respondents, 68.7 percent favored broadcasting House debates. Nearly 60 percent favored coverage by a broadcast pool, and only 30 percent favored an in-House broadcast system. Finally, a majority, 53.4 percent, favored gavel-to-gavel broadcast coverage as opposed to coverage of only selected debates.[38]

On May 27, the subcommittee met to consider concerns raised by the full committee. Representative Anderson offered a package of amendments that was adopted by voice vote. Three days later Sisk, Anderson, Pepper, Murphy, and Andrew Young introduced the new version as H. Res. 1502.

One purpose of the resolution was "the enlightenment and information of the public on the basis of accurate and impartial news coverage of the House as a legislative and representative body." The resolution inserted new "sense of the House" language that a network pool should be used to provide the coverage. It also included alternative language in the report that could be used as substitute amendments on either an in-House broadcast system or one run by the Public Broadcasting System. Finally, the new resolution called for the coverage to begin just before the 95th Congress began.

Notwithstanding the valiant efforts of the Sisk subcommittee to revive its ailing proposal, the 94th Congress adjourned without further action on it.

"Back in Business"

When the 95th Congress convened on January 4, 1977, Tip O'Neill was elected Speaker to succeed Carl Albert, who had retired. In his acceptance speech O'Neill made no reference to any plans to introduce television into the House chamber. The package of House rules changes recommended by the Democratic Caucus, H. Res. 5, was also silent on the issue.

During debate on the rules resolution, Anderson said he was "dismayed . . . that the caucus failed to adopt a rule to provide for the continuous broadcast coverage of our floor proceedings, despite a survey showing 271 Members of the 95th Congress in favor of broadcasting."[39] The Republicans, unlike the silent Democrats, presented a thirty-point House reform plan that included a new broadcast rule proposed by Anderson.[40] However, House procedures did not allow for a direct vote on the Republican alternative, and the Democrats' House rules package was adopted on a party-line vote.

It therefore came as a surprise to most members when the new Speaker announced in a press release on March 2, 1977, that a ninety-day live test of television coverage of the House floor would begin as early as Tuesday, March 15. According to the release, the test would be conducted by the Office of the Architect of the Capitol and the staff of the Joint Committee on Congressional Operations using three remote-controlled, black-and-white security cameras. The proceedings would be televised by closed circuit to offices in the Capitol and the Rayburn House Office Building where there was already a capacity to receive the signals. Coverage would continue from the opening gavel each day until the conclusion of legislative business; it would not include the end-of-the-day special order speeches. The experiment would evaluate "the feasibility of using small, fixed and remotely controlled cameras and related equipment which will not require significant or noticeable modifications to the House Chamber," as well as "the usefulness of television coverage of House proceedings as an information source in each Member's office." In addition, "the historical value of establishing a video library of House proceedings" would be assessed.[41]

The Speaker said he hoped the test would "form the basis for the eventual video coverage of the House for dissemination to the public." Such video coverage should "be kept in perspective," however. The Speaker concluded on a cautious note: "Television should be permitted to witness the operations of the House and not by its presence dominate the proceedings so as to affect the discharge of its constitutional duties."[42]

In House floor remarks on March 8, Anderson questioned whether the system was going to be primarily for the informational uses of members and perhaps only secondarily for the benefit of the public through the later dissemination of tapes. He concluded with this warning: "We will only be contributing further to public cynicism and distrust of the Congress if we initiate broadcasting more as a self-service than a public service."[43]

On March 15, the first day of the television test, the Speaker informed House members of the nature and purpose of the test. O'Neill made clear that "House rules do not permit television or radio broadcast coverage of House proceedings, or the use of audio and video excerpts outside the Capitol." He explained his "intention to seek authority from the House if it is considered appropriate to commence permanent broadcast-media coverage or to permit use of video or live coverage of the House proceedings by the news media."[44]

Immediately following the Speaker's announcement, Anderson offered a resolution, H. Res. 404, directing the Rules Committee "to investigate and evaluate the full scope and impact of the House broadcast test as it affects the safety, dignity and integrity of the proceedings of the House and the conduct and convenience of Members, and to report back to the House . . . its findings and such recommendations as it may deem appropriate, including whether such broadcast coverage should be made available to the public."[45]

Anderson again quoted from surveys showing the support of members and the general public for seeing House debates televised. "This is obviously an idea whose time has come," he said, "and I am glad you [the Speaker] have taken the first step to realize that goal."[46]

Anderson went on to mention a Harris Poll that showed 88 percent of the people thought Congress should do more to inform the public about its activities, and 76 percent thought Congress tries to hide a lot of things from the news media. He then quoted from Lou Harris's summary of these findings: "If Congress did a better job of communicating its real business, its rating might improve" since "this study shows clearly that the greater amount of information the people have about Congress, the higher they rate Congress."[47]

In a rare move Speaker O'Neill took to the well of the House to comment on the Anderson resolution. It "does nothing more than I had intended to do anyway," and "I do not know why it is before us." Anderson responded that he had offered the resolution to congratulate the Speaker on his initiative and to ensure that the Rules Committee will become involved in drafting the necessary rules to permit the public dissemination of the broadcast materials. O'Neill thanked Anderson and said:

> I know that the resolution will be adopted. I urge its adoption. In the same breath I laud the gentleman on this historical day for presenting the first resolution that had been recorded for posterity on television.[48]

The only dissenting voice during debate on the resolution was that of Rep. Leo Ryan, a third-term Democrat from California. Ryan warned his colleagues that there was no turning back on televising the House, "that unblinking eye is there; it will be there from now on." Television "now becomes part of the problem of running the House." It "will have an effect upon everything else that we do as Members."[49]

Another California Democrat and a former broadcast journalist, Rep. Lionel Van Deerlin, commended Anderson "for his diligence in pressing for the telecasting of House proceedings." Van Deerlin said that Anderson, along with Sisk, "as much as anyone has kept this issue in full public view when the inclination of some among us may have been to let it slide out of sight and out of mind."[50]

When the vote was taken, Anderson's resolution was overwhelmingly adopted, 398-10. Anderson told his hometown newspaper afterward that he was pleasantly surprised. He had expected "a whirlwind of scorn and derision from 'Tip' O'Neill, not to mention a majority of 'no' votes from the Democrats." Anderson went on, "I wouldn't have believed they'd let me get away with this." And he concluded, "We're back in business."[51]

The Home Stretch

There would be three more votes and three more reports over the next two years before the House broadcasting system would finally go public on March 19, 1979, but Ryan had been correct in saying there was "no turning back."

On September 27, 1977, Jack Brooks, chairman of the Select Committee on Congressional Operations (successor to the joint committee of the same name), filed a report on the results of the ninety-day test that had been completed on September 15. (The ninety days had been interpreted as legislative days rather than calendar days).

The report called the test of broadcast coverage "successful" and said "neither technical nor policy considerations stand in the way of early development of a permanent system for broadcasting House proceedings." A majority of members surveyed favored making complete and uninterrupted coverage of House proceedings available to the public. The report recommended that cameras focus only on the official actions of the House and not pan the chamber. The system should be operated by the House and "should not be delegated or contracted to groups outside the Congress." According to the report, only 18 of 150 members responding to its survey "preferred that a network pool provide the coverage."[52]

The select committee's report went on to recommend that the House, before the end of the first session of the 95th Congress, adopt a resolution authorizing the establishment of a permanent broadcast system that provided "complete, continuous, and unedited" coverage of the daily legislative business of the House to all members, officers, and committees by closed-circuit transmission. Use of live and recorded broadcasts should be prohibited for commercial or political advertising purposes.[53]

On October 6 Rules Committee Democrat Gillis Long of Louisiana introduced H. Res. 821, with Sisk and Brooks as cosponsors. The resolution amended House rules to authorize and direct the Speaker to "devise and implement a system subject to his direction and control for the complete and unedited audio and video broadcasting and recording of the legislative proceedings of the House." The Speaker was also asked to provide for the distribution of the broadcasts and recordings to the public and the news media. The Speaker could delegate his implementation responsibilities "to such legislative entity as he deems appropriate."[54]

Following two days of hearings on the select committee's report and Long's resolution, the Rules Committee met on October 25 and adopted, 8-7, a substitute. Rep. Trent Lott of Mississippi and Sisk introduced H. Res. 866 that same day, and it was reported by voice vote.[55]

The new resolution reflected continued resistance by Anderson and broadcasters to a House-run system. Touted as a bipartisan compromise, it required the Speaker to defer a decision on what entity should provide public coverage until after a further report and recommendation from the Rules Committee by March 15, 1978, on alternative broadcast systems. On October 27, the compromise was adopted by the House, 342-44.

The responsibility for the final Rules Committee report was entrusted to the chairman of the newly formed Rules Committee Subcommittee on Rules and Organization of the House, Gillis Long. This time Trent Lott was the ranking Republican member and Anderson the other subcommittee Republican. Subcommittee Democrats included Bolling, Young of Texas, Shirley Chisholm of New York, and, for the purpose of the report, Sisk as an ex officio member.

The subcommittee's report was adopted by the full Rules Committee on a 9-6 vote and filed on February 15, 1978. The report reaffirmed the basic principles embodied in H. Res. 866: coverage should be gavel to gavel and made available to the public and media both live and by recordings. The central rationale for broadcast coverage is quoted in the epigraph of this chapter. The central new recommendation of the report was that "the House should operate its own broadcast system following the example and building on the experience of the Canadian Parliament," which had established its own system in 1977.[56]

Sisk filed supplemental views to the report and Anderson filed dissenting views, both expressing a continued preference for allowing the networks to provide and operate the cameras. Lott filed minority views objecting to an in-House system on the grounds that it would appear to be politically motivated— "another benefit to incumbents with the taxpayers footing the bill." Installing our own system, "instead of improving our credibility with the public . . . may very well be contributing to our less than popular image."

The filing of the report technically allowed the Speaker to proceed with completing the system of his choice and making House debates public on it. But the Speaker on at least two occasions had promised the House a final vote on the matter before going public. On June 14, 1978, Representative Anderson decided to hold the Speaker to his word by offering an amendment to the legislative branch appropriations bill. It prohibited any of the funds in the bill from being used "to purchase new color television cameras and related equipment for the purpose of broadcasting the proceedings of the House except by the prior approval of the House."[57]

After Anderson explained the Speaker's promised vote on a House-run versus media-run system, Rep. Gillis Long joined the debate to suggest that immediately following the disposition of the Anderson amendment, he or someone else could offer an amendment to decide the issue once and for all as to who should control the cameras.[58] The Anderson amendment was subsequently rejected, 133-249.

The ranking Democrat on the Legislative Branch Appropriations Subcommittee, Adam Benjamin of Indiana, then offered an amendment that stipulated none of the funds in the bill could be used for implementing a House television system "under which the TV cameras in the Chamber are controlled and operated by persons not in the employ of the House."[59] During debate on the amendment, Rep. Jim Wright of Texas took issue with Anderson's calling the issue a matter of "journalistic integrity." In Wright's words, "the question at issue is the integrity of the House of Representatives. The matter at issue is not the freedom of the press. The matter at issue is the responsibility of the Congress and whether we shall assert it."[60]

Another Democrat, Rep. Romano Mazzoli of Kentucky, disagreed: "What we have fundamentally here is a question of freedom of the press" and "something usually we ourselves [as Democrats] stand in favor of—openness, candor, objectivity, let the chips fall where they may."[61]

When the chips finally fell on the Benjamin amendment, it was adopted, 235-150, and the Speaker had the final authority he needed to complete a House-owned and -operated television system. The appropriate rules were adopted by the House at the beginning of the 96th Congress in January of 1979. The newly installed system was given a final, thirty-day test, and on March 19, the House was on the air and so was the Cable-Satellite Public Affairs Network (C-SPAN), the new cable company that would carry live, gavel-to-gavel coverage of the House.[62]

The Aftermath

Pressured from outside and inside the Congress, O'Neill agreed to televising the House only once he became convinced that it could be done in a dignified manner without embarrassing or humiliating individual members or the institution. He considered House control over the cameras essential, the only way to guarantee an exclusive focus on the members speaking and to avoid shots panning the chamber for reactions or views of members engaged in other activities. In his bestselling autobiography O'Neill discusses this preferred alternative to commercial coverage:

> But what if we allowed TV cameras on the floor of the House that were controlled by us instead of the networks? And what if those cameras showed only the person who was actually at the microphone and no-

> body else? That struck me as a reasonable compromise, and that's exactly what we did in setting up the cable network known as C-Span.[63]

While it may come as news to Brian Lamb, the founder of C-SPAN, that Tip O'Neill was the real founder of his network, the point remains that C-SPAN may only show the pictures of the chamber transmitted to it by the House-owned and -operated broadcast system as captured by the cameras controlled by the Speaker. By only allowing close-ups of the persons speaking, the telecasts were nothing more nor less than an audio and visual version of the *Congressional Record* (absent the ability of members to "revise and extend" their remarks).

Televising House debates "turned out to be one of the best decisions I ever made," O'Neill later wrote. "The results of our broadcasting experiment have exceeded my wildest hopes." He was pleased because "Americans are better informed on the issues."[64]

On May 10, 1984, O'Neill made a radical departure from his commitment to showing only close-up shots of those speaking. Shortly after 7:00 P.M. on that day Rep. Robert Walker, a Republican from Pennsylvania, was in the middle of delivering a special order speech on the subject of the integrity of the *Congressional Record* when he was handed a note by Republican whip Trent Lott. Without missing a beat, Walker said:

> I do want to take note of something that is evidently happening right now which is a change of procedure here. It is my understanding that as I deliver this special order this evening, the cameras are panning this Chamber, demonstrating that there is no one here in the Chamber to listen to these remarks.[65]

Walker called the change in camera coverage "one more example of how this body is run; the kind of arrogance of power that the Members are given that kind of change with absolutely no warning." He then took notice of Rep. Tony Coelho standing at the back of the chamber, someone who "has talked in recent weeks about shutting off these special orders and not allowing them to be seen in the countryside."[66]

At the next House session on May 14, 1984, Speaker O'Neill took the well of the House to defend his new camera policy in a one-minute speech. "I took the action that I took last Thursday," O'Neill said, "because I had so many complaints and so many people had asked me to do what I did." What had enraged Democrats was a special order speech by Republican representative Newt Gingrich of Georgia the previous week. O'Neill said Gingrich "took statements that were made by 20 different Democrats going back to 1968," and suggested "that Members of Congress were Un-American." Gingrich then asked the accused members to respond, although they had not been notified that their names would be used and were not present on the floor. "A more low thing I have never seen," O'Neill said. No one challenged the Speaker's characterization because, perhaps ironically, Gingrich had not been notified by the Speaker and therefore was not there to defend himself.

O'Neill continued to explain that he had notified the chairman of his broadcast advisory committee, Rep. Charlie Rose of North Carolina, around 3:00 P.M. the afternoon of the incident to make the camera coverage change during special orders that evening. "The prerogative of the rules of this House give me the right to stop that, gives me that right to say when there will be a wide lens and when there should not be a wide lens," O'Neill explained. He did concede, in a colloquy with Minority Leader Robert H. Michel, that as a matter of courtesy he should have notified the minority leader in advance of this change in coverage policy.[67]

Tempers flared the following day when Representative Gingrich rose to a question of personal privilege to defend his actions and was recognized for one hour. He explained that he had notified by mail, in advance, the members that he would be referring to in his special order speech, but the mail apparently did not get through on time. Speaker O'Neill was again drawn into the well, this time to engage Gingrich directly on his actions. After reiterating his charge that affected members had not been properly notified and that their patriotism had been questioned (in dated statements quoted out of context), O'Neill said:

> My personal opinion is this: You deliberately stood in that well before an empty House and challenged these people, and you challenged their Americanism, and it is the lowest thing that I have ever seen in my 32 years in Congress.[68]

With that, Minority Whip Lott leapt to his feet to "demand that the Speaker's words be taken down." Under House rules, if a member's words are found by the Speaker to be unparliamentary, the offending words are stricken from the record and the member is banned from speaking for the rest of the day. Unparliamentary remarks include those that question another member's motives or integrity. Rep. Joseph Moakely, chairman of the Rules Committee and a Bay State crony of O'Neill's, was presiding as the Speaker pro tempore at the time. On the advice of the parliamentarian, he was constrained to rule that "that type of characterization should not be used in debate."

Lott then asked unanimous consent that "the Speaker be allowed to continue in order," that is, that he not be banished from the floor for the rest of the day.[69] The House agreed to the request, and O'Neill was allowed to continue in order. Before he vacated the chamber, he engaged in one parting shot at Gingrich and then at Moakley:

> I am not questioning the gentleman's patriotism, I am questioning his judgment. I also question the judgment of the Chair. I was expressing my opinion. As a matter of fact, I was expressing my opinion very mildly, because I think much worse than what I said.[70]

The "Camscam" incident boosted the political fortunes of Gingrich's group of back-benchers, known as the Conservative Opportunity Society. In part by playing to C-SPAN cameras, they went on to engineer a Republican takeover of the House in 1994. The incident also helped introduce a new era of politicization in the House. From then on both parties would exploit one-minute and special order speech periods as well as carefully drawn legislative amendments to highlight their differences with the other political party.

At the time of the Camscam incident, Democrats were torn between pulling the TV plug on special order speeches or implementing their own partisan propaganda campaign using the same techniques as the Republicans. In the face of Republicans' stiff opposition to anything less than gavel-to-gavel coverage, the Democrats retreated on turning off the cameras during special orders. The Republicans viewed the proposal as a clear breach of the original intent of the television authorization and as an attempt to muzzle the minority's one avenue for raising its issues.[71]

The Senate Proceeds with Caution

The Camscam incident and the political uses of House television that triggered it temporarily slowed momentum that had been building in the Senate for televised sessions of its own. Majority Leader Howard Baker (R-Tenn.) had introduced a resolution authorizing such coverage early in 1981, but he ran into a filibuster buzz-saw of opposition from Democratic senator Russell Long of Louisiana. Baker backed off rather than block other Senate business. Whereas concern about the imbalance between the media exposure of the president and Congress gave initial impetus to televising the House, concern about inordinate coverage of the House finally tilted the balance in favor of Senate TV. As Baker put it in 1981, "If we don't open up the Senate to radio and television, I predict that in a few years . . . in the public mind at least, the House will be the dominant branch."[72]

Minority Leader Robert Byrd eventually came around to Baker's view and was instrumental in paving the way for a vote without a filibuster. On February 27, 1986, the Senate voted 67-21 for a public trial period that began on May 1. Following the six-week trial the Senate briefly terminated video coverage in July to debate whether to make the system permanent. And on July 29, the Senate voted 78-21 in favor of permanent coverage.[73]

The Impact of TV on Congress

After nearly two decades of televised floor proceedings in the House and over a decade in the Senate, the coverage has neither lived up to the highest expectations of its proponents nor the worst fears of its opponents. Many proponents thought the increased exposure would help to restore the balance between the president and Congress. While most observers would agree that the Congress has been strengthened relative to the presidency since the 1970s, few would assert that congressional television had much, if anything, to do with it. Instead, the presidency has been diminished by the perceived excesses of the Vietnam War; impoundments by the chief executive of funds appropriated by Congress; the Watergate and Iran-Contra scandals involving Presidents Richard Nixon and Ronald Reagan, respectively; and the end of the cold war, a stage for presidential diplomacy. Congress, on the other hand, has strengthened its own hand by reasserting its prerogatives in the areas of war powers, spending, impeachment, and investigations of executive branch wrongdoing. That is not to say that Congress has now become the dominant branch of government. Presidents continue to enjoy higher job approval and confidence ratings than does Congress, even in the midst of a major campaign fund-raising scandal involving the White House.[74] However, in certain important areas, such as the economy, the public perceives that the Congress is more influential than the president today.[75]

Has television coverage of Congress increased public understanding of the issues and operations of Congress and, as a result, increased public confidence and trust in the institution? There is no hard evidence that it has.

However, 65 percent of the respondents to a 1995 poll said they received most of their news about Congress from local or network television newscasts, compared with 20 percent from newspapers.[76] And according to another poll, network news coverage of Congress has been steadily declining rather than increasing since the advent of televised floor sessions.[77] Therefore, it is highly unlikely that more Americans are better informed about Congress and its debates than they were during the pre-TV era. The exception, of course, are regular C-SPAN viewers, but they comprise only a small fraction of the TV-viewing public. Whereas 62 percent of the people in a Roper Poll said they watched a TV news program daily, only 4 percent said they watched C-SPAN daily.[78]

As for public confidence in Congress, the trend, with the exception of mid-1998, has been downward rather than upward since the introduction of congressional television. According to Gallup Poll measures of public confidence in major institutions, the percentage of people having a "great deal" or "quite a lot" of confidence in Congress was 40 percent in 1975 and 1977 (before House TV coverage began in 1979), averaged around 30 percent in 1979–84, briefly jumped back to around 40 percent in 1985–86, but hovered between 18 and 21 percent between 1991 and 1996.[79] Perhaps not coincidentally, the percentage of network news stories about Congress that were positive between 1972 and 1992 declined from 26 to 11 percent, while the percentage of negative stories increased from 74 percent to 89 percent.[80] The same survey found that the number of policy stories about Congress on the network news from 1986 to 1992 dropped from nearly 80 percent to just over 50 percent, while the percentage of stories on ethics and scandals increased from 7 percent to 17 percent.[81]

Moreover, the use of members and congressional staff as sources for commentary on Congress in network news stories dropped from 60 percent in 1972 and 1982 to just 47 percent in 1992. The networks are relying more on persons outside the Congress to comment on its actions—hardly a constructive use of the increased availability of televised floor and committee debates.[82] Those who view C-SPAN regularly and others who are knowledgeable about Congress tend to be even more negative about Congress than is the general public—at least in polls taken through 1994.[83] This could stem from the fact that such viewers tend to be more ideological and opinionated than the average voter and therefore more likely to react negatively to most of what Congress does.

As for the impact of congressional television on Congress itself, most members feel it has had an overall beneficial effect, as an internal informational device and as a stimulus for improving the quality of legislative debates. The one predictable result of televising the House and Senate floor is that it has produced an increase in nonlegislative speeches (one-minute and special order speeches) by members wishing to speak on subjects of their own choosing for home or national consumption. Not only have these speaking venues resulted in longer sessions each day, but they have been the source of coordinated political attacks on the other party's policies as well as on individuals of the other party—especially those accused of ethical problems in the Congress and the administration. The partisan wars were fueled by sharp divisions over the Reagan administration's budget cuts in the early 1980s, its support for the Nicaraguan Contras in the mid-1980s, and later by Speaker Jim Wright's ethics problems in the late 1980s, the House post office and bank scandals in the early 1990s, and Speaker Gingrich's own ethics problems in the mid-1990s.

Both party leaderships have organized "theme teams" to deliver their partisan message of the day during nonlegislative free speech periods (called "one-minutes" and special orders) at the beginning and end of each daily session. Most one-minute speeches are aimed at differentiating between the policies of the two parties, but some have deteriorated into bitter personal attacks, prompting bipartisan calls for at least postponing one-minutes until the end of each day.

It is currently in vogue to blame the "sunshine" reforms of the seventies, especially televised floor proceedings, for the public's sagging confidence in Congress. Increased public exposure is cited as a big reason for the loss of confidence. As some observers have concluded, "Familiarity breeds contempt." Televising Congress, they say, has not brought the expected benefit: "To know us is to love us." The "process is the problem," we are told, and not the product.[84]

However, the facts seem to indicate that the public sees and learns less of Congress today from television, its principal source of such news, than it did in the pre-TV era—C-SPAN viewers, perhaps, excepted. That is not to say that the people still do not have a general sense of the status and progress of the most important national issues in play between the White House and the Congress—they do. But public job-performance ratings of the president and Congress still depend more on perceived results than on process. Congressional television is here to stay. Whether it will ever measure up to its perceived potential for better educating the public on the democratic process and national issues remains to be seen.

Notes

1. "Broadcasting the Proceedings of the House: A Report of the Committee on Rules on Its Study of Alternative Methods of Providing Complete and Unedited Audio and Visual Broadcasting of the Proceedings of the House of Representatives Pursuant to Section 3 of House Resolution 866, Ninety-Fifth Congress," H. Rept. 95-881, Feb. 15, 1978, 2. This report gave the Speaker of the House final authority to devise and implement a permanent House broadcasting system pursuant to H. Res. 866.
2. Public Law 91-510, "The Legislative Reorganization Act of 1970," 91st Cong., H.R. 17654, Oct. 26, 1970, sec. 402 (a)(1).
3. *Who's Who in American Politics, 1975–76*, 5th ed., ed. Jacques Cattell Press (New York: R.R. Bowker Co., 1975), 893. No biographical information on Stewart is provided in the CRS report he wrote or in the subsequent hearings based on it. Stewart would later be listed in the hearings and reports of the Joint Committee on Congressional Operations as a research consultant to the joint committee.
4. "Congress and Mass Communications: An Institutional Perspective," a study conducted for the Joint Committee on Congressional Operations by the Congressional Research Service, Committee Print, 93d Cong., 2d sess., 1974, v.
5. Ibid.
6. Ibid.
7. Ibid., 5.
8. Ibid., 18–19.
9. Ibid., 28. H.J. Res. 209, 91st Cong.

10. Ibid., 42.
11. Ibid., 62.
12. Ibid., 64.
13. "Congress and Mass Communications: Hearings before the Joint Committee on Congressional Operations, Ninety-Third Congress, Second Session," Feb. 20, 21; March 7, 20; April 9 and 10, 1974, Opening statement of the Honorable Jack Brooks on Feb. 20, 1974, 4.
14. Ibid., opening statement of the Honorable James C. Cleveland, Feb. 20, 1974, 5.
15. Ibid., statement of the Honorable Edmund S. Muskie, Feb. 20, 1974, 15–16.
16. Ibid., statement of the Honorable Walter F. Mondale, Feb. 20, 1974, 32.
17. Ibid., statement of the Honorable John B. Anderson, Feb. 20, 1974, 55–56.
18. "Congress and Mass Communications," statement of Neil MacNeill, *Time*, March 20, 1974, 250–51.
19. Ibid., 251.
20. Ibid., 421.
21. Ibid., 422.
22. "Broadcasting House and Senate Proceedings: An Interim Report of the Joint Committee on Congressional Operations on Congress and Mass Communications," H. Rept. 93-1458, 93d Cong., 2d sess., 1–2.
23. Ibid., 57–58.
24. Ibid., 58.
25. "A Clear Message to the People: Report of the Joint Committee on Congressional Operations on Congress and Mass Communications," H. Rept. 94-539, 94th Cong., 1st sess., 3.
26. Ibid., separate views of Sen. Jesse Helms, 22.
27. "Broadcast Coverage of House Floor Proceedings: Report of the Ad Hoc Subcommittee on Broadcasting to the Committee on Rules on H. Res. 875," Rules Committee Print, Feb. 23, 1976, 3.
28. Ibid., 3–4.
29. Ibid., 4.
30. Bruce F. Freed, "House Leadership Opposes Broadcast Plan," *Congressional Quarterly Weekly Report*, March 20, 1976, 623.
31. Thomas P. O'Neill, Jr., *Man of the House: The Life and Political Memoirs of Speaker Tip O'Neill*, with William Novak (New York: Random House, 1987), 289.
32. "Broadcast Coverage of House Floor Proceedings: A Supplemental Report of the Ad Hoc Subcommittee on Broadcasting to the Committee on Rules on H. Res. 875," Rules Committee Print, March 9, 1976, 4.
33. Remarks of Rep. John B. Anderson, *Congressional Record*, March 22, 1976, E1434.
34. Freed, "House Leadership," 623.
35. "Television and Radio Coverage of the House: Hearing before the Committee on Rules," 94th Cong., 2d sess., March 24, 1976, statement of the Honorable Del Clawson in opposition to broadcasting House floor proceedings, 22.
36. Ibid., 56–64.

37. Ibid., 59.

38. "Broadcast Coverage of House Floor Proceedings: A Second Supplemental Report of the Ad Hoc Subcommittee on Broadcasting of the Committee on Rules on H. Res. 1502," Committee Print (1976), 2–3.

39. *Congressional Record*, Jan. 4, 1977, remarks of Rep. John B. Anderson on H. Res. 5, 61.

40. Ibid., "GOP Proposals for Reform of House Rules," inserted with remarks of Rep. William Frenzel, 61–62.

41. Press release of House Speaker Thomas P. "Tip" O'Neill, Jr. (D-Mass.), March 2, 1977, reprinted in remarks of Rep. John B. Anderson, *Congressional Record*, daily ed., March 8, 1977, H1852.

42. Ibid.

43. Ibid.

44. Announcement by the Speaker, *Congressional Record*, March 15, 1977, 7608.

45. H. Res. 404, 95th Cong., 1st sess., "Privileges of the House—Television Coverage of Proceedings of House," offered by Rep. John B. Anderson of Illinois, *Congressional Record*, March 15, 1977, 7608.

46. Ibid.

47. Ibid., 7609.

48. Ibid.

49. Ibid., 7611.

50. Ibid., 7612.

51. "Some More Sunshine," editorial, Rockford *Morning-Star*, March 18, 1977, a-6.

52. "Televising the House," communication from the chairman, Select Committee on Congressional Operations, to the Speaker of the House of Representatives, H. Doc. 95-231, Sept. 27, 1977, 3–5.

53. Ibid., 7–8.

54. H. Res. 821, 95th Cong., 1st sess., introduced by Mr. Long of Louisiana, Oct. 6, 1977, amending House Rule I ("Duties of the Speaker").

55. "Providing for Radio and Television Coverage of House Proceedings: Report of the Committee on Rules to Accompany H. Res. 866," H. Rept. 95-759, Oct. 26, 1977, 3.

56. "Broadcasting the Proceedings of the House," 2, 5.

57. Amendment offered by Mr. Anderson of Illinois to the legislative branch appropriations bill for fiscal year 1979, *Congressional Record*, June 14, 1978, 17657.

58. Ibid., 17659.

59. Amendment offered by Mr. Benjamin to the legislative branch appropriations bill for fiscal year 1979, *Congressional Record*, June 14, 1978, 17661.

60. Ibid., 17664.

61. Ibid., 17665.

62. For an excellent history of the development and evolution of C-SPAN, see Stephen Frantzich and John Sullivan, *The C-SPAN Revolution* (Norman: Oklahoma University Press, 1996).

63. O'Neill, *Man of the House*, 289.

64. Ibid., 288–89.

65. Remarks of Rep. Robert Walker of Pennsylvania, *Congressional Record*, May 10, 1984, 11894.

66. Ibid.

67. Remarks of Rep. Thomas P. O'Neill, Jr., *Congressional Record*, May 14, 1984, 12042.

68. Ibid., May 15, 1984, 12201.

69. Ibid.

70. Ibid., 12202.

71. See especially the May 8, 1984, letter from the chief deputy majority whip, Bill Alexander of Arkansas, to his Democratic colleagues, and three newspaper articles on a proposed telecommunications strategy, inserted in the May 10, 1984, *Congressional Record* by Republican representative Bob McEwen at 11895–97.

72. Frantzich and Sullivan, *C-SPAN Revolution*, 56, quoting Baker in Tom Shales, "The Floor Show," *Washington Post*, Dec. 1, 1981, B1.

73. Ibid., 60–64.

74. For example, a *Washington Post*–ABC News poll conducted by Chilton Research in July of 1997 showed President Clinton with a 65 percent job approval rating and Congress with a 40 percent approval rating (still relatively high for Congress). Dan Balz and Ceci Connolly, "Voters Feeling Removed from Issues in Capital," *Washington Post*, July 10, 1997, A1, A6.

75. According to a September 1996 Gallup Poll, 48 percent of the public thinks the government has more influence over the performance of the economy than nongovernmental sectors have (38 percent). Of those respondents, 59 percent think Congress has more influence over the economy than the president has. *The Gallup Poll Monthly*, Sept. 1996 (No. 372), 38.

76. Freedom Forum/Roper Poll of the general public (Sept. 1995), published in Elaine S. Povich, *Partners and Adversaries: The Contentious Connection between Congress and the Media* (Arlington, Va.: The Freedom Forum, 1996), 149.

78. S. Robert Lichter and Daniel R. Amundson, "Less News Is Worse News: Television News Coverage of Congress, 1972–92," in *Congress, the Press, and the Public*, ed. Thomas E. Mann and Norman J. Ornstein (Washington, D.C.: The American Enterprise Institute and the Brookings Institution, 1994), 134. The authors surveyed news stories about the Congress on the three major network news programs during the month of April each year from 1972 to 1992. Whereas the monthly average from 1972 through 1978 was 124 stories a month, from 1986 to 1992 the number of congressional stories averaged just 42 a month.

78. Freedom Forum/Roper Poll of the general public (Sept. 1995), in Povich, *Partners and Adversaries*, 144–45.

79. Leslie McAneny, "Public Confidence in Major Institutions Little Changed from 1995," *The Gallup Poll Monthly*, June 1996, 7–9.

80. Lichter and Amundson, "Less News Is Worse News," 138.

81. Ibid., 135–37.

82. Ibid., 137–38.

83. Frantzich and Sullivan, *C-SPAN Revolution*, 249–53. For further evidence that

those more knowledgeable about Congress are more critical of it, see Herb Asher and Mike Barr, "Popular Support for Congress and Its Members," in *Congress, the Press, and the Public*, 15–43; John R. Hibbing and Elizabeth Theiss-Morse, "What the Public Dislikes about Congress," in *Congress Reconsidered*, 6th ed., ed. Lawrence C. Dodd and Bruce I. Oppenheimer (Washington, D.C.: CQ Press, 1997), 61–80; and John R. Hibbing and Elizabeth Theiss-Morse, *Congress as Public Enemy: Public Attitudes toward American Political Institutions* (Cambridge: Cambridge University Press, 1995).

84. Frantzich and Sullivan, and Hibbing and Morse are the leading proponents of this theory of the downside of overexposure.

9

The Revival of Direct Democracy Proposals

BETWEEN 1898 and 1918, eighteen states adopted some form of initiative and referendum process for making their residents' views known on public issues (see Chapter 5). A four-decade lull followed. Until 1959 no other states adopted these direct democracy devices. Since then eight additional states and the District of Columbia have adopted some form of initiative and/or referendum (see Table 9.1). Twenty-six states now have one or both of these processes. All states except Delaware provide for a popular referendum to approve constitutional amendments recommended by the state legislatures.

The increase in the number of states joining the ranks of those with the initiative and referendum over the past thirty years has been modest. More significant and dramatic is the increase in the use of those devices beginning in the mid-1970s (see Table 9.2).

A similar survey of state initiatives and referendums on the ballot between 1900 and 1992 by David B. Magleby shows a steady decline in their number from the 1930s, when there were 246, to a low of 85 in the 1960s. But this number began increasing steadily: in the 1970s to 120, to 193 in the 1980s, and to a projected 353 in the 1990s based on the first three years of the decade.[1]

This revival of interest in direct democracy has been attributed to the climate for political reform in the wake of Vietnam, Watergate, and other political scandals that have fueled a growing crisis of confidence in government at all levels. As the use of state initiatives and referendums grew and received national attention, other states followed suit. Perhaps the biggest spur to the

Table 9.1
States with Some Form of Initiative and/or Referendum Process by Year of Adoption (1898–1992)

State	Year
South Dakota	1898
Utah	1900
Oregon	1902
Montana	1906
Oklahoma	1907
Maine	1908
Missouri	1908
Arkansas	1910
Colorado	1910
Arizona	1912
California	1912
Idaho	1912
Nevada	1912
Ohio	1912
Washington	1912
Michigan	1913
Nebraska	1916
North Dakota	1918
Alaska	1959
Florida	1968
Wyoming	1968
Illinois	1970
District of Columbia	1977
Kentucky	1992
Maryland	1992
Mississippi	1992
New Mexico	1992

Sources: Thomas E. Cronin, *Direct Democracy: The Politics of Initiative, Referendum, and Recall* (Cambridge: Harvard University Press, 1989), 51; and Lisa Oakley and Thomas H. Neale, "Citizen Initiative Proposals Appearing on State Ballots, 1976–1992," Congressional Research Service Report 95-288 GOV (Feb. 15, 1995).

Table 9.2
State Initiatives and Their Passage Rates (1904–92)

Years	Number of initiatives	Percentage of proposed initiatives that passed
1904–21	357	40.6
1922–39	386	33.7
1940–57	243	39.1
1958–75	186	44.6
1976–92	495	43.6

Source: Lisa Oakley and Thomas H. Neale, "Citizen Initiative Proposals Appearing on State Ballots, 1976–1992," Congressional Research Service Report 95-288 GOV, Feb. 15, 1995, 6.

movement was passage of the property-tax-limiting Proposition 13 in California in 1978, which will be discussed later in this chapter.

Congress Flirts with Direct Democracy

Between the 78th and 94th Congresses (1943–77), no constitutional amendments had been introduced in either house of Congress to provide for a national initiative process. During the 95th Congress that long streak was broken, mainly because of the efforts of two twenty-five-year-olds, Roger Telschow and John Forster, who were already campaign veterans in the newly resurgent use of the state initiative process. One night in February of 1977, while attending a Consumer Federation of America conference in Washington, D.C., the two concluded over a beer that what worked for state governments could work at the national level. They consequently founded a national movement for a constitutional initiative amendment, Initiative America. By that summer they had persuaded Democratic senator James Abourezk of South Dakota (the first state to adopt the initiative process, in 1898) to introduce the constitutional amendment they had drafted, even though he planned to retire the following year. Abourezk introduced the joint resolution, S. J. Res. 67, on July 11, 1977, together with Republican senator Mark Hatfield of Oregon (the third state to adopt the initiative and referendum process, in 1902).

Abourezk called the initiative process "unique among our democratic rights," and he said it was "founded on the belief that the citizens of this country are indeed as competent to enact legislation as we are to elect public officials to represent us." Because of its "workability as a democratic tool" in twenty-three states, "its extension to the Federal level [is] justified and long overdue."

Moreover, he asserted, "much of the alienation and helplessness that citizens experience can be mitigated if avenues for constructive participation exist." He praised the initiative procedure as "one means to provide direct citizen access to our governmental decision making process through a legal and democratic method."[2]

These introductory remarks by Abourezk on the Senate floor included an assurance that the proposal was not "antigovernment" but rather "a natural complement to our system of representative government." It "enhances accountability and openness of our representative process" and serves as a "'safety valve' for public concerns"—echoes of Woodrow Wilson's embrace of the device.[3]

Under the terms of the Abourezk resolution, voters could put a proposed federal law (or the repeal or amendment of an existing law) on the next general election ballot by securing the signatures of 3 percent of the voters nationally in the last presidential election, including 3 percent from at least each of ten states. The initiative process could not be used to amend the Constitution, declare war, or call out the National Guard. Signatures would have to be gathered within an eighteen-month time frame to be valid. They would be presented to the attorney general who would then have ninety days in which to validate the petition. At least 120 days would be allowed between the certification and the election in which the ballot initiative would be voted. Congress could not repeal or amend an initiative law within two years of its effective date except by a two-thirds vote of both houses.[4]

Following the introduction of the resolution in the 95th Congress, the founders of Initiative America took their campaign on the road in a school bus painted red, white, and blue and converted into living quarters and an office. Their bold and low-budget tour of the Midwest attracted significant media attention. News articles and wire stories, editorials, and broadcast commentaries on the national initiative proposal filled more than forty-five pages of an appendix to the Senate hearing record. Included were favorable pieces by Ralph Nader, David Brinkley, Pat Buchanan, Nicholas von Hoffman, and Tom Wicker. A few critical appraisals were inserted in the record as well, including columns by conservatives James J. Kilpatrick, who called the proposal "remarkably silly," and George Will, who termed it "congruent with the vague populist impulse of the day."[5] But even the critical columns helped stir the pot in the form of op-ed rebuttals and letters to the editor that were added to the hearing record.

In addition to widespread media attention, the proposal drew support from a few governors. Among them were Democrat J. J. Exon of Nebraska and Republicans Jay S. Hammond of Alaska and Tom McCall of Oregon.[6]

In the House of Representatives Republican Guy Vander Jagt of Michigan introduced his own variation on the Abourezk resolution, H. J. Res. 544, on

July 12, 1977. Vander Jagt provided a higher petition threshold of 8 percent of the last presidential vote in each of at least three-fourths of the states, but with no overall national percentage threshold. And on November 8, Democratic representative James R. Jones of Oklahoma introduced a resolution identical to Abourezk's, H. J. Res. 658. All told, fourteen House members, including eight Republicans and six Democrats, had cosponsored either the Jones or Vander Jagt resolutions by December 1977.

In the Senate, Democrat Mike Gravel of Alaska would be the lone senator to join Hatfield and Abourezk as a cosponsor of the resolution. Despite this slim support, national media attention plus Abourezk's persistence sufficed to persuade the chairman of the Senate Judiciary Committee's Constitutional Subcommittee, Birch Bayh of Indiana, to hold hearings on the proposal. It did not hurt that Abourezk, one of only four majority-party subcommittee members, could chair the hearings for two days once Bayh had made his opening remarks.

In his opening statement on December 13, 1977, Bayh pointed out that while most of the scheduled witnesses were favorably disposed to the idea of a national initiative process, "their views in no way reflect an intent upon the part of this subcommittee to narrow the range of interested witnesses." He was determined to have "a full and fair record on both the pros and cons of a national initiative process." As for himself, Bayh admitted, "I have serious reservations about the initiative proposal on the Federal level."[7]

Before turning the gavel over to Abourezk, Bayh inserted in the hearing record a letter from Assistant Attorney General Patricia M. Wald dated December 9, 1977. "While the proposed amendment certainly reflects the theory of democratic government, it is the considered judgment of the Department of Justice that it cannot be effectively implemented in the United States, at the federal level, in the Twentieth Century," she wrote. The letter recounted how the Founders had chosen "a representative or republican form of government" as opposed to a "pure democracy" for "philosophic, historical, and practical reasons." These reasons, she insisted, "remain the same today." Wald said the practical problems were even more compelling in modern times given the complexity of laws at the federal level and the increased chance of inconsistent, contradictory, or overlapping laws and other errors.[8]

In his prepared statement Abourezk said the initiative proposal is founded "on the belief in the wisdom of the American people," and "politicians who wish to oppose the initiative process place themselves in an especially difficult position . . . [of] saying that they don't trust the people or that the people are not educated enough to vote on issues." What such an argument ignores, said Abourezk, is that "these very same 'untrustworthy and uneducated' people can be trusted and are educated enough to elect politicians to office." Moreover, he went on, "the people have proven themselves worthy of this direct democratic process" through the responsible exercise of the device in twenty-three states where "the people repeatedly have shown restraint and good judgment."[9] Abourezk concluded his testimony by saying that he had introduced the amendment not because he sought to advance a particular issue or a set of liberal issues, "but because I think the American people deserve this basic democratic right" that "will help restore the people's shattered faith in their ability to effect [sic] the course of the government under which they live."[10]

He inserted in the hearing record following his testimony the results of a Cambridge Survey Research public opinion poll conducted in late November of 1977. It was based on 750 telephone interviews across the nation. Fifty-seven percent of the persons polled favored a national initiative process, only 25 percent were opposed, and 18 percent were not sure. Other results of the survey showed 74 percent saying they were more likely to vote in an election that included ballot initiatives; 45 percent agreeing that an initiative process would give them more control over their government (with 8 percent saying less control, and 42 percent saying no difference); and 77 percent saying the process would make elected representatives more responsive to the will of the people. On the other side of the ledger, 43 percent of the respondents thought the new right would result in some unfair or poor laws being adopted, as opposed to 36 percent who thought it would be exercised fairly. Sixty-one percent agreed there was a lot of truth or some truth to the statement that a national initiative process would actually weaken government because it would encourage legislators not to make hard decisions.[11] A Gallup Poll printed in the appendix to the hearing record reported results almost identical to the Cambridge survey: 57 percent of the respondents favored the Abourezk initiative proposal and 21 percent opposed it.[12]

Rep. Jim Jones, testifying on behalf of his House version of the Abourezk amendment, recalled his days as an aide in the Johnson White House a decade earlier when "the country was being torn apart by mounting popular opposition to the Vietnam war" and a "growing feeling of frustration about the bigness and the impersonality of Government." Jones speculated, "Had the American people had a national initiative process available at that time, many of the violent, wrenching aspects of our Vietnam experience could have been avoided." Proponents and opponents of the war would have had at their disposal "a peaceful but forceful way to demonstrate their feelings and their strength," and "those of us who were here in Washington would have received a clearer view—much sooner—of the people's will."[13]

Jones went on to testify that the need for such an initiative process was even more compelling today given the greater sense that "Americans feel distant from, and out of touch with, their government," because "our democratic institutions . . . have grown too big or too bureaucratic or too diffuse to deal with problems effectively and directly." Consequently, "today it is the individual citizen who lacks sufficient power to create national policy for the public good."[14]

One of the lone dissenting witnesses testifying on the Abourezk resolution was Professor Peter Bachrach, a political scientist at Temple University. Bachrach raised three arguments against the concept. First, "the political arena which it creates will be preempted by the groups that have money, that have organization, that have political skill, and that have power." He foresaw "a contest among power groups, monied power groups, over who is the most skilled in manipulating the minds of the people." Second, the proposal "presupposes that the people are in a position to make good judgments" when in fact "a significant number of them . . . are apathetic, alienated, and cynical toward the political system" and have "not had the opportunity to be politically educated." And third, "the kind of issues the elites will present to the masses will be more or less hate issues," in which there is "a strong feeling among the people, such as busing, pornography, [and] Government supported abortion." The initiative process may even make a significant group of educated voters more cynical "because issues which are raised by the liberal, radical side of the polity will be overwhelmingly defeated."[15]

The wrap-up witness at the two-day hearing, Initiative America co-director Roger Telschow, took issue with Bachrach's argument that citizens were not ready to make decisions on complex social issues: "The same argument has probably been used for blacks or any other segment of the public which once was nonvoting." In fact, added Telschow, six of the last ten amendments to the Constitution have extended the citizens' right to vote yet when each one was considered, "opponents warned of disaster, a breakdown of our governmental system, a tyranny by the majority, and so on."[16]

Telschow urged Congress to take "a major step toward renewed trust between the people and Government," because "when the Government puts more trust in the people, people will put more trust in the Government." He concluded, "ultimately, the decision to ratify this amendment must be based on trust—trust that the American people have the right and the ability to make decisions for themselves when they deem it necessary."[17]

During 1978 the list of supporters who either introduced their own resolutions or cosponsored others' grew from fourteen sponsors and cosponsors to twenty-eight, including twenty-five House members and three senators, of whom sixteen were Republicans and twelve were Democrats. One of the members who signed on as a cosponsor of the Jones resolution in the second session was a thirty-seven-year-old freshman named Richard Gephardt of Missouri, who would be elected Democratic Caucus chairman in 1985 and House majority leader in 1989 upon the resignation of Speaker Jim Wright of Texas and the elevation of Tom Foley of Washington to the Speakership. No further action was taken on the resolution in the 95th Congress.

In the 96th Congress (1979–81), interest in the initiative proposal began to wane. With Abourezk's retirement, Senator Hatfield dutifully reintroduced the proposal and collected three cosponsors: Senators Mike Gravel (D-Alaska), Dennis DeConcini (D-Ariz.), and Larry Pressler (R-S. Dak.). In the House Jones reintroduced the measure but did not bother to solicit cosponsors. Fourth-term Republican Jack Kemp of New York introduced his own version and collected five cosponsors, including Trent Lott of Mississippi who would be elected House Republican whip in 1981, Senate Republican whip in 1995, and Senate majority leader in June of 1996 upon the resignation of Sen. Bob Dole of Kansas. Kemp also made the proposal one of the central planks in his bid for the Republican presidential nomination in 1980 and of his campaign book.[18]

Nevertheless, only seventeen members of the House and Senate sponsored or cosponsored initiative constitutional amendments in the 96th Congress, including twelve Republicans and five Democrats (but not including rising star Gephardt who had temporarily latched onto an alternative device). By the following Congress, the 97th (1981–83), the total had dropped to just five House members—all Republicans, including Kemp (but not Lott). In the 98th the number of amendments introduced had dropped to just two (with no cosponsors). And from the 99th through 101st Congresses (1985–91), no general initiative amendments were introduced.

In the 102d through the 105th Congresses there were never more than two general initiative constitutional amendments introduced in any two-year period—the lone keepers of the flame being Republican representatives Gerald B. Solomon of New York and Peter Hoekstra of Michigan.[19]

Gephardt's Advisory Referendum Alternative

As the national initiative movement was losing steam, an alternative to direct democracy, a national advisory referendum, was gaining momentum. It was championed by the Missouri Public Interest Research Group. On August 18, 1980, Representative Gephardt introduced H. R. 7934 "to provide that an advisory referendum be conducted as part of each general election to give voters an opportunity to express their views on certain issues of national importance." In a press release issued the same day Gephardt said the following of his proposal:

> There is a growing feeling among the American people that their votes no longer count, that politicians fail to respond to legitimate concerns, and that they have little or no impact on policy decisions. People are frustrated. Voters stay home on election day and yearn for a clear choice

> on issues. When people are given clear choices, the evidence points to increased participation in the democratic process. A National Referendum will provide the vehicle for the re-expression of public sentiment for or against critical issues facing the Nation.[20]

The Gephardt bill called for a Joint Committee on the National Advisory Referendum composed of seven members each from the House and Senate, with the vice president participating only to break a tie vote. Not later than January 1 of each general election year, after taking testimony from the public on possible referendum items, the joint committee would report a concurrent resolution to each house setting forth the text of proposals to be submitted to the voters at the next election. The referendum proposals would be chosen from among a list in the bill of twenty-one public policy issues, ranging alphabetically from business regulation to worker health and safety.

The concurrent resolution would be subject to amendment in each house, but the number of referendum proposals could not be increased beyond three or decreased to less than one. Any differences between the versions passed by the two houses would be resolved by the joint committee. If Congress had not completed this process at least 120 days prior to an election, the president would have ninety days before the election to certify up to three referendum proposals to state election officials for inclusion on the general election ballots. The Congressional Research Service would prepare a voters' guide on the referendum issues, which would be distributed to the print and broadcast media for further public dissemination. Measures passed by the public but not enacted by the Congress within four years would be replaced on the ballot of the next general election.[21]

The idea of a national advisory referendum is not new (see Chapter 6). Sen. Robert LaFollette (the senior) introduced a bill calling for an advisory referendum on war in 1916, and his son, Sen. Robert LaFollette, Jr., forced a vote on an advisory war referendum amendment to a neutrality bill in 1939 when the Senate refused to consider his tougher constitutional amendment.

In between the two forays by the LaFollettes, the Department of Agriculture utilized advisory referendums to determine market quotas for several basic commodities in 1933 and 1936. A similar device was used in 1963 when 1.2 million farmers participated in a referendum on wheat quotas.[22] A Gallup Poll commissioned by *Direct Democracy* author Thomas Cronin in 1987 showed 58 percent public support for a national advisory referendum and only 23 percent opposition.[23]

Gephardt's proposal for a Joint Committee on the National Advisory Referendum went nowhere in the 96th Congress or in the 97th Congress (1981–83) when he reintroduced it.

National versus State Initiatives

At a time when state initiatives were growing in numbers, why did the national initiative campaign falter? Initiative America remained active through 1980, but went out of existence in 1981. According to Telschow:

> We were never that optimistic we could get the national initiative adopted. In fact, we were really surprised that it got as much attention and went as far as it did in 1977 and 1978. For a while it really was catching on. But after the 1980 election, interest seemed to wane, and those of us involved in the campaign could only go on so long living off our savings.[24]

Even though there had been no action in Congress on the proposals in 1979 and 1980 and the collapse of Initiative America looked imminent in April of 1981, the Gallup organization posed its question in the same terms as it had in 1978:

> The U.S. Senate will consider a proposal that would require a national vote—that is, a referendum—on any issue when 3% of all voters who voted in the most recent presidential election sign petitions asking for such a nationwide vote. Do you favor or oppose such a plan?

Even dangling before respondents the false prospect of Senate action the Gallup organization received a weak response. Only 52 percent of respondents expressed support—down from the 57 percent support in May of 1978—with 23 percent opposition and 25 percent with no opinion.[25] By 1987, in the Gallup Poll commissioned by Cronin, public support for a national initiative process had dwindled to 48 percent and opposition had grown to 41 percent. Cronin still concluded that "the idea plainly attracts more support than opposition."[26]

The decline in public and congressional interest was not the only factor in the movement's demise. Telschow and Forster were reportedly discouraged by the lack of support from their traditional allies in the public interest community in Washington who, they said, perceived the idea as a threat to their interests.[27]

Commenting on this explanation, *Megatrends* author John Naisbitt wrote in his 1984 book:

> Perhaps. But what is a far greater barrier to the national initiative idea is that it is simply out of tune with the larger and far more powerful trend to decentralization. A national initiative would be a highly centralized process. Initiatives are much more appropriate to the state and city level, where citizens are deciding by popular vote issues that only they will have to live with.[28]

There is no better affirmation of Naisbitt's observation than California's Proposition 13, which passed by a two-to-one margin in June of 1978, nearly a year after Abourezk introduced his national initiative constitutional amendment in the Senate. Proposition 13 garnered 100,000 more votes than all the votes cast for governor in the same election. The initiative, pioneered by Howard Jarvis and Paul Gann, cut California's property taxes by 57 percent to just 1 percent of appraised value, resulting in a $7-billion revenue loss for the state. Passage of the tax limitation proposition was a shot heard around the nation if not the world.

In the immediate aftermath of the Proposition 13 victory, there was a flurry of activity in many states for tax limiting or spending lid measures. Some were initiated by state legislators and governors hoping to preempt voter "tax revolts" at the polls, and others were sponsored as initiatives in states having such a process. However, as Naisbitt recounts, by mid-1979 "the movement for spending lids was definitely cooling down." Voters seemed to realize that "most states did not have a huge financial surplus to lean on." By late 1979 all existing spending lids were in the South or West; eastern and midwestern states were rejecting similar proposals. The real benchmark of this reversal was California's rejection of Proposition 9 ("Jarvis II," as it was called), which would have cut state income tax more than 50 percent. Although the map of support for tax limitation changed only slightly after Proposition 13, that measure was truly significant. According to Naisbitt, it signaled "the voters' discovery of the awesome power of the initiative." In 1979 alone more than 300 initiatives appeared across the country on such issues as the disposal of nonreturnable bottles and cans, and nuclear power plants.[29]

A Congressional Research Service survey of state initiatives between 1976 and 1992 reveals that of 495 initiatives on the ballot, 216, or 43.5 percent, passed. The most popular initiatives were in the areas of budgets, spending, and taxes (134); nuclear power, hazardous waste (37); lottery, gambling (31); crime and punishment (27); term limitations (20); and redistricting and legislative powers (20).[30]

In the Congress the passage of Proposition 13 sparked new interest in budget reforms, notwithstanding the relative infancy of the Congressional Budget and Impoundment Control Act of 1974. And the mood for making government more fiscally responsible and accountable did not fizzle nationally in 1980 as it had in the states, perhaps in part because Ronald Reagan had made the seemingly anomalous positions of balancing the budget and cutting taxes a centerpiece of his presidential campaign in that year.

The most popular of the budgetary reforms was a proposed constitutional amendment to require a balanced budget. Whereas in the 94th Congress (1975–77), only thirty such constitutional amendments were introduced, in the 95th Congress (1977–79), seventy-six were introduced, twenty-five of them after the passage of Proposition 13 in June of 1978. By the 96th Congress (1979–81), the number of balanced budget constitutional amendments introduced in the two houses had grown to 94.[31]

President Reagan could not deliver on his promise of balancing the budget, and federal deficits began to balloon in the 1980s. Public and congressional support for budget balancing legislative devices, as well as a constitutional amendment, grew proportionately. The Congress enacted one such process, the Gramm-Rudman "Balanced Budget and Emergency Deficit Control Act," in 1985 and another, the "Budget Enforcement Act," in 1990 as part of the budget agreement between President George Bush and the Congress. Constitutional amendments to balance the budget were forced to House floor votes by discharge petitions (requiring signatures of a majority of House members) in 1982, 1990, 1992, and 1994, falling forty-six, seven, nine, and twelve votes short of the necessary two-thirds majority for passage, respectively. The Senate also rejected balanced budget constitutional amendments in 1994, 1995, and 1997, falling short of the two-thirds requirement by four votes, one vote, and one vote, respectively. In 1995 the House easily passed a constitutional amendment for a balanced budget, one of the tenets of the new Republican majority's 100-day Contract with America agenda for the 104th Congress. Two years later the Congress struck an agreement with President Bill Clinton and enacted a package of spending and tax cuts to achieve a balanced budget by the year 2002.

Assessments of State Initiative Experiences

State governments are the laboratories of democracy, where some experiments succeed, some fail, and others have mixed or uncertain results. Even successful democratic experiments will produce different results if conducted under slightly different conditions, in different environments, or on a different scale.

The state initiative and referendum experiment has been relatively successful. It works reasonably well, it is still popular with most citizens in those states that have it, and it has not produced any memorably disastrous results—at least none that has survived court challenges.

However, as the use of state initiatives and referendums has grown in recent years, new questions have arisen as to their efficacy and desirability. They have mutated from their original conception. No longer is the initiative and referendum viewed as a "reserve power" to be used only in limited circumstances when state legislatures are not responsive to the will of the people. Today they are often used as a weapon of first rather than last resort.

As David Magleby observes, the great surge in the use of the initiative process since the mid-1970s was due mainly to its rediscovery by issue activists eager to further their policy objectives. They saw the initiative process not merely as a means to pass new laws in particular states, but as a way to bring national attention to their causes. At the outset of the renascent movement, conservatives used the initiative movement to promote tax cutting and liberals to spur interest in the nuclear freeze. Politicians used the device to bolster their political careers, stimulate voters' interest, and raise money from like-minded activists. The movement was perpetuated by initiative industry professionals engaged in a multitude of activities that became essential to success: professional managers, petition circulators, media consultants, pollsters, litigation lawyers, direct mail fund-raisers, and petition collectors. "The growth in the initiative industry raises questions about whether the process is any longer a grass-roots process," writes Magleby, noting "the initiative industry's efforts to increase business by proposing its own measures."[32]

Large amounts of money are spent to pass or defeat various initiatives. In 1988, for instance, $101 million was spent in California on five insurance initiatives. (The California governor's race in 1990 cost only $29 million.) In 1988 the cigarette industry spent $21 million in California opposing a tobacco tax increase proposition. Two-thirds of the money spent on propositions in California was from business interests, while only 12 percent was contributed by individuals. An examination of the eighteen most expensive ballot initiatives in California reveals that 83 percent of the money came from business interests and only 8 percent from individuals. In the 1992 election alone in California, 67 percent of the money came in contributions of $100,000 or more, and 37 percent in contributions of a million or more dollars.[33]

Most of this "big money" is spent on defeating ballot initiatives, and such efforts have yielded a 75 percent success rate for the wealthy interests involved. On the other hand, "big money" has only about a 25 percent success rate in promoting ballot initiatives.[34]

The 1987 Gallup Poll commissioned by Cronin reveals that 63 percent of the American people would favor limiting the amount such organized interests and wealthy individuals could spend to support their side of a ballot issue.[35] Although eighteen states at one time had laws limiting or prohibiting corporate contributions or spending in initiative campaigns, the Supreme Court has since declared these limits unconstitutional. The most prominent case was *The First National Bank of Boston et. al. v. Bellotti* in April of 1978.[36]

Another criticism leveled at the initiative process is that it is often used to target racial and other minorities, whether blacks, women, gays, immigrants, or the non-English speaking. Is direct legislation a danger to the rights of minorities? "The answer seems to be yes, unless the courts are able and willing to protect these groups from attacks by direct legislation," writes Magleby.[37] Law professor Derrick Bell notes that the referendum has been the most effect facilitator of the bias, discrimination, and prejudice that have marred American democracy from its beginning.[38] Barbara S. Gamble of the University of Michigan, in a survey of three decades of initiatives and referendums involving five major civil rights areas, concludes that voters have approved over three-quarters of such measures that restrict civil rights, compared with a one-third approval rate of all initiatives and referendums.[39]

Another factor militating against more ballot initiatives is the length of the ballots and the resulting confusion of voters. On a 1988 ballot San Francisco voters were confronted with fifty-two separate questions—twenty-nine statewide propositions and twenty-three local questions. The pamphlet accompanying this state ballot ran 159 pages, a record broken two years later when California voters were aided by a two-volume, 221-page ballot pamphlet.[40] Woodrow Wilson would probably have a difficult time today maintaining his support for both the "short ballot" and initiatives and referendums since the former was based on the premise that the more items on a ballot, the more citizens were discouraged from voting.

Many proponents of such direct legislation argue that it increases the interest of voters and turnout at elections by giving them a greater stake in their government. Magleby, however, concludes that "initiatives do not systematically increase turn-out." He cites a study of initiatives in Maine, which permits initiatives when candidates are on the ballot in even-numbered years and when there are no contested offices in odd-numbered years. The study found turnout much lower in odd-numbered years.[41]

A comparison of turnout of voting age populations in states that have initiatives compared with states that do not suggests that initiatives may increase turnout (see Table 9.3). The average voter turnout in the twenty-six initiative states in 1992 and 1996 was roughly 60 percent and 52.5 percent, respectively, whereas in noninitiative states it was approximately 56.3 percent and 50.4 percent. However, these statistics hide the wide disparity of turnout within each category. For instance, the most publicized state having initiatives, California, had a turnout of 49.1 percent and 43.3 percent in those two years, well below the national average, and well below the average turnout in noninitiative states. (See Appendix A for a breakdown of initiative and noninitiative state turnout.)

Taking a closer look at California in 1996, one can see that the drop-off rate between total turnout and those voting on propositions roughly conforms to that found in a survey of three states (California, Massachusetts, and Washington) between 1970 and 1992. That survey showed an average drop of between 8 percent and 17 percent on propositions, compared with an average drop-off rate of between 2 and 12 percent in candidate elections.[42] Similarly, in 1996, the drop-off rate on the two most controversial and most highly voted-

Table 9.3
A Comparison of Voter Turnout in States with and without an Initiative and/or Referendum Process, 1992 and 1996

	Percentage of voting age population voting	
Item	**1992**	**1996**
National average	55.24	48.99
States with initiative and/or referendum process	59.90	52.46
States without initiative and/or referendum process	56.27	50.37
Difference between states with and without initiative/referendum	–3.63	–2.09

Sources: Voter turnout data provided by the Committee for the Study of the American Electorate; list of states having an initiative and/or referendum process was provided by Congressional Research Service.

on propositions in California, Proposition 215 (to permit the medicinal use of marijuana) and Proposition 209 (to prohibit affirmative action in state programs), was nearly 13 percent. The highest drop-off rate for the fifteen propositions was 17.6 percent on Proposition 216 (relating to health fees; see Table 9.4). What all this consistently demonstrates is that the top candidate races are a greater draw than even the most publicized and controversial ballot initiatives, and not vice versa.

California is one of a few states that permit direct legislation to be voted on in special elections, usually in November of odd-numbered years when many local governments are electing their officials or deciding local measures. Magleby cites special elections in 1973, when Governor Reagan put a tax-cut measure on the ballot; 1979, when Governor Jerry Brown put a spending limit on the ballot, and 1993, when Governor Pete Wilson put a school voucher measure on the ballot. According to Magleby, California's special election experience demonstrates that only about one in four eligible voters vote in special elections. Special election voters are not very representative of voters in general elections because they tend to be better informed and more politically knowledgeable.[43]

Finally, the initiative process is criticized for not dealing with the issues that voters consider to be the most important. In 1992, for instance, California voters were most concerned about the state's economy and unemployment, and yet

Table 9.4
Votes Cast for California Ballot Propositions in 1996 as a Percentage of Total Votes Cast in the State

Proposition number	Subject of ballot proposition	Votes cast on proposition and outcome: Pass (P); Fail (F)	Percentage of total votes cast in the state[a]
204	water bond	8,655,517 (P)	86.4
205	jail bond	8,528,635 (F)	85.1
206	veterans' bond	8,425,657 (P)	84.1
207	frivolous lawsuits	8,471,078 (F)	84.5
208	Common Cause limit	8,431,417 (P)	84.2
209	CCRI (affirmative action)	8,724,015 (P)	87.1
210	minimum wage	8,723,619 (P)	87.1
211	security fraud	8,504,007 (F)	84.9
212	CalPIRG limit	8,344,010 (F)	83.3
213	uninsured drivers	8,554,163 (P)	85.4
214	health care regulation	8,354,818 (F)	83.4
215	marijuana	8,746,721 (P)	87.3
216	health regulation fees	8,257,511 (F)	82.4
217	top tax bracket	8,398,201 (F)	83.8
218	property tax limit	8,310,803 (P)	82.9

[a]Total number of votes cast was 10,019,484.

Sources: Data on voter turnout were from the Committee for the Study of the American Electorate; data on proposition results were from the Web site of California's secretary of state, Bill James (http://ss.ca.gov/vote96/html/vote/prop/page.961106073319.html).

none of the initiatives on the ballot was aimed at either issue nor could it be expected that such complex problems could be dealt with through such a process.[44]

One observer of California's initiative process, Eugene Lee, concludes that the direct democracy device has contributed to the shortcomings of the legislature, the executive branch, and the electoral process: "The initiative is part of the problem. Turned on its head, 'direct democracy' is no longer democratic."[45]

While such an assessment may be overly harsh, it has an element of truth. The modern-day operation of the initiative process would not be recognizable to its progenitors of a century ago. They intended that it be used only selectively as a safety valve when representative democracy is not functioning properly. The proliferation of complex, confusing, and even conflicting initiatives on the same ballot goes far beyond the safety valve category. Voters in initiative states are well aware of the shortcomings of the process, yet few would willingly relinquish the power to exercise it. Similarily, few would enthusiastically take on the additional responsibility of voting on national legislation as well.

Notes

1. David Magleby, "Direct Elections in the American States," in *Referendums around the World* ed. David Butler and Austin Ranney (Washington, D.C.: The AEI Press, 1994), 232.
2. Remarks of Sen. James Abourezk, *Congressional Record*, vol. 123, pt. 18, July 11, 1977, 22276–77.
3. Ibid., 22277.
4. Ibid., from text of H. J. Res. 67 inserted at 22279.
5. "Voter Initiative Constitutional Amendment: Hearings before the Subcommittee on the Constitution, of the Committee on the Judiciary, United States Senate, Ninety-Fifth Congress, First Session, on S. J. Res. 67, December 13 and 14, 1977" (Washington, D.C.: U.S. Government Printing Office, 1978), 632 and 620.
6. Rhodes Cook, "Debate Opens on Initiative System for Enacting New Federal Laws," *Congressional Quarterly Weekly Report*, Dec. 24, 1977, 2655.
7. "Voter Initiative Constitutional Amendment: Hearings," 1–2.
8. Ibid., 3.
9. Ibid., 7–8.
10. Ibid., 8.
11. Ibid., 17.
12. Ibid., 646. In the hearing record see George Gallup, "National Initiative Pro cess Favored by 57 percent of Voters," *Washington Post*, May 14, 1978.
13. Ibid., statement of the Honorable James R. Jones of Oklahoma, 19.
14. Ibid.
15. Ibid., testimony of Professor Peter Bachrach, Department of Political Science, Temple University, Philadelphia, Pa., 59–60.
16. Ibid., testimony of Roger Telschow, co-director, Initiative America, Dec. 14, 1977, 74.
17. Ibid., 75, 77.
18. Jack Kemp, *An American Renaissance: A Strategy for the 1980s* (New York: Berkeley Publishing Co., 1981).

19. The data have been derived from searches of the *Congressional Record* indexes for each of the Congresses named.

20. Thomas E. Cronin, *Direct Democracy: The Politics of Initiative, Referendum, and Recall* (Cambridge: Harvard University Press, 1989), 177.

21. Summary based on reading text of H. R. 7934, 96th Cong., 2d sess., Aug. 18, 1980.

22. Cronin, *Direct Democracy*, 177.

23. Ibid., 178.

24. Cronin, *Direct Democracy*, 187.

25. Ibid., 175.

26. Ibid., 175–76.

27. John Naisbitt, *Megatrends: Ten New Directions Transforming Our Lives* (New York: Warner Books, 1984), 170.

28. Ibid., 170–71.

29. Ibid., 166–70.

30. Oakley and Neale, "Citizen Initiative Proposals," 3.

31. Richard A. Davis, "Proposed Amendments to the Constitution of the United States of America Introduced in Congress from the 91st Congress, 1st Session, through the 98th Congress, 2nd Session, January 1969–December 1984," Congressional Research Service Report 85-36 GOV, Feb. 1, 1985, 91–143.

32. Magleby, "Direct Legislation," 234–35.

33. Ibid., 242–43.

34. Cronin, *Direct Democracy*, 109.

35. Ibid., 190.

36. Ibid., 101–2.

37. Magleby, "Direct Legislation," 241.

38. Cronin, *Direct Democracy*, 94.

39. Barbara S. Gamble, "Putting Civil Rights to a Popular Vote," *American Journal of Political Science* 41 (Jan. 1997): 245–69.

40. Magleby, "Direct Legislation," 248.

41. Ibid., 245.

42. Ibid., 246–47.

43. Ibid., 246.

44. Ibid., 240.

45. Eugene C. Lee, "Representative Government and the Initiative Process," in *California Policy Choices*, ed. John Kirlin and Donald Winkler (Los Angeles: University of Southern California, School of Public Administration, 1990), vol. 6, 248, cited in Magleby, "Direct Legislation," 256.

10

The Road to the Republican Revolution

ON November 8, 1994, the American people wielded their ultimate weapon, their vote. Its power was unmistakable, ending Democrats' long-standing control of Congress and establishing Republican control of both houses for the first time in forty years.

In the House of Representatives, Republicans gained fifty-two seats, giving them a 230-204 edge over Democrats. (Their number increased to 236 later in 1995 with five members switching parties and a special election.) Thirty-four Democratic incumbents lost, including Speaker Tom Foley, Ways and Means Committee chairman Dan Rostenkowski, Judiciary Committee chairman Jack Brooks, and sixteen freshmen. In the Senate the GOP added eight seats (including a party-switch the day after the election), giving them a 53-47 edge over Democrats.

The Republicans' unexpected rout of the Democrats has been variously described as "historic," "revolutionary," and like a "tsunami" (the Japanese word for a tidal wave)., The 36.6 million votes cast for House Republicans in 1994 did represent the largest surge in history of one party's vote from mid-term to mid-term election—a nine million vote increase over 1990, beating the previous record of a 6.3 million vote surge by the Democrats from the 1930 to the 1934 mid-term elections.[1]

Several causes are cited—ranging from anti-Clinton sentiment to anti-Democratic-Congress, anti-big-government, and pro-Republican views—with each given varying importance depending on the analyst involved. Regardless of how one weights these factors, they all boil down to the public's general disenchantment with the direction of the country and the government under unified Democratic control, and a demand for a clear change in direction that could only be provided by a different party. It was a truly national election, unusual in itself for a nonpresidential year. However, it is doubtful the same outcome would have resulted had Republicans not capitalized on three Rs to run strong, individual races: recruitment, resources, and reapportionment.

Building the Road

The Republican takeover of Congress in 1994 had its roots in the fertile soil of public discontent plowed up during the 1992 national election campaigns. The explanation for the defeat of incumbent president George Bush by Arkansas governor Bill Clinton was simple, as obvious as writing on the wall—in this case the wall of Clinton's campaign war room in Little Rock, where a sign read: "It's the economy, stupid." The national unemployment rate was running 7.5 percent, up from the 5.5 percent rate when Bush was elected president in 1988. American workers' anxiety was palpable after a rash of corporate downsizings and new uncertainties generated by the information age and global economy. The federal deficit for fiscal year 1992 was a record high of $290 billion, compared with the $155 billion deficit Bush inherited when he took office. Bush's job approval rating had dropped from 89 percent in the immediate aftermath of the Persian Gulf War in March of 1991 to 33 percent in October of 1992.

But more was at play in the 1992 election results than the predictable tendency of citizens to vote their pocketbooks during an economic downturn. Ross Perot's capture of 19 percent of the popular vote was the most for a third-party candidate since Progressive Theodore Roosevelt won 27 percent in 1912. Perot's support signaled deeper unrest among the electorate than a pocketbook protest could explain. The voters were sending a larger message that questioned both the country's future course and the government's ability to do anything about it.

Perot's popularity reflected a rising tide of public distrust and anger over government and the entire Washington establishment. In June of 1992, for example, a *Washington Post*–ABC News Poll showed the worst numbers ever recorded since the Watergate crisis on whether the public thought the country was on the right track: only 14 percent thought it was "going in the right direction," while 83 percent said it was heading "the wrong direction."

Both Clinton and Perot ran as anti-status-quo outsiders, committed to turning the country's course around by changing Washington's way of doing things. Their campaigns reflected not only national economic anxieties, but widespread and growing public distrust of government and everyone in it. The 1992

"Trust in Government Index" of the University of Michigan's American National Election Studies revealed a trust score on four questions of just 29 points (out of a possible 100)—identical to the Watergate year of 1974, as well as to the years 1978 and 1990. In 1980 the trust index was even lower, at 27, though it received temporary, Reaganesque, "morning in America" boosts to 38 and 47 in 1984 and 1986—still considerably lower than the high scores of 52 and 61 registered in 1964 and 1966, respectively.

Taken separately, the 1992 results of the four questions composing the trust index are even more disturbing. Only 29 percent of the people thought the government could be trusted to do what was right most of the time or just about always. Seventy-five percent thought government was "pretty much run by few big interests looking out for themselves," and only 20 percent thought it was being run for the benefit of all—record high and low percentages for that question up to that time. Sixty-seven percent thought "people in the government waste a lot of money we pay in taxes." On another question 46 percent thought quite a few government officials were crooked, compared with 44 percent who thought not many were.[2]

In early 1991, when Bush was still riding high in the polls, some political observers thought that Republicans had a good chance of taking control of Congress in the 1992 elections, especially given the powerful combination of favorable redistricting results and the negative impact of congressional scandals. However, with Bush's approval ratings and the economy both in sharp decline by late 1992, the pessimistic, even angry mood of the public did not produce the widespread anti-incumbent sentiment many experts had predicted. The public remained focused, laser-like on the president, the one primarily responsible, in its view, for the sorry state of affairs, and this did have a significant drag on many Republican congressional hopefuls.

Republicans picked up only ten seats in the House and actually lost a seat in the Senate in 1992. Forty-three House incumbents lost their primary or general election races, including thirty Democrats and thirteen Republicans, while the remaining 325 incumbents running for reelection won. That 88.3 percent incumbent reelection rate was the first time the rate had dipped below 90 percent since 1966. The reelection rate for House incumbents would have been even lower except for the record-setting retirement of sixty-five members, including forty-one Democrats and twenty-four Republicans, many of whom feared defeat because of their publicized overdrafts at the House bank. Seventy-seven of the incumbents who either retired or were defeated represented one-fourth of the 269 House members whose overdrafts at the House bank had been publicly disclosed.[3] As a consequence, the freshman class of the 103d Congress in 1993 was 110 members strong (63 Democrats and 47 Republicans)—the largest freshman class since the 1948 class of 118 new members.

The other reason congressional Democrats escaped a harsher than expected fate at the polls in 1992 may have been voters' unconscious desire to give the new Democratic president a Congress of the same party to produce the changes he had promised. A Republican Congress might only have perpetuated legislative gridlock, one source of public frustration with Washington during the previous Republican administrations and a prominent issue during the campaign.

After a meeting with Democratic congressional leaders in Little Rock on November 16, 1992, President-elect Clinton promised an end to the "Cold War" between the president and Congress, and House majority leader Richard Gephardt triumphantly proclaimed, "Gridlock is over, and cooperation and teamwork have begun."[4] Albert Gore, the vice president–elect, echoed this mood three days later in Washington, following a meeting with the bipartisan congressional leadership: "If you listen carefully, you can hear today the first sounds of gridlock loosening."[5]

The new administration posed a unique challenge to congressional Republicans, most of whom had never served under a Democratic president. Less than 20 percent of House Republicans and fewer than half of the Republican senators had been in Congress when Jimmy Carter was president. As California Republican representative David Dreier, a member of the class of 1980, put it, "I'm moving into uncharted waters here."[6] The dilemma was clear. On the one hand, if Republicans were too confrontational and obstructive in dealing with the president's legislative agenda, they could suffer a voter backlash at the polls in 1994. On the other hand, if they were too cooperative in helping to pass the president's programs, they would make it difficult for voters to distinguish their views from those of congressional Democrats. How could they persuade voters there was any need to change the party makeup of the Congress?

Fifth-term Texas Republican Richard Armey of Texas made no bones about where he stood just after the election:

> The politics of confrontation works, and the politics of appeasement fails. What are we going to do—bargain with them? . . . What do we say, "We'll accept your principle if you'll do just a little bit less of it?" I think it's more productive for the party to say, "Look, you're fundamentally incorrect."[7]

Armey subsequently challenged and replaced the incumbent chairman of the Republican Conference, Jerry Lewis of California, whom he claimed was soft on Democrats. This was another sign of the combative course the party would take, and it put Armey right behind Republican whip Newt Gingrich of Georgia in the leadership hierarchy. Gingrich, along with Representatives Bob Walker and Vin Weber, had founded the Conservative Opportunity Society

(COS) back in 1983 for the explicit purpose of discrediting the Democratic-controlled House and promoting conservative Republican alternatives, primarily through special order speeches broadcast by C-SPAN at the end of each day's legislative proceedings.

While still a backbencher, Gingrich made a national name for himself by filing ethics charges against Speaker Jim Wright in 1988, eventually leading to Wright's resignation from the speakership and the House in June of 1989 (by which time Gingrich had been elected whip). In 1986 Gingrich had taken from former Delaware governor Pete DuPont the reins of GOPAC, an organization dedicated to developing a farm team of Republican candidates at the state level. His conversion of GOPAC into a major recruitment and educational force would prove instrumental in building toward a Republican majority in the House.

Part of the House Republicans' new confrontational approach was to highlight the extent to which Democrats had abused their trusteeship of Congress. Republicans cited mismanagement, unresponsiveness, corruption, and procedural abuses at the expense of not simply minority rights, but of representative government and the national interest. The charges were not new to the long-suffering Republican minority. They were perennial. Indeed, they had been sounded by Democrats when Republicans controlled the Congress for two decades around the turn of the century. What was different this time was that things actually had gotten worse. The media and the public were beginning to pay some attention to the charges of an unresponsive Congress. Consequently, Republicans were pressing their case against the Democrats more aggressively and vocally, and they were beginning to see results both inside the Congress and out.

The "Republican revolution" of 1994 was more than the public overthrow of the established political order in the Congress. It was the culmination of a long-simmering, internal revolt by minority party Republicans against what they viewed as an increasingly oppressive, arrogant, and out-of-touch majority leadership bent on using and abusing power for its own self-aggrandizement and perpetuation.

While partisan rhetoric is often cast in such hyperbolic terms for maximum effect, by the fall of 1994 enough of these negative images of Congress had gained popular acceptance that they were no longer dismissed out-of-hand as political sour grapes. This time all the necessary conditions of climate and soil had came together to produce the perfect grape for wine-making. Republican revolutionaries were connecting with the masses for the first time in forty-two years with a message that rang true and promised positive change.

In the preceding 102d Congress (1991–93) freshmen House Republicans cast themselves in the revolutionary vanguard, drawing on the guerilla warfare tactics honed in previous Congresses by Gingrich's COS troops. This "gang of seven" was composed of John Boehner of Ohio, Rick Santorum of Pennsylvania, Jim Nussle of Iowa, Charles Taylor of North Carolina, Frank Riggs and John Doolittle of California, and Scott Klug of Wisconsin. They began by clamoring for various House reforms, but gained national recognition by exploiting the House bank scandal that came to light in September of 1991. Nussle even went so far as to wear a paper bag over his head during a one-minute floor speech, saying he was too ashamed of the House to show his face. The gang eventually forced full disclosure of the names of members with overdrafts by using "question of privilege resolutions," even though it jeopardized the reelection chances of several of their Republican colleagues, including Gingrich.

Member abuses at the House post office and restaurants also came to light during the scandal-racked 102d Congress. The Democratic leadership acted belatedly and incrementally in each instance, eventually caving to the calls for full disclosure and making some administrative adjustments. These included closing down the members' bank, appointing a professional, nonpartisan House administrator and inspector general, and turning the House post office over to the U.S. Postal Service. During consideration of the Democrats' House administrative reform resolution on April 9, 1992, Republican leader Bob Michel charged that the package was "a sham and a charade" and that "the real scandal is the way Congress does its legislative business." But the Republicans' substitute package that included their traditional proposals to overhaul committee and floor procedures was defeated on a 159-254 party-line vote.[8]

By March of 1992, the embarrassment caused by mounting scandals and the resulting pressures for more comprehensive reforms had grown so great that Speaker Tom Foley finally gave the go-ahead for creation of a bipartisan and bicameral Joint Committee on the Organization of Congress, a proposal he had long resisted. As introduced the previous July by Representatives Lee Hamilton (D-Ind.) and Bill Gradison (R-Ohio), and Sens. David Boren (D-Okla.) and Peter Domenici (R-N.M.), the bipartisan resolution called for the joint committee "to make a full and complete study of the organization and operation of the Congress of the United States and to recommend improvements . . . with a view toward strengthening the effectiveness of the Congress, simplifying its operations, improving its relationships with and oversight of other branches of the United States Government, and improving the orderly consideration of legislation."[9]

The measure passed the House on June 18 by a vote of 412 to 4, and the Senate by voice vote on July 30. On August 6, just before the summer recess, the House approved the Senate version of the joint committee resolution by a voice vote, even though the Senate had dropped a bipartisan, House-passed provision to permit the House members of the joint committee to make interim recommendations for House reforms to their respective party caucuses not later than November 6, 1992—well before the caucus organizational meetings for the 103d Congress in December. In its place the Senate inserted a provision prohibiting the joint committee from conducting any business prior to November 15.[10] This was a very curious and rare instance in which one house of Congress altered a legislative provision that had been approved by and applied exclusively to the other body. It is highly unlikely the Senate would have made the change without the active encouragement of someone in the House majority leadership.

Republicans were nevertheless assured during debate that the Senate language would not prohibit the House members of the joint committee from informally developing recommendations prior to the election, and then formally approving and forwarding them to the caucuses after November 15. Although Minority Leader Michel appointed the six Republican members of the joint committee on September 14, Speaker Foley waited until after the final gavel had fallen on the 102d Congress on October 9 before he quietly announced the names of the Democratic members. Foley did not want to leave any window of opportunity for the newly appointed House members of the joint committee to meet before they left town for their election campaigns.

The primary authors of the resolution creating the joint committee were appointed to lead it: Boren and Hamilton as co-chairs, and Domenici and Gradison as co-vice chairs. Shortly after taking the oath in January, Gradison unexpectedly resigned his House seat to take a job with a national health insurance association. Minority Leader Michel subsequently elevated forty-year-old David Dreier to the top House Republican slot on the joint committee. The joint committee did not hold its first organization meeting until January 6, 1993, soon after the 103d Congress convened.

By then, Democratic leaders felt the worst was behind them. The fact that they had suffered only minor setbacks at the polls was surely a sign that they had successfully weathered the storm of scandals and calls for more radical congressional reforms. With a new president of their own party, they would have their hands full processing the president's legislative agenda. Still, the large new class of freshman Democrats in the House was an unknown commodity, and their support could not be taken for granted.

House Democratic leaders decided to take the offensive by visiting their new charges at three regional meetings shortly after the election. Among other things, the freshmen were warned against participating in a proposed bipartisan freshman conference on November 24 in Omaha, where reforms of Congress were to be a major topic. At the Los Angeles meeting, Speaker Foley jokingly answered a question on the conference with his own question: "Where's Omaha?"[11] But most of the House and Senate freshmen were more intent on changing the economy and health care than on changing Congress. Freshman senator-elect and former representative Byron Dorgan of North Dakota observed that "people who ran on changing Congress by and large were not successful. The people who ran on changing the economy won."[12] Freshman representative Bob Filner of California said, "If it's the way Congress is structured that's blocking action, then that needs to be changed." "But," he added, "my sense is that what's blocked action is divided government."[13]

No urgent connection was perceived between policy priorities such as the economy and health and congressional structures and procedures. The handful of Democrats who had run on congressional reform themes were told to be patient, present their reform proposals later to their caucus and the joint committee, and wait until Congress had acted on the president's priority legislation before pressing for any internal reforms.

As a consequence, the changes reported from the Democratic Caucus and considered on January 5, 1993, the opening day of the 103d Congress, were modest and status-quo-oriented for the most part. Through a change in caucus rules, the Democrats had already imposed a lower cap on the number of subcommittees for each standing committee, resulting in the elimination of sixteen subcommittees. Ironically, despite the elimination of sixteen subcommittees and, later, four select committees, the number of House committee staff in the first session of the 103d Congress increased by 121, growing from 2,110 in 1992 to 2,231 in 1993.[14]

Unlike House Democrats, who approached reforms cautiously, House Republicans unveiled a panoply of rules changes on the opening day of the 103d Congress under the banner "A Mandate for Change in the People's House." The introductory mandate document contained the following critique of Democratic Congresses:

> The Democrats' control of the House of Representatives for 58 of the last 62 years has produced a bloated, muscle-bound bureaucracy characterized by a multiplicity of semi-autonomous subcommittees, multitudes of staff, a muddle of tangled jurisdictional lines, and a multiplication of mud-fights over turf.[15]

The mandate's forty-eight-point program included proposals to abolish proxy voting, reduce committee staff by 30 percent, limit committee chairmen and ranking minority members to three terms, apply private sector labor laws to the House, abolish all select committees, and direct the Joint Committee on the Organization of Congress to report recommendations to realign committee jurisdictions.[16]

The Democratic caucus did report one proposed change in House rules that generated considerable controversy and Republican opposition. The proposal authorized voting on the House floor by five nonmembers of the House under certain conditions. Specifically, the rule change authorized the delegates from the District of Columbia, Guam, American Samoa, and the Virgin Islands, and the resident commissioner from Puerto Rico, to vote in the Committee of the Whole. In this committee consisting of all House members, procedures are streamlined. Most floor amendments are debated and voted on in the Committee of the Whole before a measure is reported back to the House for final passage. (For a further discussion of the Committee of the Whole, see Chapters 4 and 7.)

Since all five of these nonmembers were Democrats, Republicans viewed the change as nothing more than an arrogant majority grabbing power to bolster its own voting strength. They also charged it violated the Constitution, which vested all legislative powers in Congress, the House of Representatives of which was to be comprised of members elected by the people of the several states. The constitutional issue had even made some Democrats nervous. At the last minute the proposal was changed to permit an immediate re-vote in the House on any amendment in the Committee of the Whole on which the votes of the delegates were decisive. Rep. Bob Walker thus explained this escape-hatch on close votes: "When it counts, it does not count, and when it does not count, it counts"—a description later cited as the rule's saving feature by the federal district court judge who upheld the constitutionality of the rule.[17]

Notwithstanding the inclusion of this delegate vote–nullifying device, twenty-seven Democrats voted against their own party's House rules resolution on final adoption. This was the largest number of members from either party to break party ranks on the opening-day rules vote since 1971.[18] By 1993 the old, conservative coalition had long since faded as a factor in opening-day fights over House rules, and party-line voting had been the norm for more than twenty years. Something new was afoot here, and it was not the resurrection of the old voting bloc of southern Democrats: nine of the twenty-seven dissidents were northern Democrats.

The Democratic leadership got its next wake-up call on January 26, 1993, when the House surprisingly rejected a leadership-backed resolution to extend the life of the Select Committee on Narcotics for two years—the first of four resolutions reported by the Rules Committee to extend the life of all select committees from the previous Congress.

Although intended to be temporary entities that conduct short-term oversight tasks, make their recommendations, and go out of business, select committees in recent years had taken on an almost permanent aura. The Narcotics Committee had existed since 1976, seventeen years. The Select Committee on Aging even longer—eighteen years. The two other select committees were relative new kids on the block: Children, Youth, and Families was just ten years old, and Hunger, nine years old. Together the four select committees had expended nearly $45 million over their lifetimes, and by 1992 employed close to 100 staff.[19]

The vote against reauthorizing the narcotics select committee was 180-237, with eighty-three Democrats voting against the resolution and only fifteen Republicans voting for it. The Democratic leadership was so stung by the unexpected setback that it immediately moved to table (kill) the renewal resolutions for the other three select committees. All four select committees were later given sufficient funds for an orderly shutdown of their offices by the end of March.

Despite this setback, the Democratic leadership moved ahead in using the Rules Committee to severely restrict floor amendments on every measure brought up in the House from early February through April. In the preceding 102d Congress, 34 percent of the special rules provided for an open amendment process, while 66 percent limited amendments.[20] The leadership's push for 100 percent restrictive rules in the early months of the 103d Congress was clearly designed to hand the new president some early and easy victories with minimal delays. It worked. Such bills as the Family and Medical Leave Act, the "motor voter" bill to make voter registration more convenient, and the Hatch Act amendments to ease restrictions on federal employees' political activities quickly passed the House.

The crackdown on amendments provoked a backlash in the form of dilatory votes and other obstructionist tactics, mainly spearheaded by Republican representative Dan Burton of Indiana. To channel these frustrations and put a damper on so many time-consuming votes, the Republican leadership appointed a task force on "restrictive rules strategy" in late March headed by Solomon, the ranking Republican on the Rules Committee. Known as the Republican Leadership Task Force on Deliberative Democracy, the task force included the other Rules Committee Republicans (Jimmy Quillen, David Dreier, and Porter Goss) plus Representatives Burton, Robert Walker, Bob Livingston, Jim Saxton, Scott Klug, Lincoln Diaz-Balart, and Deborah Pryce.

On April 21 the task force unveiled "the First Report of the House Democracy Project," titled "The Decline of Deliberative Democracy in the People's House." The report noted that the task force had been created "out of a growing concern that deliberative democracy was being sacrificed on the altar of political expediency." It went on to document that only thirty-two amendments offered by twenty-one members had been allowed on the first ten bills considered by the House out of 163 amendments submitted to the Rules Committee on those bills. And it concluded that "the other 414 House Members and the roughly 248-million Americans they represent have been disenfranchised during one of the most critical stages of the legislative process."[21]

The same day the report was released, the House Republican Conference gave unanimous approval to the task force's battle plan, which included press kits, op-ed articles, and graphic depictions on the House floor of the number of open versus restrictive rules under an image of the Statue of Liberty gagged. As Solomon rightly explained to the press, "The heat is already being felt."[22] The next day House Speaker Foley told reporters that there would be open rules on major legislation beginning in a few days. As he said he had told Republican leaders, "there were circumstances that were unusual in the nature of the bills that first came up. . . . We do not intend this to be the pattern for the Congress."[23]

The Republican task force's educational efforts eventually began to yield results. Editorials in national and local newspapers criticized the Democrats' stifling of democratic deliberation in the House—something Republicans considered a major breakthrough after years of complaining with little press sympathy or public recognition.

It was not until May 5, 1993, that the first open rule of the 103d Congress was brought to the floor for consideration of the National Competitiveness Act. "Hallelujah, hallelujah," Burton rejoiced. "I don't think the open rule has ever been abused. It's baloney to say open rules waste time."[24] "That strategy may have had an effect," Rules Committee chairman Joe Moakley said of the Republican task force's efforts. "But I said all along that we were going to have open rules."[25]

Although the Rules Committee did produce more open rules over the next several months, the situation was still worse than in the previous Congress. By March of 1994, only 20 percent of the rules granted were open, and some Democrats were beginning to react publicly to the overly restrictive rule strategy. Democratic representative Charles Stenholm of Texas pulled together a coalition of Democrats from the Conservative Democratic Forum that he headed, the Mainstream Forum, and the House Fiscal Caucus to form a new organization called FROG, the Fair Rules and Openness Group.[26]

Although he shunned Solomon's invitation to join with Republicans in opposing all restrictive rules, Stenholm and the others in the informal bipartisan group had an effect: six special rules were defeated in the 103d Congress. This tied the number of rules defeated in the 100th Congress and was well above the average of less than four special rule losses in the previous ten Congresses. The main reason special rules were defeated in the 103d Congress was the denial of amendments aimed at cutting spending in authorization and appropriations bills. For example, amendments were denied on an emergency appropriations bill containing nonemergency items and on an omnibus crime bill fat with pork programs. The larger message was that the Democratic leadership was losing touch with a changing public attitude toward government, notwithstanding warnings and even antileadership votes from a growing minority within its own caucus.

The Democratic leadership suffered yet another procedural setback on September 8, 1993, when fourth-term Republican Jim Inhofe of Oklahoma collared the last of the requisite 218 signatures needed on a discharge petition to dislodge from the Rules Committee a proposed change in House rules. Inhofe's action made possible House consideration of a rule that dated back to the 1910 revolt against Speaker Cannon. Signatures on a discharge petition could not be publicly disclosed by the Clerk of the House or any member until a majority of House members had signed the petition and it was placed on the discharge calendar.[27] Republicans favored public disclosure of names on a discharge petition starting on the day the petition was filed.

Although the Democratic leadership convinced six Democrats to take their names off Inhofe's petition, it was not enough. Inhofe managed to persuade forty-five Democrats to break ranks, and he enlisted all but two Republicans. Inhofe put the effort over the top with an all-out public relations effort that won support from newspapers like the *Wall Street Journal*, talk-show hosts like Rush Limbaugh, and prominent politicians like Ross Perot.[28] After Inhofe had corralled a House majority of signatures in September, the Rules Committee held a belated hearing on his resolution. At that time Inhofe revealed that during the four-week summer recess he had appeared on sixty-nine talk shows. "It wasn't much of a recess," he observed. Moreover, he claimed to have over 100 editorials from around the country in support of his proposal, and only two opposed—the *Boston Globe* (in Chairman Moakley's home district) and the *Tulsa World*, "my hometown newspaper."[29]

During the House floor debate on his resolution on September 28, Inhofe termed the discharge rule's secrecy requirement "a corrupt rule . . . a rule of fraud . . . a rule of hypocrisy." Rules Committee chairman Moakley countered by predicting that the revised rule would "alter the delicate balance that has existed over the past 60 years in the discharge process." But because a House majority clearly favored the rule change, he would not plead with other members to join him in casting a 'No' vote.[30] That signaled the leadership's "white flag" concession of certain defeat, freeing Democrats to vote as they pleased. The House adopted the resolution overwhelmingly, 384-40. No Republicans and only forty Democrats voted against it.[31]

Contrary to some dire predictions, the new sunshine discharge rule did not open the floodgates for special interest legislation to bypass committees. Only one other petition out of twenty-five filed gained the necessary 218 signatures during the remainder of the 103d Congress. That was Representative Stenholm's petition on the balanced budget constitutional amendment discussed in the previous chapter. It was the same popular proposition that had been discharged just two years earlier when the signature secrecy rule was still in effect.

Passage of the discharge "sunshine" rule over majority leadership objections was certainly not what Speaker Foley had in mind when he promised his restive Democratic freshmen in early September that October would be "reform month." He was thinking instead of the recommendations of the Joint Committee on the Organization of Congress, as well as campaign, lobbying, and gift reform legislation. As Foley put it in a letter to the freshmen, "In concentrating the scheduling of all these measures in one month, I believe that Democrats can underscore dramatically our commitment to making government fairer, more open and more responsive to the people's needs."[32]

The Joint Committee Splits

The "reform month" of October 1993 came and went without a whiff of reform on the House floor. The joint committee had fallen behind schedule as a result of partisan squabbling during an August retreat of joint committee members. The ever-patient House co-chairman Lee Hamilton felt pressure from Republican members of the joint committee for a strong bill, and he was encountering difficulties from fellow Democrats in trying to cobble together a respectable package. November proved slightly more productive with the House passing a campaign finance reform bill and a lobby disclosure and congressional gift restriction bill.

Tensions were so high between the House and Senate membership of the joint committee that the two bodies met separately to report their own bills. Since the August retreat, some of the House Democratic members of the joint committee had made clear that they would not go along with any of the House reforms proposed by the Republicans unless the Senate Republicans in turn agreed to changing the filibuster rule. The Senate half of the joint committee reported its reform bill on November 10 with relative ease. The House group went to work on November 16 but did not complete its prolonged and painful deliberations until November 22, just four days before the adjournment of the first session.

All told, the joint committee had taken 114 hours of testimony from 243 witnesses at 36 hearings between January and July of 1993. The majority and minority leaders of both houses were the lead-off witnesses, followed over the next six months by another 131 House members and 35 senators. In addition, the joint committee conducted a survey, with a 30 percent response rate from members and a 50 percent response rate from staff.[33] Ninety percent of the member respondents from both houses agreed that "major procedural and organizational improvements" were "needed in the way Congress conducts its legislative business." Over half of the respondents said they favored "a comprehensive realignment of the committee system."[34]

Despite the committee's self-adopted motto, "be bold," Hamilton had to take a bare-bones approach because the panel was composed of an equal number of Democrats and Republicans. This equal party representation on the panel would make it impossible to delete something which all the members of one party or the other opposed. "For this reason," he explained, "we have decided only to include in the markup draft proposals that are supported by a majority of the House Members on the Joint Committee. It seems to me that to do otherwise would have an element of unfairness about it."[35]

Co-vice-chairman Dreier had a different view: "Unlike the document marked up by our counterparts in the Senate, this bill is neither bi-partisan nor comprehensive, . . . something I profoundly regret. . . . Basically, from my perspective, we're back to ground zero."[36]

Republican Gerald Solomon of New York was even more critical of the bill: "I just have to say how deeply saddened I am that we have waited so long to really consider so little." Solomon went on to characterize the bill as "a minimalist approach to tinkering" instead of the "bold" approach everyone had talked about from the outset of the joint committee's work.[37]

Democratic member Sam Gejdenson of Connecticut took a different view of the items supported by Republicans that had been left out of Hamilton's base bill. "I think there is . . . a fundamental difference in what we call reform here," he observed. "Many of the proposals that my friends and colleagues on the other side proposed . . . [are] an attempt to gridlock the Congress." Singling out the Republican proposal to abolish proxy voting in committees, Gejdenson said he saw it as "an attempt to deprive the majority party, which is responsible for getting the product to the floor, . . . not as a way to reform the process."[38]

The Hamilton proposal did limit members' committee and subcommittee assignments, as well as the number of subcommittees each committee could have; provided for biennial budget resolutions; permitted the House ethics committee to appoint private citizens panels to conduct preliminary inquiries into alleged misconduct by members; and brought Congress under the same labor laws and workplace protections as the private sector. The Senate package was nearly parallel except for omission of the latter provision and the inclusion of a minor limit on filibusters relating to motions to proceed to consideration of legislation.

The most gaping omission in both packages was the lack of any change in committee structure and jurisdictions, even though the joint committee had spent eight days of hearings in April and May considering fourteeen committee reorganization proposals developed by staff. Instead, Hamilton included a provision requiring consideration of abolishing any committee whose membership dropped below 50 percent of its current size due to the new limits on members' committee assignments.

When the smoke finally cleared from the often acrimonious amendment process in the House half of the joint committee, fifteen amendments had been adopted, eight proposed by Republicans and seven by Democrats. Twenty-nine Republican amendments were rejected, most on straight, party-line votes, while two Democratic amendments were rejected. Among the Republican amendments adopted were provisions to extend the biennial budget process to appropriations bills; require the biannual publication of committee votes in the *Congressional Record;* guarantee that the minority party could offer a final amendment to legislation in a motion to recommit with instructions; and require the *Congressional Record* to be a verbatim transcript of words actually spoken in debate.[39]

Among those Republican amendments rejected were proposals to ban proxy voting in committees; impose six-year term limits on committee chairmen and ranking minority members; reduce legislative branch expenditures by 25 percent over five years (Hamilton favored a 12 percent reduction using an earlier baseline); open most committee meetings and hearings to the public and media; and permit the minority party to offer one amendment to any special rule resolution providing for the consideration of legislation.

In addition, Representative Dreier offered what he jokingly referred to as "a minor, non-controversial amendment" to reduce the number of House committees from 22 to 16 and the number of subcommittees from 118 to 96. The committees that Dreier wanted to abolish or, as he diplomatically put it, "merge" with other committees were Banking, Post Office and Civil Service, District of Columbia, Merchant Marine and Fisheries, Interior, Small Business, and Standards of Official Conduct (which would be merged with House Administration). A new Committee on Environment and Maritime Affairs would also be created. Although Hamilton and several other Democratic members of the committee commended Dreier on all his work, the amendment was eventually rejected on a party-line vote, 6-6.[40]

On the final House committee vote to report the amended bill, Republicans Dreier and Bill Emerson of Missouri voted with the six Democrats to report, with the other four Republicans voting against. As Dreier explained, he supported the motion to report "to keep the process moving forward" in the hope that, "under an open amendment process, we will be able to allow the membership to work its will."[41] Neither Hamilton nor Dreier had been able to get a commitment from Speaker Foley to bring the bill to the House under an open amendment process. Therefore, Dreier did not join Hamilton the following February in introducing the reported bill, H.R. 3801. Hamilton was already beginning to feel like the lone man out: none of his Democratic committee colleagues joined as cosponsors of the bill.

The Salisbury Conference

On Thursday, January 27, 1994, one week to the day before Hamilton dropped his modest congressional reform bill in the House hopper, the House Republican Conference boarded buses at the Capitol for a three-day planning session at Salisbury State University on the eastern shore of Maryland. The session was optimistically (and, as it happened, prophetically) entitled "The Congress of the Future," because it explored how Republicans could capture control of the Congress and how they would govern once they did. Republicans had intentionally eschewed calling the session a "retreat" because of its negative connotations. Minority Leader Robert Michel of Illinois had announced his retirement the previous October under the threat of a certain challenge to that leadership post and likely defeat by Gingrich if he did not. Michel's early announcement would allow for a year-long transition process to implement the new leadership's legislative and campaign strategies. Michel graciously allowed Gingrich to assume more and more of the planning and leadership responsibilities during this transition period.

The Salisbury conference had Gingrich's leadership style clearly imprinted on it—an amalgam of business guru Peter Drucker's style and the new planning and management theories of the U.S. Army. To better observe and absorb the process in operation, Gingrich had enlisted Washington lobbyist and former Iowa representative Tom Tauke to lead the Republican members and staff in an exercise of self-examination and definition that involved formulating guiding principles, a vision, and strategies for the party. At first, some of the more embarrassed and inhibited members, sitting around tables in small working groups, made light of the exercise as a waste of time. But it was not long before most participants became fully and seriously engaged in helping to determine what kind of governing, majority party they wanted to be. The scales of the old "minority mentality" were slowly beginning to fall from their eyes, revealing the faint outlines of a brighter horizon.[42]

When the working groups reported back to the conference, they compared notes on the guiding principles they had devised for the party and eventually reached a consensus on five principles: individual liberty, economic opportunity, limited government, personal responsibility, and security at home and abroad. From these principles the conference agreed on a vision for America's future—"to renew the American Dream by promoting individual liberty, economic opportunity, high standards of performance, and an America strong enough to defend all her citizens against violence at home or abroad." The conference demonstrated its independent judgment by agreeing to delete from an earlier draft of the vision statement one of Gingrich's favorite catchphrases, "the liberal welfare state."

Finally, the Republicans adopted a mission statement committed to "working together to offer representative governance, and to communicate our vision of America through clearly defined themes, programs and legislative initiatives to earn us the honor of becoming the Majority party in 1995."[43] The foundation for the Contract with America had been laid.

There was unanimity among the conference members and leaders alike that the party must offer a constructive agenda to the voters if it was to be a credible alternative to the ruling Democrats in Congress. As Gingrich and Armey later explained in an expanded, book version of the Contract with America, "Standing up against the Clinton administration's tax-and-spend assault on American families was worth a great deal to Republicans in the November elections, but standing up for a positive agenda to help restore the American dream and the integrity of government was worth a lot more."[44]

In between the formal sessions of the Salisbury conference, Dreier and other Republican members of the joint committee began to take the pulse of the leadership and their other Republican colleagues on how to proceed, if at all, on the House reform effort. Dreier had received some criticism from within the conference for voting to keep the process alive rather than simply pulling the plug on the package for failing the "boldness" test. Dreier and a few others pointed out that several important Republican reforms had already been incorporated into Hamilton's package, and it would therefore be wrong to renounce the bill and walk away from it. Opponents of moving the process forward, on the other hand, argued that they did not want to hand the Democrats an easy victory for what they would boast was a major reform of Congress when it was nothing of the sort.

After further give-and-take over the next two days, the leadership gave Dreier and his cohorts a green light to push aggressively for House action on the Hamilton bill provided its consideration was unconditionally linked to an open amendment process that allowed all the major Republican amendments rejected by the joint committee to be offered.

Contract with America: The Republicans' Agenda

Shortly after the late January conference, the leadership developed a detailed legislative agenda for the next Congress based on the Salisbury principles. Gingrich is credited with settling on ten agenda items since, as one aide explained, he thought the number had a "mythic power." He also decided the date for the public unveiling of the agenda, September 27, after consulting with a long-range weather forecaster in Georgia. Persuaded by Gingrich, party chairman Haley Barbour agreed to have the Republican National Committee finance an advertisement in *TV Guide* later in the fall promoting the agenda.[45]

Developing that agenda would be an inclusive, bottoms-up process, involving incumbent members, challengers, staff, and outside coalitions. Armey, the chairman of the House Republican Conference, was put in charge of pulling together the "Republican 100-day Agenda," as it was originally called. Over the July 4 recess, a six-page survey was sent to all incumbent members as well as other GOP House candidates. It asked recipients to rank in order of importance twelve general issues, roughly based on the five guiding principles adopted at the Salisbury conference. Respondents were then asked to rank in terms of respondent support and likely electoral impact roughly six subissues under each issue, for a total of sixty-seven subissues.

All told some 100 incumbents and 150 challengers answered the formal survey. According to political scientist John Bader, although it is customary for the congressional majority leadership to put forward its own legislative agenda when the president is of the other party, this survey was unprecedented in its inclusiveness and use as a national campaign document in a nonpresidential election year.[46]

On July 15, 1994, Armey sent all Republican House members a memorandum on the "GOP Contract with America agenda development." The memo urged members to return their surveys by July 22, and it encouraged them to submit "more detailed ideas and comments in writing." It also listed nine issue-oriented working groups and their respective "lead members." The working-group issue areas were the "opening day checklist" of congressional reforms, term limits, pro-family reforms, strengthening defense and foreign affairs, balanced budget amendment, common sense legal reforms, economic growth, senior citizen reforms, and regulatory reforms. "Just because other issues are not on the current working group list does not mean they are being left out," the memo stated.[47] Two additional groups, one on crime and one on welfare reform, were created shortly thereafter.

Three days prior to Armey's memorandum, Rep. Jerry Solomon, the ranking Republican on the Rules Committee, wrote Minority Leader Michel a letter, with copies going to Gingrich and Armey, urging inclusion of Michel's legislative line-item veto bill in the Republicans' fall agenda. It was an issue Solomon had championed in previous Congresses before turning it over to Michel's leadership in 1993, when it gained support. In Solomon's words, "This popular issue will be an issue in most congressional campaigns this fall and clearly draws a line between the two parties (only 33 House Democrats supported us last year while 214 opposed us)."[48]

Giving the president the line-item veto power was a good idea, Clinton said when he was a presidential candidate. But he retreated from this campaign promise at the urging of the Democratic congressional leadership shortly after his election. House leaders persuaded Clinton to support instead the House Democrats' watered-down version known as the "expedited rescission" process.

The line-item veto did not fall neatly under any of the existing working groups. At the urging of Solomon and Michel, the issue was folded into the balanced budget group as part of the "Fiscal Responsibility Act," even though it would still require the introduction of two measures since the balanced budget proposal was a constitutional amendment and the line-item veto provision was a mere statutory measure.

Armey's July 15 memo included a time line for action. The working groups were slated to submit their first drafts for discussion by an open forum of members in late July. Second drafts were scheduled for approval in early August by the Republican Conference's Policy Committee. Final legislative language was to be developed by staff during the August recess and ready for full conference debate and adoption when the House returned in early September.

The lead item on the Contract with America was an "opening day checklist" of House reforms. It would not be counted as one of the ten items in the Contract, though its importance was underscored by its placement ahead of all the others. Dreier was tapped to head the "opening day" working group with Vice-chair Jennifer Dunn of Washington, the most junior Republican from the joint committee. Four subgroups were appointed to develop various aspects of the checklist: Solomon as head of the House Rules subgroup; Rep. Wayne Allard of Colorado as head of the application-of-laws-to-Congress subgroup; Rep. Clay Shaw of Florida as head of the subgroup on a comprehensive House audit; and ranking Budget Committee Republican John Kasich of Ohio as head of the budget resolution subgroup.

What emerged from the working group on the opening-day checklist was the Contract's ambitious eight-point reform plank, most of which had been considered, if not adopted, by the joint committee the previous November. These included amendments to House rules to reduce the number of committees and subcommittees, and cut committee staff by one-third; limit committee chairmen to no more than three consecutive terms; ban proxy voting; require open committee meetings and hearings with guaranteed access by the media; require a three-fifths vote to pass any revenue increase; utilize "honest budget numbers" in the congressional budget process; and conduct a comprehensive audit of House financial records, assets, and facilities.

The checklist also called for passing a bill on opening day, the so-called "Congressional Accountability Act," that would apply to Congress the same laws that apply to private sector employers. It was practically unheard of to pass a substantive bill on the first day of a new Congress since the bill would not have the benefit of committee consideration. In this case the issue had been well thrashed out in the previous Congress.

Although Gingrich and independent pollster Frank Luntz would claim in September that all of the Contract items had at least 60 percent public support, the items were not picked on the basis of any preselection polling effort. Instead, Luntz, who had worked for presidential candidates Pat Buchanan and then Ross Perot in 1992, conducted polls and focus groups after the items had been selected to determine which phrases and slogans had the most popular appeal for use in the *TV Guide* ad and other promotions purposes.[49]

The *TV Guide* insert was especially designed and tested to be something different—not just another laundry list of campaign promises that would be forgotten after the election. Instead, it was a cardboard, tear-out checklist that invited readers to "keep this page to hold us accountable," with a box to be ticked off when each Contract item was voted on by the House. To underscore the accountability theme, the ad concluded with this startling challenge: "If we break this contract, throw us out. We mean it."

By design, both the ad and the Contract listed the balanced budget amendment and line-item veto first, and congressional term limits as the tenth item. The leaders had been advised by their consultants that people tend to look at the first and last items in a list to determine whether to read the rest, and these were the two most popular items in the Contract according to poll results.

The wording explaining each item in the ad had been carefully tested for maximum effect. The balanced budget/line-item veto item: "It's time to force the government to live within its means and to restore accountability to the budget in Washington." The third item, welfare reform: "The government should encourage people to work and *not* to have more children out of wedlock." And item five, tax cuts for families: "Let's make it easier to achieve the American Dream, save money, buy a home and send the kids to college."

With rhetoric like that and solid public support in the polls for most of the Contract items, the challenge was not to find popular issues, but rather to persuade the American people to change party control of the Congress. For congressional Republicans to run on a national party platform in a nonpresidential year defied conventional political wisdom that such races were decided district by district, based on the personalities and characters of the candidates and their stands on issues of local importance. Ironically, President Clinton helped to nationalize the Contract before it was even officially presented. As Gingrich later recounted, a White House reporter called on the Friday before the Contract event in September and alerted him that the president was about to launch a full-scale attack on the Contract. "Frankly, we were overjoyed," Gingrich wrote, since the White House response was sure to make the Contract a subject on the weekend talk shows. Coverage of the Contract event would be elevated from a possible inside-page photo opportunity to the very centerpiece of the midterm campaign.[50] "Which one of these items was President Clinton going to attack?" wondered Gingrich. "[T]he Democrats' reflexive opposition to the Contract was another example of how ideologically opposed they were to changing the status quo and how far out of touch they had become with the American people."[51]

That theme of an out-of-touch president and a Congress resistant to the changes the people wanted was echoed in nearly every campaign, and it gained resonance. President Clinton and the Democrats were unable to convince voters that unified party government was the key to ending gridlock and effecting necessary change. They also were unable to convince voters that Clinton was the kind of "new Democrat" he claimed to be. Instead of tax relief, welfare reform, and campaign and governmental reforms, he seemed to many to pursue the old Democrat "tax and spend," big government solutions of his predecessors. And this in turn provoked a mood of betrayal and distrust that helped pave the way for the Republicans' march from the Capitol steps, where they announced the Contract with America on that sunny Tuesday in late September, to the two Capitol chambers, where they assumed control for the first time in forty years.

Factors of Change

To what extent were the Contract's themes and issues responsible for the Republican takeover of Congress in 1995 and to what extent were other factors responsible? According to a *USA Today*–CNN–Gallup Poll taken in late November of 1994, only 34 percent of Americans had heard of the Contract (up from 24 percent in early October).[52] This 34 percent, what Gallup refers to as the "attentive public," was not much different from the 39 percent of eligible Americans who voted in the 1994 midterm elections. Of those who had heard of the Contract, 56 percent expressed general support, while 23 percent expressed opposition.[53]

The same poll indicated much stronger support for most of the individual Contract items, something Gingrich was eager to trumpet upon winning his party's nomination for Speaker in early December. He did so by holding aloft for his colleagues and cameras a copy of *USA Today* with the headline "Public Backs GOP Agenda." The article referred to a *USA Today*–CNN–Gallup Poll showing that six of the ten Contract items had at least 73 percent public support among those who had heard of the Contract.[54] In particular, anticrime legislation received 88 percent; a tax cut for most Americans, 83 percent; the balanced budget amendment, 84 percent; welfare limitations, 79 percent; the line-item veto, 77 percent; and term limits, 73 percent.

Those items falling just short of Gingrich's 60 percent support goal were the capital gains tax cut and the litigation rules reform, both with 58 percent support. Items with less than majority support included increased defense spending, 42 percent, and barring UN command of U.S. troops, 41 percent.[55]

When Gingrich was asked by a reporter whether the Contract had been specifically designed to pander to public opinion and attract votes, he replied, "Politics is about public opinion and gathering public support. It's like saying, isn't it pandering for Wal-Mart to stock everything people want to buy."[56]

The Contract certainly did not give people everything they wanted—its vision was not that expansive. The Republicans made a concerted effort to devise a Contract that would appeal to their traditional voting base, as well as to conservative Democrats, independents, and Perot voters. They consciously avoided including two issues (school prayer and abortion) that had substantial support within the party but might alienate some moderate Republicans as well as independent voters. It did not require a stretch in party philosophy or any special interest pandering for Republicans to identify eleven issues that were within party policy parameters and had popular public appeal.

Even if one assumes that the "attentive public" was roughly the same public that went to the polls, and that support for most individual items in the Contract was relatively high among the general populace, it does not necessarily follow that the Contract as a whole was a major factor in how people voted. An exit poll conducted at precincts across the nation revealed that the issue of most concern to those who voted for candidates of both parties was crime, which was a Contract item. Health care and jobs/the economy ranked next with those voting for Democrats. Taxes and family values and morality were the next highest concerns of those favoring Republican candidates.[57]

In 1994, unlike in 1992, the economy was not the uppermost consideration in voters' minds. During that two-year span, unemployment dropped from 7.5 percent to 6.1 percent, and the economy's growth rate was slightly improved at 3.5 percent, up from 2.7 percent. Nevertheless, Democratic voters' anxiety over jobs and the economy was still substantial. The federal deficit, another major issue in 1992, declined from its record high of nearly $300 billion to a little over $200 billion—still unacceptably high in the minds of most who tied it to the performance of the economy.

Some have misinterpreted the 1994 Republican "tsunami" as little more than a vote of no-confidence in President Clinton. But Clinton's job approval rating was actually on the rebound. From a two-year low of 39 percent in August and September, it jumped to 48 percent in late October—"the sharpest increase measured in over a year." This was "the first time since June that public disapproval of Clinton has not exceeded approval." The *Gallup Poll Monthly* saw a good omen for congressional Democrats in Clinton's comeback: "The improvement is welcome news for the Democratic party which has been suffering low expectations for the coming midterm elections."[58]

While the exit polls in 1994 showed that nearly 60 percent of voters said Clinton was the reason they voted for one party's House candidate over the other, that percentage was almost equally split between those who considered their vote a vote for Clinton (28 percent) and those who considered their vote a vote against him (31 percent). The other 40 percent of the voters said that Clinton made no difference in how they voted.[59]

The same exit polls showed 41 percent of the voters identifying themselves as Democrats and 35 percent as Republicans. Only 10 percent of the Democrats and 7 percent of the Republicans voted for candidates of the other party. Of the 24 percent who did not identify with either party, 56 percent voted for Republican candidates and 44 percent for Democratic candidates. The most telling number was the 12 percent who said they had voted for Perot in 1992; in 1994 they voted for Republican candidates by a two-to-one margin.[60] In 1992 exit polls found that the Perot voters would have divided nearly equally between Bush and Clinton had Perot not been on the ballot.

In short, Republicans had succeeded in attracting enough votes from the 1992 Perot voters and independent voters to make the difference in 1994. The Contract may not have been a deciding factor in that shift, but its general themes were in sync with those who voted to restore Republican control of Congress for the first time in four decades. As *Washington Post* writer Edward Walsh summed up the exit poll findings, "The dramatic Republican gains in yesterday's elections were fueled in large part by overwhelming support from the most alienated Americans who have little or no confidence in Congress and say the country is off track."[61] Almost 60 percent of the voters agreed that the country was on the wrong track, and they voted two-to-one for Republicans.

The National Election Studies' "Trust in Government Index" had slipped from an average score of twenty-nine in 1992 to an all-time low of twenty-six in 1994. The biggest departure from 1992 came on yet another NES question: "People like me don't have any say about what the government does." In 1992, 36 percent of the people agreed and 57 percent disagreed; in 1994 those numbers had flip-flopped, with 55 percent agreeing and 35 percent disagreeing.

In the eyes of voters in 1994, Congress was faring no better than the government in general. According to a *Washington Post*–ABC News Poll conducted one week before the election, only 21 percent of the people approved of the way Congress was doing its job.[62] In July of 1992, a CBS News–*New York Times* Poll found roughly the same approval/disapproval percentages for the Congress, 20 percent to 71 percent.[63] Only this time the verdict was different at the polls, with the majority party in the Congress taking the full brunt of voters' frustration.

Some would argue that 1994 was a mere extension of the anti-incumbent mood in 1992 that toppled President George Bush but spared most incumbents in the scandal-plagued Democratic Congress. In 1994 the anti-incumbent mood was again selective, only this time it fell overwhelmingly on the congressional majority. Thirty-four Democratic incumbents in the House and two Democratic incumbents in the Senate were defeated in the general election. Not one Republican incumbent from either house was rejected. The Republicans had successfully managed the near-impossible, with some help from President Clinton. They had nationalized a mid-term election for Congress, and the congressional Democratic Party fell big and it fell hard.

Reform's Last Gasp

Clinton dropped the mantle of change and reform that he had proudly donned during the 1992 campaign; similarly, the Democratic Congress failed to enact any of the significant reform legislation it had been working on. Campaign finance, lobbying disclosure, and gift limitation reforms were all done in by delays and dilatory tactics by both parties in both houses. Perhaps of greatest symbolic import were the failures to enact either health care reform or congressional reform legislation in the final weeks of the 1994 session.

Despite concerted public efforts by Republicans (and private efforts by Democratic representative Hamilton) to pressure the Democratic leadership into bringing the congressional reform bill to the House floor during 1994, Speaker Foley made sure that it remained bottled in the Rules Committee as long as possible. The Rules Committee and its Subcommittee on Rules of the House held eight hearings on the bipartisan Legislative Reorganization Act during the months of February through April, then sat on the bill for the next three months. The ostensible excuse for delay was the need to avoid any divisive internal reform debates that could jeopardize the fate of Clinton's health care bill, then making its way through the committee process.

On August 4, 1994, the Rules Committee finally held an initial mark-up meeting on the congressional reform bill, with the understanding that final action would be postponed until September to allow for consideration of the president's health care bill the third week in August. Ironically, the health care bill would become the poster-child for congressional reform—a victim in part of fragmented and overlapping committee jurisdictions and the inability of the majority leadership to pull things back together.

The president's bill, known as the "Health Security Act," was introduced on November 20, 1993, and referred to no fewer than ten House committees, seven of which reported their pieces in July and August of 1994. Of the two major committees of jurisdiction, the Ways and Means Committee reported two alternatives as the price of getting anything out, while the Energy and Commerce Committee could not muster enough votes to report any version. The anticipated House floor action was postponed until after the August recess.

Shortly after the Rules Committee reconvened on September 21 to resume its mark-up of the Legislative Reorganization Act, Chairman Joe Moakley abruptly recessed the committee in the middle of debate on Representative Solomon's amendment to abolish all proxy voting in House committees. That amendment, and two amendments by Dreier and Democratic representative Tony Beilenson to overhaul the House committee structure appeared to have enough Democratic votes to be adopted. Speaker Foley summoned the committee Democrats to his office and urged them to defeat both the proxy and committee overhaul amendments.

Foley's biggest fear was a repeat of the bloody battle over committee turf he had witnessed in 1974 as Democratic Caucus chairman. So brutal was the fight over the Bolling select committee's reform resolution that the scars had not healed twenty years later. Foley vowed never again to allow a destructive turf battle in the caucus to occur on his watch. Rather than risk losing on either the proxy or committee overhaul amendments, Moakley announced that the mark-up had been canceled.[64]

Five days later, on September 26, Sen. George Mitchell held a press conference to announce the demise of the president's health care bill. Eleven days after that, on October 8, the final gavel fell on the 103d Congress. The road to the Republican revolution had been well paved.

Notes

1. "Rare Combination of Forces Makes '94 Vote Historic," *Congressional Quarterly Almanac, 1995*, vol. 51 (Washington, D.C.: Congressional Quarterly, 1996), 561, 564.

2. The National Elections Studies, University of Michigan (http://www.umich.edu/~nesguide/toptables).

3. "Wave of Diversity Spared Many Incumbents," *Congressional Quarterly Almanac, 1992*, vol. 48 (Washington, D.C.: Congressional Quarterly, 1993), 17-A.

4. Ruth Marcus, "Clinton, Hill Leaders Hail New Teamwork," *Washington Post*, Nov. 17, 1992, A-1.

5. David Hess, "Clinton, Congress Pledge Cooperation," *The Miami Herald*, Nov. 20, 1992, 10A.

6. Phil Kuntz, "Soon to Lose House Clout, Republicans Rethink Strategy," *Congressional Quarterly Weekly Report*, Nov. 14, 1992, 3624.

7. Ibid.

8. Janet Hook, "Approval of Administrator Creates More Rancor," *Congressional Quarterly Weekly Report*, April 11, 1992, 929–30.

9. H. Con. Res. 192 (102d Cong., 1st sess.), to establish a Joint Committee on the Organization of Congress. The resolution was introduced by Mr. Hamilton (for himself and Mr. Gradison), July 31, 1991.

10. Janet Hook, "Congress OKs Step Toward Reform," *Congressional Quarterly Weekly Report*, Aug. 8, 1992, 2332.

11. Ronald D. Elving, "Freshmen Drawn into the Fold," *Congressional Quarterly Weekly Report*, Nov. 14, 1992, 3627.

12. Beth Donovan, "Freshmen Focus on the Product, Not on Legislative Process," *Congressional Quarterly Weekly Report*, Nov. 14, 1992, 3626.

13. Ibid.

14. "Organization of the Congress: Final Report of the Joint Committee on the Organization of Congress," 103d Cong., H. Rept. 103-413, vol. 2, 1st sess., Dec. 17, 1993, table II: Legislative Branch Employment, 1945–93, 88.

15. "A Mandate for Change in the People's House," Republican Conference House Rules Amendments, 103d Cong., *Congressional Record*, Jan. 5, 1993, H16.

16. Ibid., H17.

17. *Congressional Record*, Jan. 5, 1993, H35. See also *Michel* v. *Anderson*, 14 F. 3d 623 (D.C. Cir. 1994).

18. On that occasion in 1971, ninety-one Democrats joined with their Democratic colleague Bernie Sisk of California on a procedural vote to permit him to strike a provision from the House rules package recommended by the Democratic Caucus. The provision, subsequently stricken, would have allowed committees to bring their bills to the floor if they had been stalled in the Rules Committee for thirty-one days or more. Similar defections of large numbers of Democrats occurred on the opening-day rules votes to strike the predecessor "21-day rule" in 1965 and 1967, and over the re-adoption of a rule enlarging the Rules Committee membership in 1963.

19. *Congressional Record*, Jan. 5, 1993, table 2: House Committee Survey, 102d Congress, H25; and table 10: Funding for Current House Non-legislative Select Committees from Inception, H27.

20. Ibid., table 4: Open Versus Restrictive Rules, 95th–102d Congresses, H26.

21. Republican Leadership Task Force on Deliberative Democracy in the House, "The Decline of Deliberative Democracy in the People's House: The First Report of the House Democracy Project," April 21, 1993, 3, 5.

22. Karen Foerstel, "Republicans Unveil Strategy to Combat Restrictive Rules," *Roll Call*, April 22, 1993, 1.

23. Karen Foerstel, "Rules Will Soon Open, Says Foley," *Roll Call*, April 26, 1993, 1.

24. Karen Foerstel, "'Hallelujah,' Say Republicans, Getting First Open Rules in House for the 103d Congress," *Roll Call*, May 6, 1993, 1, 17.

25. Ibid.

26. Mary Jacoby, "Boll Weevils Won't Automatically Join GOP to Kill Rules," *Roll Call*, April 14, 1994, 3, 22.

27. "Survey of Activities of the House Committee on Rules, 103d Congress," report of the Committee on Rules, 103d Cong., 2d sess., H. Rept. 103-891, Jan. 2, 1995, "Measures Discharged from the Rules Committee," (a) H. Res. 134, 50–51.

28. Phil Kuntz, "Anti-secrecy Drive Putting Democrats on the Defensive," *Congressional Quarterly Weekly Report*, Sept. 11, 1993, 2369–70.

29. Statement of the Honorable James M. Inhofe, a representative in Congress from the state of Oklahoma, "Discharge Petition Disclosure, H. Res. 134," hearing before the Subcommittee on Rules of the House of the Committee on Rules, 103d Cong., 1st sess., Sept. 14, 1993, 9.

30. *Congressional Record,* Sept. 28, 1993, H7043.

31. *Congressional Quarterly Weekly Report,* Oct. 2, 1993, House roll call vote no. 458 on adoption of H. Res. 134, 2686.

32. "No Action Taken on Congressional Reform," *Congressional Quarterly Almanac, 1993,* vol. 49 (Washington, D.C.: Congressional Quarterly, 1994), 26.

33. "Organization of the Congress: Final Report of the House Members of the Joint Committee on the Organization of Congress," H. Rept. 103-413, vol. 1, Dec. 17, 1993, 2–3.

34. "Organization of the Congress: Final Report of the Joint Committee on the Organization of Congress," 223.

35. Opening statement by the Honorable Lee Hamilton, Nov. 16, 1993, "Business Meetings on Congressional Reform Legislation," meetings of the Joint Committee on the Organization of Congress, S. Hearing 103-320, 103d Cong., 1st sess., markup of congressional reform legislation, Nov. 10, 16, 18, 19, 21, and 22, 1993, 75.

36. Ibid., 78.

37. Ibid., 80.

38. Ibid., 82–83.

39. Ibid., 662–67.

40. Ibid., 166–201 for text of and debate on the Dreier amendment.

41. Ibid., 501.

42. These observations are based on the author's participation in the Salisbury retreat as a senior staff member of the House Rules Committee.

43. *Contract with America: The Bold Plan by Rep. Newt Gingrich, Rep. Dick Armey, and the House Republicans to Change the Nation,* ed. Ed Gillespie and Bob Schellhas (New York: Times Books/Random House, 1994), 4–5.

44. Ibid., 12.

45. Dan Balz and Ronald Brownstein, *Storming the Gates: Protest Politics and the Republican Revival* (Boston: Little Brown & Co., 1996), 37–40.

46. John B. Bader, *Taking the Initiative: Leadership Agendas in Congress and the "Contract with America"* (Washington, D.C.: Georgetown University Press, 1996), 185–86.

47. Memorandum to GOP House members from Dick Armey regarding GOP "Contract With America Agenda Development," July 15, 1994. The leadership had already chosen the title "Contract with America" by this point, and Armey's letterhead carried not only the logo of the House Republican Conference, but a bold heading "Contract with America: House GOP Agenda."

48. Letter from Gerald B. Solomon to Robert H. Michel, July 12, 1994.

49. Frank Greve, "How Poll Misstated 'Contract' Support," *The Miami Herald,* Nov. 12, 1995, 1A.

50. Newt Gingrich, *To Renew America* (New York: Harper Paperbacks, 1995), 126.

51. Ibid.

52. David W. Moore et al., "Contract with America: A Gallup Poll Special Report," *The Gallup Poll Monthly*, Nov. 1994, 19.

53. Ibid.

54. Richard Wolf, "Public Expects GOP to Honor 'Contract,'" *USA Today*, Dec. 9, 1994, 9A.

55. "Contract with America: A Gallup Poll Special Report," 19, 22.

56. Dan Balz and Charles R. Babcock, "Conservative Rebels Harassed the House," *Washington Post*, Dec. 20, 1994, A1.

57. Edward Walsh, "Many Republicans' Votes Came from Those Who Distrust Government," *Washington Post*, Nov. 9, 1994, A23. Also see "Profile of the '94 Voter; Exit Poll Results, House Races," *Washington Post*, Nov. 10, 1994, A33, for tables of the exit poll results provided by Mitofsky International of New York.

58. Lydia Saad, "Clinton Gives Democratic Party a Needed Boost," *The Gallup Poll Monthly*, Oct. 1994, 16.

59. "Profile of the '94 Voter; Exit Poll Results, House Races," A33.

60. Ibid.

61. Ibid.

62. *Washington Post*–ABC News Poll, Oct. 1997, historical comparative table 1.1 (http://www.washingtonpost.com/wpsrv/national/longterm/polls/stories/data101597.htm).

63. "Organization of the Congress: Final Report of the Joint Committee on the Organization of Congress," Approval Ratings of Congress, 1974–1992, 193.

64. For an excellent account of the work of the Joint Commitee on the Organization of Congress and the subsequent Republican takeover of Congress, see C. Lawrence Evans and Walter J. Oleszek, *Congress under Fire: Reform Politics and the Republican Majority* (Boston: Houghton Mifflin Co., 1997). Both authors served on the staff of the joint committee.

11

The Road to Governance: Revolution, Reform, and Reality

THE opening day of a new Congress in the U.S. House of Representatives is always a reminder of why it is called the "people's House." Not only is the floor of the House overflowing with new members and old, many with children and grandchildren in tow, but the visitors' galleries are packed with proud constituents, relatives, and staff from every state in the Union—all waiting to see their member of Congress take the oath of office. Once every two years, for about two hours, the House chamber is a rousing celebration of democracy. Then the chamber and galleries empty for swearing-in parties in members' offices, and the few members remaining on the floor debate the package of proposed rules that will govern the House and its committees for the next two years.

At noon on Wednesday, January 4, 1995, the hall of the House appeared no different than it did on any opening day of a new Congress—except that it was. The atmosphere was supercharged with an energy that surges at truly historic moments. And this was one of those moments. The Republicans had taken control of both houses of Congress for the first time since 1953. For one Congress, the 83d (1953–55), they controlled the House and Senate. The only returning member who had served in that Republican-controlled House was eighty-six-year-old Sidney R. Yates of Chicago, a Democrat first elected to Congress in 1948. He had served every term but two since then. Administering the oath of office to the newly elected Republican Speaker was the twenty-term dean of the House, sixty-eight-year-old John D. Dingell (D-Mich.), who had succeeded his father in office in the 1954 elections that had turned the ruling Republicans back into a minority party.

Instead of a Republican minority leader introducing and handing over the gavel to a Democratic Speaker for the twenty-first consecutive time, here was a Democratic *minority* leader, Richard A. Gephardt, performing the ritual with the traditional eloquence and grace:

> So, with partnership but with purpose, I pass this great gavel of our Government. With resignation, but with resolve, I hereby end 40 years of Democratic rule of this House; with faith and with friendship and the deepest respect. You are now my Speaker, and let the great debate begin.[1]

And here was the back-bench bomb-thrower turned Speaker, the undeniable leader of the revolution, Newt Gingrich, accepting the reins of power to chants of "Newt, Newt, Newt" from his acolytes. In his seemingly rambling, stream-of-consciousness manner, he delivered a riveting thirty-five-minute tour de force on American history, culture, literature, and political thought (replete with a recommended reading list). Into his philosophy of everything, he wrapped hopes and dreams for the future of American civilization—finally concluding:

> All I can do is pledge to you that, if each of us will reach out prayerfully and try to genuinely understand each other, then I think a year from now we can look on the 104th Congress as a truly amazing institution without regard to party, without regard to ideology. We can say, "Here, America comes to work, and here we are preparing for those children a better future."[2]

Little could Gingrich know then that a year later, instead of the nonpartisan, nonideological working House predicted, the federal government would be shut down, and the public would largely blame the Republican House. A year and a day later, on January 5, 1996, Republicans began to reopen the government and make the transition from the revolutionary Congress to the governing Congress. By the time the 104th Congress adjourned on October 4, 1996, it had enough solid accomplishments to its credit to convince voters to stay the course. The Republican Party retained control of the Congress in that fall's election—the first time since 1928 that it had held control of Congress for more than one term.

The 104th Congress was a roller-coaster ride for the new Republican majority, thrilling and frustrating, with all the highs and lows that accompany steep learning curves. A big part of that learning experience was bridging the gap between revolutionary reform rhetoric and day-to-day governing realities, between how Congress should run in theory and how it must run in practice, if anything is to be accomplished. This chapter explores the reforms adopted in the 104th Congress and how they helped or hindered the Republicans' desire to advance their agenda in the House and become more responsive and accountable to the people.

A Long Day's Journey

Newt Gingrich carefully stage managed the opening-day program for the 104th Congress just as he had the unveiling of the Contract the previous September. The Contract promised nothing less than immediate action: "On the first day of the 104th Congress, the new Republican majority will immediately pass . . . major reforms, aimed at restoring the faith and trust of the American people in their government"—a tall order for one day's work. But Gingrich did not intend to deviate one iota from that pledge or allow its completion to be overshadowed by other events of the day. During his acceptance speech as Speaker, Gingrich quoted the opening-day checklist from the Contract and joked that he had told Minority Leader Gephardt the previous evening: "If I had to do it over again, we would have pledged within 3 days that we will do these things, but that is not what we said. So we have ourselves in a little bit of a box here."[3] It was obviously the kind of box Gingrich treasured—a display case for the fruits of laboring for years in the political vineyards as a minority party.

A new House on opening day had a customary practice dating back to the turn of the century: it considered the majority party's entire package of proposed House rules for just one hour and then took two successive votes—a procedural vote by the minority party to offer its alternative rules, followed by a vote to adopt the majority's proposal. However, Gingrich was not about to allow such perfunctory consideration of the first plank in the Contract. An hour was not nearly long enough to effect substantial reforms in House structures and operations, and to apply private sector workplace laws to the Congress.

He instructed Rules Committee chairman-designate Gerald B. Solomon to draft a special rule for the extended and separate consideration of various components of the House rules package. The rule also included a section providing for the subsequent consideration of the congressional accountability bill to apply private sector labor laws to the Congress. All told, this unprecedented process would consume more than fourteen hours. Gingrich insisted that each of the eight rules changes in the Contract be given a separate vote by the House. He also insisted that each vote be preceded by a separate debate instead of "rolling" and "clustering" all the votes into a single block at the end. Those eight votes and eight debates votes would be followed by a twenty-minute discussion and single vote on Title II of the resolution containing twenty-three non-Contract sections.

Members hosting constituent parties in their offices would be repeatedly interrupted by bells calling them back to the House floor for votes from noon well into the evening hours. The objection that his opening-day legislative choreography would inconvenience members did not impress Gingrich. As he half-apologized during his acceptance speech:

> Our commitment . . . [and] absolute obligation, is first of all to work today until we are done. I know that is going to inconvenience people who have families and supporters. But we were hired to do a job, and we have to start today to prove we will do it.[4]

Just getting to opening day from election day had been an exhilarating and exhausting journey for the new majority Republicans. There were no road maps. Gingrich tapped Jim Nussle of Iowa, the former "bag man" for the "Gang of Seven," to head a seven-member transition team that would overhaul House operations from top to bottom. The irony of the appointment was not lost on Nussle. He commented that it was "almost like sticking a finger in the eye of the Democratic majority who resisted reform . . . by putting the guy who put the bag on his head in charge." Nussle referred to his freshman-year sack prank as "outrageous" but "necessarily outrageous." Now, four years later, wearing his new hat of responsibility as transition leader, he observed, "We have a mandate . . . from the voters to change business as usual in Washington. The trains have to run on time on January 4."[5]

The meetings began almost immediately between the leadership, committees, and staff to plan for the new Congress. The committees not only had to determine what portions of the 100-day Contract they were responsible for and prepare timetables for their completion. They also had to hire new staff, move offices, and switch computer systems with the former Democratic majority staff. Although the Contract called for a one-third reduction in committee staff, many Republicans would have to expand their committee staffs in order to assume the responsibilities of majority control. Under Democratic control, few committee chairmen allocated one-third of the total committee staff to the minority—a ratio Republicans had long fought for and one they now guaranteed to the new minority Democrats (though they did not go so far as to enshrine the guarantee in House rules).

Gingrich called on David Dreier, a veteran from the Joint Committee on the Organization of Congress, to develop the committee reform proposals for the opening-day package. While several had been outlined in the Contract, some were still lacking specific language. The one-third staff reduction was specific, but the pledge to reduce the number of committees was not. Dreier felt the time was finally ripe to be "bold" about rationalizing and equalizing committee jurisdictions and workload before the newly designated committee chairs became entrenched. He consequently drafted four committee reorganization options pursuant to instructions from Gingrich, ranging from incremental to major. Shortly after he accepted his new assignment, Dreier predicted, "We're going to have a bold reform plan, which is going to allow us to implement the mandate we got last week at the polls," though he admitted any bold plan would encounter some resistance in the Republican Conference.[6]

On November 16, 1994, exactly one year after the House membership of the joint committee began its mark-up, Dreier presented his four options to the leadership and transition group. His preferred plan, Option 4, would reduce the number of standing committees from twenty-two to seventeen by consolidating some committees. The plan, similar to the one he had presented to the joint committee, met with strong and immediate opposition from the incoming committee chairmen, their staffs, and allied interest groups.[7]

A few days later the leadership rejected the "bold" plan on grounds that it would be too disruptive to implement at a time when committees were already trying to process their Contract bills under tight deadlines. Gingrich knew that the majority leadership had a responsibility to keep peace in the family and forge winning coalitions for party programs; without the former, the latter would not be possible. Riling the turf sensibilities of committee chairmen at such a critical juncture could doom the Contract with America. Each committee chairman-designate had already met a November 16 deadline for submitting to the leadership a listing of Contract responsibilities within their jurisdiction, together with suggested time lines for hearings, mark-ups, reporting, and floor consideration.

Given these realities, the leadership opted for a modified version of the most incremental proposal instead of the comprehensive realignment favored by Dreier. It eliminated three committees: Post Office and Civil Service, Merchant Marine and Fisheries, and District of Columbia. The plan also shifted about one-fifth of the jurisdiction of the Commerce Committee to other committees and renamed several of the remaining committees.[8]

Solomon was the Speaker's choice to be chairman of the Rules Committee. Although Solomon was the ranking Republican member of the committee, his fate within the majority party had been the subject of considerable speculation and rumor. Solomon had challenged Gingrich in October of 1993 to succeed Bob Michel as party leader, but he quickly withdrew when he realized Gingrich had already sewn up the votes. Even before the 1994 elections, the Capitol Hill newspaper *Roll Call* quoted sources as saying that Gingrich was going to "oust" Solomon as the top Republican on Rules.[9] Adding to this speculation after the election was Gingrich's disregard for seniority when he chose Bob Livingston,

Tom Bliley, and Henry Hyde as chairmen of Appropriations, Commerce, and Judiciary, respectively. He rewarded their loyalty and aggressive styles instead of giving the chairmanships to the most senior members of the committees. Solomon had been a "pit bull" fighting for the minority party's rights and House reforms. Therefore, Gingrich put aside any thoughts of retribution he might have had after he was assured in a one-on-one meeting of Solomon's loyalty to the new Speaker.

At a November 16 press conference, Gingrich announced his selection of Solomon as Rules chairman. Solomon pledged "fair rules" and "free and open debate" to "let the House work its will." Solomon said the Republicans could afford to be more fair than the Democrats had been because Republicans were "nearly as cohesive as we were as a minority party," and not "fractionalized" as the Democrats had been in the majority.[10]

In an interview with *Roll Call*, Solomon became even more effusive. He charitably offered to grant open rules on three-fourths of all bills in 1995 since "liberal left-wing amendments" would simply die on the House floor from lack of support. "The liberal Democrat leadership was so liberal and far to the left," said Solomon, "that they couldn't afford to let bills come to the floor under open rules because their own conservative Democrats would have sided with the Republicans." In the Democratic-controlled 103d Congress (1993–95), only 30 percent of the rules had been completely open.[11]

Solomon and his Rules Committee staff collaborated with Dreier to refine the opening-day checklist of reforms.

Among the Contract provisions that needed tinkering was the one that called for a three-fifths vote on any measure containing a revenue increase. It was pointed out that this could have unintended consequences such as requiring a supermajority vote on cutting the capital gains tax. (Even by conventional budgetary scoring, such a tax cut would produce additional revenues in the first few years.) So the rule was modified to apply only to income-tax rate increases.

Many of the proposals in the non-Contract portion of the rules resolution were carried forward from previous opening-day House rules proposals made by minority Republicans. Some, such as giving the minority new rights to amend special rules or have coequal representation on certain committees, were dropped. However, the minority party was guaranteed final opportunity to amend a bill through a motion to recommit with instructions.

Many of Nussle's recommendations to overhaul the administration of the House were approved by the leadership: abolish the ancient office of doorkeeper and create a new elected post, chief administrative officer; limit members to two committees and four subcommittees; abolish the joint referral of bills and require the Speaker to designate a primary committee of responsibility for each bill introduced; require committees to adopt oversight agendas at the beginning of each Congress and assess implementation in their final activity reports; make the *Congressional Record* and committee transcripts verbatim accounts of words actually spoken; abolish delegate voting in the Committee of the Whole; publish committee roll call votes in committee reports on legislation; and require automatic roll call votes on appropriations and tax bills as well as budget resolutions.[12]

At the insistence of the freshman class, the opening-day checklist was amended to impose a four-consecutive-term limit on Speakers as a complement to the three-term limit on committee chairmen. The latter limit was extended to subcommittee chairmen as well. In addition, the freshmen successfully championed a prohibition on the introduction or consideration of time-specific commemorative legislation (such as "National Clown Week") and a ban on Legislative Service Organizations (LSOs) or special interest caucuses (such as the textile caucus) that members could fund by diverting money from their congressional office allowances.

Opening "Day" of the 104th Congress

Following Gingrich's acceptance speech as Speaker, the newly elected majority leader, Dick Armey, attempted to offer the House rules package by unanimous consent. But Minority Whip David Bonior of Michigan objected, after chiding Armey. Both the rules package and congressional accountability bill, Bonior noted, were being considered under a closed amendment process, a process Republicans had long railed against while in the minority. In response to Bonior's pointed rebuke, Armey turned things over to Solomon, who offered the special rule he had been asked to draft, H. Res. 5. It called for three and one-half hours of debate on the rules package and ten separate votes, including a vote on a minority motion to recommit with instructions.

Solomon countered Bonior's criticisms of unfair tactics by the majority party. Not since 1893 had such a special rule been used to consider an opening-day rules package. Solomon noted that the expansive special rule with its extended debates and separate votes allowed more than triple the amount of time and number of votes Democrats had ever allowed on their opening-day resolutions.

But Bonior continued to dish what Republicans had previously laid on the Democrats:

> After the years of whining and complaining on the Republican side about the damages to democracy of closed rules, what is the first thing they offer us? A closed rule. Not just one closed rule, but a closed rule within a closed rule. Where is democracy, where is open debate, where is the free flow of ideas?[13]

The Democratic minority used its time on the special rule to call for further amendments to the package, including a ban on gifts from lobbyists, a ban on book advances to members, and a limit on book royalties. The latter provisions were prompted by news that Gingrich was offered a multi-million-dollar advance on two books he was writing. (He would later turn down the advance under pressure from colleagues and the public alike.)

During his acceptance speech, Gingrich had promised that "over time we can and will this Spring rethink campaign reform, and lobbying reform and review all ethics, including the gift rule."[14] This vague commitment on opening day was not sufficient to assuage the Democrats, who proceeded to offer their gift ban and book royalty limits amendments in a motion to commit the special rule with instructions. The motion lost on a party-line vote of 196 to 235, after which the rule was adopted, 251-181. (To their credit, Republicans would pass a lobby disclosure bill and rules on House gifts and book royalties later in the first session, but only under continued pressures from the Democrats and a small group of reformers within the Republican Conference.)

It was not until 4:45 P.M. on opening day that Armey called up the House rules package, H. Res. 6, under the terms of the special rule. He said he believed the package would "dramatically alter—and I predict improve—the way in which the House conducts the American people's business" by trimming the size and costs of the institution, making it more accountable through greater openness and committee deliberation, and renewing respect for Congress through the accountability act and term limits on chairmen and the Speaker.[15]

Democratic representative John Spratt of South Carolina was dubious: "If we want to open up this institution, if we want to freshen its image, redeem its reputation among the American people, then we need to sever the ties, real and perceived, between those who work inside this institution and represent the people as a whole, and those who work Congress from the outside, the lobbyists . . . who represent special interests and limited numbers of people."[16]

Spratt was referring to the minority's amendment to ban gifts from lobbyists that was included in the final motion to commit the resolution with instructions. That final motion, offered at nearly 12:30 the next morning by Minority Whip Bonior, also included the minority's limits on book royalties, a reduction of the term limit on Speakers from four to three terms, equitable minority party representation and staff on committees, and separate votes on any Budget Act waivers contained in a special rule on legislation. The Democrats' motion to commit was rejected on a straight party-line vote of 201 to 207, after which the House adopted by voice vote Title II of the resolution.

The House overwhelmingly passed with bipartisan support the following items in the Contract: a one-third reduction of committee staff, 416-12; term limits for committee and subcommittee chairmen and the Speaker, 355-74; the ban on proxy voting, 418-13; and the open committee meeting and broadcast access guarantee, 431-0. Only the provision imposing a three-fifths majority vote requirement for tax rates increases and the procedural section of the Congressional Accountability Act pulled a majority of Democrats in opposition. But the Congressional Accountability Act (H.R. 1) passed around 2 A.M. without a dissenting vote, 429-0.

Some Democrats tried to belittle the Republicans' opening-day accomplishments. "Most of it frankly is innocuous," observed Minority Leader Gephardt. Rep. Barney Frank of Massachusetts referred to the reforms as "banishing nonexistent evils at a fast and furious pace." Liberal Democrat Pat Williams of Montana was more forthright and complimentary: "A lot of what the Republicans are doing is good," he said. "Democrats should have done this if we could have, but we couldn't. . . . We had a stake in continuing the status quo."[17]

The House finally adjourned at 2:24 A.M. on Thursday, January 5, 1995, after a marathon fourteen-plus hours. Although the House was scheduled to reconvene at 10:00 A.M. that same morning, no legislative business was scheduled. Seven committees, however, were slated that day to hold their organizational meetings. The 100-day Contract period was off and running at a frenetic pace—already well into its second day—and the clock was ticking.

Policy Performance versus Procedural Change

In 1913 Democratic Speaker Champ Clark observed that the American people are more interested in results than in the process by which they are obtained. Minority Leader Gephardt, during his remarks opening day on the rules changes, echoed the former Speaker's view:

> All of this Republican talk of reform . . . is ultimately a distraction from the real job at hand. . . . No one should pretend that these narrow procedural changes will do anything to raise incomes, to restore economic security, to revive hope and faith in America's future. . . . Meet some of the families that have given up every minute of family time working two, three, even four jobs—and still cannot make ends meet. Then ask yourself whether some new procedural change can make a difference in their lives.[18]

As gratifying as passing the Contract's opening-day checklist of House reforms had been, Republicans knew that Gephardt had a point: ultimately they would be judged by the American people on their legislative accomplishments and not on what processes or procedures were used to obtain them. Still, at least for the time being, they could take pride in bringing to fruition many of the reforms the GOP had fought for during the past four decades as the minority party.

Could the new House the Republicans had just erected deliver on promises to restore the trust and faith of the American people in their government? Could it make Congress more open, accountable, deliberative, efficient, representative, and responsive in enacting the legislative priorities of the new majority? That these goals were not always compatible and, in fact, often in conflict was not lost on the Republicans. The trick would be to strike a delicate balance between the competing objectives while advancing the policy agenda on time and intact, a feat far more difficult than anyone had imagined.

The story of the House in the 104th Congress and beyond would unfold in three parts: the initial House passage of most of the items in the Contract with America; Congress's subsequent failure to enact most of the Contract and related legislation including entitlement reforms, tax relief, appropriations bills, and an increase in the debt limit (leading to two costly shutdowns of the federal government); and finally the legislative-executive compromise that reopened the government, the enactment of several important legislative initiatives, and the reelection of the Democratic president and the Republican Congress in 1996.

Neither the revolutionary zeal behind the Contract nor the institutional reforms adopted on opening day would be as central to the outcome of this drama as the evolving leadership styles and political strategies of the Republican majority. Just as the Declaration of Independence and the Constitution were distinct documents serving two very different purposes, the revolutionary goals of the victorious Republicans in 1994 were distinct from the governing practices they adopted to ensure limited legislative successes and their political survival. The reelection imperative or "electoral connection" is a driving force in politics. The Republicans' challenge would be to maintain their idealism and sense of direction without yielding to purely pragmatic governance for the sake of holding political power. Was such an idealistic approach realistic given the demands for responsible lawmaking in a divided government, and given the reelection needs of individual party members?

Republican Reforms Put to the Test

What role did the Republican reforms play in this metamorphosis from revolutionary force to a governing party? To address this question, one must first consider the status quo and how the Republican Party expected reforms to change it.

The Democrats' reform of the House in the 1970s democratized the institution by overthrowing the entrenched, often conservative committee system, and dispersing power to the people's representatives in Congress. The "committee bill of rights" incorporated in the 1970 Legislative Reorganization Act was followed by the "subcommittee bill of rights" enshrined in Democratic

Caucus rules and reinforced by the rules of many committees. The latter reforms produced a semi-autonomous subcommittee system. Dominated by more junior and liberal subcommittee chairmen, it was intended to be more responsive to the political views of a caucus majority.

As congressional Republicans, as well as more neutral Congress-watchers and some Democrats saw it, this new regime proved to be far too fragmented and democratic to produce any coherent party program that could command majority support in the House. Subcommittees became "iron triangles" tightly linking subcommittee chairmen and their staff, the bureaucracies they oversaw, and their allied interest groups. The subcommittees were too small to be representative of the larger House, and this problem was exacerbated by the flagrant use and abuse of proxies that enabled chairmen to virtually control outcomes in their subcommittees.

Since the party caucus was too large and unwieldy to manage this system, the party looked to its leadership to bring order out of chaos through the Speaker's handpicked Rules Committee. Beginning around 1980, the leadership increasingly imposed restrictive special rules or floor procedures for major legislation that predetermined legislative outcomes by blocking amendments that could unravel carefully crafted liberal legislation. Republicans viewed this development as the height of arrogance—an abuse of power that transformed the House from a body representative of the nation to a body primarily representative of liberal factions.

Thus Republican reform efforts during the 1980s and '90s were aimed at "restoring the people's House." At the heart of this reform effort was the aim of making committees more deliberative and representative—not independent power centers but entities responsive to the wishes of the majority party caucus. At the same time, Republicans did not want to subordinate the system to a "party government" model that demanded strict party discipline and dictated the details of legislation. Instead they preferred a model of limited or selective party government. The party leadership would designate selected legislation in each Congress as party priorities, but leave the details to committees within certain policy guidelines. Beyond such general party guidance on selected bills, members would be free to act at the committee level and on the floor according to their constituents' wishes and their own consciences.

This model of limited party government was embodied in the House and party rules reforms adopted at the beginning of the 104th Congress. The Speaker would be given more say over committee chairmanships and memberships and greater control over legislation through flexible referral authority and selective intervention in the process on behalf of party priorities.

Expected to be responsive to the party leadership and program, committee chairmen would have more authority over their committees and staff. The three-term limits for chairmen would prevent committee and subcommittee leaders from becoming too independent or close to special interests. Members would have more meaningful participation in committee and subcommittee proceedings because of limits on the number of assignments they could accept. This, in turn, would make possible the abolition of proxy voting and give rise to greater deliberation in committee. If more well-conceived and representative legislation was reported from committees, it presumably would no longer be necessary for the leadership to rig the final game through highly restrictive floor procedures.

All this looked well and good on paper. It was at odds, however, with the initial Contract program that most members of the House Republican Conference had agreed to the previous September. The Contract rolled the party's major priorities into a single limited time frame. In short, the Contract was a brilliant campaign document. It nationalized the elections and served as a unifying force for the party in the critical first several months of the new Congress. As such, it enabled the majority to move forward rapidly and demonstrate that it could run the Congress and pass programs that had widespread public support.

The Contract's benefits, however, were short-lived. Neither the process for considering Contract bills in the House nor the euphoric mood it set could be sustained for long. The Contract papered over the party's traditional antipathy toward powerful, party government, the continuing fissures within the party among various factions (fiscal conservatives, supply-siders, social conservatives, and the more moderate Northeast/Midwest wing), and the desire for a more deliberative and participatory system of lawmaking.

That things held together and went as smoothly as they did during the first 100 days of the 104th Congress is something of a miracle in itself. As noted earlier, the Contract was composed of more than ten legislative proposals. Several of the ten planks included multiple legislative propositions that could not be considered together for political and practical reasons. Instead, they were divided into twenty-three more manageable pieces, seventeen of which were under the primary jurisdiction of the House Judiciary Committee. Remarkably, every committee was able to report its assigned bills according to deadlines set by the chairmen and leadership. The House actually completed its work on all the Contract items seven days ahead of the 100-day pledge, with only the term limits constitutional amendment failing to pass.

It goes without saying that most committees were not able to devote to each Contract bill the time for hearings and deliberation that would be considered advisable under more normal circumstances. But then the Contract was not designed for a deliberative process. The legislative details of each bill had been drafted and published in advance, and the Contract promised the bills would be brought to a vote essentially as drafted. Therefore, committees were given little leeway to change their bills, even if they had wanted to. The Judiciary Committee, for example, dared to adopt two substantive changes to its term limits constitutional amendment, forcing the leadership to have the Rules Committee send to the House floor an original version rather than the committee-reported one.

Although they were subject to very little deliberation at the committee level on, most of the Contract bills were given a relatively open amendment process on the House floor. The Contract had not promised that each bill would be considered under a completely open amendment process, but it did pledge that each would be given "full and open debate" and "a clear and fair vote." The leadership and Rules chairman Solomon intended to be as open as possible while operating under obvious time constraints. The Democrats, on the other hand, were intent on testing the new majority's commitment to greater openness—partly as a matter of principle, partly as payback for perfunctory consideration in committee of their views, and partly as a means of slowing down the Republicans' legislative juggernaut.

The initial test came on the very first Contract bill out of the box (after opening-day consideration of the Congressional Accountability Act). The Unfunded Mandate Reform Act was aimed at curbing federal laws that imposed new requirements on state and local governments, and the private sector, without providing the federal dollars to pay for the costs of compliance. The measure was referred to four committees in the House on opening day. Two of the four, Rules and Government Reform and Oversight, held hearings and reported their portions on January 13. The other two committees, Judiciary and Budget, waived their right to report. The Rules Committee granted a completely open rule on the bill on January 18, and the House began debate the following day.

Solomon and the chairman of the Government Reform Committee, William Clinger of Pennsylvania, split duties on managing the two hours of general debate on the bill, but it was Clinger who would be left to manage the amendment process—probably one of the most grueling experiences of his career in Congress. Of the 118 amendments printed in the *Congressional Record* during the two-week consideration of the bill, only 59 were actually offered. Of those offered, nineteen were adopted (all but one by voice vote); thirty-three amendments were rejected, all but two by roll call votes; and another seven amendments were withdrawn.[19]

As it turned out, the bill took eight days to consider, with a two-day break in the middle to debate the balanced budget constitutional amendment under a restrictive amendment process that allowed just six substitute amendments. By the time the unfunded mandate bill approached a final vote on February 1, even the Democrats were worn down and no longer insisted on roll call votes on their final round of amendments. Despite all the controversy, the bill easily passed, 360-74.

Republicans knew they could not pass the rest of the Contract bills on time if they allowed similar unlimited debate to take place, so they resorted to "modified" open rules on some of the remaining bills. This placed an overall time cap on the amendment process without specifying what amendments could and could not be offered. The minority could choose its priority amendments to offer instead of having the Rules Committee majority make the determination for them in a restrictive, structured rule.

On April 6, seven days ahead of the 100-day deadline, the House completed action on the last of the twenty-three bills that comprised the Contract. The Republicans had not fallen too far short of Solomon's goal of 75 percent open rules: of the twenty-two Contract items brought under special rules, sixteen (73 percent) were considered under an open or "modified open" amendment process (nine with completely open rules and seven with amendment time caps). The remaining six bills (27 percent) were considered under modified closed or structured rules.[20] The bill in the Contract relating to sex crimes against children was so noncontroversial that it was considered under suspension of the rules. After forty minutes of debate (no amendments), it passed, 417-0.

Obviously, the majority leadership could afford to be relatively open on the Contract legislation since all but a few Republicans had pledged their support for it in ink, if not blood, the previous fall. As expected, all of the measures except the term limits constitutional amendment passed the House. The real test would come when the Contract ties that bound were loosened, and members were left more to their own judgment on other legislation. Holding the party majority together would be difficult for the leadership, especially since it went into every battle on the assumption that it could not count on any Democratic votes.

When legislation of special importance to the majority party is at stake, the majority leadership often resorts to what political scientist Barbara Sinclair has called "unorthodox lawmaking." These unorthodox procedures to pass bills are unlike the regular order or standard legislative procedures practiced by the "textbook Congress." They include the strategic use of multiple bill referrals and omnibus bills; the creative and usually structured use of special rules; the bypassing of one or all of the committees of jurisdiction; postcommittee adjustments (for example, an entirely new substitute may be made in order for the committee-reported bill or the automatic adoption of new provisions into the reported bill may be mandated through provisions in the special rule); and presidential-congressional summits. According to Sinclair, when two or more of these special procedures are used for major legislation, the chances for passage and enactment are greatly enhanced.[21] While in the minority, Republicans had criticized most of these unorthodox procedures for perverting the deliberative and democratic process.

Another unorthodox lawmaking procedure, probably not mentioned by Sinclair because it has been around for so long, even though prohibited by parliamentary rules, is attaching legislative, policy riders to appropriations bills—a tactic that has become increasingly popular with the majority leadership during periods of divided party government. At the outset of the 104th Congress's appropriations process, Appropriations chairman Bob Livingston and Rules chairman Solomon spoke out forcefully against loading down the spending bills with legislative language. In a letter to Livingston on June 6, 1995, Solomon wrote, "I think you will agree that, given new budgetary constraints, the Appropriations Committee has its hands full enough in just finding necessary spending savings for existing programs without being saddled with rewriting underlying laws for those programs. . . . By holding a tight line against authorizing language in the bills you report, you will make it easier for both the Rules Committee and the House to resist pressures [to protect] . . . amendments various Members wish to offer to your bills."[22]

But resisting the pressures to do so proved to be a losing battle. By July 1995 Livingston was openly warning his colleagues about the practice: "The more we get sidetracked on policy issues, not fiscal issues, the harder it is to get legislation to the President's desk." And he went on, "Policy issues probably don't belong in appropriations bills. Everybody's got their own pet rock."[23] His remarks were made shortly after opposition to the National Endowment for the Arts led to the rejection, 192-238, of a special rule for the Interior appropriations bill (the only special rule loss of the 104th Congress). It portended troubles down the road with other appropriations bills.

As for the new openness promised by the Republican House, it weakened over time. By the end of the 104th Congress, only 58 percent (and not Solomon's announced 75 percent) of the special rules reported by the Republican-controlled Rules Committee were open or modified open, compared with 44 percent in the Democratic-controlled 103d Congress. Of the thirteen major bills enacted into law in the 104th Congress that were considered under special rules, only five were considered under open rules: bills on the elimination of federal speed limits, elimination of the Interstate Commerce Commission, immigration reform, lobby disclosure reform, and the line-item veto. The other eight major bills were considered under modified closed rules, including farm program reform, health insurance, minimum wage, welfare, and telecommunications bills.[24]

Perhaps because of the methods by which such bills were considered, the 104th Congress was able to enact a remarkable amount of major legislation once the midway impasse was overcome. At the end of the first session, only 88 bills had been signed into law, compared with 210 in the first session of the 103d Congress. However, at the end of the second session of the 104th Congress, another 245 bills were enacted into law, just 10 fewer than in the second session of the 103d Congress.

The Republican Congress demonstrated (albeit belatedly) its ability to compromise and work with the president to produce results and govern. This was a major factor in the party's outcome in the 1996 elections. Republicans retained control of the House and Senate, although by a slimmer majority in the House than before. According to a Gallup Poll, public approval of the job Congress was doing was higher in late October of 1996 than it had been in late October of 1994—34 percent compared with 23 percent.[25]

It is not clear the extent to which the procedural reforms adopted by the new majority affected legislative outcomes, let alone left any lasting impression on the public. The erratic pace and unique nature of the 104th Congress was not an ideal setting in which to assess whether the institutional changes, taken together, produced a more responsive, representative, accountable, or deliberative legislative body.

A survey of House committee chairmen and ranking minority members toward the end of the Congress revealed that most thought the reforms affecting their committees had produced positive results in their deliberations and operations. The only negative reactions were on the three-term limits for chairmen, and a prohibition on committee meetings while the House is considering amendments without approval of the House—a provision that would be repealed at the beginning of the next Congress.[26]

Presumably, the Republican reforms and the evolving leadership styles employed in the second half of the 104th Congress would be put to a fairer test under the more normal circumstances expected in the 105th Congress. Leaders promised their relieved members it would not be led off by a 100-day, Contract II agenda.

Notes

1. *Congressional Record*, Jan. 4, 1995, H4.
2. Ibid., H8.
3. Ibid., H6.
4. Ibid.
5. Richard Wolf, "'Bulldog' Nussle Says Status Quo Won't Do," *USA Today*, Nov. 17, 1994, 5A.
6. C. Lawrence Evans and Walter J. Oleszek, *Congress under Fire: Reform Politics and the Republican Majority* (Boston: Houghton Mifflin Co., 1997), 94.
7. Ibid., 95.
8. Ibid., 100.

9. Timothy J. Burger, "Gingrich Plots GOP Transition," *Roll Call*, Oct. 13, 1994, 21.
10. David S. Cloud, "GOP's Drive for a More Open House," *Congressional Quarterly Weekly Report*, Nov. 19, 1994, 3320.
11. Mary Jacoby, "'Chairman' Solomon Says He Plans to Grant Open Rules on 75 Percent of Bills Next Year," *Roll Call*, Nov. 28, 1994, 18.
12. See "A Contract for a New House," a section-by-section summary and analysis of H. Res. 6, adopting the Rules of the House for the 104th Congress, *Congressional Record*, Jan. 4, 1995, H32–38.
13. *Congressional Record*, Jan. 4, 1995, H11.
14. Ibid., H8.
15. Ibid., H30, 31.
16. Ibid., H31.
17. David S. Cloud, "GOP, to Its Own Great Delight, Enacts House Rules Changes," *Congressional Quarterly Weekly Report*, Jan. 7, 1995, 13, 14.
18. *Congressional Record*, Jan. 4, 1995, H18.
19. From the "Thomas" Web site (http://Thomas.loc.gov/home/thomas.html), H. R. 5, 104th Congress, bill status and summary.
20. "Survey of Activities of the House Committee on Rules," report of the Committee on Rules, H. Rept. 104-868, Nov. 26, 1996, 92–100. The six measures with structured rules included the term limit and balanced budget constitutional amendments, the habeas corpus bill, the welfare and tax bills, and the product liability/legal reform bill.
21. Barbara Sinclair, *Unorthodox Lawmaking: New Legislative Processes in the U.S. Congress* (Washington, D.C.: CQ Press, 1997).
22. Letter from Rules Committee chairman Gerald B. Solomon to Appropriations Committee chairman Robert Livingston, June 6, 1995.
23. Dan Morgan, "Chairman Wants Some Riders Off the Bus," *Washington Post*, July 14, 1995, A6.
24. "Legislation in the 104th Congress . . . What Passed and What Didn't," *Congressional Quarterly Almanac, 1996*, vol. 52 (Washington, D.C.: Congressional Quarterly, 1997), 1–13; and "Survey of Activities of the House Committee on Rules."
25. "Gallup Poll Data" from the Gallup Organization Web site.
26. "Report on Survey of House Committee Chairmen and Ranking Minority Members on Committee Operations, Staffing, and Procedures," Committee Print of the House Committee on Rules, September 5, 1996, in *Building on Change: Preparing for the 105th Congress*, hearings of the Committee on Rules, July 17, 24, and September 5, 12, 1996, 213–31.

12

Coming Full Circle: The Complete Revolution?

SHORTLY after the Republicans' 1994 election victory, Speaker-to-be Newt Gingrich announced: "On the side of House Republicans . . . we will cooperate with anyone, and we will compromise with no one."[1] By contrast, shortly after the 1996 elections, Gingrich told the Republican Conference:

> We find ourselves here with a Democratic president and a Republican Congress, and we have an absolute moral obligation to make this system work. . . . If the last Congress was the "Confrontation Congress," this Congress will be the "Implementation Congress." We bear the unusual burden of reaching out to a Democratic president and saying, "Together, we are in fact going to find common ground."[2]

Just as the confrontational style in the 104th Congress carried Republicans to the brink of disaster, so the cooperative style of the 105th Congress again imperiled the Republican leadership—especially Gingrich. Factional strife within the party continued over its revolutionary ideals versus governing realities. Discord surfaced on numerous issues, often precipitated by the procedural tactics the leadership employed to deal with them. The majority Democratic leadership had learned in previous Congresses that the use of its procedural powers not only had limits, but could backfire. Republican leaders learned this valuable lesson the hard way.

The first indication of leadership problems ahead came on the opening day of the 105th Congress, January 7, 1997. Nine Republicans broke ranks on the vote for Speaker (four voting for candidates other than Gingrich, and five voting present). The source of this unprecedented breach of party unity on an opening day was nervousness over the unresolved ethics case against Gingrich and an anticipated negative report from the ethics committee. Gingrich was narrowly elected Speaker over Democratic leader Richard A. Gephardt, 216-205.[3]

The next problem occurred on March 20, 1997, over what should have been a routine committee funding resolution. The Republicans had instituted a new committee budgeting process at the beginning of the 104th Congress by instituting a biennial, instead of annual, resolution to pay for committee operations, and by consolidating so-called statutory and investigative staff salaries under the same resolution. Previously, the statutory staff, up to thirty per committee, were separately funded through the appropriations process alone, thereby bifurcating and partially concealing the total costs of House committees.

At the beginning of the 105th Congress, the Republican leadership gave a new twist to the committee funding process: their House rules package authorized a reserve fund to be included in any biennial committee funding resolution. The reserve fund was to be available for unanticipated committee expenses, such as increased demands from an unexpected investigation, and was to be subject to majority leadership sign-off and approval by the House Oversight Committee. In the past, any additional expenses had to be approved by the full House after being reported as a supplemental expense resolution from the House Administration Committee (renamed the House Oversight Committee in the 104th Congress). Democrats objected vociferously during the opening day House rules debate of the 105th Congress to what they termed a new "slush fund" for the majority.[4]

Committee funding resolutions are "privileged" under House rules. They can be filed directly from the House floor after being reported (without prior introduction and referral), and they can be considered one calendar day after the report has been available to members. The resolution is debatable for one hour in the House, and it is not subject to amendment unless the previous question is defeated just prior to the final vote, or an amendment is put forward in a motion to recommit with instructions.

When the Democrats controlled the House, the House Administration Committee usually reported a substitute amendment for the resolution as introduced. It did this for two reasons: first, to highlight the differences between what the various committees had requested (the introduced version) and what the House Administration Committee was actually recommending (the substitute); and second, to preclude the minority on the House floor from offering a substantive amendment in a motion to recommit the resolution with instructions.

This was the practice followed by Republicans in the 104th Congress when they called up their first biennial committee funding resolution, H. Res. 107, that slashed committee staff (from over 2,000 to a little over 1,300) and cut committee funding by 30 percent (from $223.3 million to $156.3 million).[5] Although the Democrats had already taken hard hits on committee staff by moving from the majority to the minority party in the House, the committee staffing and funding processes went reasonably smoothly and fairly. The resolution was easily adopted after the traditional hour of debate, 421-6.

In 1997, however, the Republican leadership decided that even with such a tight process it was still too risky to bring the committee funding resolution for the 105th Congress directly to the floor. The resolution as reported from the House Oversight Committee authorized $178.3 million, a 14 percent increase over the previous Congress. The increase included $20 million for the Government Reform and Oversight Committee to cover its campaign fundraising investigation (a 48 percent increase from the previous Congress), and $7.9 million for the newly created reserve fund.[6]

The Republican leadership found itself caught in the middle. On one side were Democrats united against the reserve fund and scandal monies. On the other side was a small band of Republican revolutionaries, mostly from the 104th Congress's freshman class, who were outraged over the resolution's $22 million increase, which they saw as a betrayal of the Contract's commitment to cut the costs of government, beginning with the Congress.

Sensing these rumblings of revolt, the Republican leadership turned to the Rules Committee for a special rule to help extricate it from this squeeze play. To expedite consideration of the committee funding resolution, the Rules Committee on March 19 issued a special rule, H. Res. 101, that contained not one but two self-executing provisions aimed at minimizing the number of potentially embarrassing votes. First, the special rule self-executed the adoption of the House Oversight substitute, which included the reserve fund monies. Next, it automatically modified the substitute with language that promised that any increases from the previous Congress would be offset by cuts from other legislative-branch appropriations accounts. In another words, the increases would be paid for out of other entities (such as the Government Printing Office or the General Accounting Office) included in that appropriations measure. (It was unlikely that the offsets would come from members' office allowances or the leadership's allocations.) The special rule automatically ordered the previous question. This blocked further amendment. Although the special rule did allow the minority one motion to recommit, the self-executed adoption of the substitute effectively blocked any possibility that an amendment could be offered in the motion. All the motion to recommit could do was to send the resolution back to committee.

By reducing the number of opportunities for dissent on the funding resolution, the leadership opened new opportunities for dissent on the special rule, including an extra hour of debate and a previous question vote. If the vote on the previous question was rejected, the Democrats could amend the rule and make in order a further amendment of their choosing to the funding resolution. The Democrats sensed that their best strategy was to keep it simple through a straight up-or-down vote on the rule. They did not shrink, however, from lambasting both the reserve fund and the costs of the Government Reform Committee's investigation of the 1996 campaign fund-raising. None of the Republican dissenters spoke during debate on the special rule. They emerged en masse from the Republican cloakroom near the end of the vote to cast their "Nay" votes by electronic voting cards. The special rule was rejected, 210-213, with no Democrats voting for it, and eleven Republicans voting against, all but one of whom was from the freshman class of 1994.

One of the Republican rebels was Rep. Mark Neumann of Wisconsin. He told the press after the vote: "It should come as no surprise that some of us were going to say no when they want to hire more Washington bureaucrats. When we go out and tell our people we're going to balance the budget, we can't start with an increase in our own budget."[7] Other dissenters explained that they were sending a message to Speaker Gingrich and the rest of the leadership: "Our leaders are not representing the views of those who sent them." Their votes, they said, could be interpreted as a vote of "no confidence" in the leadership.

After a spirited Republican Conference that night, Republicans tried again the next day with a new special rule. This one made in order a pared-down version of the funding resolution. Only the Government Reform and Oversight Committee and the reserve fund were funded at the earlier levels. Funding for all of the other committees was extended at the previous year's level for one month. The resolution also ensured that increased costs elsewhere in the legislative branch would be offset. Both the special rule and the funding resolution were adopted with nearly unanimous Republican support. However, on the May 1 resolution to fully fund the remaining seventeen committees, nine Republican members voted no. Neumann was the only holdover from the original group of eleven dissenters. With fifty-two Democrats voting in support of the resolution this time, it passed easily, 262-157.

Procedural strategy was a major factor in two other matters in the spring of 1997: supplemental appropriations and highway funding. Taken together with the revolt over committee funding in February, these incidents eventually led to the failed coup attempt against Gingrich in early July.

The Supplemental Appropriations Fight

On May 14 the House voted 193-229 to defeat a special rule for consideration of the $8.4 billion emergency supplemental appropriations bill for domestic disaster relief and international peacekeeping operations in Bosnia and the Middle East. The rule was defeated even though it provided for an open amendment process.[8]

What sparked the opposition were special provisions in the rule. Democrats objected primarily to an amendment by Rep. George Gekas of Pennsylvania to establish an automatic funding process to block future government shutdowns. As a legislative or policy rider, the amendment needed special protection under the rule to be offered.

Among the forty-six Republicans breaking ranks with the leadership was Majority Whip Tom DeLay of Texas, the leadership's third-ranking member. The GOP defections were attributed to multiple causes. DeLay and Appropriations subcommittee chairman Jim Kolbe of Arizona were reportedly upset that the special rule had left vulnerable to a point of order a long-standing provision protecting the Massachusetts supplier of paper for U.S. currency. Others were upset that the rule self-executed the adoption of an additional $76 million in funds for the Women, Infants, and Children (WIC) nutrition program requested by President Clinton. Overall, the dissidents said the rule did not reflect commitments they believed they had from the Republican leadership. This time it was not a sophomore rebel but fourth-termer David Camp of Michigan who said, "It's important that we send a message."[9]

Late on May 14, the same day the first rule was rejected, the Rules Committee reported a new rule that protected the currency provision and provided a separate vote on the WIC amendment. The new rule was adopted the next day, 269-152; this time only eight Republicans defected. Gekas's automatic government funding amendment, identical to a Senate-passed amendment, was adopted, 227-197. This provision, along with a Republican-backed provision barring statistical sampling in the 2000 census, provoked a presidential veto of the emergency spending bill.

Speaker Gingrich and Senate majority leader Trent Lott of Mississippi quickly retreated from any further confrontation with the president over the supplemental bill. Republican rank-and-file grumbling about being led down the path of defeat and retreat intensified and soon spread to the rest of the GOP leadership. When Appropriations Committee chairman Robert Livingston called up the compromise supplemental bill on June 12, it easily passed the House, 348-74. But seventy-three of the seventy-four "nay" votes were cast by Republicans, including the second- through fifth-ranking leaders of the party (Dick Armey, Tom DeLay, John Boehner, and Chris Cox) and four committee chairmen (Bill

Archer, Dan Burton, Bill Goodling, and James Sensenbrenner).[10] The measure passed the Senate, 78-21, and was signed into law by President Clinton.

The Highway Funding Feud

The other defining incident of the first session occurred one week after the defeat of the special rule on the first emergency supplemental appropriations bill. Bud Shuster of Pennsylvania, the chairman of the House Transportation and Infrastructure Committee, told Majority Leader Armey that he wanted an amendment made in order to the budget resolution that would substantially increase highway funding. When Armey objected on grounds that it would break the just-completed, historic agreement with the president to balance the budget, Shuster was not deterred. Shuster claimed he had been promised a vote on his amendment by Gingrich. Gingrich confirmed that he had made the promise without consulting the rest of the leadership.

Both Armey and Rules Committee chairman Gerald Solomon were livid over being blind-sided. Nevertheless, Solomon knew that, as an "arm of the Speaker," he could not be the cause of the Speaker breaking his word. He insisted, though, that Shuster follow the long-standing practice by offering his proposal as an entire substitute for the budget resolution and not just as a discrete amendment to it.

After some further protests over this precedent, Shuster reluctantly agreed to redraft his amendment as a substitute when he got no further help from Gingrich. His substitute provided an additional $12 billion over the budget agreement amounts for transportation, offset by across-the-board cuts in other domestic and discretionary accounts and reduced amounts in tax cuts.

The rule reported by the Rules Committee for the budget resolution made in order five substitute amendments, three by Democrats and two by Republicans.[11] The Republicans had purposely denied a "Blue Dog Democrat" substitute by Rep. David Minge of Minnesota because they thought it posed the greatest threat to the Budget Committee's version.[12]

The budget rule did not use the "king-of-the-hill" process favored by Democrats when they were in the majority—guaranting a vote on each substitute by stacking the deck in favor of the majority's preferred version, even if it got fewer majority votes than another substitute. Nor did the budget rule follow the "queen-of-the-hill" approach of "most votes wins" that Republicans had used for substitutes on measures like term limits. Instead, the Republicans' special rules for budget resolutions in the 104th and 105th Congresses made it clear that if a substitute was adopted, it was the one that prevailed, even if others made in order by the special rule had not yet been considered. This was, after all, the normal amendment process. As Solomon put it during debate on the 1997 rule, "What that means . . . quite simply is that there are no free votes here today."

The "no free votes" policy nearly proved to be a costly disaster. Although the first four substitutes made in order were handily defeated by large margins, Shuster's substitute was actually leading during much of the vote, forcing the leadership to stretch the time allowed (seventeen minutes) to persuade some members to change their votes. As Illinois representative Ray LaHood, a member of Shuster's transportation committee, told a reporter during the vote, "Shuster has made it very clear this is the defining vote for every member's project, road or bridge. I'm telling you, this is a big vote for a lot of members. There is a lot of heartburn and anxiety around here."[13]

When the gavel finally fell on the vote shortly after three in the morning on May 21, the Shuster amendment had been narrowly rejected, 214-216. A Shuster aide complained to the *Washington Post* that the leadership was able to win the vote only after it "started breaking arms." A leadership staffer later agreed: "The only reason we had a chance to break their arms is that the Transportation Committee had already broken their legs, and they couldn't get away."[14] The Budget Committee's resolution was subsequently adopted by a comfortable margin of 333 to 99.

The Plot Thickens

The disarray among Republican leaders and followers alike reflected in these incidents provoked a round of meetings between various members of the leadership and about twenty junior dissidents who were ready to depose the Speaker. Of the fifteen rebels identified by one publication as being part of the Gingrich ouster group, twelve were members of the 1994 class of freshmen. They had gone so far as to draft a privileged resolution to vacate the speakership, identical to one unsuccessfully used by the Democrats against Speaker Joseph Cannon in the 1910 revolt.[15] They did not seem to mind that their 1910 counterparts had opposed such a resolution.

The 1997 Republican rebels said they were led to believe that Armey, DeLay, and Boehner would back their effort. But Armey reportedly changed his mind and joined with Gingrich to foil the coup attempt when he learned that Rep. Bill Paxon of New York, and not Armey, was the rebels' first choice to succeed Gingrich as Speaker.[16]

The attitude of the group of Republican rebels was perhaps best expressed by Rep. Tom Coburn of Oklahoma, who said, "The thing that binds us together is the idea that principles are more important than political expediency. By compromising, we never get defined, and we lose what we stand for."[17] Another one of the plotters, Joe Scarborough of Florida, was more pragmatic and acknowledged the political realities. He told National Public Radio after the failed coup:

"Sometimes we acted impulsively. We don't have an institutional memory. We didn't serve in legislatures before we came here. And a lot of us are not going to be around here for very long. We still need to understand we're connected at the hip to 228 people and we need to at least try to work things out."[18]

The Week That Was

One week in the 105th Congress best exemplifies the conflicting pressures on the Republicans to govern and to uphold their revolutionary ideals. It was the week of March 30, 1998, when the House considered four major issues that were so heavily wrapped in political strategies and procedural strings that the leadership nearly strangled itself and the revolution in the process.

Campaign Finance Reform

The first issue out of the box was campaign finance reform, an item Gingrich had promised to bring to a vote by the end of March in an effort to preempt a discharge petition drive gaining momentum on a bipartisan campaign reform bill.[19] The legislation was tentatively scheduled for floor consideration on March 26.

The House Oversight Committee had dutifully reported a bill on March 23, and two days later the Rules Committee took testimony from fifteen members on a dozen amendments that had been filed. It did not issue a rule pending a final leadership decision on the procedural ground rules.

On Friday, March 27, the leadership suddenly changed gears. It pulled the issue out of the Rules Committee and instead scheduled votes on four campaign bills the following Monday under the suspension-of-the-rules process usually reserved for noncontroversial measures having bipartisan support. The suspension process allows no wiggle room. Each bill is debatable for only forty minutes, is not subject to amendment or to a motion to recommit, and requires a two-thirds affirmative vote to pass. The process is therefore hardly ever used to consider a major controversial bill.

The Rules Committee had been prepared to report a highly restrictive, leadership-backed special rule that would have barred consideration of a popular alternative by Republican Chris Shays of Connecticut and Democrat Martin Meehan of Massachusetts (similar to the McCain-Feingold bill in the Senate). The leadership, however, feared a House majority might still amend the rule or offer a motion to recommit with instructions that would force a vote on the Shays-Meehan amendment.

In both the 102d and 103d Congresses, the Democrats brought their campaign finance reform bills to the House floor under modified closed rules that allowed for just one Republican substitute and prevented a motion to recommit with instructions. In both instances Republicans fought the rules tooth and nail.

The rules, they said, were "unfair" and "undemocratic" because they "gagged the people's representatives" and "disenfranchised the American people."[20]

In the 104th Congress the Republicans changed their tune. They reported a similar rule for their own campaign finance reform bill, the only difference being that Democrats were allowed a second amendment, if they wished, through a motion to recommit with instructions—a right now guaranteed to the minority party under one of the Republicans' opening-day reforms.[21]

When Majority Leader Armey announced the suspension approach for campaign bills on Friday, March 27, Democrats and Republican Chris Shays cross-examined Armey at length about the fairness and wisdom of the strategy. Armey tried to justify the process on grounds that the leaders had received "an enormous amount of requests" about the "urgency" of the issue. He lamely explained that "in order to respond to those people who have been so vocal on this matter . . . haste was more important to their concerns than the substance of the matter." Shays was incredulous. He asked Armey "to explain to me why he thinks haste is more important than substance." Armey tried to deflect the criticism. Members who insisted that it ought to be done by the end of March are responsible for placing "the emphasis on haste as opposed to substance."[22]

A flurry of critical newspaper and TV reports, editorials, and columns appeared over the weekend. Congressional Democrats resumed on Monday, March 30, where they had left off Friday with harsh one-minute and special order speeches before the measures were finally considered late that afternoon. That same day, House Oversight Committee chairman Bill Thomas had introduced a new version to overcome a criticism leveled at the reported bill. Referring to this tactic, Rep. Sam Gejdenson, the ranking Democrat on the committee, complained that "not just the substance of the legislation is bad," but the process is so "horrific" that "the Politburo under Joseph Stalin would have been proud of [it]."[23] Other members called the process a "shame," "sham," "cruel hoax," "travesty," "mockery of democracy," "fraud," and "an April Fool's Joke." Meehan resorted to a Woody Allen line from the movie "Bananas" to roll several jabs into a single punch: "a travesty of a mockery of a sham."[24]

The more telling criticisms, however, were from Republicans. Arkansas Republican Asa Hutchinson was a co-leader of a bipartisan group of freshman who were pushing campaign finance reform. Hutchinson said the suspension process "reflects the dark side of this institution" in both parties. It "sent a message to the American people that we are afraid of reform, and that we will undermine it at any price." Sophomore Republican Matt Salmon of Arizona said he was "ashamed" that the bills were being considered "in the same manner as that of the leadership who ran the House for 40 years under the Democrats."[25]

When the dust settled late that Monday night, two minor campaign bills dealing with disclosure of contributors and foreign contributions passed overwhelmingly under suspension. The two other bills, however, were resoundingly rejected. The first, a variation on the more comprehensive House Oversight Committee bill, garnered just seventy-four votes and was abandoned by the leadership. The other bill, barring the use of union dues or corporate funds for campaign purposes without the prior approval of the union members or stockholders, did not even get a majority of votes. It failed, 166-246.

But the leadership's tactics had served the unintended purpose of re-igniting interest in the languishing discharge petition that had been stuck since the fall at around 190 signatures—28 short of the magic 218 (see Chapter 10). When the House broke for a two-week recess on April 2, the number of signatories had increased to 195. Over the recess members who had cosponsored reform legislation but had not yet signed the petition were pressured to do so.

The first day back from the recess, April 21, the number of signatures shot up to 202, and the next day to 204. At that point Gingrich and Solomon sat down with a group of the Republican reformers to discuss a possible agreement. After a contentious meeting of the House Republican Conference, the leadership issued a statement announcing the deal:

> The result of the frank and focused discussion is a commitment by the Leadership that campaign finance reform will be brought to the floor in May and fully debated under an open rule, permitting substitutes and amendments. The base bill for debate will be H.R. 2183, the "Freshman Bill," a bipartisan proposal presently cosponsored by 50 Democrats and 21 Republicans.[26]

To avoid surprises, substitutes would be pre-printed in the *Congressional Record* at least two days before consideration of the legislation. To avoid the discharge process from being used, Republican members who had signed or agreed to sign the petition "agreed to remove their names." Representative Shays glowingly praised the leadership's turnaround: "This is a great day for democracy . . . for both the Republican and Democratic parties and for Congress."[27]

The leadership statement also took credit for the Republican role in the public disclosure of discharge signators: "The Leadership recognizes that the public discharge petition, which was pioneered by Newt Gingrich, Bob Walker, and Jim Inhofe, ensures that members can express their will on the scheduling of legislation."[28] The Inhofe rule change from the 103d Congress had been enhanced at the beginning of the 104th Congress by a new requirement: the instantaneous posting on the Internet of petition signatures on a daily basis. Indeed, the "discharge petition" Web page had been a frequently visited site by members, leaders, the media, and the public ever since the campaign petition was filed.[29]

Disaster Relief

On Tuesday, March 31, the day after the campaign reform bills were considered under suspension of the rules, the House debated two other matters that involved different procedural problems. The first was a $2.9 billion supplemental appropriations bill for disaster assistance and peacekeeping operations in Bosnia and Iraq. Although President Clinton had requested a single supplemental bill that included $17.9 billion in funding for the International Monetary Fund and $505 million in overdue U.S. dues for the United Nations, the Republican leadership in both houses had agreed to keep those items in a separate bill. Nevertheless, an amendment was added to the disaster bill in the Senate on March 26 providing the requested funding for the IMF, but not for the United Nations.

House Appropriations chairman Bob Livingston wanted to follow the Senate lead in giving the disaster supplemental an "emergency" designation that would exempt it from budgetary spending ceilings and enforcement. But fiscal conservatives in the party, known as the CATs (Conservative Action Team), insisted that the bill be paid for with offsetting cuts in other programs—a practice followed by Republicans in the previous three years. With the president and House Democrats opposed to such offsets, Livingston offered to include them in a self-executing special rule. In this way making the vote on the rule would be the test of whether the bill should be deficit neutral. But the idea of a special rule was vetoed by the conservatives.

What emerged from the Appropriations Committee were offsets from the Section 8 public housing reserve fund, airport grants, the AmeriCorps program, and bilingual education programs. These domestic cuts, in turn, produced resistance from moderate Republicans and a veto threat from Clinton.

To counter this, further adjustments were made through a self-executing provision in the special rule that restored some of the funds cut from airport grants, shifted further cuts to the public housing reserve fund, and gave fiscal hawks a "sense of Congress" proviso that all of the supplemental spending should be offset by cuts from other programs. The rule was adopted on March 31, 220-199, with only three Republican defections. But on the final passage vote for the supplemental bill, the measure barely squeaked through, 212-208, with seventeen Republican dissenters and only seven Democrats voting for it. The final compromise bill with the Senate retained offsets for the domestic spending, but not for the defense funds, and dropped the Senate's IMF provision.

Financial Services

The second bill that ran into trouble on that Tuesday was a major financial services bill designed to increase competition in that industry by permitting certain types of affiliations between banks, securities firms, and other financial service providers.[30] The bill had been up and down the Hill several times in the 104th Congress with no final resolution of outstanding problems among the various parties involved. The bill was reported in the 105th Congress by the Banking Committee in July of 1997 and by the Commerce Committee the following November. But by March of 1998, it was clear the measure would need further tweaking if it were to pass.

Additional negotiations were conducted and agreements reached, all of which were reflected in the complex special rule that emerged from the Rules Committee.[31] The rule made in order an entirely new amendment in the nature of a substitute for H. R. 10, the text of which was printed in the report on the rule, running 134 pages in small typeface. The rule and report were filed after midnight on the day the bill was to be considered by the House.

The new substitute included, among other things, a compromise between the Banking and Commerce versions, the text of a credit union bill reported separately from the Banking Committee, and offsets from the Federal Reserve to pay the costs of the bill.[32] The rule also made in order five amendments out of forty that had been filed with the Rules Committee, four by Republicans and one by a Democrat.

The Democrats united in opposition to the rule because it "hijacked" the popular credit union bill and because important amendments had not been allowed for consideration. In the middle of debate, Solomon initiated a quorum call to get a sense of whether his side had sufficient votes to pass the rule. The reports from the whips were not favorable. "In all my 31 years in government, I have never seen anything happen like is happening today," said Solomon about the lobbying blitz against the rule. "The phones are ringing off the hook, including my own, and they are coming from the friendly banks." He called the lobbying effort "something I have never seen in my life happen here" and warned "the country is going to regret it because this body is not going to work its will." With that, he withdrew the special rule from consideration. On March 31 the credit union bill passed handily on its own, 411-8. The financial services bill later passed the House by a cliff-hanging vote of 214 to 213 under a slightly more expansive and bipartisan rule.[33]

The Highway Bill

The fourth and final incident of the "week that was" occurred the next day, April 1, when the House considered the long-awaited omnibus highway–mass transit authorization bill. After his narrow defeat on the budget resolution the previous spring, Transportation chairman Shuster had developed a bipartisan bill that would have majority House support. It had been a long and bumpy ride to this point.

On September 4, 1997, Shuster and the Democratic leaders of his committee had held a news conference to unveil a $103 billion, three-year bill that exceeded the balanced budget agreement's levels by $17.3 billion over that same period.[34] Gingrich quickly met with Shuster, who had vowed to bring the bill up over leadership objections, "one way or another." Gingrich apparently made it clear to Shuster that he would not allow a vote on a highway bill that violated the budget agreement because "it would violate everything that the party stands for." Shuster was forced to settle for a six-month extension of the existing programs.[35]

What emerged from Shuster's committee the following spring was even more of a budget buster. The $219 billion, six-year bill included $9 billion to fund more than 1,500 special projects in members' districts. The measure represented a 42 percent increase over the funding levels of the previous six years and was $30 billion over the budget agreement levels. The bill left it to the House-Senate conference committee to find offsetting spending cuts and revenue increases to bring the bill back within the budget agreement.

The special rule for the transit bill reported by the Republican-controlled House Rules Committee on March 31 was not much different than the last special rule the Democrats had reported on the highway bill in 1991. In 1991 the Rules Committee reported a modified closed rule allowing for just twelve amendments, eight by Democrats and four by Republicans.[36] Forty-one amendments were denied. When the rule reached the floor on October 23, 1991, the ranking Republican on Rules, Solomon, blasted it as being "truly unprecedented, unjustified, and unfair," because it treated the committee's bill "as almost sacrosanct, beyond the reach of members on this floor."[37]

Armey, not yet a member of the party leadership, called the 1991 bill "a Democratic bill with a Democratic tax increase in it . . . in order to build pork barrel projects in favored congressional districts." Transportation Committee chairman Bob Roe fired back at his Republican critics for trying to "belittle" those eager to help their districts with road projects: "You could not hurt me if you hit me with a baseball bat because you people are princes of darkness," snarled Roe. "Princes of darkness is what you are."[38]

Despite the Republicans' vitriolic rhetoric, the 1991 rule was adopted, 323-102, with sixty-six Republicans supporting it and ninety-nine opposing. The bill went on to pass the House by an overwhelming vote of 343 to 83.

The 1998 highway bill was a similar bipartisan love-fest, with even less opposition to an even tighter special rule. Of the thirty-six amendments filed with the Rules Committee, it made in order only five, three by Republicans and two by Democrats.[39] One of the unsuccessful amendments, filed by Rep. Nita Lowey of New York, proposed a national drunken driving standard of 0.08 blood alcohol content. Republicans took the brunt of the blame for blocking

Lowey's amendment, which had received considerable and favorable media attention.

This time, with the shoe on the other foot, the GOP praised the modified closed rule. Republican manager David Dreier called it "a very fair and balanced rule . . . that gives the House the opportunity to debate important improvements as well as alternatives to these [transportation] programs."[40] Moreover, the minority party on Rules was more like-minded in 1998 than in 1991. Minority rule manager Joe Moakley urged his colleagues to support the rule.[41]

Speaking against the rule on grounds that the bill broke the budget agreement were fiscal conservative Democrats Charles Stenholm of Texas, David Minge of Minnesota, Budget ranking minority member John Spratt of South Carolina, and Democratic Caucus chairman Vic Fazio of California. The only Republican member to speak out against the rule was Chris Shays of Connecticut. He called it a "core debate" and "core issue" for the Republican Congress because "we are going to talk about spending surpluses before surpluses even exist." He concluded his remarks with the following:

> I hope and pray that this Republican majority finds its center again. I believe we are losing it. I believe we need to work overtime to get it back. I honestly have to say to my colleagues I think we will be judged harshly if we don't. I oppose this rule.[42]

When the vote was taken on the special rule, it was easily adopted, 357-61, with just sixteen Republicans and forty-five Democrats opposing it.

Other Republican opponents of the bill had saved their fire, preferring to voice their views during debate on the bill itself rather than on the rule reporting it. They had their chance during debate on an amendment by Rep. Lindsey Graham of South Carolina to strike out all of the special projects. Rep. Sue Myrick, former mayor of Charlotte, North Carolina, observed of the bill that, "when we came here and became a majority, we said we were going to change things. We were going to be different. We were going to balance the budget. And now we are getting ready to break that commitment by $26 billion. . . . That is, in my mind, business as usual. What has changed? It is wrong."[43]

During debate on another amendment, this one by Budget Committee chairman John Kasich to phase out most of the federal gasoline tax and turn the highway program over to the states, Republican representative Salmon complained about the bipartisan pork process, saying that the "American two-party system that we have loved so long" is "dead and gone," and "replaced by one big mammoth party called the 'republicrats'" that has "one interest, and that is business as usual."[44] Democrat Nick Joe Rahall of West Virginia called

Salmon and his colleagues "the 'RWWK,' the 'right wing whacko kids' for some of the philosophy they have been espousing here today."[45] Notwithstanding the intensity of these rhetorical exchanges, the highway bill passed by a comfortable margin, 337-80.

A final agreement between the House, Senate, and administration on the highway bill was not reached until late in the evening of May 21, the day before the House was scheduled to adjourn for its two-week, Memorial Day "district work period." Since the highway program, as extended, had already expired on May 1, Shuster had no trouble persuading the Republican leadership to expedite consideration of the bill. This required two special rules from the Rules Committee, the first of which would allow the second special rule and the conference report to be considered on the same day both were filed.[46] The massive conference report, 800-plus photocopied pages (no formal printed copy was yet available), could be considered as soon as it was filed by Chairman Shuster. This was a departure from the norm. House rules usually require a three-day interval between the release of a conference report and discussion of it.

With only two photocopies of the conference report available on the floor (one at the Republican desk and one at the Democratic desk), there was something of a feeding frenzy among members trying to discover whether their special projects had made the cut. The final conference version came in at the higher House spending level of $217 billion over six years, including $9.3 billion in special highway and bridge projects for members' districts and senators' states. Senate conferees convinced their House counterparts to reduce their 1,500 special highway and bridge projects and funding by roughly one-fourth so that the Senate could apply the amount to projects of their choosing in the states they represented.[47]

Although Shuster was forced in conference to drop a House-passed provision to take the highway trust fund off-budget, he won inclusion of a "firewall provision" that locked spending for trust fund programs in at specified levels. Remarkably, a new House point of order was instituted against any bill or amendment that attempted to reduce those levels. This is the only time a standing rule has been adopted to prevent the House from even considering reductions in spending in certain areas—a curious legacy for the same Republican Congress that boasted the first balanced budget in thirty years.

In the rush to file the conference report, conferees had improperly drafted the language to offset the excess costs of the bill by eliminating roughly $15.4 billion in veterans' disability benefits for smoking-related ailments, and by reducing social service block grants by $2.3 billion. They had omitted completely an incentive-based alternative to state-mandated programs to reduce the blood-alcohol standard for drunk driving. Both provisions were attached later to an Internal Revenue Service reform bill. The veterans' disability provision, with its inauspicious timing just before Memorial Day, turned out to be the source of greatest controversy. Democratic representative David Obey capitalized on this with a motion to recommit the conference report with instructions to find the funds elsewhere. His motion narrowly lost, 190-195. But it was smooth sailing for the pork-filled measure after that. The conference report passed the House, 297-86, and the Senate the same day, 88-5.

The late Speaker, Thomas P. O'Neill, Jr., must surely have been smiling down from heaven on this scene of bipartisan harmony. It reaffirmed his now famous aphorism that "all politics is local." Even revolutions need good roads to run on, and all roads do lead to home—especially after the enactment of the 1998 highway bill.

Notes

1. *Contract with America: The Bold Plan by Rep. Newt Gingrich, Rep. Dick Armey, and the House Republicans to Change the Nation*, ed. Ed Gillespie and Bob Schellhas (New York: Times Books/Random House, 1994), Appendix, Speech of Rep. Newt Gingrich to the Washington Research Group, Washington, D.C., November 11, 1994, 196.

2. John E. Yang, "In Conciliatory Speech, House Speaker Vows a Different Approach," *Washington Post*, Nov. 21, 1996, A1.

3. House Roll Call No. 3, Jan. 7, 1997. Gephardt also voted "present"; Gingrich was the only member not voting. House Roll Call No. 8, Jan. 21, 1997, H. Rep. 105-1, "In the Matter of Representative Newt Gingrich," report of the Committee on Standards of Official Conduct, Jan. 17, 1997. On Jan. 21 the House voted 395-28, with 5 Democrats voting present, to adopt the report of the Committee on Standards of Official Conduct. The report recommended that Gingrich be reprimanded for filing false statements with the committee and assessed $300,000 to reimburse the committee for the consequent additional costs of the investigation.

4. Ironically, when Republicans were in the minority, they complained about the "Speaker's slush fund," officially known as the "contingent fund of the House." Although the Speaker had considerable flexibility in its use (such as for foreign travel), he could not direct that it be used to supplement authorized committee expenses. Republicans had all references to the House contingent fund stricken from the rules of the House in their opening-day rules package for the 104th Congress.

5. "Providing Amounts for the Expenses of Certain Committees of the House of Representatives in the One Hundred Fourth Congress," Committee on House Oversight, H. Rept. 104-74 to accompany H. Res. 107, 104th Cong., 1st sess.

6. "Providing Amounts for Expenses of Certain Committees of the House of Representatives in the One Hundred Fifth Congress," Committee on House Oversight, H. Rept. 105-33 to accompany H. Res. 91, 105th Cong., 1st sess.

7. Guy Gugliotta, "House Dissenters Block Campaign Probe Funds," *Washington Post*, March 21, 1997, A1.

8. H. Res. 146, providing for consideration of H. R. 1469, making emergency

supplemental appropriations for recovery from natural disasters, and for overseas peacekeeping efforts.

9. John E. Yang, "Angry House Republicans Help Block Funding Bill," *Washington Post*, May 15, 1997, A9.

10. H. R. 1871, making emergency supplemental appropriations, Roll Call No. 203, June 12, 1997.

11. H. Res. 152 provided five hours of general debate on the budget resolution, H. Con. Res. 84, plus an additional twenty minutes of debate to be controlled by Representative Minge, whose substitute was not made in order. It then provided for consideration of amendments by Rep. Maxine Waters (D-Calif.), sixty minutes; Rep. John Doolittle (R-Calif.), twenty minutes; Rep. George Brown of California, twenty minutes; Rep. Joe Kennedy (D-Mass.), twenty minutes; and Rep. Bud Shuster (R-Pa.), twenty minutes.

12. A group of conservative Democrats in the House had given themselves the nickname Blue Dog Democrats in contrast to the now extinct Yellow Dog Democrats—persons supposedly so loyal to the party they would vote for a yellow dog if it were on the ticket. See Roger H. Davidson and Walter J. Oleszek, *Congress and Its Members*, 6th ed. (Washington, D.C.: CQ Press, 1998), 342.

13. Eric Pianin and John E. Yang, "Gephardt Denounces Balanced Budget Plan," *Washington Post*, May 21, 1997, A1.

14. "Heard on the Hill," *Roll Call*, May 26, 1997, 1, 14.

15. For more background and details of the coup attempt, see a series of articles by Jackie Koszczuk in the *Congressional Quarterly Weekly Report*: "Gingrich under Fire as Discord Simmers from Rank to Top," June 21, 1997, 1415–18; "Coup Attempt Throws GOP off Legislative Track," July 19, 1997, 1671–74; and "Party Stalwarts Will Determine Gingrich's Long-Term Survival," July 26, 1997, 1751–55. See also Sandy Hume, "Gingrich Foils Coup by Deputies," *The Hill*, July 16, 1997, 1, 25.

16. Because of his role in the coup attempt, Paxon stepped down as Gingrich's hand picked chairman of GOP leadership meetings and later announced he would retire at the end of the 105th Congress. The forty-four-year-old fifth termer from Buffalo already had a well-established legacy as the successful chairman of the Republican Congressional Campaign Committee, which helped the party recapture the House in 1994 after forty years of Democratic control.

17. Koszczuk, "Party Stalwarts," 1753.

18. Ibid., 1752.

19. Discharge Motion No. 3, filed by Rep. Scotty Baesler of Kentucky on October 24, 1997, on a special rule, H. Res. 259. This resolution provided for the consideration of H. R. 1366, the Blue Dog Democrats' campaign finance reform bill, as well as several substitute amendments by designated Republican and Democratic members. By the end of the first session in 1997, the petition had 187 signatures.

20. H. Res. 299, 102d Congress, providing for consideration of H. R. 3750, the House of Representatives Campaign Spending Limit and Election Reform Act of 1991; and H. Res. 319, 103d Congress, providing for consideration of H. R. 3, the House of Representatives Campaign Spending Limit and Election Reform Act of 1993.

21. H. Res. 319, 104th Congress, providing for consideration of H. R. 3820, the Campaign Finance Reform Act of 1996. The minority substitute was rejected, 177-243; the motion to recommit with instructions to tighten disclosure on independent expenditures narrowly lost, 209-212; and the Republican bill was then defeated, 162-259.

22. *Congressional Record,* March 27, 1998, H1683.

23. *Congressional Record,* March 30, 1998, H1733.

24. Jeffrey L. Katz, "All-But-Doomed Overhaul Bill Meets Its Expected End," *Congressional Quarterly Weekly Report,* April 4, 1998, 863.

25. Ibid.

26. "Leadership Statement on Campaign Finance Reform," issued by the Office of the Speaker, April 22, 1998.

27. Helen Dewar and Juliet Eilperin, "Campaign Bill Gains in House," *Washington Post,* April 23, 1998, A1.

28. "Leadership Statement," April 22, 1998.

29. The open rule on the freshman bill, adopted by the House on May 21, made in order eleven substitute amendments, each open to any germane amendment, under a "most votes wins" process. The bill was considered sporadically for eleven days, lasting into early August, with a total of forty-five amendments offered and thirty-seven roll call votes taken. When the dust finally cleared, the Shays-Meehan substitute was the only one garnering a majority of votes, 237-186. The bill went on to pass by an even larger margin of 252 to 179—with 61 Republicans joining 190 Democrats and 1 independent in support. On September 10 a final attempt to resurrect the comparable McCain-Feingold bill in the Senate fell eight votes short of the sixty votes needed to end a filibuster.

30. H. R. 10, 105th Congress, a bill to enhance competition in the financial services industry by providing a prudential framework for the affiliation of banks, securities firms, and other financial service providers. Reported by the Committee on Banking and Financial Services, July 3, 1997, H. Rept. 105-164 pt. I; and by the Committee on Commerce, Nov. 3, 1997, pt. III.

31. H. Res. 403, 105th Congress, providing for the consideration of H. R. 10, the Financial Services Act of 1998, H. Rept. 105-474, reported from the House Committee on Rules, March 31, 1998 (legislative day of March 30).

32. The credit union bill was H. R. 1151, 105th Congress, reported from the Committee on Banking and Financial Services on March 30, 1998 (H. Rept. 105-472).

33. H. Res. 428 (H. Rept. 105-531), providing for consideration of H. R. 10, the Financial Services Act of 1998. The resolution allowed for consideration of twelve amendments, printed in the Rules Committee's report on the rule. The rule was adopted, 311-105, on May 13, 1998 (Roll Call No. 142).

34. Don Phillips and Eric Pianin, "Panel Proposes $103 Billion Road Bill," *Washington Post,* Sept. 5, 1997, A4.

35. Eric Pianin, "Shuster Bows to Budget Pact," *Washington Post,* Sept. 18, 1997, A18.

36. H. Res. 252, 102d Congress, providing for consideration of H. R. 3566, the surface transportation reauthorization act.

37. Mike Mills, "House Approves Highway Bill Strewn with Obstacles," *Congressional Quarterly Weekly Report*, Oct. 26, 1991, 3117.
38. Ibid., 3118.
39. H. Res. 405, providing for consideration of H. R. 2400, the Building Efficient Surface Transportation and Equity Act of 1997 (BESTEA).
40. *Congressional Record*, April 1, 1998, H1859.
41. Ibid., H1860.
42. Ibid., H1864–65.
43. Ibid., H2014.
44. Ibid., H2024.
45. Ibid., H2025.
46. Under House rules, a two-thirds House vote is required to consider a special rule on the same day it is reported from the Rules Committee. The first rule waived this supermajority vote requirement to consider the rule for the highway bill conference report.
47. Alan K. Ota, "Senators Pile on the Take-Home Projects after Coaxing House to Reduce Its List," *Congressional Quarterly Weekly Report*, May 30, 1998, 1465.

13

Term Limits and the Scarlet Letter

THE inclusion in the 1994 Contract with America of a pledge supporting a constitutional amendment limiting congressional terms reflected a major surge in the democratic impulse to keep elected representatives close to the people. It was the outgrowth of a national movement launched around the beginning of the decade that began to use the direct democracy tool of state initiatives to impose tenure limits not only on state legislators, but on members of Congress as well.

Efforts to impose term limits on members have met with predictably chilly receptions ever since Rep. Thomas Tudor Tucker's futile foray in the First Congress, which at least provoked a House vote (see Chapter 2). It was the closest Congress would come to considering self-imposed limits on service for the next two centuries. Term limit amendments would be introduced from time to time, only to die a quiet death in committee.

That dynamic began to change in 1988, when Republicans inserted in their national party platform a plank supporting congressional term limits. In 1990 Vice President Dan Quayle stumped for congressional term limits during the mid-term election campaigns, and in December of that year White House chief of staff John Sununu announced President George Bush's intention to push for such an amendment.[1]

The states did not wait for the Democratic Congress to respond to Republican platform planks or presidents. Colorado had already adopted a ballot initiative in 1990 to exclude House and Senate members from election ballots after twelve years of service. Washington State adopted a "three-terms-and-out" rule for House members in 1991.[2] By the conclusion of the 1994 mid-term elections, twenty-two states had passed some form of term limits for congressional service, most by ballot initiative. The constitutionality of state-imposed limits on national legislators' terms had made its way on appeal to the Supreme Court in 1994 in a case from Arkansas.

Whereas prior to the 1990s, only a dozen or so term limit constitutional amendments had been introduced in both houses in any Congress, by the 103d Congress (1993–95), twenty-eight constitutional amendments had been introduced. Moreover, the most popular of the amendments, H.J. Res. 38, introduced by Rep. Bill McCollum, a seven-term Republican from Florida, attracted 102 cosponsors. McCollum filed a discharge petition on his resolution on July 1, 1993, and by the end of the 103d Congress he had collected 109 of the 218 needed to bring a discharge motion to the floor. Among the signatories were three Democrats and 60 percent of the Republican Conference.

Freshman Republican representative Peter Hoekstra of Michigan was not as successful in the 103d Congress with a discharge petition for the consideration of his bill, H. R. 3835, to conduct a national advisory referendum on congressional term limits. Hoekstra's bill had fifty-nine cosponsors, only fifty-two of whom bothered to sign his discharge petition. The object of the petition was a special rule (H. Res. 409) that would have broadened the bill to include advisory referendums on two constitutional amendments. One required a balanced budget, the other a presidential line-item veto.

Term Limits and the Contract with America

With the Republican takeover of the 104th Congress (1995–97), advisory referendums and discharge petitions would no longer be necessary: the Contract with America promised a vote on two alternative approaches to term limits during the first 100 days of the new Congress. The tenth item on the Contract, "The Citizen Legislature Act," was described as "a first-ever vote on term limits to replace career politicians with citizen legislators." As was pointed out in Chapter 10, its placement at the bottom of the list was not an indication of its priority ranking. To the contrary, as Republican pollster Frank Luntz explained, readers' eyes glance first at the first item on a list and then at the last. If they like what they see, they look in between. The first item on the Contract, the balanced budget constitutional amendment, and the last, term limits, received the highest support ratings (around 80 percent) from voters according to Luntz's survey data.[3]

When Republicans released the texts of their Contract bills on November 15, 1994, the term limit item was actually a special rule that provided for two competing versions. One was similar to McCollum's twelve-year limitation in the 103d Congress (H.J. Res. 38). The other resembled Rep. Bob Inglis's proposal from the 103d Congress (H.J. Res. 160) that limited House members to six years and senators to twelve years. Under the terms of the special rule, the Inglis measure would be offered as a substitute for the McCollum version.[4]

What emerged from the House Judiciary Committee on February 28, 1995, was a third version, an entire substitute that limited members to six *consecutive* terms of service, and senators to two *consecutive* terms. Moreover, the amendment in the nature of a substitute provided that the constitutional amendment's provisions preempted any applicable state laws containing different terms of service.

When Rep. Barney Frank of Massachusetts offered an amendment to make term limits retroactive rather than prospective, McCollum denounced it as a "killer-type amendment." The chairman of the Judiciary Committee, Rep. Henry Hyde of Illinois, voted against Frank, but he chided McCollum for his "seeming disdain for retroactivity." He went on, "If the purpose is to bring out the deadwood . . . why not sweep it clean?"[5] Frank's amendment was rejected, 15-20, with two Republicans voting for it and two Democrats voting against.

The Judiciary Committee reported the bill with the substitute amendment but *without recommendation* by a vote of 21 to 14.[6] Chairman Hyde adamantly opposed term limits as did third-ranking Judiciary Republican F. James Sensenbrenner, Jr., of Wisconsin. Moreover, the amendment to confine the limits to consecutive terms originated with a Republican, seventh-term representative George Gekas of Pennsylvania, who said it was sufficient to curb the powers of "these lifetime chairmen wielding these long gavels for ever and ever."[7] The Gekas amendment was adopted, 21-13, with five other Republicans, but not Hyde, joining Gekas.

Hyde summed up his opposition to term limits as follows:

> The nation's future depends on the caliber of the people leading it. We need individuals with the self-confidence, the experience, the wisdom and the judgment to be able to negotiate issues of war and peace. We get these people from the crucible of politics and experience. Term limits will not only deprive us of the institutional memory of Members of Congress needed to guide us, it will deprive us of the individual memories which bring experience to bear on the important issues of the day.[8]

The ten committee Democrats signing the dissenting views to the committee report characterized term limits as "anti-democratic" because they "impair without recourse a fundamental right of people to vote for whomever they choose." They also said they were "completely unnecessary" because "congressional turnover is not low." Term limit proponents claim "mutually exclusive goals": "to make legislators closer to the people," on the one hand, and "to establish constitutional distance for a more deliberative process," on the other.[9]

The group U.S. Term Limits (USTL) took a hard-line stance for a three-term limit for House members. Its TV ads criticized members who supported the twelve-year, instead of six-year, limit, and its executive director, Paul Jacob, personally attacked McCollum for supporting the six-term limit, calling him "more of an impediment to the success of term limits than anybody else in Congress."[10] The group was consequently barred from attending any more strategy meetings with the GOP leadership, Rules Committee, and their coalition allies on how to proceed.

McCollum urged that he not be required to jump through additional procedural hoops to get back to his original version from the committee's reported version. Therefore, it was decided that an entirely new resolution should be the subject of House floor debate and further amendment. McCollum obliged by introducing his old language as a new resolution (H.J. Res. 73) on March 2, 1995. The reported resolution would be jettisoned, effectively bypassing the committee product altogether. The rationale for this was that the Contract had promised that the measures would be voted on in substantially the same form as originally presented.

When the Rules Committee met on March 15, it reported a special rule making in order the newly introduced joint resolution containing McCollum's original language as the base text for amendment purposes.[11] The special rule also made in order four alternatives, one by Democrats under a "queen-of-the-hill" (or "most-votes-wins") process—a variation on the Democratic "king-of-the-hill" ("last-amendment-adopted-wins") process. If more than one alternative received a majority of votes, the one with the most votes would be reported back to the House from the Committee of the Whole for final passage. Only at that point is a two-thirds vote necessary under the Constitution. In case of a tie vote in the Committee of the Whole, the last version adopted would be reported back to the House.

The rule was reported by the Rules Committee on a 9-3 party-line vote after the committee rejected two Democratic amendments—one for a completely open amendment process and the other to apply retroactivity to the winning substitute. On the House floor, however, the rule was adopted by voice vote.

The first substitute, offered by Democratic representatives Pete Peterson of Florida and John Dingell of Michigan, would have applied the twelve-year cap *retroactively* and allowed states to set lower caps. It failed, 135-297. The amendment provoked an outburst by Rep. Martin Hoke, who called Dingell "cynical" and "hypocritical" for saying he would vote against term limits on final passage, even if his substitute was adopted. A near party-line vote of 212 to 197 was necessary to permit Hoke to retain his floor right to speak that day after this breach of House decorum.[12]

The next substitute, by Rep. Bob Inglis of South Carolina, set a six-year cap for House members, with senators limited to twelve years in office. It was rejected, 114-316. Republican freshman Van Hilleary of Tennessee offered a substitute setting a twelve-year cap for members of both houses, but allowing states to set lower limits. It lost, 164-265. The last substitute made in order by the rule was McCollum's, identical to the base text of his resolution. It was not necessary for him to offer it since no other amendment received a majority vote. The McCollum resolution passed, 227-204, 61 votes short of the two-thirds majority needed to pass a constitutional amendment. There were 189 Republicans voting in favor of passage, 40 against. Only 38 Democrats voted for passage, compared with 163 against.[13]

Among the Republicans voting against the resolution were Judiciary Committee chairman Hyde, who refused to be "an accessory to the dumbing down of democracy," and Majority Whip Tom DeLay of Texas. Republican conference chairman John Boehner, who had previously opposed term limits, reluctantly voted for them, saying it was "a bad idea whose time had come."[14]

In October of 1995, the Senate failed to approve a nonbinding "sense of the Senate" resolution on term limits. The following April the Senate fell two votes short of the sixty necessary to break a filibuster against a term limits constitutional amendment (S.J. Res. 21).[15]

On May 22, 1995, less than two months after the House vote on term limits, the Supreme Court found the Arkansas constitutional amendment imposing term limits on members of Congress to be unconstitutional. It ruled in *U.S. Term Limits, Inc., v. Thornton* that such limits imposed an additional qualification for office in violation of Article I, sections 2 and 3. The effect of the decision was to nullify similar limits adopted by twenty-two other states. But that was not enough to discourage term limit supporters around the country from trying another tack, again using ballot initiatives to achieve their goals.

The Scarlet "T"

On November 5, 1996, voters in fourteen states were confronted with ballot initiatives instructing their legislators in Congress to support a constitutional amendment limiting House members to three terms and senators to two. If federal legislators failed to follow the instructions or voted for an amendment allowing for longer terms of service, they would have printed next to their names on the next ballot the words "disregarded, failed to comply with, or violated voter instructions on term limits." Similarly, nonincumbent candidates would be given an opportunity to sign a "term-limits pledge" or one indicating that they had declined to support term limits, and the appropriate designation would appear by their names on the ballot. This tagging of term limit opponents on election ballots quickly became known as "the scarlet T" (and later as the "scarlet letter").

The ballot initiative passed in nine states: Alaska, Arkansas, Colorado, Idaho, Maine, Missouri, Nebraska, Nevada, and South Dakota. It failed in five states: Montana, North Dakota, Oregon, Washington, and Wyoming. In all but two of the fourteen states (Missouri and South Dakota), the initiative instructed state legislators to support an application to Congress for a constitutional convention to consider amendments to the Constitution. State legislators failing to vote for a call of a constitutional convention would have a designation to that effect by their names on the next election ballot.

Once more it was an Arkansas challenge to a term limit ballot initiative that made its way to the Supreme Court first. In October of 1996, the Arkansas Supreme Court held the initiative unconstitutional on grounds that it established a new, indirect means of amending the Constitution. It ruled the amendment was an attempt to give legislative powers to the people, circumventing the constitutional requirement that amendments originate with the Congress or state legislatures:

> Clearly, the proposed Amendment 9 is nothing more than a coercive attempt to compel the Arkansas General Assembly to do as the alleged majority of the people wish, without any intellectual debate, deliberation, or consideration of whether such action is in the best interest of all the people of this state.[16]

The U.S. Supreme Court initially granted a stay of the state court's order to strike the initiative from the November ballot pending resolution of the case. As it turned out, the Supreme Court would not address the matter until after the House had voted on the term limits issue the following February.

Speaker Newt Gingrich had promised that term limits would be the first significant piece of legislation to be voted on in the 105th Congress (1997–99). Accordingly, the House Judiciary Committee moved quickly in the new Congress, holding a hearing on January 22, 1997, followed by a mark-up session on February 4 at which it ordered the McCollum constitutional amendment (H.J. Res. 2) reported by a vote of 19 to 12.

Once again the committee reported the measure without recommendation. This time, however, no amendments were adopted in committee. The proposal to limit House and Senate members to no more than twelve consecutive years, adopted by the committee in the 104th Congress, offered by Rep. Jerrold Nadler of New York were rejected on a vote of 11 to 19. The closest vote, 13-15, came on an amendment by Rep. Robert Scott to allow states to adopt a term limit less than the federal limit. This time McCollum did not try to trump Scott with a federal preemption clause. Two attempts to impose a three-term limit on House members and a two-term limit on senators were roundly defeated, 4-24 and 3-25.[17]

Once again Chairman Hyde explained his continuing opposition to term limits:

> As a practical matter, each time voters go to the polls, they decide whether they should limit the term of their elected representatives. We already have term limits—they are called elections. The nation found this to be truer than ever before in the 1994 general election when, without arbitrary limits built into the Constitution, membership turnover was vastly accelerated and 40 years of one-party rule came to an end in the House of Representatives.[18]

The Judiciary Committee Democrats concurred that term limits were unnecessary. In their "dissenting views" to the report, they noted that 315 of the 435 House members in the 105th Congress had served five terms or fewer, and 63 of the 100 senators had served fewer than two terms. They went on to quote congressional scholar Thomas Mann of the Brookings Institution: "Incumbent reelection rates and margins of victory in 1992, 1994, and 1996 were low enough to encourage future challengers and put fear in the hearts of members of the Senate and House who seek reelection."[19]

While things went more smoothly in the Judiciary Committee in the 105th Congress than in the 104th, the Rules Committee faced an even greater challenge. The procedural situation was complicated by the fact that not all of the successful state ballot initiatives had identical wording for the term limit amendment. Members from several of the states felt bound to vote only for the "exact language" in their state law, as instructed.

Consequently, on February 11 the House Rules Committee reported a confusingly generous special rule. It provided for two hours of general debate followed by consideration of eleven substitute versions under the "queen-of-the-hill" or "most-votes-wins" process. Seven of the substitutes were different state variations on the same theme of six-year limits for House members and twelve-year limits for senators, with each to be debatable for ten minutes. Three other substitutes dealt with a four-consecutive-term limit for House members, the ability of states to impose shorter limits, and the retroactive application of limits. Once again, McCollum was authorized to offer the final substitute, if necessary, which was identical to the base resolution.[20]

During the Rules Committee's consideration of the sprawling special rule for the term limits resolution, Republican representative Scott McInnis of Colorado expressed concern about the most recent ballot initiatives' attempt to instruct members of Congress and the effect on their ability to deliberate. "It would alter our representative form of government," he warned. McInnis noted a worrisome development: environmental, abortion, and other interest groups in his state were already using ballot initiatives to instruct members how to vote on their issues.[21]

U.S. Term Limits had carefully pointed out the technical differences between the various state initiatives, and in response the Rules Committee had painstakingly accommodated these differences to protect members. Nevertheless, USTL executive director Paul Jacob complained: "This rule is ridiculous. There is no need for this many amendments. If they were seeking to conform with the Informed Voter Laws, there would be two options on the House floor right now."[22]

The rule sailed through the Rules Committee and the House on voice votes. Following general debate, the House began its mini-debates on the eleven alternatives made in order. All seven state versions were rejected by wide margins. The only amendment receiving more than 100 votes was offered by the unlikely bipartisan team of Joe Barton (R-Texas) and John Dingell (D-Mich.). The amendment called for twelve-year, lifetime limits for both houses, retroactively applicable to sitting members. It failed by a vote of 152 to 274.

The final passage vote on the McCollum resolution was 217-211, 69 votes short of the requisite two-thirds necessary for a constitutional amendment, and 10 votes fewer than the 227 votes it received in the previous Congress. This was due mainly to the strict instructions many members felt they were under to vote against any version that was different from the one prescribed by their state. Representative McInnis said members from the competing states were like Siamese fighting fish: "We've been bred to eat each other." He went on to say, "This is the first time I've been forced to vote against some reasonable term limits proposals."[23]

After the vote, Democrat Cleta Mitchell, a former Oklahoma legislator then serving as the director and general counsel of the Term Limits Legal Institute, criticized USTL for sowing so much confusion. "It has literally been a situation for the Republican leadership where no good deed goes unpunished. You can't ask people to keep beating their heads against the wall."[24] But Jacob was unrepentant for any responsibility in the debacle: "Congress is not going to lead the charge for limiting their own terms, not tomorrow or ever." The scarlet letter laws, he explained, will "take the wiggle room away from politicians in Congress . . . [and] term limits will become a reality."[25]

That prediction was soon thrown into doubt. On February 24, 1997, the Supreme Court, in a one-sentence order, and without comment from the justices, allowed the Arkansas court ruling to stand, thereby invalidating that state's scarlet letter law. USTL's Jacob remained undaunted. "We will continue to fight in the trenches to enact term limits on Congress," he said, expressing hope that the Supreme Court would eventually weigh in on a battle coming from another state.[26]

But challenges in the lower courts continued to chip away at the scarlet letter law. In May of 1997, federal district courts struck it down in Maine and Nebraska. In the Nebraska decision Federal District Judge Warren Urbom wrote a seventeen-page opinion backing his preliminary injunction against enforcement of the law. Suspending a state constitutional provision was "not a task to be taken lightly," he acknowledged. But "when a state law violates the United States Constitution, the amount of popular support for the law is irrelevant." He went on to write that if the law were left in place, Members would "be forced to choose between unprovoked, earnest voting and the coercive threat of the political label."[27]

U.S. Term Limits spokesman Jonathan Ferry called the decision "an affront to the voters of the state," and he said that it "wrongly classified these laws as coercive."[28] But Nebraska term limits activist Bob Wright disagreed with Ferry: "Coercive? That's the point. We know that Members are not going to vote for term limits on their own."[29]

After the Federal District Court of Maine invalidated its law a week later, term limits proponent Mitchell expressed support for the two court decisions: "I think the people who proposed the scarlet letter initiatives should lose them. It's simply against public policy to mislead people on term limits or any other issue." Her particular objection was that the laws gave negative ballot designations even to members who supported the twelve-year limits (as opposed to the presidential eight-year limit). "The courts have sent us to the political arena, whether we like it or not," she concluded.[30]

South Dakota repealed its scarlet letter law in 1997. By early in 1998, the scarlet letter was all but a "dead letter." In January Colorado's Supreme Court ruled the law unconstitutional in that state. In February a federal district court overturned Missouri's scarlet letter law, and a three-judge panel of the federal appeals court upheld that decision. In the only remaining states with scarlet letter laws (Alaska, Nevada, and Utah), the laws would not become operative until at least twenty-four other states passed similar laws so as not to disadvantage their state with more junior representatives.

After its setbacks in the spring of 1997, USTL had promised to litigate various pending state cases all the way to the Supreme Court if necessary, and to back petition drives to put the initiative on the ballots of other states. But even then, according to Ferry, USTL activists were laying the groundwork for a fall-back approach that might have a better chance of passing constitutional muster. Instead of giving opponents the coercive stigma of a critical ballot designation ("disregarded, failed to comply with, or violated voter instructions on term limits") why not reward pledge-signing proponents with a positive designation (for example, "pledged to serve only three terms")? The scarlet letter would be replaced by the equivalent of a gold star.[31]

Term Limits and the 1998 Campaigns

By February of 1998, this strategy was in full swing. U.S. Term Limits spokesman Adam Bromberg explained the shift in tactics, "We concluded, 'Hey, we ought to ask people not only to talk about term limits but to limit themselves. . . . We can't ask members to get an amendment . . . so let's ask individual members or candidates to limit the one term they do have control over, and that's their own."[32]

Eric O'Keefe, the president of Americans for Limited Terms (ALT), said the switch came "after a lot of soul searching about whether there was any real prospect of Congress passing a term limit amendment. We knew that most members voting for term limits last year hated them. So we realized that we had to change the composition of Congress, to make it [so] that it wasn't against the self-interest of someone voting on term limits to vote for it."[33]

USTL and ALT reportedly planned to budget several million dollars in 1998, primarily on issue ads targeted at congressional districts with open House seats. The first test came on January 13, 1998, when a special election primary was held for the seat of Rep. Walter Capps in California's Twenty-second District. Capps had died of a heart attack the previous October. His wife Lois was running to succeed him on the Democratic ticket. The two front-running Republicans on the all-party ballot were state representatives Brooks Firestone and Tom Bordonaro. Firestone, a tire fortune heir, was the more moderate of the two but had signed the three-term-limit pledge. Bordonaro, a social conservative, said he supported term limits but refused to sign the pledge.

Americans for Limited Terms spent $90,000 on television ads that pointed out Bordonaro's support for term limits and his refusal to sign the pledge. U.S. Term Limits backed these up with $7,000 in radio ads that echoed the ALT ads. Neither group's ads specifically urged a vote for one candidate over another. Therefore, the groups were exempt from Federal Election Commission reporting requirements for contributors.

Most of the independent spending in the primary was aimed at influencing the Republican race. Campaign for Working Families, run by social conservative Gary Bauer, gave Bordonaro $5,000 in direct contributions and spent nearly another $100,000 on television ads highlighting his opposition to the "partial birth" abortion procedure. Just before the election the Christian Coalition and Catholic Alliance produced and distributed 100,000 voter guides highlighting the candidates' positions on abortion, the death penalty, and other issues. On the other side, Planned Parenthood spent $40,000 on phone banks and a voter guide that labeled Bordonaro a "religious political extremist," without telling people to vote against him.[34]

The outcome of the single ballot race gave Democrat Capps 45 percent of the vote, followed by Bordonaro with 29 percent. Capps went on to beat Bordonaro in the March 10 special election, 53 percent to 45 percent. Ironically, Capps signed the self-limiting pledge and thus reaped the benefit of the term limit groups' largesse, even though she said she was philosophically opposed to the concept. Bordonaro, on the other hand, a self-professed supporter of term limits, continued to refuse to sign the pledge. USTL and ALT poured some $300,000 into TV and radio ads that benefited Capps.[35] A postelection poll of 500 voters taken by the Term Limits America PAC revealed that two-thirds of the voters correctly identified Bordonaro as the candidate who "refused to limit his own terms," while 21 percent said the issue "played a role in deciding who they would vote for." Of that 21 percent, 64 percent say they voted for Capps.[36]

Whatever the impact of interest groups' advertising on the election, Capps maintained it was her emphasis on local issues that won it for her, while Republican House campaign committee chairman John Linder emphasized the high success rate of widows replacing their husbands in Congress. Widows had won thirty-six of thirty-eight such contests since the beginning of the Republic.

Following the March trial run, USTL and ATL began plotting their next steps in upcoming primary states. The two groups focused their efforts on about fifteen districts holding primaries during the months of May and June 1998. ATL reportedly spent $6.5 million to get candidates to sign the pledge.[37]

The term limit groups targeted open seat races where they were more likely to get candidates to sign the pledge. But Pennsylvania's Nineteenth District was a different story. In a May 19 primary the twelve-term incumbent Republican, Rep. Bill Goodling, faced the fight of his life against Charles Gerow, an attorney and part-time college professor. Gerow had won a surprising 45 percent of the votes against Goodling in the 1996 primary. Even though Goodling promised in 1998 to serve just one more term, the term limit groups opposed him. They were irate over the fact that he had pledged in 1996 to support a three-term constitutional limit but then voted against the seven versions of six-year limits and for the twelve-year limit. Consequently, the groups poured $300,000 into radio and television ads denouncing Goodling as a career politician whose record "is a living billboard for the need for congressional term limits."

The race split conservative groups down the middle. Siding with Gerow were conservative activists Paul Weyrich, Gary Bauer, and Grover Norquist. Weighing in for Goodling were the Christian Coalition's Donald Hodel and Traditional Values Coalition chairman Louis Sheldon.[38]

Sheldon conceded that while term limits can be good, "in six years you barely get your feet wet." And he held out the example of Judiciary Committee chairman Henry Hyde, also in his twelfth term, who had played a critical role in advancing conservative interests over the years. "So if you have a person who champions a cause," concluded Sheldon, "the real issue is, let the people in the district who vote decide."[39]

Goodling, who had depended in past campaigns on volunteer workers and shoestring budgets, needed a four-alarm wake-up call from Speaker Gingrich and allied assistance from the GOP to shift to a more professional operation. Only two weeks before the election, an aide to Goodling complained that the candidate "just didn't want to raise the money." He "is still back there some place, and this is 1998 and there is a flood of money coming into the district"—mostly from the term limit groups.[40] However, Goodling's belated retooling of his campaign and the extra party help he received paid off on election day. He took 68 percent of the vote, compared with 32 percent for Gerow. Jacob tried to put the best face on USTL's setback: "Incumbent Bill Goodling found a very effective way to combat the term limits issue—he pledged to serve only one more term. We hope his tactic is widely imitated."[41]

The other Republican primary race of interest took place in Idaho's Second District on May 26. At play was an open House seat to replace GOP representative Mike Crapo, who was running for the Senate. The leading Republican candidate was the Speaker of the Idaho State House, Mike Simpson, a staunch and outspoken opponent of signing the self-limiting pledge even though all the other candidates of both parties had done so. Simpson said he opposed the pledge because it would hurt Idaho politically if members in Congress who had not signed it consequently gained greater seniority and clout. In his words, "I will not put Idaho at risk. I've never been willing to throw away principles for cheap partisan advantage and I'm not about to start now."

Simpson's three Republican opponents attacked his position in the heavily pro-term-limits state. They were aided by Americans for Limited Terms, which committed $165,000 to radio and television ads denouncing his opposition to the pledge.[42] Bauer's Campaign for Working Families ran radio ads attacking Simpson's opposition to term limits and his voting record on abortion. Bauer's ads were pulled when Republican senator Larry Craig criticized them.[43]

Other political figures in Idaho were quick to join Craig in denouncing the two groups' tactics. Popular Republican governor Phil Batt blasted the "smear campaign . . . financed in large part by out-of-state money." One of Simpson's three primary opponents, former state senator Dane Watkins, reacted to the establishment rallying around Simpson. "They wouldn't be bringing out all these big guns if he wasn't in trouble," said Watkins, whose own polls showed him with a ten-point lead in the final week of the primary race. "He's losing this thing because we've defined what he is, and he isn't a conservative. The people are going to make the decision, not the insiders and not the fat cats."[44] As it turned out, the people sided with Simpson and against the outside groups. Simpson won the primary with 40 percent of the vote, followed by state representative Mark Stubbs with 35 percent. Watkins, who had seemed to benefit most from the anti-Simpson campaign, placed a poor third with just 14 percent of the vote. Simpson went on to defeat former Democratic representative (and term limits supporter) Richard Stallings in the general election with 56 percent of the vote.

Independent issue ads by various groups in 1998 sometimes overshadowed the campaigns and issue priorities of the candidates, a matter of concern to candidates and observers alike. Particularly frustrating for the media and groups tracking campaign expenditures was issue ads' exemption from contributor disclosure requirements. In 1997, for instance, the Capitol Hill newspaper *Roll Call* attempted to follow the money used to finance the scarlet letter initiatives in fourteen states in 1996. The best it could do was to show the extent to which funds were transferred between state groups, usually with the direction and coordination of U.S. Term Limits. The investigative report questioned USTL's contention that the term limits movement is the result of spontaneous grassroots activism. This view "is called into question by what can be gleaned about its financial structure." Cleta Mitchell, then director of Americans Back in Charge, which favored the twelve-year limit for House members, also criticized USTL tactics. "There is just a pattern of USTL trying to create the impression that there are multiple organizations, when in fact they are all interchangeable. It's just them."[45]

Nevertheless, no one was charging that U.S. Term Limits or its allied organizations were violating any laws. And it was not the only group exploiting the campaign finance loopholes for issue advocacy ads as a means of influencing elections. Organized labor had pointed the way with such ads in 1995. Now other organizations were simply playing catch-up ball.

Is the Term Limits Movement Limited?

Term limits is one issue with high levels of support no matter when or under what circumstances a public opinion poll is taken. As has already been noted, a Gallup Poll taken just after the 1994 elections showed 73 percent public approval for term limits, 24 percent opposition.[46] Nearly two years later, in May of 1996, Gallup asked people whether they would vote for certain issues if presented on the ballot as a referendum. The item, "Congressional term limits amendment," polled 74 percent support and 23 percent opposition.[47]

Not as easily measured are the intensity and depth of that support at any point in time. In the 1994 survey on Contract with America items, a follow-up question asked whether it mattered if the item was passed within 100 days.

On term limits, 44 percent said yes, and 55 percent, no. Gallup extrapolated from this that popular demand for term limits was only 40 percent.[48] That is not the same, however, as asking voters whether they consider terms limits really important in the long run. Gallup points out that the support level for term limits is considerably lower when the question is asked a different way: "Do you think there should be a limit to the number of years members of Congress should serve, or do you think they should serve as long as the voters keep re-electing them?" The results in early December of 1994 were 65 percent favoring a twelve-year limit, and 36 percent favoring "as long as voters keep re-electing them."[49] When respondents to the same poll were only given a choice between twelve- and six-year term limits, 38 percent favored the longer limit, and 58 percent favored the shorter limit.[50]

Whatever the support for term limits may have been in the spring of 1998, the American people harbored less animus toward Congress than in the past. In fact, they were more satisfied with their own representative and with the institution as a whole than at any time in recent history. Those findings are based on a CNN–*USA Today*–Gallup Poll taken April 17–19, 1998. Fifty-eight percent of the respondents believed that Congress under Republican leadership since 1994 had been a "success." And for the first time in two decades, more Americans said that they approved, rather than disapproved, of the job Congress was doing.[51]

The poll also asked if respondents thought their current representative deserved to be reelected. Sixty-four percent said yes. Moreover, 56 percent said that "most members of Congress deserve another term." Such a positive response had not happened previously on this trend that dates back to 1991, according to the Gallup organization. In 1994 only 53 percent believed their own representative should be reelected, and only 39 percent thought most members of Congress should be reelected. The same 1998 poll found President Bill Clinton's approval rating at 63 percent, notwithstanding ongoing sex and fundraising scandals.[52] It was clear that both the Congress and the president were benefiting from better economic times.

Another sign that the term limits issue did not have as strong a hold as before occurred on February 23, 1998. Republican representative George Nethercutt of Washington, who used the issue of term limits to help maneuver the defeat of Speaker Tom Foley, announced he was reconsidering his own three-term pledge. "Experience has taught me that six years is too short a time to do the job the people of the 6th district elected me to do . . . balance the budget, reduce taxes, reform the IRS." He went on to say that he would not decide whether he would run again until after the 1998 election, but indicated that "many of my constituents have already encouraged me to run in 2000."[53]

USTL director Jacob responded to the news by saying that Nethercutt "has a place in history. . . . [T]he question is, which place is it going to be?" If he does decide to run again, said Jacob, he could be remembered as "one of the all-time cynical people" who used term limits to get elected, then "lost his soul."[54] In June of 1999, Nethercutt announced that he had changed his mind and would seek another term.

Cleta Mitchell, who had spent eight years with various groups championing the twelve-year House and Senate term limits, moved on to a job with the National Federation of Independent Business after the 1997 House vote. In her view USTL's and ALT's insistence on six-year House limits had shattered the coalition. "As long as those people control it," she observed, there was no hope for the movement. But she applauded the three-term limit House Republicans had put on committee and subcommittee chairmen, and the four-term limit placed on the Speaker. If those limits "stay in effect, I will have considered the term limit movement a success." She said, "The real question will be whether the Republicans stick to their guns."[55]

Perhaps more than anything else, her observation helps to refocus attention on the Republican revolution. Its intent was to change the culture of the House that had evolved over forty years of one-party rule—to do away with "business as usual" and return to an institution more responsive to the people than to the special interests.

The constitutional amendments on the balanced budget and term limits were the bookends of the Contract with America—items one and ten. They commanded a high degree of public support because they affirmed the public's disenchantment with a costly government and with self-interested elected officials preoccupied with staying in office. The reality is that both constitutional amendments cannot magically guarantee the results they symbolically promise: a balanced budget and a responsive Congress. Conversely, the desired results can be produced without the sanction of a constitutional amendment. There can be no substitute for the assertion of political will by the electors and the elected.

The Republican Congress, working with the president and aided by a booming economy, proved that it could balance the budget without the mandate of a constitutional amendment. The voters proved that they could produce not only a high turnover in office without the arbitrary guillotine of a term limits constitutional amendment, but also a change in party control of the Congress when circumstances warranted. That such a change occurred in 1994 and was affirmed in 1996 undermines one of the main arguments of term limit advocates—namely, that the voters are too satisfied with the status quo and too inattentive to congressional decision making to make informed choices and changes on their own.

The American people can resort to constitutional amendments to change their government. They have done so in the past and may do so again. But the more easily accessible and effective "club behind the door" continues to be the one they wield in the privacy of their election booths on a regular basis.

Notes

1. Michael Oreskes, "Bush Backs Move for Limiting Terms of U.S. Lawmakers," *New York Times*, Dec. 12, 1990, 1.

2. Ronald D. Elving, "National Drive to Limit Terms Casts Shadow over Congress," *Congressional Quarterly Weekly Report*, Oct. 26, 1991, 3101.

3. Katharine Q. Seelye, "Term Limits: Change Nobody Wants," *New York Times*, March 12, 1995, I28.

4. "House GOP Offers Descriptions of Bills to Enact 'Contract'," *Congressional Quarterly Weekly Report*, Nov. 19, 1994, 3379.

5. Susan B. Glasser, "Term Limits Still Sixty Votes Short," *Roll Call*, March 2, 1995, 20.

6. This was unusual. Ordinarily a committee votes out a measure on a motion "to report the bill favorably to the House with an amendment and recommend that the bill, as amended, pass."

7. "Term Limits Amendment Falls Short," *Congressional Quarterly Almanac, 1995*, vol. 51 (Washington: Congressional Quarterly, 1996), 1–37.

8. "Additional Views of Hon. Henry J. Hyde," in *Term Limits for Members of Congress: Report of the Committee on the Judiciary to accompany H.J. Res. 2* (H. Rept. 104-67), 10.

9. "Dissenting Views," Representatives Serrano, Boucher, Scott, Frank, Conyers, Bryant, Jackson Lee, Berman, Schroeder, and Watt, in *Term Limits for Members of Congress*, 13–14.

10. *Congressional Quarterly Almanac, 1995*, 1–37.

11. H. Res. 116, 104th Congress, a special rule providing for the consideration of H.J. Res. 73, the Term Limits Constitutional Amendment. The text of the amendments made in order is contained in the report on the special rule, H. Rept. 104-82.

12. *Congressional Quarterly Almanac, 1995*, vote no. 273, H80.

13. "Term Limits Amendment Falls Short," 1–37.

14. Ibid., 1–38.

15. S.J. Res. 21 was introduced by Sen. Fred Thompson of Tennessee on Jan. 19, 1995. It was ordered reported on an 11-7 vote by the Senate Judiciary Committee with amendments on Feb. 9, 1995. On Oct. 15, 1995, a report was filed on the measure (S. Rept. 104-158). It was debated on the Senate floor on April 22 and 23, 1996, and, on the latter date, a cloture motion fell two votes short, 58-42.

16. From the Arkansas Supreme Court decision in *Arkansas Term Limits v. Donovan* and *Arkansas v. Donovan*, quoted in Joan Biskupic, "Arkansas Rejection of Term Limits Rule Stands," *Washington Post*, Feb. 25, 1997, A6.

17. "Votes of the Committee," in *Congressional Term Limits Amendment*, report of the Committee on the Judiciary to accompany H.J. Res. 2 (H. Rept. 105-2), February 6, 1996, 4–8.

18. Ibid., "Additional Views of Hon. Henry J. Hyde," 11.

19. Ibid., "Dissenting Views," Representatives Conyers, Scott, Rothman, Frank, Nadler, Watt, Boucher, Lofgren, Waters, Berman, Jackson Lee, and Delahunt, 24.

20. H. Rept. 105-4, "Providing for the Consideration of House Joint Resolution 2, Congressional Term Limits Amendment," report of the Committee on Rules to accompany H. Res. 47, the special rule for H.J. Res. 2, 1-3. The seven state versions and their authors were: Representatives Hutchinson (Arkansas), McInnis (Colorado), Crapo (Idaho), Blunt (Missouri), Christensen (Nebraska), Ensign (Nevada), and Thune (South Dakota).

21. Dan Carney, "House Votes Down Amendment as Effort Loses Momentum," *Congressional Quarterly Weekly Report*, Feb. 15, 1997, 402.

22. Benjamin Sheffner, "'The End' for Term Limits Movement?" *Roll Call*, Feb. 13, 1997, 22.

23. Carney, "House Votes Down Amendment," 401.

24. Sheffner, "The End?" 22.

25. Ibid.

26. Biskupic, "Arkansas Rejection," A6.

27. Benjamin Sheffner, "Federal Judge in Nebraska Blocks 'Scarlet-Letter' Law," *Roll Call*, May 19, 1997, 22.

28. Ibid.

29. Ibid.

30. Benjamin Sheffner, "Judge Throws out Maine's 'Scarlet Letter' Law," *Roll Call*, May 22, 1997, 10.

31. Sheffner, "Federal Judge in Nebraska."

32. Robert Schlesinger, "Term Limit Groups Urge Self-Limits in Tactical Switch," *The Hill*, Feb. 25, 1998, 1.

33. Ibid., 46.

34. Alan Greenblatt, "California House Race Shapes up as a Duel of Interest Groups," *Congressional Quarterly Weekly Report*, Jan. 17, 1998, 137–38.

35. Lou Cannon, "Democrats Keep House Seat in California Special Election," *Washington Post*, March 11, 1998, A2.

36. Tim Curran, "Term Limit Groups Seek to Change Congress One Member at a Time," *Roll Call*, March 26, 1998, reproduced on U.S. Term Limits Web site.

37. Donna Cassata, "Independent Groups' Ads Increasingly Steer Campaigns," *Congressional Quarterly Weekly Report*, May 2, 1998, 1108.

38. Thomas B. Edsall, "Coming to Term Limits," *Washington Post*, May 12, 1998, A4.

39. Ibid.

40. Ibid.

41. "Term Limits Pledge Key Issue in Primaries," U.S. Term Limits press release, May 20, 1998.

42. Marc Birtel, "Leading GOP Contender for Idaho's 2d District Says No to Term Limits," *Congressional Quarterly Weekly Report*, May 9, 1998, 1222.

43. John Mercurio, "Crapo Seat at Risk?" *Roll Call*, May 25, 1998, 14.

44. Ibid., 11, 14.

45. Benjamin Sheffner, "Following the Term Limits Money Shows Dizzying Series of Transfers," *Roll Call*, March 27, 1997, 18.

46. David Moore, Lydia Sand, Leslie McAneny, and Frank Newport, "Contract with America," *The Gallup Poll Monthly*, Nov. 1994, 22.

47. Lydia Saad, "Issues Referendum Reveals Populist Leanings," *The Gallup Poll Monthly*, May 1996, 3.

48. *The Gallup Poll Monthly*, Nov. 1994, 22.

49. Ibid., 25.

50. Richard Wolf, "Public Expects GOP to Honor 'Contract'," *USA Today*, Dec. 9, 1994, 9A.

51. Lydia Saad, "Election '98: A Promising Year for Congressional Incumbents," April 25, 1998, The Gallup Organization Web site.

52. Ibid.

53. Tim Curran, "Term Limit Groups Seek to Change Congress One Member at Time," *Roll Call*, March 26, 1998, 15, 22.

54. Ibid., 22.

55. Ibid., 22.

14

The Electronic Congress

SHORTLY after noon on Friday, September 11, 1998, the House of Representatives overwhelmingly adopted a resolution calling for the immediate release of a 453-page confidential report transmitted two days earlier by Independent Counsel Kenneth Starr. The report concerned possible impeachable offenses committed by President Bill Clinton. The resolution also directed the Judiciary Committee to conduct a "deliberative review" of the report and accompanying materials, and to determine by September 28 what additional information should be released.[1]

Around 2:20 P.M., parts of the report were being read verbatim on CNN by correspondent Candy Crowley scrolling from a computer screen in a member's office.[2] Later that afternoon the report was posted on several news organizations' Web sites and on four congressional Web sites. Web traffic on House servers jumped from an average of 66,000 hits per hour to three million hits.[3] The Library of Congress's Thomas server registered more than 3.7 million hits on Friday, up from the August daily average of 236,409 hits.[4]

Before the day was out, public opinion polls assessing the president's fate were being announced on network newscasts and Internet sites.[5] As House members plowed through paper copies of the Starr report on plane flights back to their districts for the weekend, cyber chat rooms were already ricocheting with rapid-fire reactions to the report. Thanks to instantaneous communications, the American people had access to information and opinions on it way before the House could begin its "deliberative review." Since it last ventured into presidential impeachment waters in 1974, the Congress had undergone a sea change in electronic democracy.

Congress on the Web

Three days after the 1994 elections, the man who would be Speaker, Newt Gingrich of Georgia, told a Washington Research Symposium audience of his plans, not just for the new Congress, but for "renewing American civilization." America must "accelerate the transition from a second-wave mechanical, bureaucratic society to a third-wave information society." To this end, he promised to change House rules "to require that all documents and all conference reports and all committee reports be filed electronically as well as in writing . . . so that information is available to every citizen in the country at the same moment that it is available to the highest paid Washington lobbyist." By so doing, he concluded, the entire flow of information and quality of knowledge in the country will be changed, "and it will change the way people will try to play games in the legislative process."[6]

True to his word, on the morning of January 4, 1995, the opening day of the 104th Congress, Gingrich cut the ribbon on the first-ever congressional Web site, Thomas (after Thomas Jefferson). Gingrich said the site, operated by the Library of Congress, would increase public participation in government and empower people because it gives them direct access to information without the filter of the media.[7] In his acceptance speech as Speaker later that day, he made this announcement: "As of today we are going to be on line for the whole country, every amendment, every conference report."[8]

The first House document to appear on Thomas was the Republicans' rules package for the 104th Congress (H. Res. 6), together with a section-by-section summary and analysis. Not a part of that package was "one change that has had the most profound impact on the way Congress does business" and that was "the widespread introduction of electronic mail and the Internet," noted Vincent Randazzo, an aide who helped draft the new rules.[9]

Gingrich commissioned Rep. Vernon Ehlers, who had led the effort to computerize the Michigan state legislature, to put the House on-line as quickly as possible and to modernize and integrate the House's internal computer system as well. Although Ehlers had drafted an elaborate set of House rules changes to implement his plan, they had not been fine-tuned in time to plug into the opening-day rules package. Questions had been raised by committee staffers and House parliamentarians not only about the immediate feasibility and practicality of some of the requirements, but also about discrepancies likely to occur if documents were filed on-line before they were published in printed form. Since the paper record (or hard copy) is the official record of action, and corrections are often made to it after it is filed, some felt that the public might become confused or even angry if their computer-generated document turned out to be different from what the Congress said was the official document.

Nevertheless, no rule change was necessary to put Congress on the Internet immediately or to strongly encourage committees to put as much on it as they could. It was not until the beginning of the next Congress that the House finally adopted a formal rule concerning the Internet: each committee "shall, to the maximum extent feasible, make its publications available in electronic form."[10]

By mid-1998 a truly staggering amount of information was available to the public through Thomas, the House and Senate Web sites, and other Congress-related sites, such as those operated by the Government Printing Office, the General Accounting Office, the Architect of the Capitol, and the Congressional Budget Office.[11] By mid-September of 1998, 405 House members and delegates, 92 percent of the total membership, and nearly every senator, had their own "home pages" with essential biographical information, current news releases, legislative initiatives and accomplishments, issue positions, and information about the state or district, and about visiting Washington.

Every regular committee in the House and Senate had a home page by mid-1998 except the ethics and intelligence committees. The Joint Economic Committee had two home pages, one for the House and one for the Senate. Perhaps ironically, the newly formed Senate "Special Committee on the Year 2000 Technology Problem" did not have a page on the Web until a month after its formation.

The quality and quantity of information available on the Web pages of individual members and committees vary greatly. Some are updated on a weekly basis, while others have not been revised in months. Taken together, the pages are a slice of Americana. They tout the home state's virtues, products, and tourist attractions, not to mention the elected member's deep roots in the area and distinctively down-home hobbies, charities, and other civic affiliations and honors.

The Internet has given members of Congress an attractive yet inexpensive way of communicating their views and legislative activities to constituents directly, without the filter of the media. It also enables members to link their state or district pages to other useful state and federal government sites. The Senate was so sensitive about these taxpayer-paid self-advertisements that it imposed a protocol prohibiting senators from updating their sites within sixty days of a primary or general election—comparable to the current ban on mass mailings during such periods. The House has not adopted a similar prohibition, perhaps in part because its members stand for election three times as frequently as do senators, and in part because members' Web pages are not forced on constituents the way unsolicted mass mailings are.

The top leaders of both parties and houses have the benefit of double exposure on the Internet: separate home pages for the House and Senate leadership in addition to their district or state pages. These sites are a good place to learn not only what issues the two parties consider to be important, but also the individual leaders' pet projects that may not have formal party endorsement. For instance, the majority and minority leaders' Web pages contain dueling tax proposals: "Majority Leader Dick Armey's Revolutionary Flat Tax Plan" and "Minority Leader Dick Gephardt's 10% Tax Plan." The latter proposal includes a provision to require a national referendum on future tax increases, a major departure from Gephardt's earlier idea for an advisory referendum.[12]

Not available to the public on the Internet but available to members and staff on the internal computer system are Congressional Research Service (CRS) issue briefs, and longer reports and analyses of legislation and policy problems. The reports explain in simple, easy-to-understand terms the issues confronting Congress. CRS has resisted making these reports public because of its legal mandate to serve as an exclusive resource for the Congress and because of legal worries about inadvertent copyright violations. A statutory change in CRS's underlying authorizing law would be necessary to make its reports available to the general public. Bills were introduced in the 104th and 105th Congresses to overcome that hurdle. In the meantime, some committees have gone ahead and made reports they have commissioned available on their Web sites; and some enterprising "netizens" have ordered hard copies of every report from members of Congress and then made them available, for a price, on their own Web pages.

The Congressional Accountability Project, a Ralph Nader spin-off group, has crusaded to make more legislative documents available on a more timely basis, contemporaneous with, if not in advance of, amendments being offered in committee or on the floor of the House and Senate.

Committees have been cut back one-third in staff from the Democratic-controlled Congresses and thus do not have the resources to continuously feed new information into their Web pages. Moreover, requiring such electronic availability as a precondition for proceeding to consider an amendment would bring committee markups and House floor debates to a complete halt while staff hustled to comply. Despite such problems, it is expected that at least short summaries, if not the full text, of floor amendments will be readily available to the public on the Internet, just as C-SPAN now runs such summaries as crawlers on the TV screen during the debate on amendments.

In the 105th Congress Republican senator Mike Enzi requested that senators be allowed to use their laptop computers on the floor of the chamber. The Senate Rules and Administration Committee, chaired by Sen. John Warner of Virginia, vetoed Enzi's proposal on grounds that it would alter the solemn and deliberative nature of the chamber.

As things stand now, members may retire to rooms adjoining the House or Senate floor where computers are available for composing a speech or amendment, or for gathering information on pending legislation. Many state legislatures already permit their members to use computers on the legislature's floor.[13] This is not permissible, however, in the U.S. Congress because of objections raised in both houses. One is the possibility that members will use their electronic mail (e-mail) as a conduit for lobbyists to provide amendments or even speeches on pending bills. Another fear is that the noise from dozens of clacking computers will distract other members from listening to the debate and will convert the chambers in the public's eyes from debating arenas to computer labs.

Congress and E-Mail

The use of electronic mail is still in its infancy on Capitol Hill, though there are already some signs that it is not the sure cure for a detached and distant democracy that many had thought it would be. By the middle of the 105th Congress, 95 senators and 250 House members had a *public* e-mail or Web-mail address. But based on anecdotal evidence, it appears that e-mail is much more popular as a means of communication between members and staff than between members and their constituents.

Many members are reluctant to rely on e-mail, not only because of limited staff resources, but also because of the perceived loss of quality control over their responses to it. When asked whether he wanted a public e-mail address, one veteran committee chairman made his views unambiguously clear to his staff: "I hate e-mail. I don't want it in my committee office or in my congressional office. It is too distracting and too time-consuming." Very few members have the time or patience to sit at a computer and read and answer incoming e-mail; nor do they want their staff firing off instantaneous responses (other than a boiler-plate acknowledgment of receipt of the message and promise of a later replay by mail).

Most members prefer that their aides draft a written response to constituent e-mail messages on congressional letterhead to be sent through the regular mail. In that way the staffer is more likely to compose a thoughtful and informative response that can be reviewed by the member or chief of staff before the letter is signed, sealed, and sent.

Most members will candidly admit (though perhaps not directly to their computer-literate constituents) that they much prefer receiving letters to e-mail. Letters usually indicate that constituents took the time to collect their thoughts and frame them in appropriate language, rather than instantaneously letting loose on the Internet with the first angry thoughts and words that come into their heads.

Since most members already tend to answer only mail from their own state or district, they have devised ways to screen-out nonconstituent mail. The person sending the e-mail must fill out an electronic registration form. This not only filters out "spammed" messages (those sent to multiple members), but also allows the office to determine which correspondents are actually constituents and warrant a reply. Few members have the staff to answer every piece of mail that comes their way, and often refer out-of-district letters to the member from that district as a matter of "congressional courtesy." Perhaps one indication of the differing views on e-mail between the two chambers is the fact that the Senate Web site has an easily accessible e-mail directory, whereas the House site does not.[14]

Two recent polls shed further light on the emerging electronic Congress and the people. The Pew Research Center for the People and the Press surveyed presidential appointees, top civil servants, and members of Congress between October of 1997 and February of 1998 about a variety of subjects. Of the eighty-one members of Congress surveyed, 80 percent agreed that "all things considered . . . the advent of new technologies, fax machines, e-mail, Internet, cell phones" had "helped" them do their job.

When asked how often they "use a computer to go on-line to get information on current events, public issues, or politics," 26 percent of the members of Congress said "regularly"; 16 percent, "sometimes"; 26 percent, "hardly ever"; and 27 percent, "never." A large majority of members (59 percent) said they relied primarily on personal contacts as their source of information on how the public feels about issues, followed by telephone or mail from citizens (36 percent), the media (31 percent), public opinion polls (24 percent), and public meetings (21 percent).[15]

When asked whether they thought the people knew enough about the issues Congress faces to form opinions about what should be done, only 31 percent of the members of Congress said yes, 17 percent said maybe or it depends, and 47 percent said no.[16] This latter finding was played in some quarters as confirmation that members are elitists who look down their noses at their constituents for being unintelligent and uninformed, but such an interpretation is overly simplistic. It overlooks members' more realistic approach to the question. Their response probably has nothing to do with a condescending attitude toward the average citizen. Instead, members are aware of the multitude and complexity of issues they are called to vote on every week. Given that understanding, it would be unreasonable to expect anyone, other than someone paid full-time to do so, to have sufficient information to make an informed judgment about all of these diverse questions. As intelligent and conscientious as they are, most members often feel they are behind the curve when it comes to being as informed as they should be on all the matters on which they are expected to cast votes.

The other survey of interest, conducted jointly by Bonner and Associates and American University's Center for Congressional and Presidential Studies, questioned staff members from 270 congressional offices on the subject of "congressional use of the Internet."[17] The 1998 survey found that nearly 90 percent of the offices used e-mail, though no distinction was made between those who used it only for internal communications in Congress and those who also used it for external correspondence.

Nearly 69 percent reported receiving fewer than 100 e-mail messages per week, though 95 percent said that the amount of e-mail from the district had increased since 1997. Over three-fourths of the offices reported that less than half the e-mail messages they received originated in the home district. Over 71 percent said they responded to constituent e-mail through the regular mails, while 22 percent said they responded with both e-mail and "snail mail." Not surprisingly, 84.3 percent said out-of-district mail was considered less important than district mail or not important at all.

The Bonner-AU Poll found that 91 percent of the congressional offices reported using the Internet on a daily basis. Roughly the same percentage said they used it primarily to retrieve substantive information (such as bill texts, amendments, and floor schedules). Only 2.1 percent said they used the Internet primarily to ascertain interest group positions, and 6.4 percent used it primarily to connect with newspapers or conduct other legislative research.

The sites visited most frequently by congressional offices are Thomas (and other Library of Congress sites), and the sites of the Government Printing Office, Congressional Research Service, the White House, and various executive agencies. Although most offices said they did not use interest-group Web sites to find out a group's positions, 42.7 percent said they visited them to obtain information.

Staff use of the Internet is high, but the poll found that only about 57.8 percent of members use the Internet (according to their staff). Although the survey summary reports that "58% of offices reported that their members use the Internet *regularly*," the actual question that appears in the summary analysis of the report does not assess frequency of use. The question reads simply, "Does the Member in your office use the Internet?" It is difficult to believe that all the members who use the Internet use it regularly.

Finally, 56 percent of the staff surveyed agreed that the Internet would have more of an influence in the future over legislative decision making and issue outcomes than it does at present. Of those 56 percent, 77.4 percent said the influence would be good, 5.6 percent said bad, and 16.9 percent said neither good nor bad. Overall, 91.7 percent of the staff respondents said the Internet would be good for public policy formulation, citing increased access to information, a better informed electorate, and increased research opportunities. Of those who thought it would be bad for policy formulation, most cited "misinformation" as their reason.

The Internet: Communications Tool or Disinformation Device?

Perhaps the most interesting thing about the Bonner-AU survey of Capitol Hill staff is not who participated and the degree to which their offices use the Internet, but rather who sponsored the survey and why. In a press release on the survey, Bonner and Associates described itself as a "grassroots lobbying firm that, over the last 14 years, has helped America's largest corporations and associations win legislative and regulatory fights." The survey results were initially released at a National Press Club press conference on February 17, 1998. They then were used as the launchpad for an all-day "1st Annual Conference on Lobbying and the Internet" on February 23 at the Park Hyatt Hotel in Washington, at a cost of $350 per attendee.[18]

The survey provided Bonner and Associates with a base of knowledge on how it might best use electronic means to enhance its lobbying of Congress and the executive branch. The survey and the conference also attracted potential clients to the firm's high-tech operation. The Washington-based Bonner group had been best known previously for perfecting so-called "astro-turf lobbying" (lobbying techniques that creatively use phone banks and fax petitions to simulate grass-roots support for a cause).

One of Bonner's clients is the Western Fuels Association, a coalition of electric utilities formed to oppose the treaty on global warming. Bonner designed its Web site (http://www.globalwarmingcost.org) to enable specific groups, such as senior citizens and farmers, to e-mail Washington policy makers with their concerns. The groups are initially alerted to the Web site through television and newspaper advertisements. As Jack Bonner explains, "The audience has got to know you're there."[19]

The Bonner firm also uses the lobbying technique called the "virtual petition." After phone operators locate sympathetic citizens, they fax them letters of support with a box for their signatures, and ask them to fax the letter back. The signatures are then scanned into a computer and transferred onto a petition for mailing to their members of Congress. This electronic wizardry gives the impression of a genuine grass-roots, door-to-door petition effort. Some signers were surprised to find their signatures in a *Des Moines Register* advertisement as part of an "Open Letter to the Congress, President Clinton, and Vice President Gore." It looked like nineteen prominent Iowans who opposed the Rio Treaty because it would increase the cost of electricity had signed the letter. However, Bonner had legally covered itself since the fine print on the petition people signed included an authorization for Bonner to use their signatures.[20]

Not all astro-turf lobbying campaigns are as careful. One such effort aimed at derailing a major telecommunications bill in 1995 resulted in a scandal and calls for congressional and Justice Department investigations. As the House telecommunications bill was wending its way to the House floor, Hill offices were flooded with hundreds of thousands of telegrams and letters opposing the measure—all purportedly from constituents. Members began to inquire about the messages, and they learned that many of the correspondents were not aware that their names had been attached to a letter or telegram; others were not old enough to have written them or were so old they were dead. Rep. Henry Bonilla of Texas was especially surprised to receive a letter from himself in opposition to the bill. He voted for it anyway.[21]

When a reporter tracked down a woman in Chicago whose name appeared on a telegram sent to Illinois representative Michael Flanagan, opposing the telecommunications bill, she said she did not know that telegrams still existed and had never heard of Congressman Flanagan. Not only was she not aware of the telecommunications bill debate, she said she didn't really care about it "as long as we're not having a war and the government isn't going haywire."[22]

Rep. John Dingell of Michigan, the ranking Democrat on the Commerce Committee, angrily took to the floor when the bill came up for debate in August 1995. He denounced the "scandalous and outrageous behavior of the long distance lobby" as a "deliberate attempt to lie to and to deceive the Congress." The lobby had tried "to steal the government of the country from the people and from the consumers by putting in place a fraudulent system to make the Congress believe that the people had one set of feelings when, in fact, they . . . had quite a different set of feelings."[23]

The parties in this scandal were the Competitive Long Distance Coalition, which in 1993 had contracted with the public relations firm of Beckel Cowan, which later subcontracted with NTS Marketing, Inc., a telemarketing firm. In its contract NTS agreed to call more than one million constituents using some five hundred operators at the firm's headquarters in Lynchburg, Virginia. When members first began to complain about fraudulent signatures, Bob Beckel responded defensively, "Every single one of those people was called and we have the phone logs to prove it. The idea that we would make these names up is absurd."[24]

However, after further investigation, Beckel changed his story. He announced in mid-September that he could no longer stand behind his claims. NTS had made "serious errors in the implementation of the program." The firm had received verbal authorization from only about half of the 175,000 people whose names were used on the telegrams, and some 25,000 people who had approved telegrams for a previous campaign for the long-distance companies were never called for this one. Beckel apologized to the Congress and to the Competitive Long Distance Coalition. The coalition's chairman expressed regret "that this has been done to the members of the public whose names were used without permission."[25]

When the full story finally came out, NTS admitted that it had sent tens of thousands of telegrams without contacting the people whose names were used. Its president, Charles Judd, said, "There was no intent to deceive. Nobody is perfect. There were some errors, and for that we've certainly said to our client, 'You don't owe us.'" Judd went on to offer an excuse: "We were victims of the congressional schedule." The "campaign was so compressed" that instead of sending four telegrams from 175,000 people spaced over a reasonable period of time, 615,000 telegrams were sent with just a day between each of the four installments. Moreover, NTC learned that it had overbilled Beckel Cowan because of a series of computer errors. Only 495,000 telegrams had been sent using the names of about 141,000 people. Of those, 8,000 had never been contacted, though 28,000 had sent in their names.[26] Notwithstanding the flood of telegrams in opposition, the telecommunications bill handily passed the House, 305-117.

Ironically, a provision in a lobby disclosure bill in the 103rd Congress, aimed at shedding more light on astro-turf lobbying, provoked a "cultivated" grass-roots lobbying campaign that doomed the lobby disclosure legislation. The episode showed how well wired is the circuitry of the modern electronic Congress.

"Cultivated" Grass-roots Campaigns

The Democratic Party in the waning days of the 103d Congress was already feeling the lash of public and press sentiment against its lackluster legislative record. Hurriedly, it tried to salvage its failing reputation as being "pro-reform" with last-minute victories, especially on campaign and lobbying reform. Republicans, on the other hand, were hammering the Democrats for failing to bring up for a vote the comprehensive institutional reforms recommended by the GOP. Republicans, therefore, were against handing the Democrats any fall-back legislative victories on reform matters on the eve of the elections.

Most members agreed that tighter disclosure rules for lobbyists were long overdue. The two principal laws, the Foreign Agents Registration Act of 1938 and the Federal Regulation of Lobbyists Act of 1946, were widely considered to be ineffective. The Justice Department declared in 1983 that the latter law was unenforceable, and registration under the law was consequently viewed as voluntary by most lobbyists. Reform bills had been passed by one or both houses in 1967, 1976, and 1978, but none made it into law due to outstanding differences over how much disclosure should be required of whom, and whether efforts to generate grass-roots contacts with Congress should be counted.[27]

In the 103d Congress chances seemed good that a lobby disclosure bill would finally be enacted. The Senate passed its version on May 6, 1993, by a vote of 95 to 2. But in March of 1994, the Republicans turned against a bipartisan compromise that included strict new limits on gifts to members of Congress. To avoid crippling amendments, the Democrats brought out a special rule to consider the bill under suspension of the rules on a nonsuspension day. The rule narrowly passed, 221-202, and the bill then sailed to passage after forty minutes of debate, 315-110.

Most of the debate and concern had focused on the gift provisions. No concerns were raised about the lobby disclosure portions until the House-Senate compromise agreement came to the House floor late in the session on September 29. And even then the objections were not raised until the night before the rule for the conference agreement was under consideration. During debate on the rules the leading proponent of the bill, Rep. John Bryant of Texas, denounced these eleventh-hour critics:

> I was astonished to learn last night for the first time in the entire 18-month history of this bill that the Republican whip [Newt Gingrich] stood on the House floor and attacked this bill and said that somehow or another it was going to limit the ability of grassroots organizations, in particular religious organizations, to lobby. Nothing could be further from the truth. This is a ruse to protect the desire of many Members of this Congress . . . to keep on playing free golf and keep on eating free meals and keep on getting free tickets to the baseball games and the football games.[28]

The provision in question called for the disclosure of the name, address, and place of business of "any person or entity other than the client" who paid for someone to lobby on his or her behalf. It was aimed primarily at Washington lobbyists who urged constituents to contact legislators on particular matters.

Representative Bryant chided House opponents of the grass-roots provision, telling them not to "hide behind the skirts of legitimate public-interest organizations and churches" who "are happy with the bill" because "this does not hurt them." Representative Bob Walker of Pennsylvania rose to challenge him, pointing out that "the Christian Coalition, among others, does oppose it." When Walker went on to inquire of Bryant the origins of "the grassroots gag that the gentleman now brings to the floor," Bryant shot back that it was "virtually the same language that passed the House back in March." He fiercely maintained that "there is no grassroots gag, and I am not going to give you time to allow you to say that. . . . If you want to keep playing free golf, admit it." Walker assured him, "I do not play golf."[29]

Later during the debate, when Walker was given his own time to speak, he quoted criticisms from various groups opposed to the grass-roots provision. The Christian Coalition: "This legislation serves the interest of some in Congress who have targeted religious people for direct and virulent attacks over the past several months. . . . [T]his legislation represents a new 'gag rule' on democratic participation." The Americans for Tax Reform: "The chilling effect of such a vague, broad piece of legislation is unimaginable. . . . [T]he power concentrated in an unaccountable 'directorate' is frightening." And the National Committee of Catholic Laymen: "The American people who belong to organizations such as ours will be intimidated." After this litany of quotations, Walker explained the motivation behind the grass-roots lobbying provision: "Many in this body are concerned about the wave of phone calls that they get every time a controversial piece of legislation comes up. They want to stop it, and in this bill they are attempting to stop it by gagging the grassroots."[30]

Representative Gingrich concluded his remarks on the rule by saying, "This has nothing to do with lunches; this has nothing to do with gifts; this has to do with fixing some very dangerous provisions. . . . I say, do not accept the flawed document from the conferences; do not threaten the rights of our fellow citizens; do not threaten religious freedom, and do not turn over dictatorial powers of government. . . ."[31]

For a variety of reasons, the rule was only narrowly adopted, 216-205. Many members were upset about the new gift restrictions; the Black Caucus voted against the rule as a warning sign to the Democratic leadership not to take its votes for granted. An attempt by Republican representative George Gekas of Pennsylvania to send the conference report back to conference with instructions to delete the grass-roots lobbying provision lost by a similar margin, 202-215. The conference report was then easily adopted, 306-112.

Although there was no noticeable lobby effort prior to the House vote, it began soon thereafter. Gingrich had set the wheels in motion by deputizing Republican Study Committee chairman Tom DeLay to spearhead a campaign to solicit opposition from the outside. DeLay sent one of the RSC's "Talk Right" action alerts by fax to 300 religious and conservative organizations, urging their opposition to a "crackdown on grass-roots opposition." DeLay and Rep. Ernest J. Istook (R-Okla.) supplemented this appeal for help at the regular Wednesday luncheon hosted by Paul Weyrich's Coalitions for America. The luncheon was attended by representatives of thirty-five conservative and Christian groups, all with their own high-tech communications apparatuses to reach their membership. On his Friday "Dateline Washington" television show,

Weyrich appealed to listeners to "stop this monstrosity before it stops you the citizens of the United States."[32]

Gingrich also called on Christian Coalition director Ralph Reed about the bill. Reed agreed to fax the 1,000 chapter chairmen in all fifty states and asked them to mobilize their members to call Congress. Reed then talked to Pat Robertson who took time on his *700 Club* television show to lambaste the bill as "one of the most shocking attempts to limit your freedom of speech, and the rights of Christian people and other groups concerned about the out-of-control government."[33]

The result of all of these efforts was an outpouring of telephone calls to the Senate over a week's time. The Senate debate consequently became bogged down in a filibuster that went on for several days before the bill was pulled after two unsuccessful attempts to invoke cloture. Senate minority leader Bob Dole of Kansas said the bill needed further work before it left the Senate: "When you talk about grass-roots lobbying, you're not talking about high-price lobbyist lunches and legislative deals." Even the leading Republican proponent of the bill, Sen. William S. Cohen of Maine, concluded that there was not sufficient time left in the session to fix the bill to its critics' satisfaction. Due to the intense lobbying effort in which some offices were receiving as many as 1,000 phone calls a day, the votes were not there to break a filibuster and pass the bill. After four days of debate the Senate adjourned on October 8, 1994, for the election.[34]

The House had been barraged with a similar grass-roots lobbying effort the previous February over another seemingly innocuous provision in a bill. The legislation was the omnibus $12.7 billion reauthorization of the Elementary and Secondary Education Act. Embedded in the 901-page bill was a provision inserted in subcommittee by Rep. George Miller (D-Calif.) requiring school districts to have teachers certified in their subject areas in order to qualify for certain of the bill's grant money. The provision was approved by the full committee on February 8, 1994, after an amendment by Rep. Dick Armey was adopted to permit states to use "alternative" certification methods.

Things took a new twist, however, when Armey received a phone call on February 14 from a home-schooling parent from New Jersey who asked whether the teacher certification requirement applied to home-school teachers. Armey said he would look into it further and called Michael Farris, the leader of the Home School Legal Defense Association, a 39,000-member organization consisting mostly of evangelical and fundamentalist Christians and conservative Catholics. The next day the association's lawyers determined that the provision could be interpreted as requiring certification for home-schoolers. Later that day in a letter to House members, Farris warned, "This is the equivalent of a nuclear attack upon the home schooling community." He also mobilized a grass-roots network using telephone trees. In this way the group claimed it could alert 50 percent of the more than 400,000 home-schoolers in the country. The home-schoolers also utilized home-school Web sites and e-mail to get the word out. By the next day, February 16, the Capitol Hill phone lines were jammed. Armey said he couldn't even get through to his own office from the outside.[35]

When the phones first started ringing, members had already left town for the President's Day recess, but their Washington staff let them know what they were missing. Soon members were bombarded in their district offices and town meetings with questions about the issue. At a public meeting in Spokane, Washington, Speaker Tom Foley faced a meeting hall full of anxious home-schoolers. Foley promised to take care of their concerns. Nevertheless, "people came up and kept making the case again and again, said Foley, and, "I kept repeating my statement again and again."[36]

By the time the House returned on February 22, Democrats had already agreed that an amendment was needed to make it clear that nothing in the bill affected home-schooling. The next day the Education Committee and subcommittee chairmen asked the Rules Committee to make their amendment in order first. Subcommittee chairman Dale Kildee of Michigan explained why: "The goal is to spare every Member of Congress another weekend of phone calls." Armey, on the Republican side, asked for an even broader amendment to make clear that the bill did not "permit, allow, encourage or authorize any federal control over any aspect of any private, religious or home school."[37]

As it turned out, the House approved both amendments. Even though Education Committee chairman William Ford called the Democrats' amendment "an unnecessary solution to a non-existent problem," it passed the House by a vote of 424 to 1, with only the provision's original author, George Miller, voting against. Armey's amendment was subsequently adopted, 374-53, after he warned his colleagues that "the phones don't stop ringing until I pass an amendment on the floor." Members had been instructed by many of their phone callers to vote for the Armey amendment to fix the problem. Debate on the amendment took a full five hours on February 24, pushing final action on the bill over until the next week.[38]

The grass-roots campaigns on the lobby and education bills had powerful real-time effects. First, modern technologies have allowed for instantaneous, two-way communication between Congress and the public, involving a wide variety of devices. The telephone is certainly nothing new. What is new is the concentrated political force phone calls can have when prompted by other technologies: blast-faxes, spam, e-mail, Web sites, talk radio, and popular cable TV shows. In both examples, the initial stimulus for the campaigns was provoked at least in part by members of Congress appealing to their coalition allies.

Modern communications technology has greatly augmented both the responsibility of Congress to inform the people, and the people's ability to inform their representatives of their views. It would be wrong to jump to the conclusion, however, that this is a completely open and direct interactive relationship between Congress and the people. Many intermediary operators and interpreters facilitate the two-way flow of information and views.

Second, intermediaries' use of new tools of communication can rapidly spread misinformation or disinformation. Interpretations can be placed on legislative provisions that are far removed from legislative intent, yet can take on a life and truth of their own the more they are circulated. Shortly after the word was out of the possible impact of the education provision on home-schoolers, the home-schoolers convinced their allies in the private school lobby that they, too, could be vulnerable. This provoked a second wave of phone calls against the bill.

Third, interest group leaders can get the text of bills and reports directly from Thomas, but this does not mean that the group's members to whom they convey their interpretations and calls for action will check out the documents in question and draw their own conclusions before taking further action. People often may get their information, not through the media filter, but through the filter of interest groups they belong to and are consequently inclined to trust and follow.

Fourth, new technologies may have a somewhat equalizing effect on the high-powered, corporate lobbying interests. Small, grass-roots groups that are membership based are usually not in a position to expend vast sums on lobbying campaigns, let alone to make contributions to political fund-raisers. But using low-cost, computer-based communications devices to alert members to issues of concern in pending legislation is much cheaper and quicker than sending mass mailings through the regular mails.

For example, the Southern Utah Wilderness Alliance, which a few years ago could not afford to send a few hundred pieces of mail on environmental issues, can now, by advertising its Web site, mobilize some 30,000 supporters. In the summer of 1996, it used its Web site and e-mail list to contact friends and supporters. They were asked to call the White House in support of a new wilderness designation in Utah the president was considering. Within two weeks, Clinton made the announcement.[39]

Other groups—from the Christian Coalition and the National Rifle Association to the Children's Defense Fund and the National Abortion Rights Action League—mobilize support the same way. Their increasingly sophisticated

Web sites and new, high-tech lobbying techniques link their members with Washington, attract new members, and educate legislators.

Will such efforts increase the number of citizens who become actively involved in government and politics? The answer remains to be seen. Predictions that the Internet will be a magical solution to increase citizen participation in our democratic system are premature at best. There is even some preliminary evidence that those who use the Internet for information about government and national issues are those who are already politically aware and involved. The Government and Politics on the Web Project at the University of California conducted a nonscientific survey of persons who use nonpartisan public affairs Web sites such as Thomas and those of the League of Women Voters and C-SPAN. According to its initial findings, most are registered to vote and are more likely than the general public to be strong partisans. The persons contribute and become involved in campaigns, and they urge others to vote for certain candidates.[40]

The early experience with the Internet and e-mail tends to follow the pattern established by past innovations designed to open Congress to the people. Examples include requiring recorded votes on amendments, opening more committee hearings and meetings to the public and media, or broadcasting House and Senate floor sessions. Those most likely to utilize these new windows to Congress are organized interest groups with a direct interest in the details of legislation at all stages of the process. They use the resource to communicate information to their membership or clients and to inform Congress of where they stand. The great proliferation of interest groups over the past few decades is a good indication that more and more Americans are being represented in one capacity or another. But this profusion of groups and profusion of demands can lead to greater gridlock at worst or ineffective policy compromises at best.

There is no question that the "third wave" or information age is transforming our society, economy, culture, and politics, and indeed the entire world. At the same time, one of the central elements of this new age, the Internet, should not be imbued with magical powers it does not possess. It is simply a tool for the more rapid retrieval of more information, and for electronic communication and transactions between people. It is not a solution to our educational problems, any more than educational radio and television were. And it is not a solution to our governance problems, any more than telegrams, telephones, or television were.

The problem with government is neither a lack of information nor an ignorance of public needs. It has both in surplus. The real problem is determining what information is important and useful, and which public views and issues are legitimate and solvable. The Internet provides no shortcuts for the nitty-gritty work of governance: ascertaining what information is relevant and useful, thinking about what solutions will best address the problems, and convincing others of the wisdom of those solutions so that there will be sufficient understanding and acceptance to ensure their successful implementation. No electronic device, no matter how ingenious, can be a substitute for the labor-intensive work of governing in a deliberative and representative democracy. In many ways, the dawning of the information age and the advent of the electronic Congress have made that job all the more difficult.

Vince Randazzo, the House Rules Committee staffer quoted at the beginning of this chapter, sounded a cautionary note about the potential downside of new electronic technologies:

> But just as the Internet can enhance public participation and understanding, it also has the potential to undermine Congress as a deliberative institution. . . . If "electronic democracy" looms ever-larger in our system of national governance, Congress may be forced to devise new procedures or mechanisms to check the popular passions of the moment and insure that reasoned debate can continue in an environment free from the undue influence of powerful but narrow interest groups armed with the latest communications technologies.[41]

Much of what is happening today in the newly wired, electronic Congress is just what Randazzo warned about. And more of a similar nature can be expected.

Notes

1. H. Res. 525, "A resolution providing for a deliberative review by the Committee on the Judiciary of a communication from an independent counsel, and for the release thereof, and for other purposes" (H. Rept. 105-703, Committee on Rules, Sept. 10, 1998). The vote on adopting the resolution was 363-63 (House Roll Call No. 425, Sept. 11, 1998). In addition to providing for the immediate release of the report, the resolution provided for the release of the remaining materials submitted by the Independent Counsel not later than Sept. 28, 1998, "except as otherwise determined by the [Judiciary] Committee."

2. "The Starr Report: Details of the Starr Report Emerge," transcript of CNN special report from network Web site (http://www.cnn.com/TRANSCRIPTS). As CNN anchor Jeanne Meserve explained, "Candy Crowley is in a congressional office. She is looking at the internal congressional computer system which now has posted the Starr report. We still, apparently do not have it on the Internet for public viewing."

3. Linton Weeks and Leslie Walker, "Millions Drawn into the Web by Starr Report," *Washington Post*, Sept. 12, 1998, E1,7. The four congressional sites carrying the report were the House, the Judiciary Committee, the Government Printing Office, and the Library of Congress (Thomas). Some news organizations were able to post the report

earlier because they had received copies from congressional aides who had taken it off the internal House computer system where it had been posted earlier for the benefit of members.

4. "Internet Hits on Starr Report," the Associated Press, Sept. 12, 1998, 2:32 P.M. EDT, as posted on the *Washington Post's* Web site (http://search.washingtonpost.com/wp-srv/WAPO/19980912/V000723-091298-idx.html).

5. An ABC News Poll broadcast Friday night, Sept. 11, showed that 45 percent of the public thought the president should resign, 50 percent thought he should remain in office, and 58 percent thought he should be impeached if he lied under oath. By Sunday the percentage of those who thought the president should resign, or be impeached if he lied, had dropped to 39 percent and 42 percent, respectively (http://www.abcnews.com).

6. "Gingrich Address to the Washington Research Symposium," Nov. 11, 1994, reprinted from the Federal News Service in *Congressional Quarterly Weekly Report*, Nov. 12, 1994, 3295.

7. John Healy, "'Thomas' Computer Link Cuts out the Media Middleman," *Congressional Quarterly Weekly Report*, Jan. 7, 1995, 18.

8. Remarks of the Honorable Newt Gingrich, *Congressional Record*, Jan. 4, 1995, H8.

9. "Congress and the Internet," prepared remarks of Vincent Randazzo, counsel, Subcommittee on Rules and Organization of the House, House Rules Committee, before the Conference on Lobbying and the Internet, Washington, D.C., Feb. 23, 1998.

10. H. Res. 5 (105th Congress), Sec. 9, "Committee Documents on Internet," amending House rule XI, clause 2(e), by adding a new subparagraph 4; adopted Jan. 7, 1997, 222-202.

11. Thomas has the text of legislation at each stage of consideration, dating back to the 101st Congress (1989–91) as well as the text of committee reports for the 104th and 105th Congresses, bill summary and status reports since 1973, *Congressional Record* texts since 1989, and House roll call votes since 1990, Senate roll call votes beginning with the 105th Congress, and public laws dating back to 1973. Of special interest are explanations by the House and Senate parliamentarians on how the legislative process works in each body and between the two houses, and the text of historical documents including the Declaration of Independence, the Constitution, the Federalist Papers, and selected congressional documents and debates between 1774 and 1873. Thomas also provides links to the House and Senate Web sites where the public can click on to the Web pages of individual members, as well as those of most committees.

12. Gephardt's proposal would apply only after the lower tax rates proposed in Gephardt's bill were in place. H. R. 3620, 105th Congress, Title IV, "National Referendum Required for Federal Income Tax Rate Increase to Take Effect."

13. A copy of the CRS report prepared for the House Rules Committee's Subcommittee on Rules and Organization of the House, "Electronic Devices in the House Chamber," Nov. 21, 1997, can be found on the subcommittee's Web page (http://www.house.gov.rules_org/e-devices.htm).

14. While many House members do provide their direct e-mail addresses on their home pages, others refer potential correspondents to the House site labeled, "write your representative." There, instead of presenting you with the member's e-mail address, a form is provided for your member's district. Even if a person gets the member's e-mail address from another source, the same constituent screening or filtering device is used once the message reaches the House server. The Library of Congress, which does have links to private e-mail directories for members of Congress (http://lcweb.loc.gov/global/legislative/email.html), carries this advisory at the top of the directory page: "Before you send e-mail to members of Congress, be aware that because of limited staff resources, Senators and Representatives can only respond to their own constituents. Please include your name, street address, city and zip code when you write."

15. On this question, multiple answers were allowed, thus accounting for totals of greater than 100 percent.

16. "Washington Leaders Wary of Public Opinion," The Pew Research Center for the People and the Press, Trust in Government Study, Government Leaders Interviews, Oct. 1997–Feb. 1998, published on the Pew Web site (http://www.people-press.org).

17. James A. Thurber, Jack Bonner, and Dave Dulio, "Congressional Use of the Internet: A Summary Analysis of a Bonner & Associates/American University Survey of Congressional Offices," Feb. 17, 1998. The survey was taken between Dec. 10, 1997, and Jan. 16, 1998. It involved 70 Senate offices and 200 House offices. Ten- to fifteen-minute phone interviews were conducted with "key staff" according to the summary conclusions at the front of the report. However, the "General Survey Information" at the back of the report said "most staffers reported their job title as 'Systems Analyst.'" This is Hill-speak for the office computer manager, who usually is in charge of overseeing mass mailings to constituents.

18. "Most Comprehensive Survey Ever on Internet Lobbying and Internet Use by Congress: Bonner & Associates, American University to Reveal Major Findings," PRNewswire release of Bonner & Associates, American University, Feb. 12, 1998.

19. David Hosansky, "Electronic Congress: Phone Banks to E-Mail," *Congressional Quarterly Weekly Report*, Nov. 29, 1997, 2943.

20. Ken Silverstein, "Hello. I'm Calling to Mislead You," Mother Jones Interactive, MoJo Wire (http://www.mojones.com/mother_jones/ND97/silverstein_jump.html).

21. John Healey, "House Pursues Deregulation, Undaunted by Veto Threat," *Congressional Quarterly Weekly Report*, Aug. 5, 1995, 2353.

22. David Segal, "Telecommunications Legislation Sparks a Storm on the Hill," *Washington Post*, Aug. 4, 1995, B1.

23. Remarks of the Honorable John Dingell on the Communications Act of 1995, *Congressional Record*, Aug. 4, 1995, H8452.

24. David Segal, "Telecommunications Legislation," B1.

25. David Segal, "PR Firm Retreats on Telegrams," *Washington Post*, Sept. 16, 1995, C1.

26. David Segal, "The Tale of the Bogus Telegrams," *Washington Post*, Sept. 28, 1995, A1.

27. "Lobbying Disclosure Bill Dies," *Congressional Quarterly Almanac, 1994*, vol. 50 (Washington, D.C.: Congressional Quarterly, 1995), 34–35.

28. Remarks of the Honorable John Bryant on the Lobbying Disclosure Act of 1994 Conference Report rule, *Congressional Record,* Sept. 29, 1994, H10269.

29. *Congressional Record,* Sept. 29, 1994, H10270.

30. Ibid., H10276

31. Ibid., H10278.

32. Michael Weisskopf, "Senate Republicans Block Lobbyist Reform Measure," *Washington Post,* Oct. 6, 1994, A1.

33. Ibid.

34. Ibid.

35. Phil Kuntz, "Home-Schooling Movement Gives House a Lesson," *Congressional Quarterly Weekly Report*, Feb. 26, 1994, 479.

36. Ibid.

37. Ibid., 480.

38. Ibid.

39. David Hosansky, "Electronic Congress: Phone Banks to E-Mail," 2942.

40. Christopher Swope, "Mr. Smith E-Mails Washington: Constituents On Line," *Congressional Quarterly Weekly Report,* Nov. 29, 1997, 2940–41.

41. "Congress and the Internet," prepared remarks of Vincent Randazzo, 3.

15

The Curtain Falls Twice on the House

THE House of Representatives adjourned the second session of the 105th Congress not once but twice.[1] The first adjournment in late October 1998 was preceded by a vote for a presidential impeachment inquiry and an old-fashioned pork-pull on an omnibus spending bill. By the time of the second adjournment in January 1999, House Republicans had suffered a near fatal setback in the mid-term elections, the Speaker of the House and his designated successor had both resigned, and the president of the United States had been impeached. This extraordinary confluence of events led some to question whether representative democracy could survive "the politics of personal destruction," not to mention "sexual McCarthyism" and a partisan coup d'état.

Hyperbole naturally bubbles up around such unusual and emotionally charged events, but it was clear the ground had shifted again under official Washington. Whether the shock waves would have long-lasting effects beyond the epicenter remained to be seen. The American people reacted to the first news of the presidential sex scandal with greater calm and understanding than did the beltway elites, and they remained relatively unfazed, though tired and disgusted, when the whole matter came to a head. After all, they had survived the Republican "tsunami" of 1994–95 that was now barely a tidal pool. This, too, would pass, although not without leaving new cracks and fissures in the political landscape.

The Big Bang

The second regular session of the 105th Congress ended with both a whimper and a bang. The bang came first when Minority Leader Dick Gephardt of Missouri slammed down on the Democratic leadership table in the House chamber a bound bale of papers sixteen inches high. The whimper came shortly thereafter from a small band of Republicans who dared to challenge their leadership by speaking against the pending bipartisan omnibus spending bill.

In word and deed Gephardt evoked the 1988 state-of-the-union stunt in which President Ronald Reagan ridiculed the sloppy legislative bundling process using three thick budget bills weighing forty-three pounds and vowed to veto such bloated bills in the future. "Ronald Reagan was right," said Gephardt. "It was a bad way to do business in 1988, and it is a bad way to do business in 1998."[2]

Gephardt's single drop-prop was comparable in size and weight—a 4,000-page, forty-pound "Omnibus Consolidated and Emergency Supplemental Appropriations Act" with a $520 billion price tag. Technically, the legislation was the conference report for the transportation appropriations bill. But that was simply a convenient vehicle for transporting seven other appropriations bills, several emergency supplemental spending items, some tax provisions, and carloads of pork. Although he would later vote for the bill, Gephardt milked the occasion for every drop of partisan advantage:

> Mr. Speaker, it is time for a change. It is time for a Congress that works full time to help meet the challenges of our future instead of skipping town with unfilled promises and unmet priorities, and one that fulfills its constitutional role to produce a budget in a manner befitting of us all. If we want to change the agenda, it should be very clear. We have to change the leadership of this Congress.[3]

Gephardt was not alone in decrying the messiness of this consolidated appropriations approach. Appropriations Committee chairman Bob Livingston of Louisiana refused to defend the process "because I think it has been ugly."[4] Others were even less charitable. When asked whether he knew what was in the bill, Sen. Robert C. Byrd of West Virginia, the ranking Democrat on the Senate Appropriations Committee, replied, "Are you kidding? No. Only God knows what is in this monstrosity."[5] His House counterpart on Appropriations, Rep. David Obey of Wisconsin, referred to it as "this god awful mess on the floor," a "massive institutional failure," and "an incredibly outrageous way to do the country's business."[6]

As one reporter noted, "The hastily drafted document contains handwritten provisions scribbled in the margins, unnumbered and misnumbered pages, and language killed at the last minute that was crossed out but not deleted."[7]

The bill included a separate "Division A" containing $803 million in items added in conference; "thousands of other earmarks" were liberally sprinkled throughout the rest of the bill, according to the same observer. These included $750,000 for grasshopper research in Alaska, $1.1 million for manure disposal in Mississippi, and $100 million each for road projects in Alabama, Massachusetts, and Arkansas. Sen. John McCain of Arizona, who monitors such spending projects, released a fifty-two-page list of "egregious pork barrel spending," the worst he had seen in sixteen of his years in Congress.[8]

Few members were critical of all the local pork projects added during negotiations on the bill, perhaps because so many districts had been taken care of. As Obey explained the process, "hundreds of decisions on specific appropriations items" were made by the House and Senate Appropriations Committee chairmen and ranking Democrats. It was what happened later that riled members. Obey described "a laundry list of other items" that was "kicked upstairs" where "judgments were made by only one person in this House, so far as I know, that being the Speaker, and they were made on the other end of the avenue by representatives of the President." The final package was shaped by just three people: Speaker Newt Gingrich of Georgia, Senate majority leader Trent Lott of Mississippi, and White House chief of staff Erskine Bowles.

The small band of Republican opponents of the bill was led by sophomore representative Mark Neumann of Wisconsin, who claimed one-third of the debate time guaranteed by House rules when the majority and minority managers both favor a conference report. Neumann had nothing to lose and everything to gain from defying the leadership of his party in the House: he was campaigning for the Senate seat of Democratic incumbent Russ Feingold.[9]

Neumann explained that when his freshman class came to the House in 1995, it faced "$200 billion a year deficits, and we said we were going to be different in the House now. . . . [W]e are going to get . . . to a balanced budget by controlling wasteful government spending." Yet now that the budget was running a surplus, the balanced budget agreement enacted the previous year was being breached to the tune of $20 billion "under a classification called 'emergency spending' that is spending outside the budget caps." If the bill passes, Neumann concluded, "$20 billion of that surplus that we worked so hard to bring to the American people is going to disappear this evening as we cast the final vote of this . . . term."[10]

Another Republican dissenter, Rep. Chris Shays of Connecticut, echoed Neumann's sentiments when he said, "This bill represents everything I fought against as a fiscal conservative in this House, and I fought as a Republican who wanted to change this process and this place." Shays went on to recognize that the bill was a bipartisan product in which Republicans got more for defense and Democrats got more for social programs:

> Both won, so it is a big celebration. It is bipartisan. But that is what we have done since 1969. That is how we got in this mess we are in. We are right back into it. What bothers me is it is happening under my watch and our watch.[11]

To wrap up debate on the omnibus spending bill, Livingston yielded the balance of his time to Speaker Gingrich "for the last official speech of the 105th Congress" and, as it would turn out, his next to last speech as Speaker of the House. Reflecting his frustration, Gingrich referred to his backbench ankle-nippers as "the perfectionist caucus" and asked them what they would do if they had their way and the bill was defeated:

> Now, my fine friends who are perfectionists, each in their own world where they are petty dictators could write a perfect bill. And it would not be 4,000 pages, it would be about 2,200 of their particular projects and their particular interests and their particular goodies taking care of their particular states. But that is not the way life works in a free society. In a free society we have to give and take. We have to be able to work.[12]

Gingrich concluded by saying it was a "win-win bill" for Republicans because it increased defense spending, blocked the national identification system, and preserved local control of education in the hiring of new teachers. "Yes, our liberal friends get a few things," he said, but "in a free society, where we are sharing power between the legislative and executive branch, that is precisely the outcome we should expect to get. . . . [I]t is in fact, precisely how the American system operates."

The House then voted overwhelmingly to pass the bill, 333-95. Of the sixty-four Republicans voting against the measure, twenty-two were from the freshman class of the 104th Congress and another sixteen from the 103d class (over one-third of the membership of both classes). Together they comprised almost 60 percent of the negative Republican votes on the bill. The Senate cleared the bill for the president's signature the following day, 65-29, and Congress adjourned—for the time being.

The saga of the omnibus money bill is a tale about more than the 105th Congress. It provides a telling commentary on the Republican revolution, the state (and precarious fate) of its leadership, and the modern-day policy process. Not only had Republicans bested their Democratic predecessors on pork tonnage in the omnibus appropriations measure (as they had in the highway authorization); they had come close to achieving what budget process expert Allen Schick has only half-jokingly described as "H.R. 1-and-Only"—a bill in which all the work of a Congress is rolled into a single bill. In this instance, the omnibus bill provided appropriations for ten cabinet departments and numerous related agencies. It also made $9.2 billion in tax changes over nine years and enacted a number of unfinished authorization bills. The latter included bills to bring the United States into compliance with a chemical weapons treaty, reorganize several foreign policy agencies, increase foreign immigration visas for high-tech workers, curb access to Internet pornography by minors, and replenish and reform the International Monetary Fund.

Assessing the Record of the 105th Congress

What brought the 105th Congress to this juncture were many of the same landmarks on the rocky road of the 104th Congress: different tax and spending priorities than the administration, exacerbated by contentious legislative riders on appropriations bills. The problem was compounded and prolonged by the failure of Congress to adopt a budget resolution for the first time in twenty-four years. Still traumatized by negative public reactions to the government shutdowns in the winter of 1995–96, the Republican leadership was determined to keep the government open and get out of town and past the elections with its majority still intact—whatever the cost.

Part of the cost was spending more on administration priorities than the administration had originally requested. Part of the political reward was chocking the bill full of local goodies to ensure passage and contribute to the reelection of incumbents of both parties. It was as if the Republican leadership had decided that if it could not win the favor of the electorate with huge tax cuts (most of which had been blocked by the Senate), it would try the old-fashioned way of getting votes: with generous servings from the federal pork barrel.

Although House Democrats supported the omnibus bill by a margin of 170 to 31, their overall assessment of the 105th Congress was far from favorable. On the same day as the vote, the House Democratic leadership released from its Policy Committee a twenty-page special report titled "A Failed Republican Congress: Partisanship Instead of Progress." Not to be outdone, the Senate Democratic leadership released from its Policy Committee an even thicker report titled "The 105th Congress: A Legacy of Lost Opportunities."[13]

The House Democrats' report charged that the 105th Congress "had accumulated a two-year do-nothing record—with the lowest number of work-days in decades and the lowest number of laws enacted in decades."[14] When they took charge of Congress in 1995, "instead of enacting legislation aimed at the everyday problems of working families, Republicans have focused their time and resources on conducting endless, highly partisan investigations—targeted at their political enemies. That is, instead of legislating, Republicans have focused on investigating."

Republicans countered with a 157-point list of "Legislative and Oversight

Accomplishments of the Republican Congress." It highlighted "the first balanced budget in a generation, the first tax cut in 16 years, and moving people from welfare to work." (In fact, welfare reform was enacted in the preceding Congress.) The list of "accomplishments" also included presidential initiatives that had been blocked, and Republican initiatives that had been vetoed.[15]

The Election Backlash

Republicans intentionally avoided trying to nationalize the election in 1998 as they had four years earlier with their Contract with America. Candidates were left to run on their own records and issues. At the same time Republicans hoped, without overtly making it a national campaign issue, that the president's disastrous involvement with White House intern Monica Lewinsky would depress Democratic turnout and energize the Republican base.

Democrats, on the other hand, did try to nationalize the election with their mantra of Medicare, Medicaid, education, and the environment. They tried to tie every GOP candidate to the unpopular Gingrich and lump all Republicans together as a monolithic pack of right-wing, radical extremists. In addition, they attempted to pull a President Harry S. Truman by sticking the Republican Congress with the "do-nothing" label.

Their strategy, however, did not succeed in driving the GOP from power in 1998 as it had fifty years earlier. With the economy doing well, voters were not about to rock the boat. And by most measures the election reflected this general satisfaction with the status quo: only seven House incumbents lost (six of whom were Republicans) and the incoming class of forty freshmen was the smallest in a decade. Republican ranks shrank from 228 to 223, while Democrats went from 206 to 211 seats. In the Senate the election was a wash with Republicans maintaining their 55-44 edge, though two prominent Republicans, Alfonse D'Amato of New York and Lauch Faircloth of North Carolina, were defeated.

Most politicians and political experts had predicted some Republican gains in both houses based on historical patterns and relative public contentment with the way things were going.[16] On election day Speaker Gingrich predicted a Republican pickup of as many as thirty seats in the House.[17] The next day it became apparent that the Republicans had lost five seats in the House. Gingrich, who had been so accurate and so alone in predicting the 1994 Republican victory, was stunned: "I frankly don't understand all the things that happened yesterday and I'm not sure anyone else in the country does either."[18] Nevertheless, he accepted responsibility as Speaker for the loss of seats. It was a mistake, he admitted, not to "have been more consistent, more aggressive, stayed focused more on reforming government so we could cut taxes and . . . save Social Security."[19] The day after the election Republican representative

David Dreier of California told a CNN interviewer that it was a "Seinfeld election" because, like the hit TV series, it was "about nothing."

A closer look at exit polls reveals that the election must have been about something: more Democrats turned out to vote than expected, and more Republicans stayed home than expected. According to a national exit poll conducted by Voter News Service, the proportion of voters who considered themselves conservatives in 1998 dropped 6 percent from 1994, from 37 to 31 percent of all voters, while those who considered themselves Christian conservatives stayed about the same. At the same time the number of voters who considered themselves moderates rose from 45 percent of the total turnout in 1994 to 50 percent in 1998. In 1998 moderates voted for Democrats over Republicans 54 percent to 43 percent.[20]

Many conservative Republican voters, turned off by the candidates' lack of any clear message or policy positions, may well have sat on their hands. The Republican Congressional Campaign Committee attempted to re-energize the party's conservative base in thirty targeted districts with a big TV ad blitz in the final week of the campaign. This strategy may actually have backfired. Three of the ads, which indirectly alluded to the president's sex scandal by raising the issue of his character and integrity, were shown on the national networks, giving them a much higher profile than Republicans intended. Gingrich was credited with being behind the character ads, though campaign committee chairman John Linder later denied the Speaker had authorized them.[21]

Did the Clinton sex scandal and the Republican impeachment efforts figure prominently in the election outcome? Not according to the exit polls and close political observers and analysts. The Voter News Service exit poll asked voters whether they considered their vote a vote on President Clinton. Sixty percent said "no," while the 40 percent who said "yes" were evenly divided among those who said they considered their vote on congressional candidates a vote for or against the president.[22]

Still, the unexpected loss of Republican seats in the House and the attitudes of the public toward impeachment made many Republicans extremely nervous. They had reason to worry about their future as a party and as individual candidates. The same exit polls that said the Clinton scandal was not a decisive factor in the elections made it clear where the public stood on the matter. Only 35 percent of the voters approved of "the way the Republicans in Congress have handled the Clinton/Lewinsky matter," while 62 percent disapproved. By a similar margin of 58 to 39 percent, voters thought Congress should drop the whole matter as opposed to proceeding with impeachment hearings.[23]

Three days after the election, on November 6, 1998, at 2:00 P.M., Appropriations Committee chairman Bob Livingston announced that he was challenging Gingrich for the speakership. Gingrich initially accepted the challenge and set to work corralling support. But by 6:30 P.M. he reversed himself and announced he would not seek reelection as Speaker. In a brief press statement Gingrich implicitly recognized the failures of his leadership team and accepted his share of responsibility. "The Republican Conference needs to be unified," his statement read. "I urge my colleagues to pick leaders who can both reconcile and discipline, who can work together and communicate effectively."[24] Gingrich's withdrawal in the face of his likely rejection by the House vote on electing a Speaker follows a long-standing House Republican tradition from its minority days of changing top party leaders in the wake of disappointing election results.[25]

When the Republican Conference met to organize for the new Congress on November 18, Livingston got the speakership nod without opposition. He was joined in the new leadership team by two others who dared to challenge incumbent leaders. J. C. Watts of Oklahoma ousted Conference chairman John Boehner, and Tom Davis of Virginia upset John Linder to become the Congressional Campaign Committee chairman. Both of the new leaders were members of the 104th freshman class. Dick Armey of Texas, however, managed to hang onto his position as majority leader by beating back two challengers on three ballots, Jennifer Dunn of Washington and Steve Largent of Oklahoma. Whip Tom DeLay of Texas went unchallenged. Because of his efforts on behalf of Livingston and Watts, he was widely perceived as the new king-maker.

The Inexorable Impeachment Process

In mid-November 1998 it looked like the Republicans' weakened majority in the House and the upheaval in their party leadership would either derail the Clinton impeachment in the Judiciary Committee or, at the least, ensure its defeat by Republican moderates if it ever reached the full House. Judiciary Committee chairman Henry Hyde of Illinois felt the additional pressures created by his party's setback at the polls and vowed to push for expeditious final action in his committee and the House. Livingston had also made it clear he did not want impeachment still hanging around the House when he became Speaker in January.

What the conventional wisdom failed to take into account was the tremendous momentum impeachment would gain once set in motion, even against strong, countervailing political pressures. More than one observer remarked that impeachment seemed to take on a life of its own, as if the constitutional machinery was unstoppable and irreversible. That is not to say that conviction and removal of the president were inevitable. Few thought that. But the process designed by the Framers would play itself out as intended, despite numerous attempts to short-circuit it.

What triggered this seemingly inexorable process was the "referral" to the House by the Office of the Independent Counsel, Kenneth Starr, described at the beginning of Chapter 14. A provision in the Independent Counsel Reauthorization Act of 1994 requires the independent counsel to "advise the House of Representatives of any substantial and credible information," received in carrying out the responsibilities of the office, "that may constitute grounds for an impeachment."[26]

The thirty-six sealed boxes containing two complete sets of the independent counsel's narrative report, appendices, and supporting documents and evidence were delivered in two government vans to the Capitol on September 9, 1998. The mountain of material that was literally left on the doorstep of the House was not something the House could ignore. The question was, what to do with it?

Two days later the House voted overwhelmingly (363-63) for a resolution directing the immediate release of the narrative portion of the Starr report, without any prior review of the contents by anyone. The resolution gave the Judiciary Committee two weeks and some discretion on the release of the remaining materials. It also required the committee to report to the House concerning whether a formal impeachment inquiry should be launched.[27]

Once it became known that the report contained sordid and salacious details about the president's relationship with Monica Lewinsky, a public backlash set in, and the Republican majority bore the brunt of the criticism, notwithstanding the bipartisan vote to release the report. It was the first in a long string of ironies that would plague House Republicans throughout the process.

The day the materials were delivered, Chairman Hyde had vigorously argued before a bipartisan leadership meeting that they not be released until the Judiciary Committee had reviewed them. As the Judiciary Committee's impeachment report documents, "a chief proponent of immediately releasing the information was Minority Leader Gephardt." He "favored release because of his concern about leaks coming from the Committee." In fact, Gephardt said "there was a general need to release all the material in the referral—including the appendices and supporting evidence—to the public as soon as possible."[28] Gephardt's views prevailed with the bipartisan leadership, notwithstanding the concerns raised by Hyde and ranking Judiciary Democrat John Conyers about the sensitivity of secret grand jury materials.

The House vote on the resolution to release the Starr report (H. Res. 525) and begin a preliminary impeachment inquiry was a weathervane that clearly showed the way the winds would be blowing in the Judiciary Committee. While 138, or 69 percent, of the Democrats who voted supported the resolution, eleven of the sixteen Judiciary Committee Democrats (69 percent) voted against the resolution—an exact mirror image of the House caucus. These votes reflected the Democrats' concern about the sensitive nature of the materials being released as well as their stronger attachment to President Clinton than the average House Democrat. According to nonpartisan vote studies by *Congressional Quarterly* in 1998, the average House Democrat supported the president's position on House floor votes 74 percent of the time, while the average Judiciary Committee Democrat supported the president 81 percent of the time.[29]

The Judiciary Committee is one of the most ideologically polarized committees in the House. Its members tend to be persons with strong views on the volatile issues under its jurisdiction (race, crime, abortion, flag-burning, and government ethics, for example). Not surprisingly, a presidential impeachment inquiry had a strong electromagnetic effect in driving partisans to their respective poles. Contrary to popular myth, the 1974 impeachment inquiry of President Richard Nixon was not a bipartisan love-fest. It, too, began on shrill notes of partisan protest from the Republican minority in the winter of 1973–74. But these objections were soon muffled when the committee voted to conduct the remainder of its hearings and arguments in private over the next several months. The committee did not deliberate in public until the end of the process in late July of 1974, when members explained where they stood on the proposed articles and voted.[30]

Two decades later such secret deliberations were unthinkable in the modern era of government in the sunshine. Republicans would continue to pay the price as Democrats exploited the opening to paint the most partisan picture possible. The public had long been convinced that all this impeachment talk was nothing more than partisan politics as usual. Cries of partisanship and unfairness coming out of Washington only confirmed their suspicions. When Judiciary Committee Democrats insisted on following the "Rodino model" from the 1974 impeachment inquiry, Republicans complied in the House resolution authorizing the formal inquiry and in committee rules of procedure. But the Democrats then complained that the Rodino model was not good enough: it was too open-ended in scope and jurisdiction, and not fair enough in granting minority rights. The Republicans could not win no matter how far they bent over backward to be fair: they always came out on the short end as being the source of the nasty partisanship.[31]

In fact, there was little difference between the two parties' competing versions of the resolution authorizing the formal impeachment inquiry. Public attention focused on the near party-line vote on October 8, 1998, authorizing the Judiciary Committee to conduct a formal impeachment inquiry into President Clinton's conduct. But the more significant story was lost in the shuffle: only five House members voted against having any form of impeachment inquiry.[32] Put another way, 429 of the 434 House members voting that day supported the proposition that the Judiciary Committee should "investigate whether sufficient grounds exist for the impeachment of William Jefferson Clinton, President of the United States."

The Democrats' version required the Judiciary Committee to review the constitutional standard for impeachment first and then determine whether the facts presented in the independent counsel's referral could constitute grounds for impeachment if assumed true. It also called for the Judiciary Committee to report back to the House sufficiently in advance of December 31, 1998, to give the House time to act on any recommendation.

In short, the Democrats wanted to ensure that the inquiry was confined to the Lewinsky matter and that it be concluded by the end of the year. The Republican version, on the other hand, like the Rodino model, did not limit the scope of the inquiry. However, the authority in the resolution would naturally expire at noon on January 3, 1999, with the end of the 105th Congress. So it did not authorize an open-ended probe, the claim of some critics. The two parties were quibbling over a two-and-one-half-day difference in the duration of the authority. The majority version prevailed on a vote of 258 to 176, with 31 Democrats joining 227 Republicans in favor.

As it turned out, the Judiciary Committee and the House completed work on impeachment within the time frame and jurisdictional scope recommended by the Democrats. Only once was it hinted that the committee might expand its inquiry to other matters such as the president's campaign financing practices and his Whitewater land development involvement, perhaps in response to Gingrich's view, expressed early on, that the Lewinsky charges alone would not be sufficient to impeach and remove the president. But that trial balloon was quickly shot down, not just by the media and Democrats, but by House Republicans already nervous about the political fallout from even a limited impeachment inquiry.

On December 10, 11, and 12, 1998, the Judiciary Committee conducted its final deliberations and favorably reported all four proposed articles of impeachment on party-line votes. The articles charged the president with grand jury perjury, perjury in a civil case, obstruction of justice, and abuse of power. Chairman Hyde's repeated comments earlier in the year that any impeachment of President Clinton "has to elicit bipartisan support" or it is doomed would be thrown back at him by the Democrats and haunt him through the remainder of the process.[33] Making a final bow to fairness, Hyde let Democrats offer a censure resolution in the Judiciary Committee after the four articles had been adopted. But, like the articles, the censure proposal did not attract any bipartisan support. It failed 14-22, with one member voting present.

Three months had passed since the Starr report was referred to the House, and public opinion on the president's fate had hardly wavered during that time. Clinton's job approval ratings remained consistently high, in the 60 to 70 percent range over much of the year, and these were matched by similar percentages of Americans opposed to either his impeachment or resignation. Neither the weight of evidence in the Starr report nor any subsequent disclosures or arguments in the Judiciary Committee budged the public from its steadfast stand, even though a majority of Americans came to believe that the president probably was guilty of perjury and obstruction of justice, the two most serious charges contained in the articles of impeachment.[34]

What was changing, though, was public opinion about the Congress's job performance generally, and the Republicans in Congress and as a party specifically. Those indicators were all going south the longer the impeachment ordeal dragged on. In late August of 1998, a Pew Research Center survey found 48 percent public approval for the "the job the Republican leaders in Congress are doing," and 36 percent disapproval. Within two weeks after the release of the Starr report in September, Pew found approval and disapproval even at 44 percent. By the time of the House vote on impeachment on December 19, 1998, public approval of the job Republican leaders were doing in Congress had sunk to 39 percent. Disapproval had shot up to 56 percent.[35]

And yet the inexorable machinery of impeachment continued to grind forward. The House was summoned back for the special impeachment session on Wednesday, December 16. The impeachment debate was delayed for a day because of the president's announcement of American bombing raids over Iraq, retaliation for its expulsion of U.N. arms inspectors. On Saturday, December 19, after two days of debate, the House adopted two of the four articles of impeachment on near party-line votes. Only five Democrats and five Republicans broke party ranks on the grand-jury-perjury article, and five Democrats and twelve Republicans on the obstruction-of-justice article. Before the votes on the articles, the Democrats attempted to substitute censure language for the impeachment articles, a move that was ruled out of order as nongermane based on long-standing precedents from the parliamentarian's office. An attempt to overturn the ruling was beaten back on a near-party-line procedural vote, with just two Republicans siding with the Democrats and four Democrats voting with the Republican majority.[36]

The final votes to impeach the president and send the matter to trial in the Senate led many observers to wonder whether Republicans had lost all touch with political reality. Some concluded that the Republicans were simply playing to an activist party base that wanted Clinton removed and were gambling that the rest of the public would soon forget and not hold their impeachment votes against them in the 2000 elections. Certainly party identity played a major role in how each side *viewed* the controversy. As the popular saying goes, "Where you stand depends on where you sit." Republicans tended to think the matter as centering on the integrity of the administration of justice and the primacy of "the rule of law" on which it rests. Democrats, on the other hand, tended to see the controversy as revolving primarily around lying about a private, consensual affair that posed no threat to the state and therefore did not rise to the level of impeachable conduct.

But it would be wrong to conclude that impeachment was driven solely or even primarily by partisan motivations. This was not some partisan vendetta, manufactured out of whole cloth. Dozens of members in both parties now agonized over how to vote. They believed it was their first duty to uphold the Constitution rather than to represent party or popular viewpoints. Some two dozen moderate Republicans had not made up their minds, or at least not announced their decisions, until a day or two before the final vote on impeachment. This spoke volumes about what a close call they considered the matter to be. Moreover, most of them ended up voting for impeachment, at considerable political risk given the political makeup of their districts. This was also a sign of the gravity they attached to doing what they considered to be the right thing. As many of them would indicate when they announced their decisions, they were not convinced that the president had yet fully understood the seriousness of the wrong he had done. What had pushed many of them over the edge was the president's continued legal hairsplitting and defiant attitude toward questions put to him by members of Congress. What they were looking for was not another expression of contrition (Clinton kept apologizing), but rather a frank admission from the president that he had lied. Had he done so in a timely fashion, the vote might well have gone the other way in the House.

Another indication that the impeachment outcome was not purely partisan can be found in the wording of the Democrats' own censure resolution. Offered on the House floor by Rep. Rick Boucher (D-Va.), the resolution charged that the president had "egregiously failed" to "set an example of high moral standards and conduct himself in a manner that fosters respect for the truth." Through his actions he "violated the trust of the American people, lessened their esteem for the office of President, and dishonored the office which they have entrusted to him." In addition, he "made false statements concerning his reprehensible conduct with a subordinate," "wrongly took steps to delay discovery of the truth," and "brought upon himself, and fully deserves, the censure and condemnation of the American people and this House."[37] In many ways the Democrats' censure resolution was harsher than the Judiciary Committee's articles of impeachment because it condemned not just his public and official actions but his personal and private conduct as well.

Another Speaker Falls

The impeachment votes in the House that Saturday were all but overshadowed by another momentous development—the announcement by Speaker-designate Bob Livingston of Louisiana that he was withdrawing his name from nomination as Speaker and would be resigning from the House because of revelations he had made public two days earlier concerning several marital infidelities since he had come to Congress. Livingston dropped this bombshell toward the end of his House floor speech in support of the impeachment resolution. He had just set off an uproar on the Democratic side of the aisle by suggesting that the president could terminate the damage and heal the wounds he had created by resigning. Some Democrats began to chant, "No, you resign, you resign." Livingston held up his hand, and when the chanting subsided he continued:

> And I can only challenge you in such fashion if am willing to heed my own words. To my colleagues, my friends and most especially my wife and family: I have hurt you all deeply, and I beg your forgiveness. I was prepared to lead our narrow majority as Speaker, and I believe I had it in me to do a fine job. But I cannot do that job or be the kind of leader that I would like to be under current circumstances, so I must set the example that I hope President Clinton will follow. Mr. Speaker, I will not stand for Speaker of the House on January 6.[38]

The day before, Minority Leader Gephardt had indirectly referred to Livingston's disclosure that his infidelities were about to be made public by *Hustler* publisher Larry Flynt. Gephardt told the House he was saddened by recent events. He went on:

> We are now at the height of a cycle of the politics of negative attacks, character assassination, personal smears, of good people, decent people, worthy people. It is no wonder to me and to you that the people of our country today are cynical and indifferent and apathetic about our government and about our country. The politics of smear and slash and burn must end. This House and this country must be based on certain basic values: Respect, trust, fairness, forgiveness. We can take an important step today back to the politics of respect and trust and fairness and forgiveness.[39]

A bipartisan, standing ovation followed those remarks. Now, less than two hours after Livingston's startling announcement, Gephardt rose again to speak. He expressed regret at Livingston's decision to leave Congress, calling it "a terrible capitulation to the negative forces that are consuming our political system and our country," and he urged him to reconsider. Gephardt reminded his colleagues that the Founders had created a government of men, not angels, and that no one in Congress today could pass the puritanical test of purity that some are demanding of elected leaders. "If we demand that mere mortals live up to this standard," he continued, "we will see our seats of government lay empty and we will see the best, most able people unfairly cast out of public service."[40]

The minority leader said it was time to "stop destroying imperfect people at the altar of an unobtainable morality" and to stop the rapid descent "into a politics where life imitates farce, fratricide dominates our public debate, and America is held hostage to tactics of smear and fear." And then, in his most powerful appeal, he underscored his message of the previous day:

> Let all of us here today say no to resignation, no to impeachment, no to hatred, no to intolerance of each other, and no to vicious self-righteousness. We need to start healing. We need to start binding up our wounds. We need to end this downward spiral which will culminate in the death of representative democracy.[41]

The Aftermath

Gephardt's remarks were not powerful enough to stop the impeachment train from rolling on to the Senate, but they did strike a sympathetic chord in members on both sides of the aisle. The Republicans' choice of their deputy whip, Rep. J. Dennis Hastert of Illinois, to replace Livingston as their nominee for Speaker bespoke an earnest desire for a "kinder, gentler" speakership than the partisan lightning rod that Gingrich had been. Hastert already had a solid reputation in the House as a calm conciliator, able to work with persons of all political and ideological persuasions to accomplish mutually desirable goals.

The perceived partisanship and bitter residue of the House impeachment ordeal helped to bring senate majority leader Lott and minority leader Thomas Daschle of South Dakota together to forge bipartisan agreements on impeachment-trial procedures, if not on the final outcome. The outcome was nearly foreordained—no one realistically expected a two-thirds vote to convict and remove the president—some members of both parties even favored cutting the Senate trial far short of a full-scale, formal proceeding.

Senator Byrd, one of the staunchest defenders of constitutional processes, surprised nearly everyone on January 22 by submitting a motion to dismiss the case before a decision had even been made on whether to depose witnesses or allow the House managers to present their final arguments. Byrd's motion was rejected on January 27, 44-56, and the trial ground on until the two articles were finally rejected on February 12, 1999, with neither gaining even a majority vote.[42] Byrd would later reflect on how the process had played out, saying, "The Constitution is a cul-de-sac when it comes to impeachment. There is no escape exit. There is only one way and that is to deal directly with the articles of impeachment."[43]

Historians will grapple for years to come over the significance of it all. How could a president, at the time enjoying a high public approval rating between 60 and 70 percent, be impeached? How could the House of Representatives, said to be one of the most poll-driven legislative bodies in history, ignore the polls and commit what seemed to many a politically suicidal act? Was this the final disconnect of the Congress from the people or the beginning of a new era in representative democracy?

Notes

1. H. Con. Res. 353, 105th Cong., 2d sess., adopted Oct. 20, 1998, adjourning the second session of the 105th Congress. The resolution authorized the Speaker and Senate majority leader to reassemble the House and Senate, or the Speaker to reassemble the House, with two days notice, "whenever the public interest shall warrant it."
2. *Congressional Record*, Oct. 20, 1998, H11589.
3. Ibid.
4. Ibid., H11586.
5. George Hager, "House Passes Spending Bill," *Washington Post*, Oct. 21, 1998, A1.
6. *Congressional Record*, Oct. 20, 1998, H11585.
7. Andrew Taylor, "Congress Wraps up and Heads Home on a Trail of Broken Budget Caps," *CQ Weekly Report*, Oct. 24, 1998, 2887.
8. Ibid., 2888.
9. In fact, four of the seven Republicans who dared to speak against the bill were running for other offices: Representatives Neumann, Ensign (Nev.), Christensen (Neb.), and Linda Smith (Wash.). The returning Republican bill opponents to speak were Representatives Shays (Conn.), Istook (Okla.), and McIntosh (Ind.).
10. *Congressional Record*, Oct. 20, 1998, H11642.
11. Ibid., H11644.
12. Ibid., H11648.
13. The reports were posted on their respective leadership Web pages (http://www.house.gov.90/democrats/dpc/failed.html and http://www.senate.gov/-dpc/landfill/sr-79.html).
14. Compared with the last Democratic Congress (the 103d), the House in the 105th Congress was in session fewer days (248 vs. 265) but more hours (1,979 v. 1,887). It enacted more substantive laws (394 vs. 384), if one subtracts the 81 commemorative resolutions enacted in the 103d Congress. Republicans abolished commemoratives at the beginning of the 104th.
15. "Building on Our Achievements: The Legislative and Oversight Achievements of the Republican Congress," House Republican Conference (http://hillsource.house.gov).
16. Since World War II the party not controlling the White House has averaged a gain of twenty-seven seats in mid-term elections. A mid-October 1988 CNN-*Time* Poll found likely voters supporting Republicans and Democrats for Congress in equal

measure (47 percent). The job approval rating of Congress stood at 50 percent (down from 63 percent in mid-September). President Clinton's job approval rating was 64 percent. Eighty-four percent of respondents said economic conditions in the country were good. Keating Holland, "Poll: Equal Support for Democratic, Republican Candidates," allpolitics.com story page (http://www.cnn.com/ALLPOLITICS/stories/10/16/poll/).

17. Charles Pope, "Hollow 'Victory': A Chronology of Rebellion," *CQ Weekly*, Nov. 14, 1998, 3062.

18. Jeffrey Katz, "Shakeup in the House," *CQ Weekly*, Nov. 7, 1998, 2990–91.

19. Pope, "Hollow 'Victory'," 3062.

20. Terry M. Neal and Richard Morin, "For Voters, It's Back Toward the Middle," *Washington Post*, Nov. 5, 1998, A33.

21. Ceci Connolly and Howard Kurtz, "Gingrich Orchestrated Lewinsky Ads," *Washington Post*, Oct. 30, 1998, A1, 18.

22. R.W. Apple, Jr., "Analysis: In the End, Voters React to Issues," *New York Times*, Nov. 4, 1998, archives (http://www.nytimes.com/library/politics/camp/110498eln-assess.html).

23. Neal and Morin, "For Voters," A33.

24. "Gingrich Statement," *Roll Call*, Nov. 9, 1998, 21.

25. Charles Halleck defeated Joe Martin in 1959; Jerry Ford defeated Halleck in 1965; in 1981 Bob Michel replaced John Rhodes (who did not seek reelection as leader but remained in the House for another term); and Gingrich forced Michel's retirement in 1994.

26. Independent Counsel Reauthorization Act, 28 U.S.C. Sec. 591.

27. H. Res. 525, providing for a deliberative review by the Committee on the Judiciary of a communication from an independent counsel, and for release thereof, and for other purposes, introduced by Mr. Solomon and reported by the Rules Committee on September 10, 1998 (H. Rept. 105-703), and adopted by the House on September 11, 1998 (Roll Call No. 425).

28. "The Impeachment of William Jefferson Clinton, President of the United States," a report of the Committee on the Judiciary, House of Representatives, to accompany H. Res. 611 (H. Rept. 105-830), Dec. 16, 1998, 124–25.

29. David Hosansky, "Clinton's Biggest Prize Was a Frustrated GOP," *CQ Weekly*, Jan. 9, 1999, 86, 90, 91. Data are derived from Congressional Quarterly's presidential support score vote studies in 1998 based on eighty-two House roll call votes on which the president took a position.

30. See, for instance, Guy Gugliotta and George Lardner, Jr., "Arguments the Same, Only Places Switched; Bipartisanship Eluded Hill in Watergate," *Washington Post*, Oct. 2, 1998, A16; and Donald R. Wolfensberger, "Partisanship Nothing New When It Comes to Impeachment," *Roll Call*, Oct. 8, 1998, 5.

31. For a more detailed comparison of the Hyde and Rodino models, see the "Additional Views of Mr. Coble, Mr. Gallegly, and Mrs. Bono," in "The Impeachment of William Jefferson Clinton, President of the United States," 148–50.

32. Based on a comparison of the votes on the Democrats' motion to recommit H. Res. 581 with instructions to report back a substitute authorization of an impeachment

inquiry (Roll Call No. 497), and the final adoption of H. Res. 581 recommended by the Judiciary Committee (Roll Call No. 498), Oct. 8, 1998.

33. See, for instance, a reference to Hyde's comment to this effect in a January television interview, in Guy Gugliotta, "Partisanship Carries the Day," *Washington Post*, Dec. 13, 1998, A1.

34. According to a Dec. 10, 1998, Gallup Poll, on the eve of the Judiciary Committee's vote, 71 percent of the respondents thought the president had committed perjury compared with 23 percent who thought he had not; and 50 percent thought he had obstructed justice compared with 43 percent who did not think he had. In both instances only 40 percent thought the charge was serious enough to justify impeachment, while 57 percent thought it was not. "Presidential Crisis: Public Opinion on the Crisis," the Gallup Organization Web site (http://www.gallup.com/polltrends/opinion.htm).

35. Pew Research Center for the People and the Press Surveys from 8/21–24/98, 9/21–22/98, and 12/19–21/98, cited in "Congress: Job Ratings," PollingReport.com (http://www.pollingreport.com/congjob.htm).

36. It is ironic that the Democrats were able to make so much political hay in the media over Republicans' unfairness in denying them a vote on censure when Republicans were simply following the usual impeachment process and precedents. Moreover, as Judiciary Committee Republican James Sensenbrenner would point out during the debate, when Minority Leader John Rhodes tried to get Majority Leader Thomas P. (Tip) O'Neill to allow Republicans to offer a censure substitute to the Nixon impeachment articles in 1974, O'Neill turned him down flat, saying, "I'm bitterly opposed to that." *Congressional Record*, Dec. 18, 1998, H11792, quoting from Jimmy Breslin, *How the Good Guys Finally Won: Notes from an Impeachment Summer*.

37. Motion to recommit offered by Mr. Boucher, *Congressional Record*, Dec. 19, 1998, H12031.

38. Remarks of Mr. Livingston, *Congressional Record*, Dec. 19, 1998, H11970.

39. Remarks of Mr. Gephardt, *Congressional Record*, Dec. 18, 1998, H11777.

40. Remarks of Mr. Gephardt, *Congressional Record*, Dec. 19, 1998, H12031.

41. Ibid.

42. Wisconsin senator Russ Feingold cast the lone Democratic vote against dismissal.

43. Frank Ahrens, "Robert Byrd's Rules of Order," *Washington Post*, Feb. 11, 1999, C8.

16

The Future of Deliberative Democracy

THE day before the impeachment trial of President Bill Clinton ended in the Senate, the *Washington Post* ran a lengthy front-page article on the likely impact of the scandal and impeachment on the presidency, the Congress, the press, and the public. The lead paragraph drew the bleak conclusion that the year-long ordeal had "reinforced negative trends in politics and the news media, widened the gulf between Washington and the American people and left the leaders of the country's major institutions on trial."[1]

By the end of the forty-six-paragraph article, the picture was not any brighter. Don Eberly, director of the Civil Society Project in Harrisburg, Pennsylvania, said he was "deeply pessimistic" about the long-term political effects on the public. In his words:

> I think this is another Vietnam and Watergate that will degrade and divide our politics for years to come. It will further hollow out our institutions. Trust is eroding. Goodwill is gone. I think there is a thick cloud of moral corruption overhanging all our political institutions.[2]

Polls in the immediate aftermath of the impeachment trial had conflicting results. Some showed that a majority of the American people did not think the experience would have a long-lasting negative effect on the country.[3] Other polls indicated that the impeachment ordeal further weakened faith and confidence in government.[4] Some are still referring to a "crisis of confidence" three decades after Vietnam and Watergate supposedly created this condition.

This may be a sign that the phrase has been so debased as to lack any real meaning, or that we are perpetually on the precarious brink of a national collapse. Following the impeachment trial, most Americans still thought the country was on the right track, which argues against the imminent collapse explanation.[5] Still, low public confidence in government in the midst of economic prosperity and optimism about about the country's future is cause for serious concern.

Explaining the Confidence Gap

Most experts trace the decline of confidence back to the sixties and seventies, especially to the twin tragedies of the Vietnam War and the Watergate scandal that forced Richard Nixon to resign from the presidency. Those events alone, however, can hardly account for the "confidence gap" or "trust deficit" more than a quarter of a century later. A cottage industry in books, polls, commissions, foundation grants, and symposiums is exploring the causes for such persistently low levels of public trust in government—and remedies as well.

One impressive book on the subject, *Why People Don't Trust Government*, examines the issue from every conceivable angle.[6] Eighteen Harvard scholars fill ten chapters exploring some seventeen hypotheses only to conclude that (1) they do not know enough "to draw a single conclusion about what has happened to confidence in government (and other institutions) over the past three decades"; (2) they do not know "if the problem is really threatening"; and (3) a research agenda should be developed "that reduces the unknowns."[7]

Having conceded this fundamental gap, the editors of the book offer one "plausible" explanation involving a combination of causes. Like most, they identify the precipitating causes as Vietnam and Watergate, but they say the effects of those experiences have been broader and more long-lasting than anticipated because of the transformation of the economy in the third industrial revolution, which has created anxiety and dissatisfaction among large sectors of the public. Another factor is the long-term, socioeconomic, and secular trend away from community toward greater individualism. This trend, which came to a head in the 1960s, was responsible for undermining authority, on the one hand, while, on the other, making government "a lightning rod for social concerns" and an "arbiter of social relations."[8]

According to the editors, two changes in American political processes contributed to the decline of confidence in government. The first was the replacement of political party organizations by movements and interest groups and the simultaneous growth of inflexible partisanship within the Congress. This has increased the sense of distance between the political elites, playing to their extreme bases, and the people, most of whom are in the middle of the political spectrum.

The second change was the more intrusive and negative coverage of government by the mass media—what some have called the "the spiral of cynicism."[9] This media-generated negative image of a "bad, disconnected government" is reinforced by those who run for government office by running against government. Even incumbents do this. As the editors put it, "Cynicism about government becomes the new conventional wisdom."[10]

And the Answer Is . . .

The Harvard scholars have made a good, educated guess. At the least they deserve an "A" for admitting that they really do not know the full answer to why the public distrusts government. Different individuals have different reasons for distrusting government at different times. Therefore, a single, coherent, "right" explanation can never be adduced at any point in time.

If there is any constant among all the variable causes for distrust, it is the feeling itself: Americans have distrusted their government since before the Revolution. And yet the Harvard study dismisses this as a given without even placing it among its seventeen possible causes. In the book's introduction the editors observe that "the United States was founded with a mistrust of government." In the concluding chapter they recognize that "a certain level of mistrust is a long-standing and healthy feature of American life" since "too much trust may be a bad thing for our liberties." But how do you distinguish the "healthy mistrust" from the dangerous distrust that "may mean a government incapable of performing well the tasks that most people want government to do"?[11] How do you know when the line has been crossed if the people's whole attitude toward government is based on a certain lack of trust?

Distrust (by whatever name) is the very dynamic that has driven Congress to be more responsive to the people when it has felt particularly threatened by an intensification of public anger and alienation. At such times the Congress has endeavored to improve its policy performance, often by changing its internal processes, leaders, or leadership styles to better respond to perceived public needs. Internal reforms have usually been promoted and sold as necessary to restore public trust and confidence in the government. Although the American people have been generally oblivious to institutional innovations and therefore have not rewarded Congress with the expected boosts in approval and confidence, they have taken notice of the more prominent national policy decisions that these process changes have made possible. Neither have significant failures to act on perceived policy problems escaped them.

The key to forging successful and acceptable national policies has always been the ability of Congress to deliberate. Deliberation is defined here as "a reasoning together about the nature of a problem and solutions to it," and "a careful consideration of all the alternatives."[12] Deliberation has required a sufficient distance between representatives and their constituents to allow for an honest airing of opinions, doubts, and differences among legislators and ultimately sufficient latitude for them to compromise those differences for the common good. As the country enters the twenty-first century, it again finds deliberative democracy on trial and threatened by a variety of forces, much as it was at the turn of the twentieth century.

The increasing polarization between the two political parties in Congress, as the Harvard project noted, is a major cause of declining confidence in the system. No one seriously argues that parties should not have different positions on the issues; that is what parties should be about, and that is what has made our democracy so vibrant and durable. But when opinions are so adamant and rigid that compromises cannot be reached, then the parties are failing in their principal responsibility of national governance. This is particularly important when the executive and legislative branches are controlled by different political parties, something that has become more the norm than the exception during the last half of the twentieth century.[13]

The Perpetual Campaign

What are the causes of this increasing partisanship that militates against, rather than for, deliberation in the national interest? The new partisanship reflects a larger cluster of party activists at their respective ideological poles, mainly a result of the parties' shifting demographics. This polarity has made for fiercer and more sharply defined political races. In Congress in recent years there has been a slow but steady cultural change—from a culture of governing through deliberation to one of perpetual campaigning through confrontation. This culture of campaigning is not confined to one party or the other, or even to one branch or the other. The president and the Congress seem to be following the same patterns and tactics, and listening to the same or similar political advisers and pollsters.[14]

This cultural shift would not be so bad if campaigns were primarily about competing political philosophies and ideas of how best to solve our most pressing national problems. But, more and more, campaigns are driven by polls, promises, pandering, personalities, and peccadillos. Candidates are now told by their professional managers that to wage a successful campaign they must demonize their opponent, define all issues as a choice between good and evil, avoid discussing the tough issues, oversimplify and magnify the importance of their key "wedge" issues, and attack, attack, attack.

American Enterprise Institute president Christopher DeMuth recently lamented this trend:

> Serious deliberation among representatives of different regional and economic factions is what our Constitution was designed for, and has

> sometimes achieved. But republican deliberation—meaning mutual enlightenment and compromise—is increasingly difficult in the face of instant mass communication, incessant polling, ferociously well-organized interest groups, perverse campaign finance rules, and other developments conducive toward plebiscitary political and servile government.[15]

To the extent that governing becomes a mere extension of political campaigns, our deliberative system will suffer, since there will be no middle ground left for the kind of compromise that is essential to effective governance. Congress should be a place where competing political philosophies clash, but unlike in a campaign, it is not a zero-sum game in which your opponent must be destroyed for you to succeed. Members of Congress must continue to work with their counterparts in the opposition party; they are not vanquished by legislative defeats. The more partisan campaign tactics and wedge issues are allowed to replace genuine political differences and deliberation in the Congress over truly vital issues, the more there will be a decline in the decorum and comity necessary to sustain the system.

The Decline of Comity and Civility

When former senator Russell Long of Louisiana was asked in 1989 which of the new technologies he thought had the greatest impact on the modern Congress, he surprised those present who thought he would say television, given his long-running opposition to televising Senate floor debates. Instead, he answered, "the jet airplane."

Long explained that in the old days members returned home only once or twice a year and therefore "got to know each other both as representatives from the various states and as human beings." But jet air travel changed all that because "there was little excuse not to go back to the district every weekend." Consequently, by the time he left the Senate in 1986, there were senators he barely recognized since he saw them for only a few days in the middle of each week.[16]

Ironically, it took the ordeal of a Senate impeachment trial in early 1999 for senators to realize just how much things had changed from those "good old days" that most had only heard about from a few remaining old timers. Shortly after the trial, Sen. Byron Dorgan of North Dakota observed that "the Senate is closer today, one member to another, having . . . gone through this together."[17] Sen. Carl Levin of Michigan agreed: "We've come through the fire together. We worked together many times across the aisle. In a very important way for the country, the Senators are closer personally."[18]

A combination of factors produced this strange bonding experience: the emotional nature of the trial, the fact that senators were forced to sit together in the same room for hours on end (something that rarely happens during legislative debates), and the reported soul-baring that took place in a closed, bipartisan caucus and in subsequent secret deliberations just prior to the final votes. Sen. Charles Schumer (D-N.Y.) described this effect of closed deliberations: "When you close a proceeding, you get more interactive dialogue because people are just talking to one another, as opposed to talking to a much larger audience."[19] Moreover, senators were even forced to meet some weekends, blocking their normal escape routes back to their home states and opening unique opportunities to socialize together. Whether this newfound spirit of bipartisan bonding would last beyond the immediate afterglow of the trial remained problematic. But at least it had given senators a glimpse of the past and the possible.

House members, who debated impeachment for just two days in December under much less amicable circumstances, had to view with some envy the relative camaraderie produced by the Senate trial. The House has always been less collegial than the Senate. But the weekend homing tendencies of senators and representatives in recent years have made it even more difficult for them to get to know each other.[20] The very need for House bipartisan "civility retreats" in 1997 and 1999 reveals how weak the glue of comity has become. Moreover, the extended weekends at home have compressed the actual work week in Washington. No wonder there is not enough time for sufficient deliberations in committee and on the floor. And it is doubtful that members want longer work weeks, as Speaker-designate Bob Livingston found in late 1998 when he suggested more five-day work weeks.

Politics versus Policy

Another byproduct of the new congressional culture of the perpetual campaign is the scheduling of so-called "bumper sticker bills" aimed more at scoring political points than at serious policy making. Consider, for instance, the month of June 1998. A budget resolution was already two months overdue and the appropriations process was at least a month behind schedule. Nevertheless, the House found time to consider bills that recognized "the importance of fathers in the raising and development of their children," urged the president to "reconsider his decision to be formally received in Tiananmen Square by the Government of the People's Republic of China," required a vote on all of the user fees in the president's budget (without the new initiatives they were designed to fund); amended the Constitution to permit the imposition of campaign spending limits (introduced by a Republican leader who opposed the measure); expressed the sense of the House that social promotion in America's schools should end; and declared that the Internal Revenue Code should be replaced by a tax system that is "simple and fair" (without specifying what or how).

This position taking on issues in a symbolic but not substantive sense is designed to put members on the right side of the most recent public opinion polls or highlight some basic difference between the parties. Legislative posturing for partisan advantage is nothing new, though in the past members usually used floor speeches and amendments rather than inflating the issue into a separate legislative bill—a party balloon with bright colors and markings, filled only with air.

New Reliance on Leaders

Not surprisingly, the growth of the perpetual campaign tracks the onset of the postreform Congress in which members have increasingly turned to their party leaders to pull together the overly democratized and fragmented system of subcommittee government. In an attempt to bring coherence and order to a disorderly and uncertain floor situation, leaders tightened their management of legislation on the floor and even in committee. These majority tactics naturally provoked resistance from the minority, resulting not only in sharper party policy differences, but in more frequent procedural confrontations over the ground rules for floor debate and amendment.

As has been well-documented by political scientist Barbara Sinclair, the use of special rules in the House restricting the offering of floor amendments has been one arrow in the leadership's quiver. Other devices include the use of postcommittee adjustments that provide for the automatic adoption of an amendment to a bill without a separate vote, the bypassing of committees altogether, the increasing reliance on omnibus bills that help to sugarcoat the bitter pills inside, and the use of leadership summits with the executive to circumvent unwieldy and divided House-Senate conference committees. In addition, the leadership has increasingly relied on two long-available tactics: the suspension of the rules process that limits debate and prohibits all amendments; and the inclusion of legislative or policy riders in appropriations bills, the latter having been as much the cause for presidential vetoes as different spending priorities between the president and Congress.[21]

The confluence of a more constituency-oriented membership and a more politically sensitive and tightly managed legislative agenda has been a self-reinforcing and self-perpetuating trend since it benefits committee and party leaders and followers alike. It enables the majority leadership to perform its two principal responsibilities of institutional maintenance and party maintenance or, as others have described the roles, building winning coalitions for passing legislation and keeping peace in the family by helping members with their projects and campaigns. The majority the Republicans held in the 105th Congress was thin: the defection of any eleven members could spell defeat. Therefore, peace-keeping involved a labor-intensive task of micromanaging multitudes of potential controversies.

The temptation to manipulate the process to produce desired policy results is hardly a recent development. For years historians, political scientists, and activist partisans have encouraged such behavior as a sign of a strong party leadership, dedicated to advancing its party's legislative agenda. James Madison foresaw this prospect: "In all legislative assemblies the greater [the] number composing them may be, the fewer will be the men who will in fact direct their proceedings." Too many representatives, he wrote in the Federalist Papers, could bring the assembly to a point at which it could no longer protect the people against a government by the few: "The countenance of government may become more democratic, but the soul that animates it will be more oligarchic. The machine will be enlarged, but the fewer, and often the more secret, will be the springs by which its motions are directed."[22]

Animal Farm

The prevalence of a strong party leadership militates against a freely functioning committee system and the kind of deliberation associated with it. In 1885 Woodrow Wilson noted that floor debates are public exhibitions, while committee sessions are where the real work of Congress is done.[23] His observation retains its essential kernel of truth today. Wilson's complaint that committee deliberations were secretive and too responsive to special interest demands led him to call for greater party control over the legislative agenda. The result, however, was that policy was forged in secret sessions of the party caucus. This prescribed antidote to committee government not only contradicted his antipathy toward secrecy, but has proven in modern times to be a fundamental fly in the ointment. Party caucuses are not well suited for thrashing out sound national policies. They tend to focus on how pending legislation will affect members' reelection chances and the continuing support of their natural allies among outside groups or coalitions.

Despite the Republicans' promise in the 1994 campaign of a more open and deliberative process in committees and on the floor if they took control of the House, they have not been very different from the Democrats in leadership operating styles or procedural tactics (see Appendix B). By concentrating more powers in the hands of its leadership at the expense of committee control and deliberation, the razor-thin Republican majority found it necessary to expend more energy to achieve favorable outcomes, even if it meant overriding certain key players and committees or shutting out certain legislative alternatives. As Newt Gingrich himself admits in his 1998 book, *Lessons Learned the Hard Way*, the new leaders, upon taking majority control, realized how enormous the pressures were to round up votes. This pushed them into the mode of inducing conformity. "Thus there is a permanent danger," he writes, "that like the animals in George Orwell's *Animal Farm*, we might gradually come to resemble the very machine we had replaced."[24]

He quickly adds, however, that Republicans would never become like Democrats had been when they were in the majority in Congress because the GOP was a party of ideas, and it was in its best interest to promote a "continuing debate in which these ideas can be modified, improved and tested." Republicans encouraged independent thinking and welcomed dissent and argument. They were "entrepreneurs of social policy" rather than "spear carriers of conformity."[25]

Notwithstanding Gingrich's eloquent ode to deliberation, reporter Ronald Elving drew exactly the analogy that Gingrich claimed would never become reality. Elving accused the Republicans of reverting to the ways of their former masters who were Democrats. In an article published just before the release of Gingrich's book, Elving also refers to Orwell. Surveying the Republicans' handling of the disaster supplemental, highway, campaign, and banking bills in the 105th Congress, Elving observed:

> Like the elevated animals that overthrew the farmer in George Orwell's "Animal Farm," they have learned how the experience of power transforms "four legs good, two legs bad" into "four legs good, two legs better."

In a similar fashion, Republicans began to imitate the ways of their former Democratic masters in handling legislation. Although the 1994 election of a reform regime in the House was based on Gingrich's personality and critique of Democratic management, "the demands of regime have taken precedence over the idea of reform," Elving concludes. "So it is that revolutions age."[26]

Public Expectations of Congress

It is doubtful that the public is even vaguely aware of the extent of Republicans' "animal farm" reversion to the ways of their former masters in the Democratic Party. But the public is keenly aware of the din that arises between the two parties and two branches over what the legislative process is or is not producing. The shorthand for this is "partisan bickering," and the public has one response: "stop it."

The general public pays very little close attention to the actions and activities of its government. According to a Pew Research Center survey in June 1998, only 36 percent of the people say they follow what is going on in government and public affairs most of the time, and half of those respondents agree that they are generally bored by what goes on in Washington.[27]

How, then, can the people still give such high ratings to their own representative in Congress? A *Washington Post* poll taken on February 14, 1999, two days after the Senate acquitted President Clinton on impeachment charges, found that 46 percent of the people approved of the way the Congress was handling its job, and 50 percent disapproved. At the same time the same poll revealed that 70 percent approved of the way their own representative was handling his or her job, and only 21 percent disapproved.[28]

This seeming paradox has always been with us: the virtuous hometown representative up against that evil, big city organization—in this case the U.S. government in Washington, D.C.: "We love our congressman or congresswoman but hate the Congress; too bad all the rest aren't like our Joe or Jane." The shift in Congress from deliberative lawmaking to perpetual campaigning has exacerbated what constituents dislike about Congress and like about their representative. Members spend more time in their districts attending to constituents' needs and winning votes and less time in Washington attending to their lawmaking responsibilities in committee and on the floor. While members become more representative (especially when it comes to paying attention to the well-organized groups within their districts), Congress becomes less deliberative in assessing and legislatively addressing the serious problems facing the nation.[29]

Only part of this paradox can be attributed to the media, though it is true that the hometown representative gets more favorable treatment from the local media than Congress does from either the local or national media. People tend to hold the institution of Congress to higher standards and expectations than they do their individual representative. They have an idealized notion of Congress: it should be the embodiment of the collective will and judgment of all the people, and therefore should always act in the national interest. The whole is expected to be greater than the sum of its parts when in reality it will rarely equal the sum of the strengths and virtues of individual members.

A closely related view is that the Congress, acting in concert with the president, will fulfill all the expectations the people have of government, many of which have been raised by politicians themselves in their campaign promises. Under this concept, acting in the national interest means effectively addressing all the interests, needs, and concerns of the nation as perceived by the citizenry. The problem is, not all citizens agree on the needs to be addressed.

It is therefore not surprising that Congress usually falls far short of the idealistic expectations the people have of it. Instead, Congress is seen as manifesting the basest of self-interested motives, the lowest of institutional ethical values and performance standards, and, consequently, a very disappointing record when it comes to meeting national policy needs.

The ideal concept of Congress is grounded in something that James A. Morone calls the "democratic wish." It "imagines there is a single, united people, bound together by a consensus over the public good which is discerned through direct citizen participation in community settings." According to Morone, the central image of this "democratic wish" is of a "united people pursuing a shared communal interest," with the people as "governors as well as constituents, political agents as well as principals." This is possible because, as a "single, united political entity," they are wiser than their governors and thus capable of solving the troubles that plague the nation.[30]

Morone has it half right. The people do cling to the "myth" that there is an easily discernible public good or national interest solution for every problem, if only the politicians would stop playing politics and do what is right rather than what is politically expedient. The people, however, do not see themselves as governing the nation more ably than their elected officials. The people have no illusions about legislating or governing themselves on the national level. From their direct participation in community settings, they certainly have no specific idea of what the public good would be on any given national problem. If they did, they would realize that decisions at both the national and local levels require the contentious and often prolonged process of deliberation—of thinking, arguing, and ultimately deciding together on a solution that will be both broadly acceptable and effective. And therein lies the conundrum of deliberative democracy. Just as everyone wants to go to heaven but nobody wants to die to get there, everyone wants the Congress and the president to act in the national interest, but no one wants the messiness, noise, and delays of deliberative decision making.[31]

In a 1942 radio address, Speaker Sam Rayburn of Texas captured the essence of deliberative democracy as well as the people's antipathy toward it. Congress is the place, he said, where the "varied needs and interests of the people find expression" and where, "out of the clash of contending opinions is forged the democratic unity of a democratic people." And yet, "too many people mistake the deliberations of Congress for its decisions." Such deliberation is essential because "common consent in democratic government springs from common understanding. It is out of the airing of conflicting opinions in hearings, debates, and conferences that a people's Congress comes to decisions that command the respect of a free and democratic people."[32]

Perceptions of Special Interests

Many Americans believe the government is run more for the benefit of a few big interests than for ordinary people, or in the national interest. The clamoring and clawing of competing interests for the attention and largesse of the government make the system seem to them so tawdry and unsavory. There is too little understanding, however, of the pluralistic nature of our society. People tend not to view themselves as part of organized interests vying for the government's attention, action, and benefits. Yet almost everyone today is part of one or more such groups that are placing increasing demands on the government on a daily basis.

The agglomeration and accommodation of all the organized interests should not be equated with the national interest or public good. Far from it. But such interests (or "factions," as Madison called them) are a natural byproduct of liberty which is designed to protect individuals who have different abilities and goals. It is only natural, then, that such individuals will form different opinions and gravitate to different leaders based on these differences.[33]

Madison recognized that you can neither eliminate the cause of factions, which is liberty, nor the differences in people's abilities, interests, and opinions. Therefore, the job of modern legislation is to regulate these competing interests by involving them in the necessary and ordinary operations of government.[34] Madison saw the republican form of government as being best suited for this since, under a pure democracy, it would be too easy for a single faction or opinion to form at the expense of a minority's rights. A republican system delegates government to a small number of elected representatives. The effect "is to refine and enlarge public views by passing them through the medium of a chosen body of citizens, whose wisdom may best discern the true interest of their country and whose patriotism and love of justice will be the least likely to sacrifice it to temporary or partial considerations."[35]

Statesmanship alone would not subdue these competing interests: "It is in vain to say that enlightened statesmen will be able to adjust these clashing interests and render them all subservient to the public good," Madison wrote. Moreover, "enlightened statesmen will not always be at the helm."[36] The virtuous, disinterested republican was already a dying breed. Few citizens of independent wealth remained in the new republic, and therefore everyone had some particular interest.

But Madison did not see this as a problem so long as the country continued to grow and congressional districts got larger and more diverse. A representative would be required to represent a district with diverse interests and therefore could not easily side with one at the expense of another. The greater the multiplicity of interests in the country, the less likely would be the danger that factions would ever combine to form a majority: "Extend the sphere and you take in a greater variety of parties and interests; and you make it less probable that a majority of the whole will have a common motive to invade the rights of other citizens."[37]

What Madison did not anticipate was the concentration of so many interests at the seat of the federal government. He anticipated "great and aggregate interests being referred to the national, the local and particular to the State legislatures." Nor did he anticipate the miracles of modern communication that link impassioned citizens of like mind to each other simultaneously: "if such a common motive exists, it will be more difficult for all who feel it to discover their own strength and to act in unison with each other."[38] As we have seen from earlier chapters, grass-roots groups today can inundate Congress with phone calls and e-mail messages hours after their memberships have been alerted through phone trees, e-mail bombs, and blast faxes.

A Virtual Direct Democracy?

Is Madison's concept of deliberative democracy relevant to the information age of instant and interactive communications? Or is it as obsolete as the quill pen with which the Founders wrote the Constitution?

There is already mounting evidence that we have arrived at a state of "virtual direct democracy." Public opinion polls increasingly dictate not only major campaign themes and national legislative agendas, but also specific policy solutions. The legislative and executive branches use party-commissioned polls and focus groups to shape their political messages and legislative initiatives. In addition, interest groups are increasingly using unscientific public opinion polls on their Internet Web sites to attract new members and impress Congress with the strength of their positions.

Moreover, some members of Congress are including national opinion polls on their Web pages to advertise and demonstrate support for their pet causes. Republican senator John Ashcroft of Missouri ran such a poll on his Web page on the term limits constitutional amendment. He wanted to promote that cause and, some maintained, his own presidential aspirations (which he subsequently abandoned).

According to a House report on "CyberCongress Accomplishments in the 104th Congress," the staff of the House Oversight Committee "has provided intensive marketing and educational efforts to champion Members' ability to use their web sites to communicate with their constituents." Interactive sites could use electronic surveys "to find out how constituents would vote on pending legislation."[39] Can the day be far off when public interest groups demand that electronic surveys be made available on every member's Web site so constituents can register their votes on every pending bill and amendment? If such instantaneous surveys are combined with the proposal that members be allowed to have their own laptop computers on the floor, the potential for direct democracy will become a virtual reality.[40]

Direct Democracy?

Does the growth of virtual direct democracy portend in the not too distant future some form of direct democracy involving citizen lawmaking through national initiatives and referendums? The likelihood of this form of direct democracy has never been great and is not great now. The potential that modern communications technology holds for a more informed electorate being able to initiate and vote on federal laws electronically does not make it inevitable, let alone desired or desirable.

The democratic impulse still strongly prefers representative democracy over even a limited form of direct democracy. Notwithstanding the relative popularity and arguable success of state initiatives and referendums, there is no evidence that the people are clamoring for such devices at the national level. Most people regard the prospect of direct democracy much like Oscar Wilde viewed socialism: "It sounds like a good idea, but it takes too many evenings."[41]

The experiences of the states with the initiative and referendum process has been mixed, especially in trend-setting California. This should make anyone think twice about extending this device to the national level.[42]

Redefining Deliberation

For better and worse, the American character that has emerged in this country since the Revolution has been about the freedom and liberty of individuals to pursue their own interests and happiness, and to be left alone by government, rather than to be the government. The idea that a majority of U.S. citizens were ever fully engaged in politics and government is a popular myth.[43] One would have to swim against a very strong tide of national history and habit to expect a "revival" of classical republican virtue in which disinterested leaders combine forces with an altruistic citizenry to promote national interests over special or personal interests.

However, the problem of persistently low levels of public confidence in government remains. What can be done to address this condition and the attendant feelings of alienation from and distrust of government and its leaders? The system depends on the continuing support of the people for its survival, "deriving," as it does, "its just powers from the consent of the governed." But more direct forms of democracy are not the answer. History tells us direct democracy inevitably leads to tyranny and destruction.

The best antidote to calls by some for direct decision making by citizens is a restoration of representative and deliberative democracy. It must adhere to our basic, founding principles yet encourage greater participation in the policy process through the use of information age technologies, techniques, and resources. Deliberative democracy can no longer be confined to the halls and backrooms of Congress or justified on the grounds of the great physical distance between lawmakers and their constituents. The new reality is that very little deliberation currently takes place in the Congress anyway. Representatives are intent on serving their constituents and running for reelection on the basis of their record of constituent service. The distance between representatives and their constituents has shrunk to nothing, even in Washington. On Capitol Hill the public, at least through its agents in a multitude of interest groups, is literally breathing down the necks of legislators in real time, scrutinizing, second guessing, and often criticizing every significant decision in committee or on the floor.

Some argue that this reality is the greatest impediment, if not permanent obstacle, to restoring any form of deliberation. It is unrealistic to think that the clock can somehow be turned back to an age when members of Congress had the time, distance, and privacy from public intrusions to seriously deliberate among themselves. There is no need to restore a mythical golden age of deliberation (which should not be confused with what might have been a golden age of oratory).

Nevertheless, an effort to re-create some semblance of deliberation can help to transcend or at least counterbalance the ever-present special interests and the influence they have on the decisions made (or blocked). Such a deliberative window can provide lawmakers with an opening to work for solutions that are in the larger, national interest through compromise and consensus building both within the institution and without. Such outcomes are not a gauzy, unattainable ideal. They are what is often produced when public frustration over legislative gridlock reaches a boiling point, and Congress is forced to deal with a major, pressing problem or suffer the consequences at the polls.

Too often such solutions have not been forthcoming until matters have reached a national crisis that does not easily lend itself to rational, long-term planning and action. By engaging the people early on in a public discussion of a problem and possible solutions (the heart of a deliberative process), Congress can help pave the way for a rational, consensus solution before the problem reaches the crisis stage. One promising example of early engagement of the public in policy deliberation occurred in 1998, when President Clinton initiated four national forums around the country on the future of the Social Security system. Cosponsored by the Concord Coalition and the American Association of Retired People (AARP), the forums involved randomly selected citizens as participants. Members of Congress from both parties also participated. That initiative, in turn, has borne fruit. Members of Congress have organized district town hall meetings on Social Security, and private groups and foundations have contributed to the national discussion through forums and Web site information, polls, and chat rooms.

One should not expect legislators or the president, even with the substantial aid of public-minded foundations and organizations, to involve citizens in discussions of all the major policy issues that must be dealt with in each two-year term of Congress. However, by engaging the public in just two or three pending issues that directly affect individual citizens, their families, and communities, the president and Congress could make significant progress in reconnecting the people with their government. By demonstrating that the government does care about what the people think and by encouraging their participation in such policy debates, government can begin to reestablish the vital ties of trust.

More interactive teleconferencing between congressional committees and groups of citizens could be employed. Many committees and subcommittees already conduct periodic field hearings in members' districts to hear from a variety of individuals and groups on particular problems of mutual concern. As telecommunications technologies become more readily available and easy to use, two or three field hearings could be conducted simultaneously and linked in real time with committee members in Washington. In this way citizens could interact, not only with the policy makers, but also with citizens in other parts of the country. By comparing their situations with regard to federal programs affecting them, constituents could gain a better understanding of the conflicting views their own representative often receives when attempting to reach compromises with members of different viewpoints and regions of the country. Just as important, it would give members new incentives to participate in committee hearings held in Washington. Today these hearings are often sparsely attended and boring—featuring, as they do, the usual collection of administration officials and lobbyists.

No matter how much Congress may attempt to increase citizens' awareness, knowledge, and involvement in public policy issues, there can be no substitute for the deliberation that still must take place among the people's representatives before an acceptable national solution can be reached. Just as in Woodrow Wilson's time, committees are the place where the real work of Congress is done—gathering information, marshaling arguments, and persuading colleagues. These essential elements of deliberation are ideally employed with maximum force and effect at this stage of the process. There is already some evidence that committees are being given more leeway for deliberation under the new Speaker, J. Dennis Hastert (R-Ill.) than they were under Gingrich's regime. Moreover, House floor debates and the amendment process were more open in the 106th Congress (at least in the early months) than they were in the previous Congress.[44] All this could augur well for a more deliberative Congress in the long run.

Conclusion

This is not the first time party control of one house of Congress has been tenuous, or divided government has frayed relations between the legislative and executive branches. The country and the Congress, especially in the past century, have endured much more partisan, raucous, and rancorous times, and both have emerged the better for it.

Through all these tumultuous periods, most members of Congress have been hardworking and reputable. Good policy making has taken place in the quiet committee rooms and solemn chambers of the Capitol. Most of this work goes unheralded by the media because it is done in relative obscurity with little controversy or crowing. It is frequently overshadowed by political skirmishes that have more symbolic than real value. But this unsung work often has more lasting impact on the lives of average citizens than the "great" political debates of the day.

Out of our turbulent history as a nation, Congress has adapted and drawn closer to the people while expanding individual rights, liberties, and opportunities. Despite such gains and progress, the people have always exhibited a measure of suspicion toward their elected, representative government. It is an inherent aspect of the American character, dating back to the new nation's revolt against authority. The Constitution practically advertises in boldface that neither the government nor the people should be left to their own devices—they had better keep a close eye and check on the possible excesses of the other if domestic stability and unity are to be preserved amidst all the constant change.

Upon being elected Speaker of the House in 1925, Ohio Republican Nicholas Longworth told his colleagues that there was nothing new about how the people regarded Congress. He had been a member of the House for twenty years, and during the whole of that time "we have been attacked, denounced, despised, hunted, harried, blamed, looked down upon, excoriated, and flayed. I refuse to take it personally." Congress had been unpopular when Lincoln was a congressman, when John Quincy Adams was a congressman, and even when Henry Clay was a congressman. Congress has always been unpopular, Longworth concluded: "From the beginning of the Republic it has been the duty of every free-born voter to look down upon us, and the duty of every free-born humorist to make jokes at us."[45]

So it has been and likely always will be. Deliberative democracy has been on continuous trial from the beginning. And, over the long haul, members of Congress have acquitted themselves honorably. Whether the information age will yield a higher level of democratic dialogue within the Congress and between the people and their elected officials may well determine whether our system of government will regain the trust of the people that is so essential to the survival of this great and ongoing experiment in self-rule.

Notes

1. David S. Broder and Dan Balz, "Scandal's Damage Is Wide, If Not Deep," *Washington Post*, Feb. 11, 1999, A1.

2. Ibid., A16.

3. According to a *Los Angeles Times* Poll conducted on the day of President Clinton's acquittal, only 34 percent of the respondents felt the impeachment episode would have a lasting negative effect on the country. Another 11 percent thought it would have a lasting positive effect, while 50 percent thought it would have no effect at all. See the "Cloakroom—Poll Track" of the *National Journal* (http://www.cloakroom.com/members/polltrack/todays/).

4. Ibid. According to a CBS Poll on Feb. 12, 1999, 62 percent of the respondents felt the impeachment and trial weakened their faith in the government's ability to handle charges of lawbreaking by a president. Fifty-seven percent of the respondents in a Feb. 12–13, 1999, Fox News–Opinion Dynamics Poll thought Clinton's presidency, as revealed in the impeachment process, "damaged the country's moral values," while only 32 percent thought it had no effect. In the same poll 61 percent said that based on what they'd seen coming out of Washington over the past year, they did not think they "would ever be able to think of politicians as positive role models again."

5. A *Washington Post* Poll taken on Feb. 14, 1999, two days after the conclusion of the Senate impeachment trial of President Clinton, found 55 percent of the people agreeing that "things in this country are generally going in the right direction," down six percentage points from the beginning of 1998, but still way ahead of the 19 percent agreement in January of 1992, the 31 percent agreement in January of 1994, and the 21 percent agreement in January of 1996. "Washington Post Poll: Clinton Acquitted," Feb. 15, 1999 (http://www.washingtonpost.com/wp-srv/politics/polls/vault/stories/data021599.htm).

6. Joseph S. Nye, Jr., Philip D. Zelikow, and David C. King, eds., *Why People Don't Trust Government* (Cambridge, Mass.: Harvard University Press, 1997).

7. Joseph S. Nye, Jr., and Philip D. Zelikow, "Conclusion: Reflections, Conjectures, and Puzzles," in *Why People Don't Trust Government*, 268, 279.

8. Ibid., 270–71.

9. See Joseph N. Cappella and Kathleen Hall Jamieson, *Spiral of Cynicism: The Press and the Public Good* (New York: Oxford University Press, 1997). The authors lay most of the blame for voter cynicism on the press for its sensational rather than substantive approach to covering politicians and policy issues.

10. Nye and Zelikow, "Conclusion," 273.

11. Ibid., 2, 276.

12. Steven S. Smith, *Call to Order: Floor Politics in the House and Senate* (Washington, D.C.: Brookings Institution Press, 1989), 239.

13. The same political party controlled the presidency and both houses of Congress in only eighteen years between 1951 and 2000.

14. This paragraph and the succeeding three paragraphs are adapted from the author's testimony before the Subcommittee on Rules and Organization of the House of the House Rules Committee, on "Civility in the House of Representatives," April 17, and May 1, 1997.

15. Remarks of Christopher C. DeMuth before the annual dinner of the American Enterprise Institute for Public Policy Research, Dec. 5, 1996, Washington, D.C.

16. Stephen E. Frantzich, "Technology and the Future of Congress" (paper delivered at the annual meeting of the American Political Science Association, Washington, D.C., Aug. 28–31, 1997), 5.

17. Amy Keller, "The End Is Here—Senators Come Together at Trial's Close," *Roll Call*, Feb. 15, 1999, 1.

18. John Bresnahan and Amy Keller, "Senate Acquits President; Neither Article Gets Majority; Censure Effort Goes Nowhere," *Roll Call*, Feb. 15, 1999, 12.

19. Katharine Q. Seelye, "Secrecy Is a Working Tool in the Hands of the Senate," *New York Times*, Jan. 31, 1999, "Week in Review," 3.

20. The number of annually authorized trips to the district by House members has increased steadily from two round trips a year in the 1950s, to six in the mid-1960s, to twenty-two in the 1970s, to thirty-two in the 1980s. In the 1990s the limit on the number of trips was lifted and members could decide for themselves how much of their office budget to use for trips.

21. Barbara Sinclair, *Unorthodox Lawmaking: New Legislative Process in the U.S. Congress* (Washington, D.C.: CQ Press, 1997).

22. James Madison, "The Federalist No. 52," in *The Federalist Papers* (New York: Mentor Books, 1961), 360–61.

23. Woodrow Wilson, *Congressional Government: A Study in American Politics* (Baltimore: The Johns Hopkins University Press, 1885; 1981 paperback edition), 69.

24. Newt Gingrich, *Lessons Learned the Hard Way: A Personal Report* (New York: HarperCollins, 1998), 166.

25. Ibid., 167–69.

26. Ronald D. Elving, "CQ Roundtable: The Revolution at Twilight," *Congressional Quarterly Weekly Report*, April 4, 1998, 918.

27. "Compared to 1994, Voters Not So Angry, Not So Interested," The Pew Research Center for the People and the Press, survey of 1,012 adults conducted by telephone, June 4–8, 1998.

28. "*Washington Post* Poll: Clinton Acquitted," Feb. 15, 1999. (http://www.washingtonpost.com/wp-srv/politics/polls/vault/stories/data021599.htm). By contrast, on the eve of the 1994 election, the public's approval of the job Congress was doing was just 21 percent, and approval of the job the respondent's own representative was doing was 51 percent.

29. See Anthony King, *Running Scared: Why America's Politicians Campaign Too Much and Govern Too Little* (New York: The Free Press, 1997). King argues that the American system is "too democratic" and suffers from "hyper-responsiveness." He believes politicians should be given "just a little *more* political leeway, [and] just a little *more* room for policy maneuver" (166).

30. James A. Morone, *The Democratic Wish* (New York: Basic Books, 1990), 7.

31. For more on deliberation and its decline, see Joseph M. Bessette, *The Mild Voice of Reason: Deliberative Democracy and American National Government* (Chicago: The University of Chicago Press, 1994); idem, "Deliberative Democracy and the Citizen: The Majority Principle in Republican Government," in *How Democratic is the Constitution?* ed. Robert A. Goldwin and William A. Schambra (Washington, D.C.:

The American Enterprise Institute, 1980), 102–16; George F. Will, *Restoration: Congress, Term Limits and the Recovery of Deliberative Democracy* (New York: The Free Press, 1992); and George E. Connor and Bruce I. Oppenheimer, "Deliberation: An Untimed Value in a Timed Game," in *Congress Reconsidered*, 5th ed., ed. Lawrence C. Dodd and Bruce I. Oppenheimer (Washington, D.C.: CQ Press, 1993), 315–30.

32. The Honorable Sam Rayburn, "Texas Forum of the Air" (radio broadcast, Nov. 1, 1942), reprinted in 88 *Congressional Record* 3866 (1942) by Representative Wright Patman.

33. James Madison, "Federalist No. 10," in *The Federalist Papers*, 78–79.

34. Ibid., 79.

35. Ibid., 82.

36. Ibid., 80.

37. Ibid., 83.

38. Ibid.

39. "CyberCongress Accomplishments During the 104th Congress: A Progress Report on the CyberCongress Project," submitted to the Committee on House Oversight by the Computer and Information Services Working Group, 7–8.

40. See Hugh Heclo, "Hyperdemocracy," *The Wilson Quarterly* 23 (Winter 1999): 62–71.

41. Quoted in King, *Running Scared*, 166.

42. For more on the California experience with the initiative process, see Peter Schrag, "California, Here We Come," *The Atlantic Monthly* (March 1998): 20–31, and his book on which it is based, *Paradise Lost: California's Experience, America's Future* (New York: The New Press, 1998).

43. This is certainly one of the themes in Alexis de Tocqueville's *Democracy in America* (New York: Knopf, 1994). It is also convincingly developed in the Pulitzer Prize–winning book by Gordon S. Wood, *The Radicalism of the American Revolution* (New York: Vintage Books, 1990), and in Michael Schudson's *The Good Citizen: A History of American Civic Life* (New York: The Free Press, 1998).

44. After the first three months of the 106th Congress in 1999, seventeen of the first twenty special rules reported by the House Rules Committee (85 percent) provided for an open or modified open amendment process on legislation. That compares with 60 percent of the first twenty rules in the 105th Congress in 1997; 85 percent of the first twenty rules in the 104th Congress in 1995; and 30 percent of the first twenty rules in the 103d Congress in 1993, the last Democratic-controlled House.

45. Quoted in Neil MacNeil, *Forge of Democracy* (New York: David McKay Co., 1963), 11.

Appendix A

Voter Turnout in States with and without Statutory Initiatives and/or Referendums, 1992 and 1996 General Elections

State	Voter turnout as a percentage of voting age population	
	1992	1996
States with statutory initiatives and/or referendums		
Alaska	65.44	56.85
Arizona	54.09	45.39
Arkansas	53.77	47.54
California	49.11	43.31
Colorado	62.74	53.14
District of Columbia	49.58	42.70
Idaho	65.15	58.19
Kentucky	53.72	47.49
Maine	71.98	64.53
Maryland	53.38	46.73
Massachusetts	60.21	55.30
Michigan	61.75	54.46
Mississippi	52.76	45.58
Missouri	61.99	54.22
Montana	70.07	62.92
Nebraska	63.35	56.08
Nevada	49.98	39.35
New Mexico	51.63	45.96
North Dakota	67.28	56.32

(continued)

State	Voter turnout as a percentage of voting age population	
	1992	1996
States with statutory initiatives and/or referendums *(continued)*		
Ohio	60.64	54.25
Oklahoma	59.72	49.88
Oregon	65.71	57.50
South Dakota	66.98	61.10
Utah	65.15	50.31
Washington	59.93	54.68
Wyoming	62.30	60.11
Average	59.90	52.46
States without statutory initiatives and/or referendums		
Alabama	55.24	47.58
Connecticut	63.76	56.43
Delaware	55.19	49.51
Florida	50.20	48.00
Georgia	46.89	42.60
Hawaii	41.94	40.83
Illinois	58.94	49.19
Indiana	55.22	48.88
Iowa	65.28	57.72
Kansas	63.03	56.60
Louisiana	59.83	56.87
Minnesota	71.63	64.26
New Hampshire	63.14	58.03
New Jersey	56.27	51.22
New York	50.90	46.51
North Carolina	50.06	45.75
Pennsylvania	54.34	49.00
Rhode Island	58.44	52.03
South Carolina	45.00	41.47

State	Voter turnout as a percentage of voting age population	
	1992	1996
States without statutory initiatives and/or referendums *(continued)*		
Tennessee	52.41	47.11
Texas	49.14	41.20
Vermont	67.53	58.61
Virginia	52.84	47.49
West Virginia	50.65	45.01
Wisconsin	68.99	57.43
Average	56.27	50.37
National average	55.24	48.99
States with initiatives and/or referendums	59.90	52.46
States without initiatives and/or referendums	56.27	50.37
Percent difference between states with and states without initiatives and/or referendums	3.63	2.09

Sources: Voter turnout data were provided by the Committee for the Study of the American Electorate; the state lists were provided by the Congressional Research Service.

Appendix B

House Legislative Data for 103d–105th Congresses

Item	103d Congress (1993–95)	104th Congress (1995–97)	105th Congress (1997–99)
Days in session	265	289	248
Hours in session	1,887	2,445	1,979
Average hours per day in session	7.1	8.5	7.9
Total public measures[a]			
Introduced	5,739	4,542	5,012
Reported	544	518	511
Passed	757	611	710
Total unreported measures passed	291	165	282
Unreported measures passed as a percent of total	38%	27%	40%
Total public laws enacted	465	333	394
Commemorative measures enacted	81	0	0
Commemoratives as a percent of total	17%	0%	0%
Substantive laws (minus commem- oratives)	384	333	394
Total roll call votes	1,094	1,321	1,157
Roll call votes per measure passed	1.4	2.2	1.6
Congressional Record pages	22,575	24,495	22,682

(continued)

Item	103d Congress (1993–95)	104th Congress (1995–97)	105th Congress (1997–99)
Record pages per measure passed	29.8	40.1	31.9
Session hours per measure passed	2.5	4.0	2.8
Open or modified open rules (as percent of total)	46 (44%)	83 (58%)	75 (54%)
Structured or modified closed rules	49 (47%)	40 (28%)	41 (29%)
Closed rules	9 (9%)	22 (15%)	23 (17%)
Self-executing rules	35	27	45
Committees/ subcommittees	23/118	20/86	20/83
Committee staff (2d session)	1,800	1,171	1,265
Appropriations for House (in millions)	$1,477,945	$1,355,025	$1,442,709

[a]"Public measures" refer only to bills and joint resolutions and not simple or concurrent resolutions.

Sources: "Résumé of Congressional Activity," Daily Digest, *Congressional Record;* "Survey of Activities," Committee on Rules; Congressional Research Service reports on "Committee Numbers, Sizes, Assignments and Staff" and "Legislative Branch Appropriations"; House Calendars; and Rules Committee Calendars and Web site. Compiled by the author.

Bibliography

Bader, John B. *Taking the Initiative: Leadership Agendas in Congress and the "Contract with America."* Washington, D.C.: Georgetown University Press, 1996.

Balz, Dan, and Ronald Brownstein. *Storming the Gates: Protest Politics and the Republican Revival*. Boston: Little, Brown and Co., 1996.

Bessette, Joseph M. *The Mild Voice of Reason: Deliberative Democracy and American National Government*. Chicago: University of Chicago Press, 1994.

Bibby, John F., and Roger H. Davidson. *On Capitol Hill: Studies in the Legislative Process*. 2d ed. Hinsdale, Ill.: The Dryden Press, 1972.

Bowen, Catherine Drinker. *Miracle at Philadelphia: The Story of the Constitutional Convention, May to September, 1787*. 1966. Reprint, Boston: Little, Brown and Co., 1986.

Browning, Graeme. *Electronic Democracy: Using the Internet to Influence American Politics*. Wilton, Conn.: Pemberton Press, 1996.

Cheney, Richard B., and Lynn V. Cheney. *Kings of the Hill: Power and Personality in the House of Representatives*. New York: The Continuum Publishing Co., 1983.

Congress, the Press, and the Public. Edited by Thomas E. Mann and Norman J. Ornstein. Washington, D.C.: The American Enterprise Institute and the Brookings Institution Press, 1994.

Congress Reconsidered. 5th ed. Edited by Lawrence C. Dodd and Bruce I. Oppenheimer. Washington, D.C.: CQ Press, 1989.

The Constitution of the United States of America: Analysis and Interpretation. Edited by Johnny H. Killian. Senate Document No. 99-16. Washington, D.C.: U.S. Government Printing Office, 1987.

Contract with America: The Bold Plan by Rep. Newt Gingrich, Rep. Dick Armey and the House Republicans to Change the Nation. Edited by Ed Gillespie and Bob Schellhas. New York: Times Books, 1994.

Cronin, Thomas E. *Direct Democracy: The Politics of Initiative, Referendum and Recall*. Cambridge: Harvard University Press, 1989.

Davidson, Roger H., and Walter J. Oleszek. *Congress and Its Members*. 7th ed. Washington, D.C.: CQ Press, 1999.

Deschler's Precedents of the United States House of Representatives. Edited by

Lewis Deschler. House Document No. 94-661. 94th Cong., 2d sess. Washington, D.C.: U.S. Government Printing Office, 1977.

Documents Illustrative of the Formation of the Union of the American States. Edited by Charles C. Tansill. Washington, D.C.: U.S. Government Printing Office, 1927.

Encyclopedia of the United States Congress. Edited by Donald C. Bacon, Roger H. Davidson, and Morton Keller. New York: Simon & Shuster, 1995.

Evans, C. Lawrence, and Walter J. Oleszek. *Congress under Fire: Reform Politics and the Republican Majority*. Boston: Houghton Mifflin Co., 1997.

The Federalist Papers. New York: Mentor Books, 1961.

Frantzich, Stephen, and John Sullivan. *The C-SPAN Revolution*. Norman: Oklahoma University Press, 1996.

Galloway, George B. *History of the United States House of Representatives*. House Document No. 250, 89th Cong., 1st sess. Washington, D.C.: U.S. Government Printing Office, 1965.

Garay, Ronald. *Congressional Television: A Legislative History*. Westport, Conn.: Greenwood Press, 1984.

Gingrich, Newt. *Lessons Learned the Hard Way: A Personal Report*. New York: HarperCollins Publishers, 1998.

———. *To Renew America*. New York: Harper Paperbacks, 1995.

Grossman, Lawrence K. *The Electronic Republic: Reshaping Democracy in the Information Age*. New York: Penguin Books, 1995.

Hibbing, John R., and Elizabeth Theiss-Morse. *Congress as Public Enemy: Public Attitudes Toward American Political Institutions*. Cambridge: Cambridge University Press, 1995.

Hinds' Precedents of the House of Representatives of the United States. Edited by Asher Hinds. Washington, D.C.: U.S. Government Printing Office, 1907.

A History of the Committee on Rules. House Committee on Rules, Committee Print. 97th Cong., 2d sess. Washington, D.C.: U.S. Government Printing Office, 1983.

Inaugural Addresses of the Presidents of the United States: From George Washington, 1789 to George Bush, 1989. Senate Document 101-10. Washington, D.C.: U.S. Government Printing Office, 1989.

Kemp, Jack. *An American Renaissance: A Strategy for the 1980s*. New York: Berkeley Publishing Co., 1981.

King, Anthony. *Running Scared: Why America's Politicians Campaign Too Much and Govern Too Little*. New York: Martin Kessler Books, 1997.

The Life and Selected Writings of Thomas Jefferson. Edited by Adrienne Koch and William Peden. New York: The Modern Library, 1944.

Malbin, Michael J. *Unelected Representatives: Congressional Staff and the Future of Representative Government*. New York: Basic Books, 1980.

Morone, James A. *The Democratic Wish*. New York: Basic Books, 1990.

Naisbitt, John. *Megatrends: Ten New Directions Transforming Our Lives*. New York: Warner Books, 1984.

National Party Platforms. Edited by Donald Bruce Johnson. Urbana: University of Illinois Press, 1978.

Nevins, Allan, and Henry Steele Commager. *A Pocket History of the United States*. New York: Washington Square Press, 1956.

O'Neill, Thomas P., Jr., with William Novak. *Man of the House: The Life and Political Memoirs of Speaker Tip O'Neill*. New York: Random House, 1987.

Origins of the House of Representatives: A Documentary Record. Edited by Bruce A. Ragsdale. Washington, D.C.: U.S. Government Printing Office, 1990.

Papers on the Constitution. Edited by John W. Elsberg. Washington, D.C.: Center of Military History, United States Army, 1990.

The Papers of Woodrow Wilson. Edited by Arthur S. Link. Princeton, N.J.: Princeton University Press, 1974.

Paxon, Frederic L. *American Democracy and the World War: The Pre-War Years, 1913–1917*. New York: Cooper Square Publishers, 1966.

Povich, Elaine S. *Partners and Adversaries: The Contentious Connection between Congress and the Media*. Arlington, Va.: The Freedom Forum, 1996.

Referendums around the World. Edited by David Butler and Austin Ranney. Washington, D.C.: The AEI Press, 1994.

Rieselbach, Leroy N. *Congressional Reform: The Changing Modern Congress*. Washington, D.C.: CQ Press, 1994.

Schrag, Peter. *Paradise Lost: California's Experience, America's Future*. New York: The New Press, 1998.

Schudson, Michael. *The Good Citizen: A History of American Civic Life*. New York: The Free Press, 1998.

Sinclair, Barbara. *Unorthodox Lawmaking: New Legislative Processes in the U.S. Congress*. Washington, D.C.: CQ Press, 1997.

Smith, Steven S. *Call to Order: Floor Politics in the House and Senate*. Washington, D.C. The Brookings Institution Press, 1989.

Why People Don't Trust Government. Edited by Joseph S. Nye, Jr., Philip D. Zelikow, and David C. King. Cambridge, Mass.: Harvard University Press, 1997.

Will, George F. *Restoration: Congress, Term Limits and the Recovery of Deliberative Democracy*. New York: The Free Press, 1992.

Wilson, Woodrow. *Congressional Government: A Study in American Politics*. 1885. Reprint, Baltimore: The Johns Hopkins University Press, 1981.

———. *The New Freedom: A Call for the Emancipation of the Generous Energies of the People*. New York: Doubleday, Page & Co., 1913.

———. *The State and Federal Governments of the United States*. Boston: D.C. Heath & Co., 1891.

Wood, Gordon S. *The Radicalism of the American Revolution*. New York: Vintage Books, 1990.

Yankelovich, Daniel. *Coming to Public Judgment: Making Democracy Work in a Complex World*. Syracuse, N.Y.: Syracuse University Press, 1991.

Index